The Social Processes of Aging and Old Age

ARNOLD S. BROWN

Northern Arizona University

PRENTICE HALL, ENGLEWOOD CLIFFS, NEW JERSEY 07632

Library of Congress Cataloging-in-Publication Data

Brown, Arnold S.
    The social processes of aging and old age / Arnold S. Brown.

    Includes index.
    ISBN 0-13-817537-3
    1. Gerontology.   2. Old age--Social aspects.   3. Aged--Social
conditions.   4. Aging--Psychological aspects.   I. Title.
HQ1061.B77 1989
305.2'6--dc19   88-30694
                                                              CIP

Editorial/production supervision and
    interior design: *Marjorie Borden Shustak*
Manufacturing buyer: *Carol Bystrom*
Cover design: *Ben Santora*

To my wife, Harriet,
for her love and commitment

 © 1990 by Prentice-Hall, Inc.
A Division of Simon & Schuster
Englewood Cliffs, New Jersey 07632

Printed in the United States of America

10 9 8 7 6 5 4 3 2 1

ISBN 0-13-817537-3

Prentice-Hall International (UK) Limited, *London*
Prentice-Hall of Australia Pty. Limited, *Sydney*
Prentice-Hall Canada Inc., *Toronto*
Prentice-Hall Hispanoamericana, S.A., *Mexico*
Prentice-Hall of India Private Limited, *New Delhi*
Prentice-Hall of Japan, Inc., *Tokyo*
Simon & Schuster Asia Pte. Ltd., *Singapore*
Editora Prentice-Hall do Brasil, Ltda., *Rio de Janeiro*

Contents

Preface

The inspiration for this book has come from a variety of experiences related to gerontology that it has been my privilege to have had over the past 20 years. Studying aging and old age theoretically, teaching it academically, working with it practically in program and policy development, researching it with different methods, and observing it interculturally during those years has taught me that gerontology is a truly dynamic and exciting field of endeavor.

I have learned that what it means to age and become an old person is not a static entity, but is constantly changing in today's world. I have learned that theories, practices, and policies related to aging continue to influence each other and, therefore, can never be understood as separate entities. I have also discovered that we have much to learn about aging through intercultural comparisons.

In this book I have attempted to be comprehensive in the selection of age-related topics. I have also tried to discuss each topic with special emphasis on social processes and social change. The history of how each subject emerged as important to aging is given. How policy, practice, and theory interact is also analyzed. In addition, special attention has been paid to intercultural comparisons with each topic.

I want to express my special appreciation to several important people for the help and support they have given me on this project. My thanks go to

Kooros Mahmoudi and Michael Kanan (departmental chairmen) and Earl Backman (college dean) for the patience they have shown me and the released-time they have given me to write. Thanks, too, for the enthusiastic encouragement given me by staff members of the Northern Arizona Regional Gerontology Institute: Jackie Goodman, Debby Harmon, Jane Alley, and Bonnie Anderson; they gave me the confidence I needed. Two colleagues, Margrette Nelson and Renee Nelson, encouraged me and gave me insights concerning my writing style, for which I am grateful. Also, several of my graduate and undergraduate students read some of the chapters and gave me constructive feedback from their perspective.

I am especially appreciative of the opportunity I was given to visit the People's Republic of China with a team of other United States gerontologists. It was that experience that sparked my interest in intercultural aging. Thanks to Susan Mercer, our leader, for inviting me, and to *People to People, International,* our sponsoring agency. I am also indebted to Shi Jianming, one of our interpreters, for his willingness to share all that he knew about aging in China.

The person to whom I am the most grateful is my loving and patient wife, Harriet. She not only believed in me, but spent endless hours helping me with the typing and editing processes. I could not have done it all without her help.

Finally, Bill Webber, Nancy Roberts, and Marjorie Shustak, at Prentice Hall, have been very helpful. Bill patiently saw me through a major redirection of my writing project, and they have all been consistently supportive.

1

The Emergence of Aging: An Important Area of Study

INTRODUCTION

What does it mean to grow older? What happens to us physically as we age? How does aging change our relationships with others? How does aging affect how we feel about ourselves? What happens to us financially as a result of getting older? How are families and other social institutions affected by the aging processes? What happens to the political and economic priorities of nations as their populations become older? These kinds of questions are becoming increasingly important to us as humans. They are also the kinds of questions that are being studied in the rapidly expanding field of gerontology.

Aging has emerged as a vital area of concern in the modern industrialized nations of the world during the twentieth century, and it is rapidly becoming important throughout the rest of the world as well. It is a subject that concerns humans because of our unique ability among the family of animals to have an awareness of ourselves and others and to conceptualize the future as well as the past and present.[1] Because we have that unique capacity, we are all aware that we are experiencing the processes of aging, and those processes have some kind of meaning for everyone. No one has ever been able to totally ignore them. The aging processes have not always been a major social concern, however. It has been only in recent years that aging has emerged not just as something of which humans are aware, but as a vital social matter and a major area of academic and scientific study.

Two somewhat different but closely related concerns have come to orient the field of gerontology. The processes of aging constitute one area of gerontological interest. We are interested in studying these processes because of the many ways in which they affect our lives (physically, socially, psychologically, economically, philosophically, religiously, and so on). The other area of interest to gerontologists and others is old age. The study of what it is like to be old is becoming of interest to virtually everyone, especially in the present era, when most nations of the world are modernized or becoming modernized. A special interest in old age has thus far dominated the field of gerontology, but there has recently been a growing interest in the aging processes as well. As the likelihood that most of us will reach old age has increased (something that was not nearly as true in the past), an understanding of how we arrive at that position in life becomes much more vital to us.

The subject of aging has become increasingly important at many levels of modern social life. Growing numbers of individuals, especially from middle age on, are asking what will happen to them as they age. The impact of aging and of dealing with the aging processes has also become a major concern to families, to the economic structure, to communities, to healthcare professionals, to welfare agencies, to religious institutions, to the scientific community, and to entire nations. One cannot help but wonder why so much of the attention of such a broad spectrum of the world has been drawn to the subject of aging in such a relatively short period of time.

WHAT MAKES AGING AN IMPORTANT ISSUE?

In attempting to determine why aging has rapidly become such an important concern, gerontologists have discovered a number of factors that seem to be taking place on quite a broad cross-cultural basis. Together these factors have begun to rapidly and drastically change the experience of being old.

Perhaps the most important reason that aging is receiving so much attention is the substantial shift in the composition of populations that is taking place in most parts of the world today. At a time when the general populations of the industrial nations of the world are growing at relatively slow rates, the aged populations of those nations are growing rapidly. The elderly populations of nations are growing not only in sheer numbers, but also in the percentages that they represent of the total populations of those nations.[2] This growth is beginning to take place even in a few of the world's developing countries. These trends have been developing in the United States and in Europe since the turn of the century, but the rates of growth in numbers of elderly people have been increasing since World War II in other parts of the world as well and are expected to increase even more dramatically during the next 50 years.[3,4]

The elderly population is increasing at such a rapid rate partly because of increased life expectancy, due in large measure to improved health care and health maintenance. Improved health care practices and advances in life-saving technology have made it possible for most people to avoid death from ailments that once took the lives of many.[5,6] Thus, many people are now living to advanced ages to which only a privileged few once lived. Although the life span of humans has not yet increased (there were always those few who lived to be over a 100 years old), the life expectancy has increased dramatically.

A growing consciousness of the aged as a distinct and definable group is another factor that has helped to make aging an important issue today. The sheer numbers of old people have increased our awareness of them. With so many elderly people in our midst, we have not only become more cognizant of them, but we have also been influenced to think of them as a special category of people and to interact with them less as individuals and more as members of the age group into which they fit. That grouping tendency itself has served to draw attention to the aged.

Grouping people into age-related groups is, in fact, a growing tendency for entire populations. In modern societies, increasing emphasis is placed on stages of the life cycle.[7,8,9] We not only tend to think about and discuss life in those terms, but we also tend to organize our life styles around those stages, so that it is necessary to make major social and psychological adjustments as we move from one stage to the next.[10,11] All of this inevitably draws attention to and helps to define the aging processes throughout life. Aging has become a sociological fact of life and a major social issue.

A third factor that has made aging an issue is the way in which the aged have become characterized today. We have become aware of the aged not only because of their numbers and our tendency to group them as aged, but also because of the tendency in the recent past to define them as a group with unmet needs which neither they nor their families can meet with their own resources alone. The aged are defined as needy, and it is assumed that the society as a whole must respond to their needs.[12,13]

CHANGING CHARACTERIZATIONS OF OLD AGE

As attention has been drawn to aging and particularly to those labeled as aged, we have changed our conceptualization of what it means to be old and of what constitutes old age. It is important to understand these changes because, ironically, the way in which elderly people are characterized helps to a large extent to create the situation and social conditions in which elderly people live.

There are traditionally two opposite conceptualizations of old age. According to the positive conceptualization, to be old is to be wise, to have high social status, to be respected, and to be in a position to exert family and community influence. Much has been made of the fact that this conceptualization of old age is especially prevalent in Oriental cultures.[14] In fact, this has tended to be the prevailing way of thinking about the aged in the traditions of most cultures in the times when extended families served as the basic social and economic structure of society.[15,16]

The second, essentially negative view of old age, is that old age inherently involves major and irreversible losses. To be old is to be physically incapacitated, to suffer the loss of mental capabilities, to become economically dependent, to experience social isolation, and to lose social status.

Both of these characterizations have always been experientially legitimated.[17,18] On the one hand, the survival of societies and the preservation of the cultural wisdom of those societies have depended upon the experiential wisdom of older members. Surviving into old age was itself seen as a sign of having special qualities of wisdom. It could be argued that not all old people had great wisdom and that not all experiences necessarily brought wisdom. Nevertheless, it was certainly true that cultural wisdom did not come without experience, and old age was therefore the most important sign of wisdom; being old was defined positively as a result.

On the other hand, physical and mental losses have always been more prevalent among the elderly than among the young. Until recently, senility has been thought to be not only related to but caused by the aging process. Even though modern science has largely discounted that notion, it is still clear that such losses are related to age. The older one gets, the more apt one is to experience physical and mental losses.

Both characterizations of old age have thus been used in the past, depending upon the circumstances of those being defined as old. A positive definition was applied to those whose physical and especially mental capacities were intact. A negative definition was applied to those experiencing mental and physical losses. In recent years, though, negative views of old age have increasingly prevailed at the expense of the traditionally positive views. When they become old, individuals—even those who are still physically and mentally capable and vigorous—tend not to be afforded high social status, nor are they considered wise. Instead, regardless of their capabilities, they are considered dependent. Even if they need no special care or assistance, they tend to be ignored and treated as irrelevant by the rest of society.

Cowgill and Holmes have theorized that this change has come about across a number of cultures as a result of modernization.[19] They note that as societies modernize, regardless of their past cultural traditions, the elderly members of those societies will tend to lose status and will be defined as dependent. One cannot help but wonder what there is about modernization that determines that that kind of social loss will come about. Among other contributing factors, Cowgill mentions modern education.[20] Perhaps, then, it has to do most of all with the source of cultural knowledge on which societies depend. In nonmodernized societies, tradition plays a vital role in supplying the necessary knowledge base for survival and advancement. The experience that comes with age tends to be the best source of such knowledge. In today's modernized, mechanized, computerized, and scientifically oriented societies, perhaps it is assumed that the great amount of knowledge that is available in books and on microfilms and computer tapes surpasses the knowledge that individuals acquire through personal experience. Perhaps the dominant perception today is that the wisdom of old age is relevant only to the past. If so, one has to wonder whether it is possible to restore the positive social status of the aged, and about what place experience may still play in the learning and maintenance of cultural traditions.

THE DEVELOPMENT OF MAJOR CONCERNS ABOUT AGING

Aging in America became an important area of study in the mid-twentieth century, but not primarily because it represented a subject of great academic interest or fascination. Few scientists became involved from that perspective. Instead, it became an important subject to study not only because the aged emerged as an increasingly large and visible part of the population, but also because, as a group, their social problems seemed serious enough to require the attention of the whole society.[21,22] Scientific studies on aging were called for to help answer the puzzling questions surrounding those problems.

First, in contrast to a time in the past when the aged were an integral part of family and community life, it appeared that a substantial pattern of social disengagement and isolation had emerged during the middle part of the twentieth century. This pattern was disturbing to people in societies oriented to high levels of social activity and involvement. It seemed to suggest either that many of the aged were suffering some kind of psychological pathology, or that they were experiencing some kind of social deprivation, or both. The question of why disengagement tended to correlate with age dominated the theoretical work among social and psychological gerontologists in the United States for a quarter of a century.

A second problem area that developed, seemingly very closely associated with the problem of isolation, was what appeared to be quite severe social-psychological losses among elderly people. They seemed to be losing their sense of independence, their social status, and their self-esteem, and they were even developing an increase in the incidence of mental disorders.[23,24] It seemed that as the respect accorded them by the rest of society declined, their own sense of their importance also declined, and they tended to acquiesce to placement in a dependent situation. There are clear indications that old age has been perceived in terms of these kinds of losses for almost two centuries,[25] but not until the middle of the twentieth century did those perceptions pose serious problems. Social scientists, along with social workers and others, became interested in finding out why these kinds of losses were becoming so common a part of the experiences of old age in modern societies.

A third problem area concerning the aged was the experience of major losses in physical and mental functioning. With changes in life expectancy and increasing percentages of the population being made up of the very old, more attention was drawn to the rather unique physical and mental problems of the aged. People were beginning to survive the acute health problems that once took the lives of many at younger ages. Now, however, they faced other, more chronic and debilitating health problems. These problems usually did not directly kill them, but they tended to impair their functioning capacities and to make health care a long-term issue.[26] This has become an area of concern that neither the aged themselves nor the rest of society can ignore. It has greatly contributed to the perception that the aged are a dependent group of people and to the growing belief that they place an excessive burden of care on the rest of the population. Long-term care has become defined as one of the most serious social problems associated with aging.[27]

A fourth problem area has to do with economic losses among the aged population. This began to emerge as a serious social problem in the United States in the early part of the twentieth century, concurrent with industrialization and urbanization.[28,29] More and more elderly workers became unemployed, with few, if any, prospects for reemployment and with virtually no source of income. In more recent years, even after the establishment of the social security program, the development of other pension programs, and some general improvement in the income levels of elderly people,[30] the financial situation of a fairly large percentage of the aged in the United States remains inadequate, especially among women, the very old, and minorities.[31] This problem has been perceived as even more serious in just the last few years, with the belief of many that social security is too expensive and cannot and will not survive. Even with all of the attention being paid to this problem up to now, the number of impoverished and nearly impoverished among the aged remains unacceptably high.[32,33] The continued existence of this problem also contributes to and helps define the persistent perception of old people as dependent.

A pervasive and complicating factor is that, because of the strong attention paid to these interrelated social problems, it has come to be assumed that the aged as a group are dependent and have needs that neither they nor their families are able to meet. This assumption itself strongly influences society's treatment of the aged and to a large extent becomes a self-fulfilling prophecy and a perpetuation of the problems that have created the assumption.

The notion of unmet needs has prompted the interest and involvement of politicians, government bureaucrats, program planners, and social service practitioners. It has influenced the creation of a vast network of program planning and service delivery. It has resulted in the allocation and expenditure of vast sums of money in order to meet the needs of the aged. It has further prompted the creation of self-interest groups that stand to benefit professionally and financially from all of the activity in behalf of the aged.[34,35]

Many social scientists are now exploring the ways in which the emphasis on unmet needs, and the potential changes in that emphasis, are affecting the aged. It is one of the primary concerns to be addressed in this book. How do the typical intervention processes being used to serve the aged affect the elderly recipients? Do the intervention processes serve to make them more independent, as they are expected to do, or do they, in fact, create new dependencies? How are these intervention processes perhaps changing the structures of the families and family relationships of elderly recipients? Do they help build or diminish family ties and interdependencies between the older persons and others within the families? Do they tend to create substitute nonfamily relationships that may provide more, or less, security?

In the search for answers to these kinds of pressing questions, gerontologists are beginning to look comparatively at aging in other cultures. Until very recently, the cross-cultural literature on aging has focused on somewhat utopian cultural situations, especially those in which old people enjoy high social status and have exceptionally high rates of longevity, as illustrated by Benet's analysis of the Abkhasian people in the Soviet province of Georgia.[36] This literature has not served as a very useful source of comparison, however. It generally represents societies in which the people do not face the problems that we in the United States do. More importantly, this kind of literature often does not include comprehensive data that can be used for point-by-point, problem-by-problem comparisons of societies.

A growing volume of excellent cross-cultural literature on aging now makes comprehensive comparisons much more possible. Cross-cultural studies of aging were begun in the 1960s by an international group of researchers who simultaneously studied western cultures.[37] The work done in recent years by Palmore and by others on aging in Japan expanded the cross-cultural literature to a very different part of the modern world.[38-40] Even more recently, the work of Davis-Friedmann on aging in the People's Republic of China has added still another important dimension to this literature.[41] The work of Cowgill and Holmes on the relationship between modernization and loss of social status among the aged added an important theoretical component.[42-44] In addition, Fry and Palmore have compiled valuable collections of articles on aging in a great variety of cultural settings.[45,46] Cross-cultural comparisons will be a major theme of this book.

CONTRASTING APPROACHES TO THE STUDY OF AGING

As social scientists become involved in the study of aging, it is important that we pay close attention not just to the empirical data available but also to how we approach the subject of aging. The set of assumptions that we make in order to make sense of the data may determine more about our predictive conclusions than the data themselves do. Different approaches often begin with contrasting assumptions about the phenomena under study. These sets of assumptions, or *theories*, are descriptions of what societies are like. There are a number of possible theories to guide the study of a subject such as the sociology of aging. Points of most of these theories overlap, to be sure, but often the main orienting or definitive concepts of the theories not only differ from but contrast with one another. This is especially true of two particular approaches used by social gerontologists.

One sociological approach, which is quite widely applied to the study of aging, emphasizes *social structures* or *systems*, including societal values and norms and such social institutions as the family, the economy, and government.[47] The basic assumption of this approach is that we are all born into already existing and well-established social structures or systems. It is further assumed that the social stiuations or conditions in which we find ourselves are and will continue to be largely determined by those structures or systems. The social systems, therefore, are the primary focus of any social phenomenon being studied from this approach.

In applying this approach to the study of aging, attention is given to such social systems as work, retirement, welfare, health care, and the nuclear family. Studies with this kind of focus typically indicate that the involvement of the aged in these social systems is statistically correlated with such variables as social isolation, low social status, dependency, and low self-esteem. When this situation is compared to the past, when most societies were basically agrarian, there was no retirement, the extended family was emphasized, and the family was responsible for welfare, one readily draws the conclusion that such social systems cause the conditions found among the aged. It is quite apparent that such a conclusion is based not simply on the data, but also on the study's focus on social systems, as illustrated by Rosow's analysis of "The Social Integration of the Aged."[48]

The other approach sometimes applied to aging is what we might call the *social-processes* approach. While not denying that social systems are realities for humans, those who advocate the social-processes approach choose another factor on which to focus their studies. They believe it is more appropriate to focus on the social processes that are related to the phenomena being studied, such as communicating through language, negotiating and performing social roles, and learning. Rose's projection of the emergence of a subculture of aging out of peer interactional processes illustrates this approach.[49] The basic assumption underlying this approach is that social systems are never fixed. Rather, they are constantly changing and are themselves the products of something else. Social changes and the social processes that bring them about are much more important realities than social systems. If it is indeed found that elderly persons have low social status, are socially isolated, and have low self-esteem, then examining the social processes related to the development of those conditions would not only explain a lot more about why these conditions exist, but should also reveal trends for the future. Retirement, for example, is not a fixed social entity. It is itself a social and economic process and will continue to change and emerge as something quite different than it has been in the past.

A distinct advantage of the social-processes appraoch is that it does not confine us to the necessity of either returning the aged to an ideal past or locking them into a deterministic and unsatisfactory present. Instead, predictions for the future depend entirely on current social processes inevitably changing present conditions. Whether the future represents improvement or not depends upon what the processes are, who is manipulating them, toward what ends, and for whose benefits.

CONCLUSION

Social processes will be the main analytical focus throughout this book. It is hoped that the use of this approach will enable the reader to recognize that conditions of the aged are not pessimistically determined but are products of dynamic social processes that are subject to manipulation and change. They may indeed be manipulated to the detriment and deprivation of the aged population, but that is by no means a foregone conclusion. They may just as readily be manipulated in the best interests of that segment of the population. The result depends upon how well we understand the dynamics of those processes and upon the good will and intentions of those who are best able to manipulate them. It is important to understand, though, that most of these processes are not just natural occurrences over which we have no control. Instead, they are processes that are increasingly manipulated to the advantage of some individuals and groups, often other than the aged themselves. An understanding of how the processes are manipulated and to whose advantages, then, is as important as an understanding of the processes themselves.

NOTES

[1] John P. Hewitt, *Self and Society: A Symbolic Interactionist Social Psychology* (Boston: Allyn & Bacon, 1984), pp. 89–137.

[2] Donald O. Cowgill, *Aging Around the World* (Belmont, Calif.: Wadsworth, 1986), pp. 21–22.

[3] Sally L. Hoover and Jacob S. Siegel, "International Demographic Trends and Perspectives on Aging," *Journal of Cross-Cultural Gerontology,* 1, no. 1 (1986), 5–30.

[4] Cowgill, *Aging Around the World,* pp. 22–27.

[5] Hoover and Siegel, "International Demographic Trends, " pp. 5–30.

[6] Russell A. Ward, *The Aging Experience: An Introduction to Social Gerontology* (New York: Harper & Row, Pub., 1984), pp. 32–33.

[7] Eric H. Erickson, "Eight Ages of Man," *International Journal of Psychiatry,* 2, no. 3 (1966), 281–97.

[8] Gail Sheehy, *Passages: Predictable Crises of Adult Life* (New York: Dutton, 1976), pp. 20–32.

[9] Marion Perlmutter and Elizabeth Hall, *Adult Development and Aging* (New York: John Wiley, 1985), pp. 4–29.

[10] Irving Rosow, *Social Integration of the Aged* (New York: The Free Press, 1967), pp. 35–40.

[11] Georgia M. Barrow, *Aging, the Individual, and Society* (St. Paul: West, 1986) pp. 59–63.

[12] Harold Cox, *Later Life: The Realities of Aging* (Englewood Cliffs, N.J.: Prentice-Hall, 1984), pp. 18–20.

[13] Joseph A. Kuypers and Vern L. Bengtson, "Social Breakdown and Competence: A Model of Normal Aging," *Human Development,* 16, no. 2 (1973), 181–201.

[14] Erdman B. Palmore, "The Status and Integration of the Aged in Japanese Society," *Journal of Gerontology,* 30, no. 2 (March 1975), 199–208.

[15] Jennie Keith, *Old People as People: Social and Cultural Influences on Aging and Old Age* (Boston: Little, Brown, 1982), pp. 3–4.

[16] Martha Baum and Rainer C. Baum, *Growing Old: A Societal Perspective* (Englewood Cliffs, N.J.: Prentice-Hall, 1980), pp. 105–6.

[17] Ibid., pp. 106–10.

[18] Marjorie M. Schweitzer, "The Elders: Cultural Dimensions of Aging in Two American Indian Communities," in *Growing Old in Different Societies: Cross-Cultural Perspectives,* ed. Jay Sokolovsky (Belmont, Calif.: Wadsworth, 1983), pp. 168–78.

[19] Donald O. Cowgill and Lowell D. Holmes, *Aging and Modernization* (New York: Appleton-Century-Crofts, 1972).

[20] Donald O. Cowgill, "Aging and Modernization: A Revision of the Theory" (1974), in *Aging in America: Readings in Social Gerontology,* eds. Cary S. Kart and Barbara B. Manard (Sherman Oaks, Calif.: Alfred, 1981), pp. 111–32.

[21] Robert C. Atchley, "Aging As a Social Problem: An Overview," in *Social Problems of the Aging: Readings,* eds. Robert C. Atchley, S. L. Corbett, and Mildred M. Selzer (Belmont, Calif.: Wadsworth, 1978), pp. 4–21.

[22] Carroll L. Estes, *The Aging Enterprise* (San Francisco: Jossey-Bass, 1979), p. 4.

[23] Marjorie Fiske Lowenthal, "Social Isolation and Mental Illness," in *Middle Age and Aging: A Reader in Social Psychology,* ed. B. L. Neugarten (Chicago: University of Chicago Press, 1968), pp. 220–34.

[24] Kuypers and Bengtson, "Social Breakdown and Competence," pp. 181–201.

[25] David Hackett Fischer, *Growing Old in America* (New York: Oxford University Press, 1978), pp. 77–99.

[26] Tom Hickey, *Health and Aging* (Monterey, Calif.: Brooks/Cole, 1980), pp. 33–37.

[27] Nancy Eustis, Jay Greenburg, and Sharon Patten, *Long-Term Care for Older Persons: A Policy Perspective* (Monterey, Calif.: Brooks/Cole, 1984), pp. 1–4.

[28] Fischer, *Growing Old in America,* pp. 157–87.

[29] W. Andrew Achenbaum, *Shades of Gray: Old Age, American Values, and Federal Policies Since 1920* (Boston: Little, Brown, 1983), p. 15.

[30] James Schulz, *The Economics of Aging* (Belmont, Calif.: Wadsworth, 1980), p. 2.

[31] Robert C. Atchley, *Aging: Continuity and Change* (Belmont, Calif.: Wadsworth, 1987), pp. 105–7.

[32] Schulz, *The Economics of Aging,* pp. 34–39.

[33] John R. Weeks, *Aging: Concepts and Social Issues* (Belmont, Calif.: Wadsworth, 1984), pp. 150–59.

[34] Estes, *The Aging Enterprise,* pp. 72–75.

[35] Robert H. Binstock, "The Politics of Aging Interest Groups," in *The Aging in Politics: Process and Policy,* ed. R. B. Hudson (Springfield, Ill.: Chas. C Thomas, 1981), pp. 47–85.

[36] Sula Benet, *Abkhasians: The Long-Living People of the Caucasus* (New York: Holt, Rinehart and Winston, 1974).

[37] Ethel Shanas et al., *Old People in Three Industrial Societies* (New York: Atherton Press, 1968).

[38] Erdman B. Palmore, *The Honorable Elders* (Durham, N. C.: Duke University Press, 1975).

[39] David Plath, " 'Ecstacy Years'—Old Age in Japan," *Growing Old in Different Societies: Cross-Cultural Perspectives,* ed. Jay Sokolovsky (Belmont, Calif.: Wadsworth, 1983), pp. 147–53.

[40] Daisaku Maeda, "Family Care in Japan," *The Gerontologist,* 23, no. 6 (December 1983), 579–83.

[41] Deborah Davis-Friedmann, *Long Lives: Chinese Elderly and the Communist Revolution* (Cambridge, Mass.: Harvard University Press, 1983).

[42] Cowgill and Holmes, *Aging and Modernization.*

[43] Donald O. Cowgill, *Aging Around the World,* (Belmont, Calif.: Wadsworth, 1986).

[44] Lowell D. Holmes, *Other Cultures, Elder Years: An Introduction to Cultural Gerontology* (Minneapolis, Minn.: Burgess, 1983).

[45] Erdman B. Palmore, ed., *International Handbook on Aging: Contemporary Developments and Research* (Westport, Conn.: Greenwood Press, 1980).

[46] Christine Fry, ed., *Aging in Culture and Society: Comparative Viewpoints and Strategies* (Brooklyn, N.Y.: J. F. Bergin, 1980).

[47] Rosow, *Social Integration,* pp. 8–30.

[48] Ibid.

[49] Arnold M. Rose, "The Subculture of the Aging: A Topic for Sociological Research," in *Older People and Their Social World,* eds. Arnold M. Rose and Warren A. Peterson (Philadelphia: F. A. Davis, 1965), pp. 3–16.

2

Changing Demographics of Aging

INTRODUCTION

On a recent trip to the People's Republic of China, a group of U.S. gerontologists, of which this author was a member, was told by Chinese officials about their elderly population. They explained that life expectancy was increasing dramatically, that the elderly composed an ever-increasing part of the Chinese population, and that generous retirement policies were being implemented throughout the country. They also related that the rapid growth of their population was quickly being brought under control with their new one-child-per-couple policy. The officials expressed much pride as they spoke of these facts.

Members of the group asked the Chinese officials how these changes had become possible, why the policies had been set, and what some possible future implications (negative and positive) of these policies and population trends might be. They explained that the policy of restricting numbers of children would help the country avoid the numerous problems related to uncontrolled population growth. They also explained that their elderly population had increased because of the success of a healthcare system that equally served the entire population. However, they expressed very limited understanding that the policies and population trends might bring about some undesirable changes as well as desirable ones. Some of the elderly people with whom the group visited expressed serious misgivings about how the one-child-per-couple policy might affect their great tradition of family solidarity, upon which even the government depended. Officials did not appear to have considered that that might be a negative consequence of their present situation.

Much of what the U.S. gerontologists learned about the Chinese elderly had to do with demographics. Questions were raised about (1) how populations are changing and will probably change in the future; (2) what policies were being implemented; (3) how the changes had come about and why the policies were set; (4) how policies and population trends might be interrelated and might produce even further unanticipated changes in the future; and (5) how certain kinds of people might be effected by those changes, negatively as well as positively.

Demographic analysis, then, is not just a matter of juggling statistics. It is a valuable way of making sense out of changes in given populations, the reasons for those changes, and the potential implications.

A thorough demographic study could help officials in the People's Republic of China anticipate future problems with their elderly population, for example. A distinction has been made between formal demography and population analysis. *Formal demography* is defined as "the gathering, collating, statistical analysis, and technical presentation of population data." *Population analysis* is defined as "the systematic study of population trends and phenomena in relation to their social setting."[1]

Formal demography population distributions and trends tend to be treated from a factual perspective, as though they were due only to natural processes. Any study of human history clearly shows, however, that this is hardly ever the case. The situations in which we humans find ourselves are to a large extent the results of actions that we take, either individually or collectively, as we define our circumstances and make decisions about appropriate actions.[2] Therefore, in order to understand a phenomenon such as a growing elderly population, we must examine its development and its consequences (intended or unintended). We will thus be better prepared to assess, in turn, the future implications of present population distributions and trends.

DEMOGRAPHIC TRANSITIONS AND THE POPULATION CONTROL MOVEMENT

Why are the numbers of old people throughout the world growing? Why are elderly populations growing in proportion to the rest of the world's populations? Why are societies as a whole growing older as the years go by? Why are these trends more applicable in some countries and much less so in others? Statistically these things are true because of changes that have taken place in the death and birth rates. The question of why they have changed, though, can best be answered by looking at two processes related to population changes that

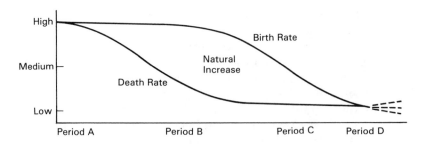

FIGURE 2–1 The Demographic Transition (From *Population Dynamics: Causes and Consequences of World Demographic Change* by Ralph Thomlinson. Copyright © by Random House, Inc. Reprinted by permission of the publisher.

have been unfolding throughout the world in recent years: demographic transition and the population-control movement.

Demographic transition is both an explanation of a historical process and a theory of population change.[3] As a historical process, it involves three periods (see Figure 2–1).

The first period represents a time of relative population stability, when death rates were about equal to birth rates and both were relatively high. Statistics show that this was the situation throughout the world for thousands of years. As Figure 2–2 shows, the world population grew only slightly for more than 9,000 years of human history. This was true because although the birth rate remained high, so did the death rate. In fact, there were times in parts of the world when famine or the spread of infectious diseases sent the death rate soaring, populations declined, and the survival of some societies was threatened.[4]

The second period of the demographic transition represents a time when death rates and birth rates became imbalanced. The death rate is lowered as a result of a number of economic and social changes, while the birth rate remains

FIGURE 2–2 Historical Growth of the World's Population (*Source:* R. H. Wheeler and L. F. Bouvier, *Population: Demography and Policy* (New York: St. Martin's Press, 1981), p. 24.)

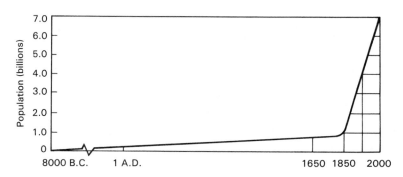

relatively high. The result is a rapid rate of population growth. This stage has largely taken place in the nineteenth and twentieth centuries, and especially since World War II, when the growth of the population took on the label "the population explosion"[5] or "the population bomb."[6]

This has been a phenomenon without historical precedence. It was clearly caused not so much by natural events, as some have contended, but rather by two sets of human actions. First, as societies became urbanized and industrialized, the quality of food, shelter, and clothing improved. Secondly, and even more importantly, medical technology and public health were developed to save lives and to overcome the centuries-old problem of infant mortality. In effect, science solved one severe problem and created another.

One of the results of this phenomenon was a dramatic increase in life expectancy at birth and in the number of people who lived to become part of the elderly population. Consequently, the aged population began to grow rapidly both in size and in proportion to the rest of the population.[7]

During this stage, an intensive social movement has begun for the purpose of controlling population growth throughout the world. Dire predictions have been made of mass starvation and death, economic depression, and world-wide poverty if growth of the world's populations are not controlled. Severe measures have been boldly suggested.[8]

The early stages of this movement were initiated in the developed nations of the world, especially in the United States, with particular focus on third-world countries, where populations were growing at the highest and most dangerous rates. The initial responses from third-world countries were either indifferent or negative. Some national officials in Africa even accuse those leading the movement of a conspiracy of racial genocide.[9]

Demographic transition as a theory also emerged during this period, and a heated dialogue on its validity took place.[10,11] One expression of the theory (the projected third period of demographic transition) was that nature itself will eventually control birth rates as the world becomes too crowded. This theory was based on a scientific experiment with fruit flies in a bottle that contained a given amount of food. The fruit flies' propagation increased until the food supply began to run out, when the growth essentially ceased. The assumption was that the human population would follow the same determined pattern.[12] The counterargument was, first, that humans do not behave as fruit flies do. As Peterson suggested, if human populations decline, they do so because parents decide for a variety of reasons not to have children.[13] Many also contended that immediate action must be taken to avoid the enormous problems that overwhelm the earth's environment. Whatever natural birth controls there might be would simply be too late. Human intervention was seen as absolutely vital.[14]

As a direct result of the birth-control movement, specific programs were initiated in many parts of the world. The major program emphasis has been on family planning. National governments have been urged to develop programs to make contraceptive methods available and to educate the public about birth control and family planning. In spite of substantial indifference and some opposition in developing countries, over 20 countries had implemented some form of family-planning program by 1970.[15]

For some time, some analysts have doubted that the family-planning approach would be effective enough to solve the population problem.[16] That skeptical attitude, coupled with the influence of such other factors as the women's movement, has made population control quite effective in the most industrialized nations. The birth rates have lowered substantially and the growth of those populations has been checked.[17,18] In those parts of the world, there have thus been fewer babies being born while the number of elderly has continued to increase. The more the problem of population growth was solved, the older the populations of those countries became.

In recent years, the great concern about the population-control movement has, ironically but encouragingly, shifted location from the developed to the developing countries.[19] By the 1980s, many of the developing countries had begun to become increasingly interested in economic development and increasingly aware that uncontrolled population growth was a major deterrent to economic prosperity. Consequently, some of these countries have also begun to substantially cut their birth rates.[20] Some have taken more drastic measures than would be acceptable in most industrialized countries. Problems related to extremely high world-wide population growth rates have by no means been solved.[21,22] Some countries have, nevertheless, begun to join the industrialized countries in moving into the third period of the demographic transition through very deliberate means. Consequently, their populations are also getting older, and the proportions of their populations who are old are rapidly increasing.

TRENDS AND DISTRIBUTIONS OF AGED POPULATIONS

In 1960, the total world population was about 3 billion; by 1980, it had increased to nearly 4.5 billion. Projections are that by the year 2000, the total population will be approximately 6 billion; in 2020, the world will have reached to a population of nearly 8 billion. The world population will have increased by 157 percent in just 60 years, yet the rate of increase each 20 years continues to decline (45 percent from 1960 to 1980; 38 percent from 1980 to 2000; and 28 percent from 2000 to 2020).[23] Progress is being made in controlling the growth of the population as a whole.

We see a different pattern, though, when we examine the world's elderly population. In 1960, those 60 years old and over numbered 250 million (8.2 percent of the total population), and by 1980, the number had increased to 376 million (8.5 percent of the total). Projections indicate that those 60 and over will number nearly 600 million (almost 10% of the total) by the year 2000 and over 950 million by 2020 (12.5 percent of the total). Instead of a declining rate of increase, as is the case with the population as a whole, those 60 and over are increasing at accelerated rates (50.4 percent from 1960 to 1980; 57.1 percent from 1980 to 2000; and about 65 percent from 2000 to 2020).[24]

Of all the age groups, the percentages of increase over the 60-year period from 1960 to 2020 will have been far higher for the oldest of the old—those 80 years old and over. In 1960 they numbered nearly 20 million (less than 0.7 percent of the total population), and in 1980 there were 35 million of them (0.8 percent of the total). The projections for the years 2000 and 2020 put them at about 60 million (just under 1 percent) and about 100 million (1.3 percent), respectively. Those over 80 increased from 1960 to 1980 by as much as 77.6 percent. Between 1980 and 2000, they will have increased by about 69 percent, and between 2000 and 2020, by another 70 percent. Over the 60 years being analyzed, they will have increased by an astounding 410 percent, compared with only 157 percent for the total population.[25] The population of the world as a whole is an aging population, and the future of the world will depend upon how we cope with the changes implied by this fact.

It is noteworthy that in none of the regions of the world are the numbers of aged or their percentages relative to total populations decreasing. The extent of their increases do differ from one region of the world to another, however. These differences are greatest between those regions classified in terms of economic development.

In comparing the more-developed regions (MDRs) and the less-developed regions (LDRs) of the world, we note that more of the aged live in the LDRs than in MDRs (205.3 million versus 170.5 million in 1980). The opposite is true of those 70 and over, and especially of those 80 and over. As many as 6.5 million more of those 80 and over lived in MDRs than in LDRs in 1980. Projections for the year 2020, however, are that by then even more of those over 80 will live in LDRs than in MDRs.[26] The population of the world, even elderly populations, tends to be concentrated in those countries that are the least prepared to support their citizens, especially those who are old.

The MDRs have had, and will continue to have, much higher proportions of elderly than the LDRs, however. For example, those 60 and over in MDRs represented almost twice as high a percentage of the total populations as those in the LDRs in 1960 (12.5 percent versus 6.3 percent). The percentage gaps between LDRs and MDRs became even wider in 1980 (15.0 percent versus 6.2 percent) and will continue to be wide in the year 2000 (18.1 percent versus 7.4 percent) and in 2020 (21.8 percent versus 10.5 percent). Those differences are even greater for those in the older age groups. Since 1960, those 80 years old and older in MDRs have represented percentages of the total populations about three times larger than those in the LDRs, and will continue to do so, at least until the year 2020. The region with the largest proportion of elderly is Europe, and the region with the lowest proportion is Africa.[27]

Obviously, the LDRs of the world continue to have younger populations even though the numbers of elderly are growing rapidly in those areas as well in the MDRs. The regional differences in percentages of elderly people are due

TABLE 2–1   Life Expectancy at Birth and at Age 60, by Sex and Region, 1995–2000

	At Birth		At Age 60	
Region	Male	Female	Male	Female
World	61.9	65.1	15.4	17.1
More-developed regions	71.8	79.2	17.6	21.4
Less-developed regions	60.5	63.1	15.2	16.8

Source: Adapted from J. Treas and B. Logue, "Economic Development and the Older Population," *Population and Development Review,* 12, no. 4 (December 1986), 648, Table 2.

partly to the fact that the birth rates remain high in those areas. They are also due partly to differences in life expectancy.

Life expectancy can be measured from birth or from any age after that. Table 2–1 compares the life expectancies in various regions of the world at birth and at age 60, as calculated in 1982. These two sets of data are essentially the products of two kinds of mortalities. Infant or childhood mortality has the greatest influence on life expectancy at birth, while adult mortality determines life expectancy at age 60. Obviously, the causes of those two types of mortality are quite different.

There are much greater differences between MDR and LDR at-birth life expectancy figures than the at-age-60 life expectancy. On the one hand, the at-birth life expectancy for males living in MDRs is over 11 years more than those living in LDRs and over 16 years more for females. On the other hand, the at-age-60 life expectancy for males in MDRs is only 2.6 years more than for those in LDRs and 4.6 years more for females.[28] As a whole, then, life expectancy and the bulging aged populations are more the results of saving children's lives than of elongating elderly people's lives.

Much has been made of the claim that people in certain places in the world enjoy especially high longevity. Two specific areas have been particularly cited: the Soviet Caucasus Republics of Georgia, Azerbaydzhan, and Armenia,[29] and the village of Vilcabamba in Southern Ecuador.[30] Claims have been made in the Soviet press that several thousand centenarians live in the Caucasus areas of the USSR. In Vilcabamba, Ecuador, the claim in the early 1970s was that as many as 16.4 percent of that population was made up of people over 60 years old.

The environments of these areas, the living conditions of the people, and their life-styles have been analyzed for clues to the longevity they enjoy. It has been noted that all of the areas are rugged and mountainous, that the people are hard-working and live simple, stress-free lives, and that their diets tend to be especially balanced and nutritious.

The claims of longevity in these areas have been severely challenged in recent years as having little or no factual basis.[31–33] The challengers argue that the claims have been extremely exaggerated. Palmore concludes that the claims have been so exaggerated, in fact, that "gerontologists must look elsewhere to find the 'secret of longevity.' "[34] Even if there were some truth to the claims of greater longevity in some unique environments, giving them much analytical attention serves very limited purpose, simply because they are unique (not typical) environments. Most of the world's citizens do not and never will live in those kinds of environments, and there is good evidence that it would be fatal for many to try. Neither are most in the world today apt to live in socially simplistic communities. The much greater likelihood is that life for most of us, in old age as well as when we are younger, will become more, not less, complex.

Part of what the world's life-expectancy statistics imply is how the various age levels balance out in given populations. One way of analyzing this is in terms of what is called the *old-age dependency ratio*. It is based on the assumption that the elderly are economically dependent upon younger adults in any society. It is typically measured by comparing those in given populations who are 65 or older with those between the ages of 15 and 64.

Table 2–2 provides comparisons between the MDRs and the LDRs of the world on existing and projected old-age dependency ratios. As these figures show, projections are that the old-age dependency ratios will increase to the year 2030. Not surprisingly, the old-age dependency ratios are, and will continue to be, more than twice as high in the MDRs compared with the LDRs. The increase between 1985 and 2030 will be about equal in both areas, however. These ratios are projected to increase most markedly in Europe (208.8 percent). The next-highest increase will be in East Asia (88.5 percent). Projections are that Africa will be the only part of the world where the old-age dependency ratio will decline during that 35-year period. The reason for that projected decline is primarily that the birth rate in African countries is expected to remain extremely high at least to the year 2030. China's concerted efforts to control its birth rate are

TABLE 2–2   Estimated and Projected Old-Age Dependency Ratios (population aged 65+/population aged 15–64 × 100), 1985–2000

Region	1985	2000	2020
World	9.5	10.5	12.8
More-developed regions	16.7	20.0	25.2
Less-developed regions	6.8	7.8	10.3
Africa	5.9	5.9	5.0
East Asia	8.7	10.9	16.4
South Asia	6.0	7.0	9.3
Northern America	16.9	17.6	24.0
Latin America	7.7	8.4	11.0
Europe	19.4	48.8	56.9
Oceania	13.0	14.0	17.5

Source: J. Treas and B. Logue, "Economic Development and the Older Population," *Population and Development Review*, 12, no. 4 (December 1986), 649, Table 3.

undoubtedly the major reason for the projected increase of the old-age dependency ratio in East Asia.

The composition of the aged population is another significant demographic factor. The composition of a given population is determined by a number of factors, including the following: (1) geographic distribution of the population, (2) the specific characteristics of the population (age, sex, marital status, racial and ethnic backgrounds, income, and health status), and (3) the migration patterns in which the members of given populations have engaged, which tend to change the distribution structures.

The geographical distribution of the elderly population in terms of residence in rural versus urban areas is important. While the general population of the world is becoming increasingly urbanized, that pattern does not necessarily characterize the older population. Hoover and Siegel report, for example, that during the years from 1965 to 1975, 65 percent of the 25- to 29-year-old population in MDRs and 37 percent in LDRs were urbanized, compared with only 57 percent in MDRs and 30 percent in LDRs among those over 60 years of age.[35] These differences were largely due to the greater tendency among younger adults to migrate from rural to urban areas. The tendency for proportionately more elderly people to remain in rural areas and younger adults to leave has serious implications for the social support needs of elderly populations. We will discuss these needs later. We should realize, however, that rural versus urban distributions in the future may well be determined as much by the migration patterns of the aged themselves as those of young adults. The aged may well become as urbanized as the rest of the population. Frey makes the case, for example, that the migration patterns of particular cohorts of the elderly population can be expected to differ from those of other cohorts.[36] Demographic predictions must therefore consider both types of migration patterns.

One type of migration among the aged is related to retirement; this type is common in the United States. Flynn and colleagues studied this kind of migration from 1960 to 1980.[37] Their findings reveal that, indeed, the migration of the aged may be radically changing from the pattern indicated by past analyses. It was discovered that, overall, interstate migration of those 60 and over increased more during both decades (1960 to 1970 and 1970 to 1980) than migration of the population as a whole, and the increase in migration among the elderly from 1970 to 1980 was nearly twice the increase among the total population (50 percent versus 26.6 percent). Greater percentages of the total population than of the population over 60 still migrate from state to state, but the present pattern indicates that the older adults are catching up.

Another finding from Flynn's group shows changes in where retirees tend to migrate. Florida has had, and continues to have, by far the greatest number of elderly retirees in-migrating than any other state. In 1980, more than one-fourth of all those over 60 who migrated from one state to another moved to Florida. Furthermore, the numbers of the over-60 group moving to Florida had more than doubled from 1960 to 1980, and the percentages of interstate migrants over

60 moving to Florida also increased. However, there was also an increasing tendency toward out-migration from Florida during that same period. In 1980, a total of 92,000 people age 60 and over moved out of the state, representing as many as 21 percent of the number who moved to the state that year. The number moving out of Florida doubled between 1970 and 1980.[38]

California is the state where the second-highest numbers of elderly Americans move. The popularity of California as a state in which to retire is also clearly declining, however. The percentages of all 60-and-over interstate migrants moving to California went from 13.6 percent in 1960 to 10 percent in 1970 to 8.7 percent in 1980. In addition, there was a sizable out-migration pattern from California among the aged—a total of 141,000 moved out in 1980. That was only 4,000 less than moved to the state that same year, and it represented a 62 percent increase in out-migration from 1970. Apparently many of these out-migrants return to their states of origin, a growing tendency especially for those from southern states.[39]

Arizona and Texas are rapidly becoming the two most attractive states for retirees. Between 1960 and 1980, the numbers moving to Arizona more than tripled, and those moving to Texas increased by 191 percent. Furthermore, both states had relatively few elderly who left the state in 1980.[40] These "sun-belt" states are clearly attracting the greatest numbers of retirees in the United States. Within the pattern of migration to the sun belt, though, shifts are emerging in terms of which states are most desirable, and those shifts merit explanation.

An analysis of rural–urban migration patterns among aged Americans should help to explain the meaning of the shifts in selected states. After the 1970 census, it was discovered that the U.S. population as a whole had begun to reverse its well-established pattern of migrating from rural areas and small towns to cities—and it was elderly interstate migrants who took the lead in that tendency. The pattern of elderly people moving from one state to another, some leaving metropolitan areas and choosing to live in small rural communities, began in the 1960s and continued through the 1970s and 1980s.[41–43] This pattern has been specifically noted in the state of Arizona. Although more elderly people migrating into Arizona tend to settle in Maricopa (the Phoenix area) and Pima (the Tucson area) counties, by far the most rapid growth in the state is taking place in the rural areas of such counties as Yavapai and Mohave. In some of the very small towns in those counties, the aged populations now represent over 40 percent of the total town populations. Most of the elderly in these communities have moved there by choice, partly for economic reasons but also to avoid the congestion of metropolitan areas.[44]

Age and sex distributions of elderly populations are also important parts of demographic analysis. It is well known that the ratio of men to women declines with age. This is true in all parts of the world, regardless of culture, economic conditions, or any other factors.[45,46] The truth is that women universally tend to live longer than men.

It is true, however, that the sex ratios (number of males per 100 females) of the countries of the world vary greatly. Cowgill reports, for example, that they "vary from a high of 136 in Senegal to a low of 42 in Russia."[47] They generally tend to be higher in the world's LDRs than in MDRs, but, with few exceptions, they are dropping in both.[48] The basic reason for these differences is that the life expectancies are lower in the LDRs than in the MDRs, and thus the populations are generally much younger in the LDRs. As life expectancy increases in the LDRs and their populations become older, the ratios of men to women will also decline. Hoover and Siegel explain that by the year 2000, "sharp declines are expected to occur in some less-developed areas that now have relatively high sex ratios (e.g., South Asia, especially Pakistan, India, Bangladesh, and the Philippines)."[49] The older a given population, the higher the percentage of women. Old age is primarily a woman's world.

SIGNIFICANCE OF DEMOGRAPHIC TRENDS IN AGING

Present trends in world population indicate that the explosive and potentially destructive growth patterns are beginning to be controlled, not only among the developed nations but throughout much of the world. Birth rates as well as death rates are decreasing, and the rates of population growth are declining. Although not all of the predicted social and economic disasters resulting from rapid population growth have been avoided, population as a future social problem is apparently on the way to resolution,[50] primarily because of deliberate and sometimes drastic measures being taken to reduce birth rates to match the already lowered death rates.

It is good news indeed that a potentially very destructive problem is being brought under control. What we must also realize, however, is that, in so doing, we have created dynamic forces of social change, and that social change inevitably has negative consequences as well as desirable ones. Even as the problem of rapid population growth is beginning to be solved, new problems related to aging are already emerging. Furthermore, the more rapidly the overall population problem is solved, the more difficult it will be to deal with developing age-related problems.

In general, the more rapidly both death and birth rates are reduced, the more rapidly life expectancies rise, and the more rapidly populations age. Consequently, the oldest segment of the population grows the most rapidly. These dynamic processes are already in force, and they raise serious questions about physical, mental, social, and economic dependencies related to old age.

The dependency ratios previously discussed have the most to do with the question of economic dependency that is being raised by many analysts today. Many see it as a severe threat to modern economic systems.[51,52] An important question concerning the so-called dependency ratio is whether its assumption is valid. Is it fair to assume that, as a whole, those 65 and over are economically dependent upon those between the ages of 15 and 64? There are, in fact, good reasons to question this assumption. After analyzing the extent to which old-age dependency ratios exist internationally, Treas and Logue concede that the ratios "are inadequate measures for gauging the true burden of old-age dependency." They reason that we don't yet know enough about the cost of supporting elderly people and that obviously not all elderly are dependent.[53] Our lack of knowledge about economic dependency is not the best reason for challenging the validity of the old-age dependency ratio assumption, however.

Measures of dependency ratios often include children under age 15 as well as adults 65 and over. The implication here is that children and old people are equally dependent on the rest of the population for economic support. Cowgill reports on a study that compared the amount of dependency of children and elderly people in 87 nations and territories throughout the world. It was discovered that children were much more dependent than the aged. Cowgill concludes, therefore, that overall economic dependency does not increase as populations age, as some would contend, since caring for elderly people actually costs less than caring for children.[54] While this evidence is important, it does not, as such, challenge the basic assumption of the old-age dependency ratio.

The key issue to consider in challenging the old-age dependency ratio assumption is whether the aged contribute to the economy, and the extent to which they do so. Contrary to the popular notion that old people represent only an economic burden, there are in fact two ways in which they contribute to the economy. First, millions of those in retirement take on productive volunteer roles within the family and community as well as in the marketplace. This is a growing pattern in developing and developed countries alike,[55] and the economic contribution is enormous.

The other major economic contribution made by the aged, especially in modern industrial nations, is in terms of capital investments. Private pension funds, into which more and more elderly people paid as workers, have become one of the most vital sources of economic development.[56] These funds typically remain as sources of capital even after retirees draw pensions from them. (These issues will be more completely discussed in Chapter 11.)

The use of the old-age dependency measure is simply based on false and misleading assumptions. That does not mean, of course, that old age carries no economic dependency. The very old, who now represent the most rapidly growing part of the population, typically have the highest rates of poverty of any age group. In addition, they are typically the least able to use their skills productively. The fact that the majority of them are women also contributes to their deprived economic condition. It is no secret that women enjoy far fewer financial resources than men, especially if those women are single, widowed, and old.

The migration patterns of today's elderly raise further questions about their social dependency. The aged have the same, and perhaps more, need for social support from others in their most intimate environments. Yet at least part of the migration patterns in which the elderly are involved have a great potential to deny them the social supports they need. As we have seen, some are opting not to migrate, but to remain in the communities in which they have lived for most of their lives. These are typically small, rural communities from which younger people tend to migrate. Many of these aged find themselves being left behind by their families in communities that are diminishing in size and support services. This pattern is found internationally.[57]

Increasing numbers of elderly are now migrating, particularly those in the more developed regions of the world. The migration pattern tends to be associated with social support deficits. Many choose to move to nonmetropolitan, small, rural communities or suburbs where they join others of their age peers. In these cases they tend to leave behind their social support networks and move to communities or neighborhoods with few support services and limited potential for the development of new support networks.[58,59] In these situations, which have been labeled "gerontic enclaves," the support networks are increasingly needed but are less available with the passage of time. All of this raises a very important question about the effect of increased longevity on quality of life.[60]

CONCLUSION

The demographic trends of the aged present both hope and challenges for the future of the aged. Life expectancies are on the increase. The elderly are increasingly free to make choices about where they want to live. If they are fairly well-to-do, they readily migrate from colder areas to warmer climates in retirement communities, where they can interact with their age peers. Even those with limited financial resources are finding it increasingly possible to choose the environments in which they prefer to live.

As we have seen, many of the aged still choose to remain in the communities where they have lived most of their lives. Increasing numbers of them are opting to move to more desirable environments. Many move to urban areas, but compared with their younger migrant counterparts, a larger percentage of them are moving to small communities in areas with mild climates.

That the aged are becoming more free to choose where they will live is encouraging. Some of their choices are beset with potential problems, however. Their tendency to move to small communities is one such problem. Many of these communities lack the social and health facilities that will be increasingly necessary as the elderly cohorts grow older. This kind of demographic information is therefore important as nations make policy decisions that affect their aging populations.

NOTES

[1] William Peterson, *Population* (New York: Macmillan, 1975), p. 3.

[2] John P. Hewitt, *Self and Society: A Symbolic Interactionist Social Psychology* (Boston: Allyn & Bacon, 1984), pp. 75–81.

[3] John E. Farley, *American Social Problems: An Institutional Analysis* (Englewood Cliffs, N.J.: Prentice-Hall, 1987), p. 330.

[4] Peterson, *Population*, pp. 416–29.

[5] Donald O. Cowgill, *Aging Around the World* (Belmont, Calif.: Wadsworth, 1986), p. 22.

[6] Paul R. Ehrlich, *The Population Bomb* (New York: Ballantine, 1968), pp. 3–17.

[7] Paul T. Schultz, *Economics of Population* (Reading, Mass.: Addison-Wesley, 1981), pp. 39–43.

[8] Ehrlich, *The Population Bomb*, pp. 127–57.

[9] Clayton A. Hartjen, *Possible Trouble: An Analysis of Social Problems* (New York: Praeger, 1977), pp. 188–91.

[10] Ibid., pp. 181–82.

[11] Kingsley Davis, "Population Policy: Will Current Programs Succeed?" *Science*, 158 (November 10, 1967), 730–39.

[12] Peterson, *Population*, p. 337.

[13] Ibid., p. 338.

[14] Hartjen, *Possible Trouble*, pp. 181–82.

[15] Kingsley Davis, "The World's Population Crisis," in *Contemporary Social Problems*, eds. Robert K. Merton and Robert Nisbet (New York: Harcourt Brace Jovanovich, Inc., 1971), pp. 363–405.

[16] Davis, "Population Policy," pp. 730–39.

[17] Joseph Julian, *Social Problems* (New York: Appleton-Century-Crofts, 1973), p. 525.

[18] Donald J. Bogue and Amy Ong Tsui, "Zero World Population Growth?" in *Social Problems: The Contemporary Debates*, eds. John B. Williamson, Linda Evans, and Anne Munley (Boston: Little, Brown, 1981), pp. 392–400.

[19] Farley, *American Social Problems*, p. 333.

[20] T. Paul Schultz, "An Economic Interpretation of the Decline in Fertility in a Rapidly Developing Country: Consequences of Development and Family Planning," in *Population and Economic Change in Developing Countries*, ed. Richard A. Easterlin (Chicago: University of Chicago Press, 1980), pp. 209–88.

[21] Lester R. Brown, Kathleen Newland, and Bruce Stokes, "Twenty-Two Aspects of the Population," *The Futurist*, 10, no. 5 (October 1976), 238–45.

[22] Farley, *American Social Problems*, pp. 327–28.

[23] Sally L. Hoover and Jacob S. Siegel, "International Demographic Trends and Perspectives on Aging," *Journal of Cross-Cultural Gerontology*, 1, no. 1 (1986), 5–30.

[24] Ibid.

[25] Ibid.

[26] Ibid.

[27] Ibid.

[28] Judith Treas and Barbara Logue, "Economic Development and the Older Population," *Population and Development Review*, 12, no. 4 (December 1986), 645–73.

[29] Sula Benet, "Why They Live to be 100, or Even Older in Abkhasia," in *Aging in America: Readings in Social Gerontology*, eds. Cary S. Kart and Barbara B. Manard (Sherman Oaks, Calif.: Alfred, 1981), pp. 176–88.

[30] Alexander Leaf, "Getting Old," *Scientific American*, 229 (September 1973), 45–52.

[31] Joseph T. Freeman, "The Old, Old, Very Old Charlie Smith," *The Gerontologist*, 22, no. 6 (December 1982), 532–36.

[32] Erdman B. Palmore, "Longevity in Abkhazia: A Reevaluation," *The Gerontologist*, 24, no. 1 (February 1984), 95–96.

[33] Neil G. Bennett and Lea K. Garson, "Extraordinary Longevity in the Soviet Union: Fact or Artifact?" *The Gerontologist*, 26, no. 4 (August 1986), 358–61.

[34] Palmore, "Longevity in Abkhazia," pp. 95–96.

[35] Hoover and Siegel, "International Demographic Trends," pp. 5–30.

[36] William H. Frey, "Lifecourse Migration and Redistribution of the Elderly Across U.S. Regions and Metropolitan Areas," *Economic Outlook USA*, 2nd qtr. (1986), pp. 10–16.

[37] Cynthia B. Flynn et al., "The Redistribution of America's Older Population: Major National Migration Patterns for Three Census Decades, 1960–1980," *The Gerontologist*, 25, no. 3 (June 1985), 292–96.

[38] Ibid.

[39] Charles F. Longino and Jeanne C. Biggar, "The Impact of Retirement Migration on the South," *The Gerontologist*, 21, no. 3 (June 1981), 283–90.

[40] Flynn et al., "The Redistribution of America's Older Population," pp. 292–96.

[41] Charles F. Longino, "Changing Aged Nonmetropolitan Migration Patterns, 1955 to 1960 and 1965 to 1970," *Journal of Gerontology*, 37, no. 2 (March 1982), 228–34.

[42] Charles F. Longino et al., "Aged Metropolitan-Nonmetropolitan Migration Streams over Three Census Decades," *Journal of Gerontology*, 39, no. 6 (November 1984), 721–29.

[43] Ellen Bryant and Mohamed El-Attar, "Migration and Redistribution of the Elderly: A Challenge to Community Services," *The Gerontologist*, 24, no. 6 (December 1984), 634–40.

[44] Arnold S. Brown, "The Problem of Housing for the Elderly in Arizona," in *Report of the Arizona 1981 White House Conference on Aging* (Phoenix: Governor's Advisory Council on Aging, 1981), pp. 107–13.

[45] Hoover and Siegel, "International Demographic Trends," pp. 5–30.

[46] Cowgill, *Aging Around the World*, pp. 27–28.

[47] Ibid., p. 28.

[48] Hoover and Siegel, "International Demographic Trends," pp. 5–30.

[49] Ibid.

[50] Bogue and Taui, "Zero World Population Growth?" pp. 392–400.

[51] Treas and Logue, "Economic Development," pp. 645–73.

[52] Carolyn L. Weaver, "Social Security in Aging Societies," *Population and Development Review*, 12, suppl. (1986), 273–95.

[53] Treas and Logue, "Economic Development," pp. 645–73.

[54] Cowgill, *Aging Around the World*, p. 35.

[55] Treas and Logue, "Economic Development," pp. 645–73.

[56] Robert C. Atchley, *Social Forces and Aging: An Introduction to Social Gerontology* (Belmont, Calif.: Wadsworth, 1985), p. 308.

[57] Hoover and Siegel, "International Demographic Trends," pp. 5–30.

[58] Bryant and El-Attar, "Migration and Distribution," pp. 634–40.

[59] Hoover and Siegel, "International Demographic Trends," pp. 5–30.

[60] Marie R. Haug and Steven J. Folmar, "Longevity, Gender, and Life Quality," *Journal of Health and Social Behavior*, 27, no. 4 (1986), 332–45.

3

Physical and Psychological Aspects of Aging

INTRODUCTION

The question of why living organisms change with age, eventually lose their capacities to function, and die is not merely an interesting scientific question; rather, it is vital to each of us and to our understanding of the meaning of life and death.

Each of us has a very large stake in what happens to us physically and mentally as we grow older. The processes of physical and mental aging, and the results of these processes in terms of the length of our lives, our decreasing abilities to function, and the changes in our appearances, are subjects that none of us dares to ignore.

For that reason, the aging processes have become very important areas of study for gerontologists. They are increasingly significant and challenging areas of study for biological and psychological gerontologists. They are equally significant to those in other areas of gerontology in terms of how they affect the economic, health, and social policies of aging.

The physiology and psychology of aging are of interest to gerontologists in a number of ways. They are important in terms of the knowledge they provide about the age-old question of longevity. Although the question of why we age has not been answered and may never be, biologists and psychologists have provided us with some increasingly informed and promising theories. A great deal is now known about the environmental and dietary factors that make it possible for more people to live and function normally much longer than has generally been true in the past. Studies of these aspects of aging have raised serious questions about physical and mental functioning throughout the life cycle. Physical and mental aging processes also have serious social, psychological, and economic implications, and the study of those aspects of aging are important for that reason as well.

There are many excellent books on the biology and psychology of aging, and it is not our purpose to even attempt to match or duplicate that literature. Instead, the main purposes of this chapter are to (1) analyze the processes of data collection and theory development regarding physical aging and (2) discuss the social and psychological implications of the physical and mental changes that we humans experience as we live our lives.

AGING AND DISEASE

We have become increasingly capable of differentiating between physical and mental changes that are due to diseases and those that are due to aging processes themselves. In the past, except for well-known and well-understood acute diseases that young people quite commonly acquired, the distinctions between diseases of the body and mind as compared to the normal physical and mental aging processes were blurred. Some physical and mental problems (particularly chronic problems) were seen as natural consequences of growing old. It was not at all uncommon, in fact, for old age itself to be thought of and treated as a chronic disease and a major cause of death. One of the early theories of biological aging clearly reflected this view. According to this theory, it was assumed that becoming old was simply a matter of "wear and tear."[1-3] Like a machine, the human body was thought to be limited to a certain amount of use, and the more active one's life, the faster one's body and mind would wear out.

In more recent years, a much greater distinction between aging and disease processes has been made. Along with that distinction, a very strong belief has developed among biological and medical gerontologists that diseases and other environmental factors—and not aging—cause infirmity and death. Their contention has been that, although the acquisition of chronic diseases and other debilitating factors in the environment may be associated with age (the older one is, the greater the chance of acquiring chronic diseases and becoming debilitated), age itself does not cause them. Chronic diseases can be acquired by people of all ages. Moreover, not all older people acquire these diseases or become debilitated in specific ways.

The distinction between disease and aging has been well articulated by Kohn.[4] According to his definitions, the basic difference between disease and aging is that aging involves universal, inevitable, and therefore normal physio-logical changes, whereas diseases are abnormal in that they do not happen to every member of the species. Troll makes the same distinction in her use of the terms *primary* and *secondary* aging.[5] She describes primary aging as bodily changes that are "inevitable and universal," and secondary aging as those changes that "are more frequent in the later years of life," but "are not inevitable," such as various kinds of mental and physical illnesses.

Many who have come to make these distinctions will concede that the aging processes themselves do result in diminishing physical, sensory, and cognitive capacities.[6] However, their contention is that the results of aging happen only gradually and only minimally throughout life and are never the direct causes of physiological malfunction or death. Instead, diseases and environmental factors are the causes of debilitation and death.[7,8] It is pointed out, for example, that many respiratory problems are the result of pathology rather than of normal aging. Biologists indicate that the respiratory system is the most vulnerable to damage from outside forces, such as air pollution, tobacco smoke, obesity, and respiratory diseases.[9,10] It is difficult to distinguish between the impact of pathological and normal aging factors, but, according to this view of aging, respiratory problems have more to do with the life-style one chooses than with aging as such.

These kinds of clear distinctions between disease and aging constitute the theoretical perspective of the Duke Longitudinal Studies, as the concepts that were used to guide those studies—"normal aging" and "pathological processes"—illustrate.[11] The expectations of those studies apparently were that pathological processes would have more to do with functional losses and death than would the normal aging processes.

Torack uses this same viewpoint, as it relates to cognitive processes, in his book *Your Brain is Younger than You Think.* He mentions critically the time when "any serious decline in mental alertness was considered to be a normal consequence of age." In contrast, he states his belief that "there is no evidence to show that aging per se causes changes in the brain that are responsible for the development of mental illness." In fact, he contends that "the rate of occurrence of mental illness in the elderly should be no greater than that of younger populations."[12]

Studies have shown that, beyond the age of 30, the older one is, the less brain mass one tends to have.[13] The total difference in brain weight between those who are middle-aged to those who have reached old age is about 7 percent. Elderly persons also tend to have fewer neurons and to have greater amounts of abnormal protein substances within the brain than those who are younger.[14] Some researchers conclude from these data that a natural process of brain atrophy occurs with age due to biological deterioration.[15] Those who see the environment, rather than aging, as the basic problem point out that almost all of these studies are cross-sectional and that the differences between the age groups are more likely due to the fact that older people have had, up to now, much less intellectual stimulation and brain usage than those who are younger.[16]

One of the mental capacities that is functionally vital to humans is the ability to remember people, events, and experiences from the past. Without that capacity, humans have no means of interpreting or finding meaning in the present. Accounts of our experiences as we observe and interact with our environments are somehow recorded and stored in our brains. Remembering those events requires that those stored records be recalled to consciousness. It has not fully been known whether loss of the ability to remember past events and acquaintances is due to the loss of stored records, the loss of the capacity to recall, or both. A neurosurgeon, Wilder Penfield, shed some light on that question a number of years ago, when he was able to stimulate a patient's memory by means of electronic probes into the brain. The patient suddenly remembered a long-forgotten and uneventful day from her childhood in vivid detail.[17] Thus it would seem that most of our past is stored in our brains and remains there throughout our lives, unless we experience some form of neurological damage as a result of trauma or some form of dementia. Our difficulty in remembering the details of the past, then, seems to be related to our inability to recall them.[18] Research indicates that, overall, the elderly are less capable than those who are younger of efficiently exercising the recall process, at least with short-term memory, even when the time for recalling is somewhat extended from what is normally used in such tests.[19]

Somewhat surprisingly, the elderly tend to have better long-term than short-term memory.[20] The reason for this is not clear, but some believe that it is simply because they are more oriented to the past than to either the future or the present. Or, perhaps they most readily recall those events and objects (1) that they share with others in their social environments, (2) that mean the most to them, and (3) that arouse the greatest emotional response.[21,22] Once again, environmental circumstances, not aging, are seen as the primary causal factors.

Hickey points out that this is basically an optimistic perspective on aging.[23] If disease, and not aging, is seen as causing functional losses and death, then the great advances in medical technology, disease control, and environmental safety over the past 50 years give us plenty of reason to be confident about improving the physical and mental conditions of old age.

This perspective on aging has been labeled "the bioscientific, medical model,"[24] presumably because it has been promoted largely by medical science—a branch of science that (1) is oriented to solving medical problems and is unable to accept the notion that aging and death are inevitable and (2) has gone through an era of outstanding advancement. Medical scientists probably want to be able to deny that aging and death are inevitable, and they seem to have plenty of reason to be optimistic. From this perspective, it is believed that the losses of old age can not only be prevented, but they can even be reversed.

Schaie and Willis's experimentation with a program of cognitive training to restore intellectual functioning among elderly subjects illustrates this point. Indeed, one of the conclusions they drew from their research was that "cognitive training techniques can reverse reliably documented decline over a 14-year period in a substantial number of older adults."[25]

A theoretical expression of this optimistic perspective is the "autoimmune theory."[26,27] The contention of this theory is that interaction between the human body and the environment tends to cause cellular damage and the failure of the body's immune system. In turn, this failure renders us increasingly susceptible to the chronic problems commonly related to old age. Implied in this theory is the assumption that finding ways to protect the body's immune system would help to eliminate the relationship between age and disease.

In recent years, the optimistic assumptions about the physical aging process have increasingly been challenged. This challenge is supported by many studies comparing adults at various age levels in virtually every physical and mental function. Data from these studies tend to show a steady and seemingly inevitable loss of the ability to function, both in terms of speed and efficiency. This evidence has led many biologists and psychologists to conclude that, regardless of the presence of disease, functional losses with age are universal and inevitable among humans as well as all other forms of life. As Fries puts it, "the bioscientific, medical model of disease, our prevalent model, assumes that death is always the result of a disease process; if there were no disease, there would be no death." However, he contends that "this view is hard to defend."[28]

Kohn describes both aging and disease as "progressive processes" that steadily progress toward a final result that is essentially harmful to the person experiencing them.[29] Both are harmful in that they result in the loss of functional capacities. In fact, Fries describes chronic diseases as "conditions that originate in early life and develop insidiously" and that are "inescapably linked with eventual mortality."[30] According to this more pessimistic view, aging is ultimately the more devastating of the two processes because aging inevitably results in steadily accelerated losses and death, while diseases are, at least in theory, preventable, treatable, and reversible.

A theory that helps to explain this perspective has been called the "deliberate biological programming theory,"[31] or what Rockstein and Sussman termed the "running-out-of-program theory."[32] It is the contention of this theory that within each normal cell is stored the capability to terminate its own life. (Cancer cells are the only ones that are immortal.) It is believed that each human has a genetically programmed life span, and that the closer we come to the end of that life span, the more rapidly we will experience physical losses, purely as a consequence of aging itself.[33] While many have contended for some time that diseases were the major causes of death, aging itself is now believed by others to bring inevitable functional losses and eventual death.

AGING: DECLINE OR DEVELOPMENT?

According to Kohn, aging can be distinguished not only from disease but from development as well. Development is quite the opposite of aging, by his definition. Development is the process that brings one to one's highest level of maturity and thus enhances one's functioning capacity. In contrast, aging processes begin at the high point of maturity and cause the functional capacities to continuously diminish.[34] Similarily, Rockstein divides life into three stages: (1) embryological development, (2) growth and maturation, and (3) senescence.[35] He describes senescence as the stage when "the body's ability to reverse the degenerative changes in structure and function becomes less effective, and ultimately fails."[36] Thus, the inevitable direction of the physical and mental aging process is toward degeneration and failure. Obviously, this is a negative definition of aging. The most encouraging statement that can be made from this perspective is that the functional losses are gradual for most of the life span and that most people are able to adjust to the changes as they take place.

A number of factors can, and often do, cause degenerative processes to take place rapidly and even quite abruptly. Harmful life habits, accidents, and the acquisition of certain diseases all contribute to degenerative processes. However, it is the view of many biologists today that, regardless of the environmental encounters of the human body, degenerative aging processes remain inevitable. The available evidence would seem to support the idea that humans do indeed have a finite life span,[37] and that we not only die within a somewhat predictable period of time, but our bodies also experience several very typical changes as we age.

One typical change that takes place is in the appearance of our bodies. Our skin wrinkles, sags, and develops spots. We tend to become stooped and walk with a shuffling gait. Our hair becomes coarser and loses its color, and our voices change.[38] The evidence indicates that, although these changes are affected by environmental factors (including exposure to the sun and wind, smoking, and diet), internal atrophic processes and cell loss are also involved. Biologists are convinced that these kinds of changes are inevitable, regardless of the use of cosmetics and cosmetic surgery and despite all efforts to avoid environmental exposure.

Another basic characteristic of aging is the declining ability to function physically and mentally and to maintain oneself in daily living without assistance. Although the times, rates, and severities of functional decline vary greatly from one individual to another and between different parts of the body, analysts insist that this decline eventually happens to all of us as we grow older and that it happens in all parts of our bodies. The nervous, cardiovascular, respiratory, gastrointestinal, excretory, reproductive, and skeletal systems and the sensory organs all experience functional decline to some degree, and according to some typical pattern, the longer the human organism remains alive.[39-41] Kohn is adamant that "decline with age in function of the major organ systems responsible for maintaining homeostasis . . . is unequivocal," and that "every organ system in the body and every physiological process could be discussed in terms of aging."[42]

Some are now challenging the view of aging as the inevitable net loss of function. While no one denies that many physical and mental functions diminish with age, the assumptions that aging results in net functional losses and that aging does not include development or maturing processes are being challenged. Those who challenge these assumptions argue, in fact, that every age represents both functional losses and new functional developments. They would contend that the studies that seem so clearly to support the notion that aging represents net losses have simply ignored those functional capacities that may develop in the later years of life. For example, Kitchener and King found evidence to support their notion that wisdom, in the form of what they defined as reflective judgment, "really does come only with age."[43] From this viewpoint, there would be no distinction between development (maturity) and aging.

Ager and others argue for a more positive interpretation of aging in an analysis of what they characterize as "creative aging."[44] Their main point is that, contrary to the idea that aging is a process of decline and a deterrent to growth, virtually all aspects of aging are a creative process of continuous adaptation. These analysts might be accused of trying to establish a situation of "mind over matter" as a way of helping elderly individuals to hang onto their capabilities as long as possible before they finally have to face the inevitability of decline, or of trying to help individuals adapt to inevitable functional decline and helplessness with as little trauma as possible. Their analysis is much more than wishful thinking, however. They point out that adaptation is an integral part of one's physical and mental constitution. Basic to their argument is what they call the "plasticity" of the central nervous system, which makes it possible for individuals to integrate and adapt to new experiences. They point out that, while the number of neurons in the central nervous system indeed decreases with age, the central nervous system tends to respond to functional demands by sprouting new synaptic endings at given neural junctions. Another adaptive process within the central nervous system is what they term "engram formation," which makes it possible to develop skills through experiential repetition, through a dual process of "divergence" (one neuron influencing multiple other neurons) and "convergence" (each neuron being influenced by multiple other neurons). These processes, then, make it possible for one's experiences to compensate for the fact that a slower functional pace accompanies old age.

Physical and mental adaptation is greatly dependent upon the continuous exercising of the physiological and mental functions.[45] It is well known that, for people of all ages, physical exercise acts to stimulate metabolic processes that restore and rebuild body tissue. Ager and her colleagues point out that it also brings the neurological processes into play and thus helps individuals to adapt to environmental stresses.[46]

It has been noted that as we age, the speed and accuracy with which we are able to respond to environmental stimuli decreases.[47–50] A major factor that is sometimes noted but is seldom stressed in studies of physical and mental aging is that older adults seem to be much more able than younger people to adjust to their physical and mental losses. For example, in studies comparing persons over 60 with younger adults in the length of time to extract information from a display flashed on a screen, it was found that even though the older subjects were slower, they often compensated for their slowness by using cues from their surroundings or by taking advantage of advance information, or both.[51] Macht and Buschke found, too, that under given controlled conditions, "certain kinds of complex mental processes do not show age-related slowing."[52] Apparently then, even in a biological sense, the experience and knowledge that can come only with age are often a distinct advantage.

It is important to note that the functional changes that elderly people tend to experience do not take place at uniform rates and by no means always take place in a steadily declining pattern. Rockstein and Sussman point out that there are two principles to remember about physical aging: (1) In any one organism, all organs do not age at the same rate; and (2) any one organ does not necessarily age at the same rate in different individuals of the same species.[53] Furthermore, for many people these declines do not become debilitating until the final months or few years of their lives.[54] Thus, for most people, the degree of decline throughout most of the life span tends to exert a relatively insignificant effect upon their abilities to function—far less significant, at least, than we generally assume. Chirikos and Nestel found, in fact, a surprisingly high level of restored functional capability over a five-year period in a longitudinal study.[55]

COMPRESSED AGING

A growing concern in gerontology, and especially among those responsible for setting policy on aging, is how to afford the costs of providing care for the rapidly growing number of aged as the life expectancy continues to increase. This problem is complicated by the fact that the fastest rate of growth is taking place among the very old (those 85 and over). The assumption is that as more and more people live longer, each person will need increasingly intensive care for longer periods of time.

This is an argument that would seem to find support among those who contend that aging itself is a debilitating process that disease control is powerless to stop. According to an analysis by Fries, however, this is an unnecessary worry for the future. He argues instead for what he calls "the compression of morbidity," and "the compression of senescence."[56]

As previously noted, Fries insists that we humans have a somewhat predictable life span, and that "the inevitable result is natural death, even without disease." The "ideal" is for humans to live out their total life span. A statistical analysis (see Figure 3–1) shows that, through the control of disease, progress has already been made toward a "rectangular survival curve," or, as

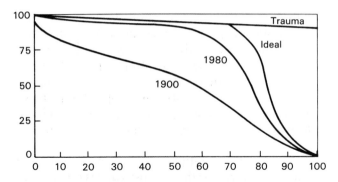

FIGURE 3–1   The Increasingly Rectangular Survival Curve* (*Source:*
J. F. Fries, "Aging, Natural Death, and the Compression of Morbidity," *The New
England Journal of Medicine*, 303, no. 3 (July 17, 1980), 130–35. Reprinted by
permission of *The New England Journal of Medicine.*

Fries explains it, "the elimination of premature death."

It is also Fries's contention, however, that it is basically the acquisition of disease, rather than aging as such, that creates long-term physical and mental dysfunction during much of the life course. Disease control has the potential to postpone the dysfunctional impact of even chronic (incurable) diseases. Thus, not only is morbidity compressed, but so is senescence. Therefore, natural dying and death generally take place in a truncated period of time at the end of the life span. Based on this analysis, Fries foresees a society "in which life is physically, emotionally, and intellectually vigorous until shortly before its close, when, like the marvelous one-hoss shay, everything comes apart at once and repair is impossible."[57]

CONCLUSION

Old age in modern society has become a period of life that most people dread. That is due in no small part to how the physical and mental aspects of aging are defined and what the physical aging processes have come to symbolize.

If the assumption is, as much of the research findings would seem to indicate, that growing old inevitably results in the loss of physical and mental capacity to function, then old age is a time of social dependency. One of the most inevitable and most visible age-related physical changes is the change in the skin. Ironically, even though it results in virtually no functional loss, it, more than any other physical change, symbolizes old age as functional loss and almost invariably has negative personal and social consequences. Aside from actual functional losses, the changes in appearance that symbolize old age can serve as the primary source of age-related job discrimination.[58]

---

* About 80 percent of the difference between the 1900 curve and the ideal curve had been eliminated by 1980. Trauma is now the dominant cause of death in early life.

In addition, actual losses in abilities to function serve as a major source of loss of social status, even among age peers. According to Rose, in his analysis of an emerging subculture of aging, being healthy (functionally active) is one of the most important social values, and the lack of health results in the loss of status within that subculture.[59] The psychological results of functional loss, therefore, are apt to be the loss of a sense of self-worth and self-esteem. Kuypers and Bengtson hypothesized, for example, that the elderly become labeled incompetent, and eventually internalize that label, as a result of the "atrophy of previous skills" and "role loss."[60]

A logical extension of the "bioscientific, medical model" of disease and aging, which assumes that disease, rather than aging, causes death, is that every known lifesaving technology ought to be used to keep people alive. This is clearly the prevailing philosophy and policy in modern medicine today. This policy raises serious practical and ethical questions, however. Is it worth what it costs? Can we continue to afford a practice that serves relatively few people and that increases all healthcare costs? Is it fair that relatively few receive the benefits while many others do not? Does it improve or diminish the quality and dignity of life? Is it even based on realistic assumptions about life and death? Our answer to the latter question is basic to our answers to the others.

The limited life span and compressed morbidity and senescence perspectives on aging have quite different social and psychological implications. Logically, these perspectives raise serious questions about the extent to which we as a society ought to go in lifesaving techniques. It makes sense to spend a great deal of our resources on the prevention and control of diseases in order to keep people as physically and mentally functional as possible throughout the life course. Devices whose only function is to artificially maintain life are logically questionable, however. If we humans have programmed life spans, then we have a right to two basic expectations. First, we have the personal right and the social obligation to remain as physically and socially functional as possible for the duration of that life span. Second, we have the right to die naturally and with dignity. Such a right is increasingly being defined as the right to reject artificial lifesaving technologies and to choose to die in our homes among our loved ones rather than in hospitals. As Fries concludes, "The hospice becomes more attractive than the hospital."[61]

Defining which among all of the available medical technologies are artificial and which are natural is not easy, to be sure. Neither do we know fully which decrements in old age are caused by diseases and which are the results of natural aging processes. We are rapidly moving toward claiming the right to individually define what provides us with or cheats us of dignity in life and death, and to admit that death is as natural as life.

There is much to be learned from a comparison of the theoretical assumptions and practices of modern medicine in the West with those of traditional medicine in the Orient. The basic philosophy on which traditional Chinese medicine is based is in basic agreement with the notion, previously discussed, that humans have fixed life spans and that this has important implications about the meaning and practices of life.

It is significant that much more emphasis is placed on the prevention of physical problems and less on treatment in the People's Republic of China compared with the United States. The Chinese have also deliberately and systematically developed a healthcare system that is much less technologically sophisticated but that is much more readily available to everyone. The results are that (1) their life expectancy is less than that in the United States, but (2) there are far fewer elderly who are debilitated and dysfunctional. Consequently, in China old age is not perceived as a time of decrements and dependency. The social status of even those in retirement remains intact and is in some cases enhanced. Death is viewed as a natural process and not as something to be feared.[62]

NOTES

[1] Howard J. Curtis, *Biological Mechanisms of Aging* (Springfield, Ill: Chas. C Thomas, 1966), pp. 15–16.

[2] Morris Rockstein and Marvin Sussman, *Biology of Aging* (Belmont, Calif.: Wadsworth, 1979), pp. 42–43.

[3] Molly S. Wantz and John E. Gay, *The Aging Process: A Health Perspective* (Cambridge, Mass.: Winthrop, 1981), p. 43.

[4] Robert R. Kohn, *Principles of Mammalian Aging* (Englewood Cliffs, N.J.: Prentice-Hall, 1978), p. 10.

[5] Lillian E. Troll, *Early and Middle Adulthood* (Monterey, Calif.: Brooks/Cole, 1985), pp. 22–23.

[6] Ibid.

[7] Tom Hickey, *Health and Aging* (Monterey, Calif.: Brooks/Cole, 1980), p. 3.

[8] W. A. Marshall, "The Body," in *The Seven Ages of Man*, eds. Robert R. Sears and Shirley S. Feldman (Los Altos, Calif.: William Kaufmann, 1973), pp. 117–22.

[9] A. S. Dontas et al., "Longtitudinal versus Cross-Sectional Vital Capacity Changes and Affecting Factors," *Journal of Gerontology*, 39, no. 4 (July 1984), 430–38.

[10] Rockstein and Sussman, *Biology of Aging*, p. 87.

[11] Ewald W. Busse and George L. Maddox, *The Duke Longitudinal Studies of Normal Aging* (New York: Springer, 1985), pp. 4–8.

[12] Richard M. Torack, *Your Brain is Younger than You Think* (Chicago: Nelson-Hall, 1981), pp. vii–ix.

[13] Rockstein and Sussman, *Biology of Aging*, p. 58.

[14] John W. Santrock, *Adult Development and Aging* (Dubuque: Wm. C. Brown, 1985), pp. 121–23.

[15] Shumpei Takeda and Taiju Matsuzawa, "Age-Related Brain Atrophy: A Study with Computed Tomography," *Journal of Gerontology*, 40, no. 2 (March 1985), 159–63.

[16] Troll, *Early and Middle Adulthood*, pp. 47–62.

[17] "Exploring the Frontiers of the Mind," *Time*, 103, no. 2 (January 14, 1974), 50–59.

[18] Marion Perlmutter and Elizabeth Hall, *Adult Development and Aging*, (New York: John Wiley, 1985), p. 219.

[19] Fergus I. M. Craik and Jan C. Rabinowitz, "The Effects of Presentation Rate and Encoding Task on Age-Related Memory Deficits," *Journal of Gerontology*, 40, no. 3 (May 1985), 309–15.

[20] Perlmutter and Hall, *Adult Development and Aging,* pp. 217–19.

[21] Alfred R. Lindesmith, Anselm L. Strauss, and Norman K. Denzin, *Social Psychology* (New York: Holt, Rinehart and Winston, 1977), pp. 201–2.

[22] Marcel Proust, *Remembrance of Things Past,* vol. 3, trans. C. K. S. Moncrieff, T. Kilmartin, and A. Mayor (New York: Random House, 1981), pp. 709–10.

[23] Hickey, *Health and Aging,* p. 2.

[24] James F. Fries, "Aging, Natural Death, and the Compression of Morbidity," *The New England Journal of Medicine,* 303, no. 3 (July 17, 1980), 130–35.

[25] K. Warner Schaie and Sherry L. Willis, "Can Decline in Adult Intellectual Functioning be Reversed?" *Developmental Psychology,* 22, no. 2 (1986), 223–32.

[26] Roy L. Walford, *The Immunologic Theory of Aging* (Baltimore: Williams & Wilkins, 1969).

[27] Rockstein and Sussman, *Biology of Aging,* pp. 43–44.

[28] Fries, "Aging, Natural Death," pp. 130–35.

[29] Kohn, *Principles of Mammalian Aging,* p. 10.

[30] Fries, "Aging, Natural Death," pp. 130–35.

[31] Ewald W. Busse and Dan Blazer, "The Theories and Processes of Aging," in *Handbook of Geriatric Psychiatry,* eds. E. W. Busse and Dan Blazer (New York: Van Nostrand Reinhold, 1980), pp. 3–27.

[32] Rockstein and Sussman, *Biology of Aging,* p. 39.

[33] Fries, "Aging, Natural Death," pp. 130–35.

[34] Kohn, *Principles of Mammalian Aging,* pp. 9–10.

[35] Rockstein and Sussman, *Biology of Aging,* p. 103.

[36] Ibid.

[37] Daniel J. Wallace, "The Biology of Aging," in *Dimensions of Aging,* eds. Jon Hendricks and C. Davis Hendricks (Cambridge, Mass.: Winthrop, 1979), p. 76.

[38] Rockstein and Sussman, *Biology of Aging,* p. 132.

[39] Perlmutter and Hall, *Adult Development and Aging,* pp. 93–97, 188–89.

[40] Rockstein and Sussman, *Biology of Aging,* pp. 65–94.

[41] Dontas et al., "Longitudinal versus Cross-Sectional Vital Capacity Changes," pp. 430–38.

[42] Kohn, *Principles of Mammalian Aging,* p. 181.

[43] "Can College Teach Thinking," *Time,* 129, no. 7 (February 16, 1987), 61.

[44] Charlene L. Ager et al., "Creative Aging," in *Annual Editions: Aging,* ed. H. Cox (Guilford, Conn.: Dushkin, 1983), pp. 31–36.

[45] Richard R. Powell, "Psychological Effects of Exercise Therapy Upon Institutionalized Geriatric Mental Patients," *Journal of Gerontology,* 29, no. 2 (March 1974), 157–61.

[46] Ager et al., "Creative Aging," pp. 31–36.

[47] J. K. Belsky, *The Psychology of Aging: Theory, Research, and Practice* (Monterey, Calif.: Brooks/Cole, 1984), p. 85.

[48] Kohn, *Principles of Mammalian Aging,* p. 181.

[49] Rockstein and Sussman, *Biology of Aging,* pp. 55–59.

[50] Gary W. Evans et al., "Cognitive Mapping and Elderly Adults: Verbal and Location Memory for Urban Landmarks," *Journal of Gerontology,* 39, no. 4 (July 1984), 452–57.

[51] Perlmutter and Hall, *Adult Development and Aging,* 186.

[52] Michael L. Macht and Herman Buschke, "Speed of Recall in Aging, *Journal of Gerontology,* 39, no. 4 (July 1984), 439–43.

[53] Rockstein and Sussman, *Biology of Aging,* p. 10.

[54] Fries, "Aging, Natural Death," pp. 130–35.

[55] Thomas N. Chirikos and George Nestel, "Longitudinal Analysis of Functional Disabilities in Older Men," *Journal of Gerontology,* 40, no. 4 (July 1985), 426–33.

[56] Fries, "Aging, Natural Death," pp. 130–35.

[57] Ibid.

[58] Stanley Brandes, *Forty: The Age and the Symbol* (Knoxville: The University of Tennessee Press, 1986), pp. 44–49.

[59] Arnold M. Rose, "The Subculture of the Aging: A Framework for Research in Social Gerontology," in *Older People and Their Social World,* eds. Arnold M. Rose and Warren A. Peterson (Philadelphia: F. A. Davis, 1965), pp. 3–16.

[60] Joseph A. Kuypers and Vern L. Bengtson, "Social Breakdown and Competence: A Model of Normal Aging," *Human Development,* 16 (1973), 181–201.

[61] Fries, "Aging, Natural Death," pp. 130–35.

[62] Myrna Lewis, "Aging in the People's Republic of China," *International Journal of Aging and Human Development,* 15, no. 2 (1982), 79–105.

4

A Social Psychology of Aging

INTRODUCTION

We humans are apparently unique among living organisms in one very important sense: We have an awareness of and curiosity about our environments. We can attempt to understand and assign meaning to the many environmental elements. Even more astounding is the fact that we learn to understand ourselves in the context of our environments.

Curiosity is clearly a part of human nature. Human life is full of puzzles that we seem compelled to solve.[1] We need to learn about, understand, and be able to explain the relationships between the objects of our environments. We are then able to know how we can relate to and cope with environmental components, including ourselves. The search for explanations is universal to humans through a process that has been described as "common sense."

Scientific investigation is very much a part of human curiosity and the search for answers about the puzzles of life. Scientists have simply systematized common sense by adding more sophisticated data collection processes and defining concepts more specifically. While other sciences focus on other parts of nature, social sciences ask the puzzling questions and seek explanations about human behavior. Social psychology is one of the branches of social science; as the name implies, it has a focus that draws from two already-established social sciences—sociology and psychology.

In order to more fully comprehend a particular science, we must examine the explanatory factor that is most central to that science. For example, if traditional sociologists were asked what best explains why humans feel and act as they do, they would answer that it is social structure or the social order. It is the social order into which individuals are born and are socialized that influences, and even determines, individual behavior. Traditional psychologists, on the other hand, contend that behavior stems from individual personality traits. The difference between these two fields is not so much that they study different phenomena; rather, it is what they see as the most important explanatory factor of human behavior. In that sense there has always been disagreement between the two fields.

Social psychology has emerged because students of both psychology and sociology have recognized the limitations and the important emphases of both.[2] It has become increasingly apparent that individuals influence the social order and that the social order in turn influences individuals. Social psychology is an attempt to find a middle ground and take both emphases into account. To some extent, though, in attempting to accommodate two somewhat opposing explanatory emphases, it has failed to come up with an explanatory focus of its own. One author of a social psychology textbook readily admits this when he says, "In all candor, you shouldn't expect too much from social psychological theories. Our formulations obviously are not as highly developed as those in the natural sciences."[3] Nevertheless, social psychology has succeeded in questioning the adequacy of both the psychological and the sociological explanations. Specifically, individual personality traits are treated by psychologists as if they were given entities that do not themselves need to be explained. Likewise, sociologists have treated the social order as if it were a given entity that needed no explanation. To fully understand human nature, in fact, both of those phenomena need to be explained, as does any other part of the human environment. Both need to be treated, not so much as given entities that cause other phenomena but are themselves never caused, but as processes with definable sources.

Social psychology with an emphasis on interaction views the human experience as a process of symbolic interaction. According to this theoretical perspective, interaction is the most central explanatory factor. As humans continuously and symbolically interact with one another in all possible situations, both individual identities and social order are produced. As processes, however, both personalities and social orders are continuously subject to change as the result of further interaction.[4]

The interaction perspective offers a dynamic view of all aspects of life, including aging. This is the social psychological perspective that will be used in this chapter to analyze the lives of the elderly in various cultural settings. We will examine their sense of self, their relationships, their roles, their attitudes, their feelings, their motivations, and their definitions of the situations in which they find themselves.

CHANGING PERCEPTIONS OF SELF WITH AGE

One of the central social psychological issues related to aging is what characterizes individuals as they age. Social psychologists generally agree that there are individual differences between people in their attitudes, behaviors, and modes of interaction. There are disagreements, however, in conceptualizations of individual differences. Some use *personality* and others use *self* as the concept that best explains individual differences. While the definitions of these two concepts have some aspects in common, there is much variation in their typical treatments. Those who analyze individual differences in terms of personalities tend to categorize them into fairly well-defined and fixed traits that individuals are assumed to possess.[5] In contrast, those who use the term *self* to account for individual differences tend to define the self as a process and assume that individuals are unique and do not fit into one category of personal traits or another. This is an important distinction because it helps us to understand what the unit of analysis is in assessing changes in individual characteristics. In analyzing people in terms of the self, the processes through which the self develops constitute the important units of analysis. We must focus on the processes, not on specific characteristics that may be assumed to be related to various ages.

If we assume that the self is a developmental process, then, we need to understand the elements of that process in order to comprehend how the self may change as individuals age. Of first importance is to recognize that the process is a cognitive one. No such phenomenon as the self emerges or becomes a reality without the ability to learn language, to conceptualize and make sense out of the environment, and to interact with others on the basis of how we perceive the world. The use of language is what gives our lives meaning and makes it possible for us to plan and sustain life, and yet it is not a skill with which we are born. It is a skill that we must learn, and we are totally dependent upon others in our social environment to learn it.[6,7]

It is in an environment of ongoing symbolic interaction that we initially learn the use and the meanings associated with language. We are also largely dependent upon that environment to maintain these cognitive skills throughout our lives. It is in the social realm that the dynamics of life are played out and that our sense of self emerges. Helen Keller's account of her early years illustrates this truth. The symbolic environment in which she lived simply did not reach her because, until she learned a sign language based on touch, she was locked into a world of deafness and blindness in which she simply responded directly to external stimuli just as an animal would.[8]

Several components of the self emerge from this interactive process. They can be divided into two basic concepts of self: (1) those that provide us with a sense of ourselves as "objects" in relationship to other objects in our midst and that give us a sense of our location and (2) those that are evaluative and provide us with a sense of our worth.[9,10]

Probably the most basic self-concept is that of self-awareness. Until we are aware of ourselves as objects or persons separate from but related to others, no other characteristics of the self can develop. Furthermore, to the extent that we lose awareness of ourselves throughout life, we also tend to lose elements of the self. It has been pointed out, for example, that we often act with very little immediate awareness of what we are doing because many acts become habitual or routine, especially in isolation, where they are never subject to social scrutiny. The result of self-awareness, then, is more accurate self-perceptions.[11] By implication, the loss of self-awareness will result in less accurate self-perceptions. This is especially applicable to the problem of disengagement among the elderly.

Aside from those among the elderly who suffer dementia-type cognitive losses, loss of self-awareness is actually not as great a problem among this population as many in modern society imagine. The false assumption that aging brings loss of self-awareness was illustrated in a number of television commercials in the mid-1980s. Particularly offensive were commercials advertising eye clinics in which elderly persons were portrayed as being so unaware of themselves that they became totally dependent upon a son or daughter to explain their problems to them, list their insurance benefits, choose the right clinic, take them to the clinic, and speak for them at the clinic.

This kind of portrayal is thought by some to serve as a labeling process, with the effect of creating isolation which, in turn, often does lead to actual loss of awareness, loss of a sense of competence, and even loss of communication skills.[12] Studies show that this series of events is not typical for most elderly people, however.[13]

Loss of awareness among the elderly is often a product of some types of institutionalization, even among those who do not suffer from dementia. For example, Kutner has described the situation of terminally ill patients in hospital wards who had been deliberately isolated from one another and from everyone else except hospital attendants. Although none suffered from organic brain damage, most had lost confidence, interaction skills, and an awareness of themselves and the world around them. These losses had resulted not from their illnesses, but directly from the isolating practices of the hospitals. Through a specifically designed rehabilitation program, Kutner was able to turn the wards into social groups in which all of the patients actively participated. As a result, their communication skills were effectively restored and they again became keenly aware of and vitally interested in themselves and their environments.[14]

Another concept having to do with the self as an object is *self-perception.* Although this concept does not connote a fully developed sense of self, it goes one step beyond a simple awareness of self. With self-perception, individuals are able to take themselves into account much as they do others.

There are two somewhat different ideas of how self-perception contributes to the development of self. Bem describes the process from a purely behavioristic perspective. In essence, he contends that self-perception results from, rather than leads to, behavior.[15] According to this theory, humans often act in direct response to external stimuli. They then account for or rationalize their acts by inferring that the actions came from some internal disposition. That inference then becomes part of one's self-perception. This idea is similar to what Hewitt calls "motive talk,"—giving after-the-fact accounts of acts that are questioned[16]—although it is questionable whether human behavior ever results from direct responses to external stimuli. Instead, as Hewitt explains it, rationalized, after-the-fact self-perception is more likely to result from situations in which established normative guidelines are absent and actions are based on norms that emerge within the situations themselves.[17] The process is nevertheless a real one, especially for those in the midst of social adjustment, as many elderly people are in facing such life events as retirement and widowhood.

The other way of describing self-perception is as the product of actively interacting with oneself. Mead described the self as containing two active elements, the *I* and the *me,* which are in constant dialogue with each other. According to Mead, the *me* is that part of the self that represents established values and norms, while the *I* is the impulsive aspect of the self and the main source of innovation and creativity.[18] Mead's I and me should not be confused with Freud's concepts of id and superego. The I and the me are not at war with each other, as Freud depicted the id and superego. Neither is the I antisocial, as the id was described to be. As Bolton suggests, the I is not just a matter of an organism impulsively reacting to stimuli, as a result of some biologically innate drive. Instead it represents an alternative perspective to that represented by the me, and may be equally socially acceptable.[19] The truth is that societies expect individuals to think and even act impulsively as much as they expect them to adhere to established social values. Also, the me is not necessarily an internalization of societal norms that have been forced upon the individual, as Freud viewed the superego. Most of all, it is part of the self that may or may not reflect given social values or norms.

In setting forth his ideas of the I and the me, Mead simply wanted to indicate that the processes involved in symbolic interaction work internally, with oneself, as much as they do externally, with others. In that sense the self has all the attributes of a social group. We can talk to ourselves, challenge our own ideas, argue with ourselves, make decisions, and plan our actions. Because we humans have this capability, we are not merely reactive or responsive to our environments, but inevitably and constantly active participants. Even at times when we may outwardly appear to mindlessly respond to environmental stimuli, we are internally actively involved at least to some degree. This is just as true for the elderly as for the young.

It is through the interaction processes, internal as well as external, that we gain a sense of our own identities—what we are like, who we are, where we belong, what we should think, and how we should feel and act. Turner contends that we come to have a "real self"—a core set of feelings, attitudes, and values that we are willing to claim as our own—which we cumulatively acquire from all of the interactions in which we have been involved throughout our lives. Having acquired a "real self," we tend to distinguish between those feelings and actions that emanate from us spontaneously but are really foreign to us, and those that come from our real selves. We are ready to claim ownership of the latter but not the former.[20]

The real self, according to Turner, tends to be either institutionally or impulsively oriented—to find personal fulfillment either in pursuing the goals of social institutions or in pursuing personal goals. Turner's analysis is limited by a rather narrow definition of institutions. The truth is that there are very different types of institutions, and not all of them are committed to established social order. Some, such as the 1960s social revolution (which became quite institutionalized), entrepreneurship, and journalism, exist for the very purpose of challenging the status quo. Others, such as retirement, are structured in a way that, in fact, encourages the pursuit of self-interest. The truth is that all of us are institutionally oriented, and our individual identities are greatly influenced by the particular institutions to which we become attached. Also, when individuals shift their orientations from one type of social institution to another, they can easily become confused about their basic identities.

The quest for "personal identity" is a relatively new phenomenon. Karp and Yoels point out that the search for identify has spread rapidly, and has become something of a social movement.[21] They suggest that this movement has emerged at a time of great geographic and social mobility, and of a shift in emphasis in our social lives from a work ethic to a consumption ethic. Mobility tends to result in a sense of rootlessness, and the consumption ethic pushes us to try to find fulfillment and identity in the consumption of goods and services with built-in obsolescence. The movement is fed by those who promote and market consumption as the answer to the search for identity. These authors contend that this movement especially touches young adults, but it might well have even greater impact on the elderly population in the experience of retirement.

Much of the literature on identity crisis is related to aging. Sheehy wrote about identity crises at various points in life that she contended were very predictable.[22] Brandes strongly suggests that age 40 is so prominent as a symbol of midlife crisis that just becoming 40 itself often triggers such a crisis.[23] Atchley hypothesizes that identity crises tend to take place in times of such great change that it is difficult to integrate one's experiences into one's sense of self.[24] Similarly, George suggests that in times of social change, adjustment and identity become closely related dynamic processes and not just static states of being.[25] It would seem, then, that identity would be even more of a problem for older adults than for others. As Atchley puts it, "the longer one has an adult identity, the more times one's theory of self can be tested across various situations."[26]

George points out that our identities are largely related to the statuses (positions) we occupy in society and the social roles we perform. Furthermore, the fact of having acquired a sense of identity greatly influences the positions and roles that we continue to select. This selection process in turn serves to solidify our existing identities.[27] By the same token, a loss of positions and roles would logically create a loss of identity.

Aging typically brings not only major changes, but also major losses. The combination of both changes and losses would seem to indicate that challenges to identity constitute a particular problem of the aged. This can be illustrated by the experience of becoming widowed, which involves both loss and challenges to one's social identity.[28,29] Most elderly people who are widowed are women, and most elderly women today tend to identify themselves in ways intimately connected to marriage and family.

What, then, are the facts about identity among the elderly? There are at least two important types of identity issues relating to aging: (1) the extent to which established, life-long identities are maintained into old age, and (2) the extent to which individuals take on new age-related identities. With regard to maintaining life-long identities, many investigators have been convinced that the many changes and related losses experienced in old age would translate into major losses in identity, with consequent negative impact on self-concept.[30–32] However, the available evidence clearly shows that, as a whole, this is not the case.[33,34] There is a surprisingly high level of maintenance of identity among the elderly.

How can identity maintenance in old age be explained? Several factors help to answer that question. One is the emphasis placed on reminiscence among elderly people. Their experiences provide them with much material for self-interaction focused on past accomplishments. Reminiscence is a particular kind of self-interaction that tends to keep elderly people oriented to the past and reinforces their past identities. In addition, as George suggests, it may be that the elderly somewhat deliberately select identity-maintaining strategies. Identities are inevitably formed and maintained with the encouragement and approval of the significant others in our lives. Aware of the importance of others, many elderly deliberately elect to interact with those who will continue to support them in their established identities.[35] Retired teachers may associate with other retired teachers and serve as volunteer tutors in order to maintain their teacher identities, for example.

The contexts in which elderly people adopt new age-related identities, and the extent to which they do so, also deserve to be examined. For example, is it part of being elderly to personally admit the fact of being old and to willingly internalize that identity? Under what circumstances and with what consequences to the sense of self might this happen or not happen? A study of this issue was recently conducted among Yoruba elderly in southwest Nigeria.[36] A significant positive correlation was found between chronological age and age identification, but there was no relationship between age identification and life satisfaction, as the investigator expected. The Yoruba culture is a rather primitive one in which the older adults never retire and in which the roles they perform in old age carry a substantial amount of authority within the family and community. Togonu-Bickersteth speculates that it is likely that the harshness of their lives explains why life satisfaction does not tend to increase with increased old-age identity. He sees it as at least somewhat significant that life satisfaction does not decrease with increased-age identity, however. He concludes that "in Yoruba culture advanced age confers mystical and social privilege." Thus, being old is not viewed as a socially negative experience."

Such findings in traditional cultures are probably not surprising, but what about age identification in more modern societies? The People's Republic of China cannot yet be considered one of the world's industrially developed countries, but some of the Chinese practices related to the aged are similar to those in developed countries. For example, most Chinese citizens now retire at even younger ages than elsewhere in the world. Nevertheless, age identification in China certainly is not something to be denied or avoided. This is due, in part, to the long tradition of filial piety which has not been totally destroyed during the years of Communist rule. Just as important, though, is the fact that most elderly people in China continue to perform socially significant roles. Although these roles are often quite different from those they previously performed at work, many of them carry substantial authority.[37]

It has long been assumed that there is a strong tendency in the most industrialized countries for the elderly to resist being identified as old for as long as possible. In addition, the assumption is that when the aged finally identify themselves as old, they see the identity as a negative one because of the prevailing negative stereotypes about older people.[38] Based on his observations of elderly people in Japan, Palmore reported that, despite advanced industrialization in that country, negative stereotypes of the aged did not exist. He concluded that this was because they had effectively adapted their ancient traditions of honoring and respecting their elders to their modern way of life.[39] More recent analyses indicate an increasing breakdown in the application of their traditions and an increase in negative stereotypes of the aged, however.[40] Presumably, this trend will also lead to decreased age identification among the aged themselves.

Evidence concerning age identity in the United States is mixed. While many elderly Americans view old age more negatively than do the elderly in Oriental societies, Ward found that accepting that identity was related neither to the prevalence of negative stereotypes nor to loss of self-esteem. Instead, age identification was mostly related to actual age-related deprivations.[41] In a longitudinal study, Bultena and Powers found substantial denial of age identification among people over 60, but a tendency to accept that kind of identity as those in the sample grew older. There was also a significant tendency for age identification to be seen as positive when respondents assessed their situations as advantageous compared with those of other elderly people with whom they interacted.[42]

From these analyses, it seems apparent that the greatest deterrents to the acquisition of age identity among the elderly are (1) their relative ability to function adequately, compared with others in their own peer group and (2) their relationships with significant others, especially age-related peers. Having meaningful roles to perform in old age, especially as they themselves individually or corporately define them, also seems to be important. Generally, the opinions and stereotypes held by the rest of society seem to have very little effect on whether such identities are formed and on whether they are negative or positive.

In the 1960s and 1970s, much emphasis was placed on the negative aspects of old age and its affects on aspects of the self among the aged. It is noteworthy that almost no up-to-date literature exists on the problem of old-age denial and the unwillingness to be identified as such. Perhaps that is in part because of actual changes in the impact of the negative aspects of aging from then to now. It is also due in part to a fundamental misunderstanding of what is involved in the development of self in old age.

Even in the era of age-related negativism, to which he himself contributed, Rose hypothesized the development of what he called a "subculture of aging."[43] As Rose saw it, a central issue in the development of this phenomenon was the increasing interaction of elderly people with one another rather than with those in other age groups. He predicted that, as this happened, regardless of whether it took place as a result of rejection by others or a result of feelings of affinity toward one another, elderly people would begin to establish their own unique set of values and norms. A by-product of this process would be an increasing reliance on age-related peer groups for a sense of self-concept and identity. Since the major orientation of this kind of structure is old age, adaptation of age identification would logically be expected on the part of those involved. Perhaps this, more than any other factor, helps to explain why age identification seems to be increasingly prevalent, and why that identification seems to be increasingly positive today.

Another vital component of the self is the evaluative aspect. This is typically referred to as self-worth or self-esteem and can be defined as the way in which individuals assess their own worth to themselves and to others. The question of whether elderly people maintain a sense of their own personal worth while suffering the many physical, social, and mental losses commonly associated with old age has been a consistent theme of inquiry among gerontologists for many years. In the minds of most social-psychologically oriented gerontologists, it is probably thought of as the most vital factor in the maintenance of a healthy self in old age. It is commonly assessed by the use of a self-esteem scale and is treated as an indicator of life satisfaction and morale. The association between one or more of these measures and every conceivable age-related loss has been studied to determine the impact of the various types of losses on this aspect of the self. The basic assumption behind most of these investigative efforts is that age-related losses lead to negative assessments of personal worth among the aged. Remaining is the question of which of the many losses cause the greatest loss of self-esteem or self-worth.

If this is such a vital issue, then it behooves us to understand it from a theoretical as well as an empirical perspective. Two such perspectives will be examined here. One of the most comprehensive theoretical explanations of the loss of the self-worth has been provided by Kuypers and Bengtson (discussed more fully in Chapter 5).[44] According to this theory, three major losses are typically associated with age: (1) loss of roles, (2) loss of normative guidance, and (3) loss of reference groups. As a result of the loss of productive roles the elderly become publicly labeled as useless, incompetent, and obsolete. As a result of the loss of normative guidance and reference groups, from which we tend to get clues about actions that are appropriate, elderly individuals become susceptible to public labels. As a result, the aged typically fail to use their functional skills and eventually lose them. The final, defeating result is that the public labels become personally internalized. Elderly people judge themselves as useless, incompetent, and worthless. These authors expressed their belief that a negative sense of self-worth would predominate among the elderly in the modern world.

As much sense as this may make from the perspective of labeling theory, the prevailing empirical evidence does not tend to support it as the normal pattern among the aged in the United States.[45] Self-esteem is consistently found to be high among the aged. In one study, it was found to be almost twice as high among the elderly as among teenagers.[46] In fact, evidence indicates that self-esteem tends to increase with age.

One cannot help but wonder about the source of such optimism among the aged. It may be related in part to their particular perspective on the life course. Based on a recent study on life purposes, it has been suggested, for example, that remembering past accomplishments is an important source of feelings of contentment and a sense of integrity, even among the very old.[47] In addition, evidence does not indicate that there is a major loss of reference groups among the aged, as Kuypers and Bengtson predicted. Peer-group networks are an ever-increasing pattern among the elderly. The formation and maintenance of social networks has been described as "negotiated order."[48] Involvement in such networks is often a result of what the elderly see as needs in new situations. Social networks can easily become the source of new forms of self-esteem and self-worth. In that context, an individual's sense of worth might not be at all apparent to an outsider. For example, this author once observed an elderly woman who came to a senior center daily to do nothing but play Chinese checkers with a few choice friends. She very rarely missed a day. She lived alone and so, on the surface, it appeared that she came purely because she liked the game and to avoid being lonely. Her life seemed to have little or no purpose or worth. However, she revealed in an interview that, in fact, she was gaining a whole new sense of self-worth by coming to the center each day. She explained that the others with whom she played often told her that they were dependent upon her for their enjoyment of the day's activities. She had come to accept it as her duty to be there every day.

It is clear that self-esteem and a sense of worth among the aged has many possible sources and takes many different forms. Maintaining established or developing new forms of self-worth are dynamic social processes that often cannot be understood without first understanding the social worlds of the elderly themselves.

ROLE TRANSITIONS WITH AGE

Role change is a central issue in the social psychology of aging. As we have seen, roles have a profound effect on an individual's self-concept and sense of worth. They are also vital to the positions of the elderly in society.

In the many analyses of roles among the aged, the concept of loss is an assumption that has consistently been made.[49-52] The validity of that basic assumption is now being questioned. Perhaps *role transition*, rather than role loss, better represents what people experience as they age. Part of that difference in perspective depends upon how roles are defined.

The definition of roles on which much of the role-loss literature has been based is structural. This is the most prevalent view and one that has been very well articulated in social gerontology by Rosow.[53] From this perspective, roles are related to statuses, or the socially defined positions that each person is assigned. Roles are the socially prescribed ways that individuals are expected to act in fulfilling the requirements of their positions. From this perspective, variations in role performance are viewed as deviant.

In analyzing changes in roles through the life course, Rosow explains that role expectations differ from one stage of life to another and that adjustments must be made as we move from one stage to the next. In general, these adjustments are made possible through a well-defined socialization process that rewards individuals for adjusting to the new role expectations of the next stage of life. The one exception to this process is old age. Society provides neither adequate role expectations nor rewards for taking on the old-person status. Old age is the one stage of life for which we are not properly socialized. Consequently, Rosow contends, old age represents a major loss of roles and is seen by the aged themselves as a negative experience that most would prefer to avoid. Not all analysts who have emphasized role loss are structuralists. Yet most have tended to use this kind of description of roles in their analyses.

A very different definition of roles is provided by symbolic interactionists. While they admit that some roles do become fairly well socially established, their contention is that none are ever prescribed fully enough to be considered social structures. Some roles are not defined at all before they are performed. Roles are therefore not social structures that individuals must either conform to or deviate from. Instead, they are negotiated in our interactions with those in our social environments. In order for us to make sense of them, every interaction requires the definition and performance of some kinds of roles. As Turner puts it, "The role beomes the point of reference for placing interpretation on specific actions, for anticipating that one line of action will follow another, and for making evaluations of individual actions."[54] We may come to some situations with fairly well-established notions about the roles that we are expected to perform as we engage in interaction. In many other situations, however, the roles have to be negotiated almost entirely from the situations themselves. Regardless of the situations, though, the very processes of interaction include an element of role negotiation. As Colomy and Rhoades explain, "An essential feature of role-taking and role-making processes in the interactionist model is the grouping of behavior into meaningful and intelligible units."[55] As a professor who has taught a course in sociocultural aging a number of times, for example, I have come to have a good idea of what my role is in teaching that course. From one semester to another, however, the teacher role in that course changes quite drastically, from predominantly lecturing to predominantly discussion, depending upon the number and kinds of comments made by students. According to this perspective, then, the definition and performance of roles are not entities that are prescribed in advance but are dynamic processes that carry great potential for change even in situations that may seem to be governed by tradition. Viewing the roles of the elderly from this perspective, we cannot assume that the movement out of certain roles will constitute a net loss of roles. Instead, we need to examine more fully their continued interactions to discover what new roles they may be acquiring.

What, then, characterizes the interaction patterns of the aged in the world today? As we will learn in Chapter 7, family relationships continue to be vital to the elderly in all parts of the world. This is particularly true in Oriental countries, but it is also true in the United States and other Western societies. Relationships with spouses are by far the most vital. The evidence is, in fact, that marital satisfaction tends to be at its highest point among couples in retirement.[56] The elderly also continue to insist on the privilege of having regular contact with their adult children and grandchildren.[57,58] This tends to be true even for those who no longer live in close proximity to their children and grandchildren. As a whole, interaction with other extended family members does not seem to be as important. At least part of the reason that family relationships continue is their meaning with regard to role transitions, some of which are viewed positively and some negatively by the aged. In the People's Republic of China, elderly family members who are retired and living with one of their children's families find themselves in partnership with their children in child-rearing roles.[59] In the West, even though some are unable to do so, elderly parents and their adult children prefer to live in close proximity to one another but not in the same household.[60] This allows them to interact regularly, to develop new types of nonauthoritative grandparent roles, and, at the same time, to avoid the problem of the role reversal between themselves and their adult children by becoming dependent upon their children in their daily lives. Problems with intergenerational relationships in the family have been noted even in cultural groups in which strong emphasis is placed on the family. This is true in China, where the three-generation household is still preferred,[61] and on the Navajo reservation, where intergenerational support is still strongly emphasized.[62]

Fear of, and resistance to, becoming dependent is an overriding concern among the elderly, especially in the United States, and it influences both how they interact and with whom.[63,64] As a result, a growing tendency among the elderly is to select as friends others who are similar in background and experience. Relationships with people their own age are becoming the most attractive to them.[65] These types of relationships are also increasing among those cultural groups in which family intergenerational interdependency is still strongly emphasized, such as in China and among the Navajo elderly.

What, then, are the results of these kinds of relationships with regard to role changes among the aged? For one thing, adjustment to retirement (the loss of the work role) has been found to be relatively easy for the vast majority of elderly people. A great deal of evidence on retirement among American workers indicates that their morale and life satisfaction does not decline with retirement, as many have predicted that it would.[66,67] One investigator found that both community involvement and life satisfaction increased following retirement.[68] Atchley contends that retirement itself represents a role that includes behavioral expectations.[69] Along with societal expectations, the retirement role has also come to encourage peer interaction and activities, such as traveling and recreation. Retirement is becoming a whole new way of life for many elderly people in those communities where retirement has become national policy.

CONCLUSION

We have analyzed the social psychological conditions of elderly people in the world today. We have examined how their perceptions of themselves and the roles they perform have changed, and we have discussed the interactional situations in which those changes have taken place. It has been noted that in the past, most such analyses have concluded that old age generally means "loss" in the social psychological sense. However, the available evidence, especially that produced in recent years, shows that what elderly people tend to experience is not so much loss as it is change and transition. The sense of self often changes markedly in old age, but self-perception and self-esteem tend to remain positive (and are sometimes even more positive) in old age. For increasing numbers of elderly people, the roles of old age are very different than those they had as younger adults. For them, retirement does not mean the loss of roles but a transition to new and different roles.

The changes and transitions that the aged are experiencing today tend to be mostly positive and are prevalent cross-culturally and across social classes, despite the vast cultural and class differences. The basically positive nature of social psychological well-being of elderly people today can be attributed largely to their patterns of interaction. Particularly important is the fact that they increasingly prefer and choose age-peer interaction. Interaction among those in common situations, such as retirement and old age, is a dynamic process that inevitably produces new self-perceptions and new roles that are appropriate and directly applicable to those common situations. To ignore those very dynamic processes in analyzing the social psychology of aging is to misunderstand what becoming old today is really like.

NOTES

[1] Robert H. Lauer and Warren H. Handel, *Social Psychology: The Theory and Application of Symbolic Interactionism* (Englewood Cliffs, N.J.: Prentice-Hall, 1983), p. 4.

[2] Cookie W. Stephan and Walter G. Stephan, *Two Social Psychologies: An Integrative Approach* (Homewood, Ill.: Dorsey Press, 1985), p. 12.

[3] Leonard Berkowitz, *A Survey of Social Psychology* (New York: Holt, Rinehart and Winston, 1986), p. 13.

[4] John P. Hewitt, *Self and Society: A Symbolic Interactionist Social Psychology* (Boston: Allyn & Bacon, 1984), pp. 5–8.

[5] Louis A. Penner, *Social Psychology: Concepts and Applications* (St. Paul, Minn.: West, 1986), pp. 99–101.

[6] Hewitt, *Self and Society*, pp. 102–6.

[7] Alfred R. Lindesmith, Anselm L. Strauss, and Norman K. Denzin, *Social Psychology* (New York: Holt, Rinehart and Winston, 1977), pp. 312–23.

[8] Helen Keller, *The Story of My Life* (New York: Doubleday, 1917), pp. 22–24.

[9] Ralph H. Turner, "The Real Self: From Institution to Impulse," *American Journal of Sociology*, 81, no. 5 (March 1976), 989–1016.

[10] Hewitt, *Self and Society*, pp. 117–25.

[11] Penner, *Social Psychology*, pp. 175–76.

[12] Joseph A. Kuypers and Vern L. Bengtson, "Social Breakdown and Competence: A Model of Normal Aging," *Human Development*, 16 (1973), 181–201.

[13] Linda K. George, *Role Transitions in Later Life* (Monterey, Calif.: Brooks/Cole, 1980), pp. 41–43.

[14] Bernard Kutner, "The Hospital Environment," *Social Sciences and Medicine*, 4, suppl. 1 (1970), 9–12.

[15] Daryl J. Bem, "Self-perception Theory," *Advances in Experimental Social Psychology*, vol. 6, ed. Leonard Berkowitz (New York: Academic Press, 1972), pp. 2–62.

[16] Hewitt, *Self and Society*, pp. 163–70.

[17] Ibid., p. 216.

[18] Ibid., pp. 72–74.

[19] Charles D. Bolton, "Some Consequences of the Median Self," *Symbolic Interaction*, 4, no. 2 (1981), 245–59.

[20] Turner, "Real Self," pp. 989–1016.

[21] David A. Karp and William C. Yoels, *Symbols, Selves, and Society: Understanding Interaction* (New York: Lippincott/Harper & Row, Pub., 1979), p. 204.

[22] Gail Sheehy, *Passages: Predictable Crises of Adult Life* (New York: Dutton, 1976), pp. 20–32.

[23] Stanley Brandes, *Forty: The Age and the Symbol* (Knoxville: The University of Tennessee Press, 1986), pp. 3–15.

[24] Robert C. Atchley, *Aging: Continuity and Change* (Belmont, Calif.: Wadsworth, 1987), pp. 100–101.

[25] George, *Role Transitions in Later Life*, pp. 21–22.

[26] Atchley, *Aging: Continuity and Change*, p. 100.

[27] George, *Role Transitions in Later Life*, p. 18.

[28] Arnold S. Brown, "Socially Disruptive Events and Morale Among the Elderly" (unpublished paper presented at the Gerontological Society 27th Annual Meeting in Portland, Oregon, October 1974), Abstract printed in *The Gerontologist*, 14, no. 5, pt. 2 (October 1974), p. 72.

[29] Robert C. Atchley, *Social Forces and Aging: An Introduction to Social Gerontology* (Belmont, Calif.: Wadsworth, 1985), pp. 224–31.

[30] Arnold M. Rose, "A Current Theoretical Issue in Social Gerontology," in *Older People and Their Social World*, eds. Arnold M. Rose and Warren A. Peterson (Philadelphia: F. A. Davis, 1965), pp. 359–66.

[31] Kuypers and Bengtson, "Social Breakdown and Competence," pp. 181–201.

[32] Irving Rosow, "The Social Context of the Aging Self," *The Gerontologist*, 13, no. 1 (Spring 1973), 82–87.

[33] Atchley, *Social Forces and Aging*, p. 225.

[34] George, *Role Transitions in Later Life*, p. 21.

[35] Ibid., pp. 17–18.

[36] Funmi Togonu-Bickersteth, "Age Identification Among Yoruba Aged," *Journal of Gerontology*, 41, no. 1 (January 1986), 110–13.

[37] Myrna Lewis, "Aging in the People's Republic of China," *International Journal of Aging and Development*, 15, no. 2 (1982), 79–105.

[38] Rosow, "The Social Context of the Aging Self," pp. 82–87.

[39] Erdman Palmore, "The Status and Integration of the Aged in Japanese Society," *Journal of Gerontology*, 30, no. 2 (March 1975), 199–208.

[40] "The Japanese-style Welfare System," *Japanese Quarterly*, 30 (July–September 1983), 327–30.

[41] Russell A. Ward, "The Impact of Subjective Age and Stigma on Older Persons," *Journal of Gerontology*, 32, no. 2 (March 1977), 227–32.

[42] G. L. Bultena and E. A. Powers, "Denial of Aging: Age Identification and Reference Group Orientations," *Journal of Gerontology*, 33, no. 5 (September 1978), 748–54.

[43] Arnold M. Rose, "The Subculture of Aging: A Framework for Research in Social Gerontology," in *Older People and Their Social World*, eds. Arnold M. Rose and Warren A. Peterson (Philadelphia: F. A. Davis, 1965), pp. 3–16.

[44] Kuypers and Bengston, "Social Breakdown and Competence," pp. 181–201.

[45] George, *Role Transitions in Later Life*, p. 43.

[46] Atchley, *Social Forces and Aging*, p. 104.

[47] Gary T. Recker, Edward J. Peacock, and Paul T. P. Wong, "Meaning and Purpose in Life and Well-Being: A Life Span Perspective," *Journal of Gerontology*, 42, no. 1 (January 1987), 44–49.

[48] Gary A. Fine and Sherryl Kleinman, "Network and Meaning: An Interactionist Approach to Structure," *Symbolic Interaction*, 6, no. 1 (Spring 1983), 97–110.

[49] Jacquelyne J. Jackson, *Minorities and Aging* (Belmont, Calif.: Wadsworth, 1980), pp. 119–25.

[50] Kuypers and Bengston, "Social Breakdown and Competence," pp. 181–201.

[51] Rose, "Current Theoretical Issues," pp. 359–66.

[52] Irving Rosow, "Status and Role Change Through the Life Course," in *Handbook of Aging and Social Science*, eds. R. H. Binstock and Ethel Shanas (New York: Van Nostrand Reinhold, 1976), p. 462.

[53] Ibid.

[54] Ralph H. Turner, "Role Taking: Process versus Conformity," in *Human Behavior and Social Processes*, ed. Arnold M. Rose (Boston: Houghton Mifflin Company, 1962), pp. 20–40.

[55] Paul Colomy and Gary Rhoades, "Role Performance and Person Perception: Toward an Interactionist Approach," *Symbolic Interaction*, 6, no. 2 (1983), 207–27.

[56] Boyd C. Rollins and Harold Feldman, "Marital Satisfaction over the Family Life Cycle, *Journal of Marriage and the Family*, 32, no. 6 (February 1970), 20–28.

[57] Arnold S. Brown, "Satisfying Relationships for the Elderly and Their Patterns of Disengagement," *The Gerontologist*, 14, no. 3 (June 1974), 258–62.

[58] Ethel Shanas et al., *Old People in Three Industrial Societies* (New York: Atherton Press, 1968), pp. 192–97.

[59] Deborah Davis-Friedmann, *Long Lives: Chinese Elderly and the Communist Revolution* (Cambridge, Mass.: Harvard University Press, 1983), pp. 47–54.

[60] Shanas et al., *Old People in Three Industrial Societies*, pp. 192–94.

[61] Davis-Friedmann, *Long Lives*, pp. 71–84.

[62] Arnold S. Brown, "Report on Navajo Elder Abuse" (unpublished research report submitted to the Navajo Office on Aging, Window Rock, Arizona, Fall 1986), pp. 14–15.

[63] Arnold S. Brown, "Problems of Dependence and Independence Among the Elderly" (unpublished research report presented at the 25th Annual Western Gerontological Society Meeting in San Francisco, April 1979).

[64] Atchley, *Aging: Continuity and Change*, pp. 89–91.

[65] Ibid., pp. 203–4.

[66] Brown, "Socially Disruptive Events," p. 72.

[67] Linda K. George and George Maddox, "Subjective Adaptation to Loss of the Work Role: A Longitudinal Study," *Journal of Gerontology*, 32, no. 1 (July 1977), 456–62.

[68] Bill D. Bell, "Role Set Orientations and Life Satisfaction: A New Look at an Old Theory," in *Time, Roles and Self in Old Age*, ed. Jaber F. Gubrium (New York: Human Sciences Press, 1976), pp. 148–64.

[69] Atchley, *Aging: Continuity and Change*, pp. 223–24.

5

The Emergence of Social Theories of Old Age

INTRODUCTION

Scientific interest in the social aspects of aging is almost exclusively a twentieth-century phenomenon, and much of this type of scientific work has lacked a theoretical base. Furthermore, indications are that most of the theoretical work that has been done among social scientists has been initiated in the United States, and has been applied cross-culturally only to a limited extent. As Maddox and Campbell point out, even the social scientific research that has been done and reported internationally has been "national rather than comparative."[1] What theoretical foundation there was for the study of "Old People in Three Industrial Societies," for example, was clearly from the United States.[2] To understand the important contributions that social theories of aging have made to gerontology, therefore, we must begin by examining the contexts in which the various social theories have emerged in the United States and then examine their cross-cultural adequacy.

Very limited attention was paid by social scientists to the social and psychological issues of aging during the early part of this century. Those few who became interested did so out of concern for their own personal aging problems.[3] Special attention began to be paid to this area of gerontology in the United States during the 1950s. Throughout that decade, U.S. citizens became increasingly aware and alarmed that the social lives of the aged were changing. It appeared that the elderly were becoming socially isolated and concomitantly seemed to be losing their sense of purpose and self-worth. There seemed to be no ready or adequate explanations for this, but deep concern for older people began to pervade society as a whole. There was an underlying suspicion that the rest of society must be at fault, and something of a societal guilt complex seems to have been partly behind the widespread concern.

Social gerontology began to develop as a discipline during that era. It became the task of this new discipline to study and provide scientific explanations for the disturbing phenomena related to aging. As a result of the work done by social gerontologists from that time until the present, a number of different and often conflicting theories of aging have been offered to explain the social psychological losses that tend to accompany old age.

The generating of theories of aging since the 1950s has in itself been something of a social process. It is a process that has been very much related to the changing perceptions of aging and to the social policies related to aging that have been developed. It has, on the one hand, reflected the changing perceptions and policies of old age and, on the other hand, contributed to those definitions and policies. As the Hendrickses have written about social gerontologists, "The crucial dimensions of their conceptual frameworks are but reflections from the larger social matrix. At the same time, however, gerontologists strive to reach beyond the world of common sense to discover consistent patterns of aging in the social world."[4] The theories that have emerged, then, must be analyzed, not so much as purely scientific work that provides factual explanations, but more realistically as an integral part of the changing phenomena of aging. In that sense, then, a comparative look at the major theories of aging and the social milieu out of which they have risen is an important aspect of the study of aging in modern society.

In the attempts by social gerontologists to find answers to the puzzling questions about why we tend to experience such social and psychological losses as disengagement and low self-esteem as we become older, several potentially causal factors became the focus of research. Such obvious contributors to disengagement as physical and mental health and loss of income were repeatedly researched, with the result that it became generally well established that these were indeed major causes.

It was soon discovered, however, that the physical and material variables alone could not account for all losses among the aged. Sociocultural and psychological variables such as status and role, self-concepts, and personality were, therefore, also investigated. Largely on the basis of these investigations, the major social theories of aging were developed.

When social gerontology began to become an important area of study for social scientists, research was basically descriptive in nature and lacked the discipline of explicit or formalized theory. Most of the social scientists who became interested in aging were involved in providing answers to the practical problems faced by the elderly. It soon became clear, however, that the practical answers tended to be based on quite definite theoretical assumptions. One set of these assumptions was later more clearly defined and stated as one of the major theories. Since then it has been defended, changed, and even quite severely challenged as other more formalized theories were offered and defended as viable explanations of the social aspects of aging.

ACTIVITY THEORY

While the early years were somewhat void of formal theory, the work that was done seemed to be based consistently on the underlying assumption that the elderly have the same social and psychological needs to be active as younger adults. This notion was especially emphasized by Burgess, Havighurst, and Tobin at the University of Chicago in the 1950s and was subsequently termed the *activity theory*.[5] According to this theory, inactivity is closely related to low levels of happiness, little sense of usefulness, and an inadequate adjustment to life in general among the aged.[6] The key to successful aging was thus said to be the maintenance of optimal levels of activity.[7]

The assumption that the elderly need to remain active was certainly not an original idea with the theorists. It very much fit what most Americans at that time believed and were concerned about in behalf of the elderly people being observed. It was thus not an empirically established, scientifically tested, or proven theory. Instead it was a quite popular assumption on which actions in behalf of the aged were being strongly proposed. This kind of emphasis influenced a major social policy effort. It contributed directly to the establishment of activity centers for senior citizens across the country. This was purely a nationally based theory, with no attempts made to give it a cross-cultural focus.

Despite substantial evidence that such social psychological factors as lack of a sense of self-worth were indeed related to low levels of activity,[8] it could not be adequately established that the relationship was a directly causal one. Even though there were positive results from the establishment of activity centers for many elderly, the theory turned out to be rather weak as an adequately comprehensive explanation of disengagement and personal loss among the aged. It failed to have the practical results that were anticipated. If the assumption of the theory that inactivity causes these problems were sound, then providing opportunities for them to become active in activity centers should have attracted most of the elderly, especially those who had become the most inactive. Yet, not even a majority of the elderly population were reached as participants of activity centers even among the most isolated.[9,10] At this point in time we can think of a number of possible reasons that some of the elderly would choose not to participate in activity center programs, but those reasons were not included as activity theory assumptions.

The inadequacy of the activity theory was its failure to consider a number of important issues. First, it failed to ask whether or not inactivity among the aged was voluntary on their part or was involuntarily thrust upon them. Second, it failed to distinguish among the various types of activities that may have been available to the elderly and to assess which did and did not provide meaningful roles in later life. As Atchley later stated, "No single standard can be used to determine the adequacy of activity patterns among mature adults."[11] The activities that middle-aged people value may not be what elderly people value. Third, it failed to consider what level of activity might be desirable for the aged. Fourth, it failed to analyze the processes of inactivity in old age in order to discover the major causal factors of inactivity among the aged.

DISENGAGEMENT THEORY

After a decade in which it had become apparent to most Americans that many of the aged were becoming socially isolated and psychologically troubled, there was an obvious need for some kind of comprehensive explanation to alleviate some of the guilt attached to that awareness. Such an explanation was provided by Cumming and Henry in their 1961 book, *Growing Old: The Process of Disengagement*, in which they outlined their *disengagement theory*.[12] If accepted, it would have gone a long way toward alleviating the sense of responsibility that many Americans felt about the plight of older citizens.

Cumming and Henry's book was also a report of an extensive study of the social lives of the aged conducted in the Kansas City area. Thus, their theory was dignified by the claim of having a solid empirical basis. In analyzing the validity of the theory, though, it must be realized that it was as much a product of their structural functionalist frame of reference as it was of the empirical data they cited as support for the theory.

Directly challenging the assumptions of activity theory—that the elderly have the same need to be active as others—Cumming and Henry contended that social disengagement for the aged is socially and psychologically functional and a natural part of the processes of aging. As people age, according to their theory, their most basic social psychological need changes from one of active involvement to one of inactive contemplation about the meaning of life in the face of impending death. This change is mutually advantageous to both society and the aged themselves. For the aged, it means the opportunity to retreat from the demands of society and quietly contemplate the meaning of life and death. For society as a whole, it provides a way to partially alleviate part of the social psychological trauma of the impairment and inevitable death of elderly people. By implication, the contention of the theory is that disengagement is inevitable, typically gradual, and preferred by and satisfying to the aged. Another implication of this theory was that it applies universally, and therefore cross-culturally, to all aged persons.

The practical and social policy implications of disengagement theory in the

United States should have been clear. If, as Cumming and Henry proposed, the social and psychological needs of the aged are quite different from those of the rest of the population, and disengagement is natural and preferred, then feeling guilty about the inactivity of the aged would be useless. To attempt to keep them active would actually be counterproductive for both the aged and the society as a whole. The condition of social isolation among the aged, then, was not something to try to change or about which to despair, but rather was something that ought to be accepted and even encouraged.

Disengagement theory very quickly became well known among gerontologists, but it was accepted and supported by almost none of them. It represented the first comprehensive and definitive social theory of aging, and for that it was respected. Most social gerontologists simply did not believe it, however, despite the empirical data provided by the authors to support it. In effect, it became the theoretical orientation for virtually all theorists for many years, primarily because it was the theory to challenge and to try to disprove. Many who did the challenging did so with moral indignation and passion. It was as though we as industrious and socially active Americans could not bring ourselves to believe that social isolation and noninvolvement was right or acceptable for anyone, regardless of what evidence there might be to support such an argument. It seemed much better to admit that the condition of old age in the United States was abnormal, to accept the blame, and to do all we could to alleviate the problem. It should have been an explanation that gave societal reassurance about our aged, but it seemed to do precisely the opposite.

The explanation provided by disengagement theory did have verification, as well as nonacceptance problems, however. Cumming and Henry failed to provide adequate evidence that the aged actually prefer to disengage or that they are even satisfied with conditions of disengagement, as the two theorists implied would be true. They also failed to adequately establish that all people do, as they contended, naturally and gradually disengage as they move into old age. Although their statistical analysis made it appear to be a gradual process, subsequent analyses of the actual experiences of the aged have shown that it is socially abrupt and psychologically disturbing. Furthermore, by no means do all older people disengage.[13,14] The theory has also been criticized as being simply inadequate as a social theory of aging. As Maddox and Campbell noted, "The theory tended toward biological reductionism and hence dealt inadequately with both the social context of aging and the personal meaning of aging."[15]

Despite the claim that it was universal in scope, disengagement theory has also been criticized because it is culturally bound to the situation of the aged in the United States. In fact, analyses of the theory have been made in at least two other countries, and it was found to be largely invalid in each case, because of different cultural characteristics. Simic found, for example, that disengagement simply has not been a social pattern among the aged in Yugoslavia. He attributes the difference to the very different socialization patterns in the two countries. According to him, Americans are socialized throughout their lives toward "self-realization, independence, and individualism," all of which is apt to separate the generations and lead to social isolation, especially among elderly people. In contrast, Yugoslavians are socialized toward "kinship corporacy, interdependence, and familial symbiosis and reciprocity," all of which tends to ensure continued intergenerational relationships throughout life.[16]

Vatuk studied disengagement in India, where the culture itself tends to emphasize old age as a time of inactivity, when "one should be able to sit back and let oneself be cared for by others" and when one can disassociate oneself "from direct involvement in the management and direction of household affairs." Presumably disengagement theory ought to apply there if any place. In fact, it was found that elderly people in India typically had personal problems adjusting to the societal expectations of becoming inactive and relinquishing authority, and that their overall levels of social participation did not decline.[17]

LOSS OF MAJOR LIFE ROLES THEORY

What might be called the *loss of major life roles theory* clearly fit the prevailing societal attitude of the early 1960s in the United States much better than did disengagement theory. While the loss of major life roles has never been clearly defined as a theory, it was a major theoretical and socially accepted theme during that time. It emerged in the early 1960s and remained a dominant emphasis for more than a decade.

The loss of major life roles is one of the main explanatory factors developed as a direct challenge to the disengagement theory. It implied that certain social trends and socioeconomic policies of that time were to blame for the existing conditions of the aged. This seemed to be the kind of moral indictment in which the majority of Americans tended to believe and which they were ready to accept.

Advocates of this theory challenged the basic assumptions of disengagement theory—that social withdrawal was a natural process of aging and that it was basically satisfying to those who become disengaged. Rather, they claimed, disengagement was a form of behavior imposed upon the aged as a consequence of societal goals in which older citizens were systematically and abruptly denied a part. The result was a severe loss in life satisfaction. Disengagement and the personal losses that tended to be related to it were not primarily a matter of being inactive, as stressed by activity theory. More important, the crux of the problem was the loss of those roles in life that provide people with meaning, purpose, and identity.

Specifically, Rose claimed that the policy of compulsory retirement meant that those who retired were suddenly cut off from their major life roles in society—that of employee or worker. By then, compulsory retirement was the policy of virtually all employers in the United States, including the federal government. According to Rose, this was a serious loss, not merely because of the loss of the work role alone, but also because of its derivative effects on auxiliary roles such as club member and community leader. Typically, personnel for these auxiliary roles were recruited from the ranks of major role participants and almost never from among retirees. The loss of worker roles almost inevitably meant the loss of the auxiliary roles as well. While Rose did not clarify why that kind of role loss should necessarily take place, his research at that time showed that it did take place.[18]

Lopata made the case that culturally determined loss of major life roles was also applicable to elderly women. She pointed out that as their children left home or their husbands retired—typically quite abrupt occurrences in their lives—women's housewife roles suddenly declined in importance and involved them in fewer related community activities. The result of what she called the "life cycle of the social role of housewife," which typically left women widows, was that there were no role expectations left for her to perform. She was no longer expected to participate in any of the activities typically related to the housewife role.[19] According to these analysts, then, disengagement and loss of life satisfaction for both men and women resulted from the culturally forced loss of those major life roles that tended to provide identity, purpose, and meaning to their lives.

Rosow made a similar point a few years later in his book *Socialization to Old Age*.[20] Socialization, he said, is the process of society assigning status (social positions) to its members and outlining the role specifications for those status positions. With the major source of status in our society still being one's occupation and the work that one does, he said, status among the aged is so minor and unimportant that few, if any, roles are specified for them. He contended that the aged have status of sorts, but that theirs is essentially a roleless status. This was something of the same point Burgess had previously made by referring to old age as a "roleless role."[21] Leisure activities, which had sometimes been mentioned as a possible new source of status for the aged, Rosow claimed, represented not a separate source of status, but simply a reward for work. Leisure activites provide prestige only if one's work status is high enough for one to claim leisure as a part-time reward, according to Rosow. He also made the point that elderly women suffer the loss of roles and fulfilling identity not only when their specific housewife roles decline but even more so as their husbands retire, since their identities are closely related to their husbands' work roles.

Havighurst, Neugarten, and Tobin, in arguing against disengagement theory, made the point not only that disengagement is a matter of a lack of role participation among the aged, but that dissatisfaction is a typical correlate of the lack of role activity.[22] Maddox also found, in studying the relationship between role activity and satisfaction among the elderly, that those who had the least amount of activity were generally also the least satisfied with life.[23]

The emphasis on the loss of major life roles as the primary causal factor of disengagement and loss of life satisfaction served to point up the influence that cultural factors seemed to have on these matters. The advocates of this theoretical position convincingly argued that disengagement is much more than a simple lack of activities. They also offered persuasive evidence that quite successfully challenged the notion that disengagement was a natural process preferred by the elderly themselves.[24]

In recent years, Atchley has challenged Rosow's contention that there is nothing to which to socialize the aged, and that the loss of roles results in depression, anxiety, and anomie for the older person. Atchley contends that the role of retired person is not as vague as Rosow claimed. Recent research, he asserts, reveals that older people are no worse off than the general population.[25]

There is undoubtedly some truth to Atchley's argument that socialization for the aged is toward "particularistic" roles rather than toward more general roles, such as occupation. In part at least, the differences between Rosow's and Atchley's arguments may well be the products of change over time, however. In the early years of mandatory retirement policies in the United States, the loss of major life roles seems to have been very real and quite devastating to many retirees, both personally and socially as well as economically. However, this theory ignored the possibility, as discussed in Chapter 4, that retirement might become institutionalized and that new societal expectations, new roles, and new opportunities for social interaction in old age might develop. Corrective action stemming from the theory itself undoubtedly helped to make disengagement much less culturally forced than it once was and much less a social problem.

That many elderly people suffered greatly and unfairly from the loss of major life roles became a widely accepted idea during the 1960s and 1970s, and there was much concern that something should be done about that problem. Consequently, providing "meaningful roles" for the aged became one of the many goals that were discussed and for which recommendations for congressional action were made. The result was that the federal government established, and allocated funding for, a number of programs to provide volunteer and paid work opportunities. These programs included the Retired Senior Volunteer Program (RSVP), the Service Corps of Retired Executives (SCORE), Foster Grandparents, and Title VII of the Older Americans' Act. This kind of volunteerism became an important source of meaningful and fulfilling social roles and personal satisfaction for many retired people. Thus, the loss of major life roles theory tends to be much weaker today than it once was, even in the United States.

The weakness of the loss of major life roles theory is made especially clear when it is applied cross-culturally. Loss of major roles does seem to take place in India. As previously noted, elderly people are expected to eventually relinquish their authoritative work and household roles to those in the next generation. Difficult as it may be for individuals to give up those roles, however, the process apparently does not result in social withdrawal or personal loss.[26] In the

People's Republic of China, there seems to be no pattern of role loss. While retirement at relatively early ages is becoming common, there seems to be no net loss of roles as a result. Instead, socially important and personally meaningful roles are readily available both in the family and in the community.[27] Schweitzer found that, among two Native American tribes in Oklahoma, the roles of elderly tribal members are especially prestigious and powerful. They are culturally functional roles that also keep the elders socially active.[28]

The loss of major life roles theory was clearly both time bound and culturally bound. It was at least partially valid during the 1960s in the United States, but it was less valid both as time passed and in other cultures. Nevertheless, the emphasis on this theory did have an effect on how Americans thought of retirement and the conditions of the elderly in general. Aging and retiring became experiences that many Americans came to dread, even though a sizable majority of those who were retired, even in the 1960s, claimed to enjoy retirement and to be highly satisfied with life in old age. This discrepancy in how retired people and others judge old age and retirement still exists today.

CONTINUITY THEORY

Some U.S. gerontologists were still unwilling to believe that all of the aged were either willing to disengage or forced to disengage and lose their sense of purpose in life. The evidence indicated that many elderly people did not inevitably disengage as they aged. Many others did so simply as a continuation of "tendencies toward inactivity" that had been established earlier in their lives. Some theorists concluded that neither the activities theory, nor the disengagement theory, nor the loss of major life roles theory adequately accounted for how people tended to experience old age. Instead, they looked at personality types to explain whether or not disengagement was part of an individual's old-age experience, and they developed what they called the *continuity theory*. Their contention was that the reason that some elderly people disengaged while others did not was that the personalities and life-long behavioral tendencies of each group influenced them to do one or the other. Some had tendencies to be active, while others had tendencies toward social noninvolvement. Whether people disengaged in old age, then, was due simply to the continuation of these tendencies throughout the life course.[29,30]

This, too, was a theory that should have been popular among Americans because it had the potential to alleviate society's sense of responsibility for causing the problem of isolation and loss of morale among the aged. There was a problem of logic connected to the theory, however, and it never became very influential. There was nothing in the theory that helped to explain why people would necessarily disengage more in old age than earlier in life. That, after all, was what troubled Americans the most about old age.

SOCIALLY DISRUPTIVE EVENTS THEORY

Disengagement is an issue that seems to have declined in importance in recent years. The problem was probably never as widespread as it seemed to be, and programs have been developed and somewhat successfully implemented to alleviate the problem for many elderly people. Nevertheless, disengagement and the loss of self-esteem still prevail on the part of many elderly people. Therefore, the challenge to gerontological theorists is to provide a more generic explanation for this phenomenon than those provided by the previously discussed theories, and one that would have validity over time.

Evidence for such a theory, which could most appropriately be called the *socially disruptive events theory*, was produced by research carried out in the late 1960s and early 1970s in two unrelated projects. Research by Tallmer and Kutner showed a clear and strong association between disengagement and what they described as "the stresses of aging."[31] In research carried out by this author a few years later,[32] it was discovered that disengagement was related to a number of events (especially loss of spouse, loss of physical capacity, and retirement) that tended to be severely disruptive of elderly people's lives. It was found that the experience of even one of these events typically resulted in disengagement that was often severe immediately following the event but that eventually tended to be reversed. The accumulation of a number of these events in a short period of time (a pattern more and more prevalent with increasing age), however, almost universally resulted in relatively permanent disengagement and an accompanying loss of morale and sense of self-worth.

From this perspective, disengagement is neither totally voluntary and satisfying, as Cumming and Henry assumed, nor totally forced by social processes. Rather, it stems from the types of social interaction processes that the aged experience as a result of the disruptive events in their lives. Dissatisfying as it may be, it is part of the social order that is negotiated and accepted in their interactions with others who are associated with those disruptive events.[33] Specifically, when one's social life is severely disrupted in a number of ways in a brief period of time, relationships with others not only change but also tend to become strained and personally disturbing, and social withdrawal becomes the most appropriate response. Once the pattern of disengagement becomes established, it tends to become part of one's social order and becomes increasingly difficult to alter, even though it is not a preferred life-style for most people.

The validity of this theory clearly is not confined to the unique cultural experiences of a given time. It provides an explanation of disengagement, when it occurs, that would be valid across time, since it is based on experiences that are especially typical of older persons. As was the case with the others discussed, however, this theory is limited as a comprehensive theory of aging because it, too, focuses on a specific issue and emphasizes a negative view of old age.

RECONSTRUCTION THEORY

The rather persuasive belief that the elderly have been unfairly treated in American society and that being old is essentially a negative social experience persisted into and throughout much of the 1970s. Another theory, emphasizing the impact of labeling processes on old people, was developed in the early part of that decade. It elaborated on the negative aspects of old age even more than did the theories emphasizing socially disruptive events and the loss of major life roles.

Kuypers and Bengtson, the proponents of the new theory, which they titled the *reconstruction theory,* borrowed Zusman's social breakdown syndrome model of mental illness[34] to explain their view of the situation of the aged in modern society. The elderly are quite successfully labeled incompetent, they noted, by both societal and self-labeling processes.[35] They suggested that the primary sources of that very negative label were role loss, lack of reference groups, and ambiguous normative guidance. These experiences, which they contended are typical of the elderly, tend to render old people vulnerable to society's negative labels.

In developing their theory, Kuypers and Bengtson maintained that the labeling processes applied to elderly people in modern society have been quite effective (see Figure 5-1). They concluded that old people (presumably more than others) tend to become dependent upon external, societally established labels for their identity. On this basis, old people internalize society's definitions and expectations of them. This, these theorists contend, leads to a "vicious spiral of negativism." Barrow summarized Kuypers and Bengtson's position in these words: "Since the self-concept of the elderly is formed in interaction with

FIGURE 5–1 System representation of the social breakdown syndrome as applied to old age, with negative inputs from the external social system. (*Source:* J. A. Kuypers and V. L. Bengston, "Social Breakdown and Competence: A Model of Normal Aging," *Human Development* 16 (1973), 181–201.) Reprinted with permission of S. Karger AG, Basel.

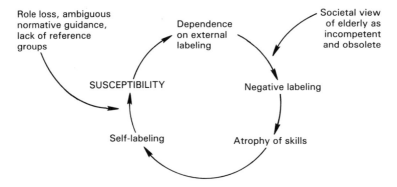

others and this society labels the elderly in a negative way, they come to see themselves as others see them: incompetent."[36]

Kuypers and Bengtson were trying to explain not only disengagement but also the loss of morale and life satisfaction that seemed to be related to social isolation. They elaborated a process that in a sense said what society already believed: that we in modern society were adding insult to the injury of the experience of being old. We had not only placed the elderly in vulnerable positions, but then we gave them negative labels, which they in their vulnerability tended to internalize as their own perceptions of themselves.

As Kuypers and Bengtson saw it, extensive societal intervention and even quite drastic reconstruction would be necessary to reverse the results of the negative labeling of the aged. Specifically, they called for (1) substantially improving the social services offered to the aged, (2) teaching them how to have better internal control and greater self-confidence, and (3) redefining the importance of work in society. If labeling, and not sheer survival needs, is the basic problem of the aged, however, one cannot help but wonder how providing further social services would not serve to make them even more, not less, dependent, and thus even more vulnerable to the negative labels. Furthermore, the assumption that the aged must be taught by the rest of us to have better internal control and self-confidence would actually seem to be another subtle way of labeling them incompetent. Ironically, even though these men contended that role loss was part of what makes the elderly vulnerable to the negative labels, they did not propose the reestablishment of meaningful roles as a way out of the negative dilemma that they described.[37]

The early 1970s, when the reconstruction theory was offered, was probably the culminating point of the negative analysis of old age. At the heart of the 1971 White House Conference on Aging was the desire to do all we could do to overcome the many forms of that negativism. That conference was later described as covering a "laundry list" of problems associated with being old that needed to be corrected.

Toward the end of the decade of the 1970s, the negative aspects of old age began to be challenged. George's 1980 book, *Role Transition in Later Life,* for example, emphasized the concept of role change rather than role loss. George challenged the negativism of reconstruction theory. She contended that "available evidence suggests that negative self-evaluation in later life is the exception rather than the rule" and that the elderly "meet the demands of personal well-being" and "maintain a positive sense of self."[38] She criticized the social breakdown syndrome (labeling) perspective for not recognizing the importance of what she called "personal resources or coping skills."

The plight of most of the aged was probably never as negative as Kuypers and Bengtson outlined it. Yet to a very large extent the negative theories were not so much wrong as they were products of the times in which they were conceived. The evidence of later years cited by George does not necessarily disqualify the validity of labeling, but only its negative results. The personal resources and coping skills that George discussed but did not attempt to explain are themselves undoubtedly at least partially the products of positive labels that have developed in recent years but that were largely absent in the past.

The formation of age-peer groups in recent years is one major source of more positive labels. As mentioned in Chapter 1, Rose predicted a number of years ago that, as the ever-increasing numbers of elderly people come together in groups and interact more with one another than with others, something of a subculture of aging would emerge, and that those who participated would gain new identities and new sets of values and norms not supported by the rest of society.[39] While some have argued that a subculture of aging has not developed in the ways that Rose predicted,[40-42] it is obvious that increasing numbers of exclusively age-related groups and communities are forming and that increasing numbers of the elderly do indeed interact more with one another in those groups than with others. The relative amount of age-peer interaction itself implies a value preference among those who choose to engage in it and clearly suggests a source of positive labeling and image building. This analysis also suggests the opposite conclusion: that those who choose not to participate in age-related peer interactions are less likely to maintain or reformulate positive self-images.

The labels "helpless" and "incompetent" are not logically or practically necessary, even for the majority of those who are institutionalized. As Kalish has pointed out, becoming dependent in one way does not necessitate becoming dependent in other ways.[43] Most of those in need of long-term physical care are in no way mentally incompetent or incapable of making decisions. Rather, it is the labeling process and the policies of long-term care institutions to make decisions for their patients that create conditions of dependency and apparent incompetence among the institutionalized elderly. That long-term care patients can indeed make competent decisions in institutions has been demonstrated by Kutner's environmental therapy program, discussed in Chapter 4, in which chronically ill patients have learned to have some control over their environments.[44]

This analysis of the application of labeling theory to the elderly in the United States today suggests that both negative and positive sources of labeling are present. The negative sources are apparently associated with the ways in which society tends to respond to the elderly as a group. The positive sources seem to be initiated by the elderly themselves. Ironically, that fact in itself logically refutes the validity of the negative labels that society tends to apply to the elderly. Indeed, aging has been viewed with an increasingly positive emphasis in the United States in recent years. Elderly persons have not only discovered sources of positive labels among themselves, but they, along with a number of gerontologists,[45-47] have also highlighted and challenged what they see as the myths or negative stereotypes of old age.

AGE STRATIFICATION THEORY

In the early 1970s, Riley led the development of *age stratification theory*, to provide a basis for explaining whatever forms and levels of inequality might exist between the young and old in given societies. Sociologists usually conceptualized the unequal distribution of social power, prestige, and economic resources in terms of social class distinctions. Riley contended that age was another important criterion on which inequality is determined. The basic assumption was that societies are inevitably stratified by age as well as by class.

The theory did not assume, however, that the conditions of old age are necessarily always the same. They may differ from one society to another. They may also change over time within given societies, as, indeed, they have done and continue to do. According to this theory, the relative inequality of the aged at any given time and in any cultural situation depends upon two types of experiences: (1) their typical life course experiences, due mostly to the physical and mental changes that take place and (2) the historically based experiences they have as part of the age cohort to which they belong.[48]

What happens to the members of given age cohorts depends primarily on external events, such as wars, economic changes, and technology, that tend to mold their aging experiences, compared to the experiences of the age cohorts that follow them. For example, Riley expressed concern about the effect of "the rapid pace of educational advancement" in this century. She pointed out that "the age pattern of education today is a reversal of that in earlier societies where the old were honored for their great knowledge." While she obviously did not want to be pessimistic about the conditions of today's elderly, she nevertheless concluded that "If one looks ahead from today's knowledge explosion, the information gap between the very young and even the not-so-young is deepening."[49]

The substance of stratification theory seems to allow for changes to occur between age strata that could once again favor the aged. Practically, however, Riley seems to imply that it is the younger, rather than the older, age cohorts that determine the direction of change.[50] It would seem, then, that younger cohorts will continue to have the advantage, according to this theory. This conclusion seems at first to be refuted in Yin and Lai's application of this theory to aging in China. They concluded that the present aged cohort tends to have a power and status advantage over the cohort that follows. They explain, though, that that advantage is obtained only because of setbacks to the younger cohort due to the cultural revolution, and that future younger cohorts will undoubtedly regain the advantage.[51]

An important question to put to stratification theorists, if their theory is to provide an adequate explanation of old age in the future and across cultures, is: What is the nature of the outside factors that tend to determine what the different age strata will be like? From the practical illustrations provided by

Riley, today's outside influences seem to be parts of what Cowgill and Holmes conceptualized as "modernization."[52] Yin and Lai's analysis indeed reflects an overlap between the two theories.[53] In a practical sense, it is difficult to see how age stratification theory differs much from modernization theory in explaining old-age experiences.

MODERNIZATION THEORY

The early theories of aging emphasized the negative definitions of aging so thoroughly and convincingly that they even became the dominant definition of aging in the first efforts to look at aging cross-culturally. Cross-cultural gerontologists focused primarily on the loss of social status among the aged. The assumption was that such a loss was being experienced not only in the United States, but also in Western European countries and indeed in many other places in the world, and always for the same reason. Thus, the idea that old age was a basically negative experience was being defined and treated not just as a culturally bound phenomenon, but as universally applicable.

As the most definitive spokesmen for cross-cultural aging with a negative perspective, Cowgill and Holmes developed what they termed the *modernization theory of aging*. They outlined their theory in their book *Aging and Modernization*, published in 1972.[54] According to this theory, loss of social status was not peculiar to Western societies. Instead, it is a universal experience in all cultures (regardless of economic, religious, political, or social traditions) in which modernization processes are occurring.

These authors based their theory on the findings of their descriptive study of status changes in 15 societies with different levels of modernization. Recognizing their lack of a specific definition of modernization, Cowgill later offered a more definitive restatement and a further defense of the theory.[55] In making a case for the cross-cultural application of the theory, he selected what he saw as the four "most salient aspects of modernization with reference to aging":

1. The development of health technology, which he claimed favors the young by allowing more infants to live into childhood and adult life even though it also results in greater longevity in the long run;
2. economic modernization or development, which he said encourages greater specialization and increasingly complex job skills and leaves the aged not only without work roles but also without the traditional role of providing vocational guidance to the young (also see Achenbaum[56]);
3. urbanization, which he said tends to separate work from the home and the aged from their younger family members; and
4. formalized education, which he said targets the young and leaves the aged at literacy and educational disadvantages.

All of this, wherever it occurs, inevitably leads to an ever-increasing generation gap and a deprived elderly population.

Palmore and Whittington found support for modernization theory in a study carried out in the United States in the early part of the 1970s.[57] They found not only that the aged had lower status than younger adults, but also that there had been a significant decline in the status of the aged relative to the rest of the population between 1940 and 1969. The decline of status was worsening, according to the conclusions drawn from these data. These authors believed that massive intervention in terms of improved income, work opportunities, and education for the aged would be necessary to stop the steady decline of status for the aged in the United States.

Cowgill seemed to be even more pessimistic than Palmore and Whittington. He insisted that the relationship between modernization and declining social status was "not a mere statistical correlation, it is a functional relationship that can be analyzed."[58] Loss of status is nothing less than a function of the very structures of modernizing societies, according to this view.

Data gathered from various countries, both modernized and nonmodernized, during the 1970s and 1980s seemed to quite strongly support the theory. Some who studied aging in Japan found, for example, that, while tradition called for family and corporate support and respect for the aged, tradition was increasingly being challenged on a practical level.[59,60]

The modernization theory of aging began to be challenged rather quickly, however. Palmore also studied aging in Japan and concluded that, because of the continued emphasis in that country on the Oriental tradition of honor and respect for the aged, the modernization that had been taking place at a rapid rate since World War II was not causing a decline in status among the Japanese aged.[61] In fact, according to his analysis, even corporations treated workers as family and provided them with life-long social and economic security. Similarly, in a study of aging in Samoa, Holmes and Rhoads found that respect for the aged among the Samoans had been preserved in the midst of quite rapid and otherwise socially disruptive modernization processes.[62]

The potentially most significant and telling criticism of the modernization theory of aging, though, came from a set of data that have been treated in a rather low-key manner and with some uncertainty about their meaning. In a study of the loss of status among the aged in a number of societies at various levels of modernization, Palmore and Manton discovered a tendency for status among the aged to be somewhat regained in the most modernized societies, particularly as status was related to occupation and education.[63]

These data were only a minor part of those produced by the study as a whole, most of which clearly supported the modernization theory of aging. Yet they probably provide a greater challenge to the theory than anything else. They imply that in the long run, the processes of modernization do not, as proponents of the theory have clearly stated, necessarily lead to ever-declining status for the aged. Instead, the expectation would be that those very processes will eventually act to restore that status.

It would seem, then, that what appeared to be such a strongly predictive theory that would apply across cultures and over time has turned out to be both time bound and culturally bound. It is time bound in that its basic premise is based on how modern societies are structured at present, how they emerged in the West, and how they are being transplanted into other parts of the world. Notions that are particularly apt to change in future modernized societies and that may serve to date this theory are that work and occupations are the primary sources of social status, and that formal education will continue to favor young people. Both of these ideas are already being substantially challenged in the United States, with increased importance being placed on volunteer leisure activities, and with the astounding growth in educational programs for senior citizens in recent years. The modernization theory appears to be culturally bound in that its proponents have failed to recognize the power of well-established cultural traditions and to consider the fact that old traditions often take on new forms and are at least somewhat preserved in the midst of change.

CONCLUSION

Theories of aging have played an important part in the evolution of the field of social gerontology in the brief history of that area of study. Without them we would be even less sure than we now are of how to interpret the social and psychological meaning of growing old and being old in today's world.

The theories that gerontologists have thus far developed have by no means provided all of the answers to the questions that trouble us and that we would like to have answered about aging. As we have seen, some give different and even conflicting answers to the same questions. Some lack an adequate data base to claim much validity and scientific respect, even though most have made substantial practical contributions.

Two basic problems have kept the existing theories of aging from being universally applicable. First, they have largely been time bound and culturally bound, finding their validity only in issues related to particular times and places. Second, they have typically addressed specific issues related to aging and being old and have failed to consider the experiences of aging in an inclusive sense. As previously noted, these issues have been largely negative ones. While these problems can never be completely overcome (theorists are as much a part of the times and places in which they live as anyone), what seems to be needed are less time-bound and culturally bound theories related to specific issues, and more theories that comprehensively address the experiences of aging and old age.

We have treated the theories from quite a different perspective than they are normally treated. The reason for that was to make the point that the gerontological theories, valuable as they have been and still are, are not so much right or wrong, valid or invalid explanations of the aging experience; more accurately, they have been products of the particular times in which they emerged. That is, although they may have been valid at one point in time, they tend not to remain valid over time. Instead of merely confining them to history as unimportant relics of particular times, however, we must recognize that many of the theories themselves, because they dealt with the vital issues of their times, have helped to bring about the changes that tended to make them invalid for the future. Loss of major life roles theory, for example, had an unquestionable influence on the U.S. policy of developing volunteer programs for the elderly through which they could begin to find meaningful substitute roles.

While gerontological theory has made an important contribution, it is also important to recognize that there is a dire need for more universal (that is, more comprehensive and valid across cultures and over time) theories of aging. At this point in the evolution of gerontology, that might be too much to expect. The need for such theories is nevertheless a real one, and such theories are worth the search.

NOTES

[1] George L. Maddox and Richard T. Campbell, "Scope, Concepts, and Methods in the Study of Aging," in *Handbook of Aging and the Social Sciences*, eds. Robert H. Binstock and Ethel Shanas (New York: Van Nostrand Reinhold, 1985), p. 10.

[2] Ethel Shanas et al., *Old People in Three Industrial Societies* (New York: Atherton Press, 1968), pp. 3–7.

[3] Cary S. Kart, *Realities of Aging: An Introduction to Gerontology* (Boston: Allyn & Bacon, 1985), pp. 10–11.

[4] Jon Hendricks and C. Davis Hendricks, "Theories of Social Gerontology," in *Dimensions of Aging*, eds. Jon Hendricks and C. Davis Hendricks (Cambridge: Winthrop, 1979), pp. 191–208.

[5] Robert J. Havighurst, Bernice Neugarten, and Sheldon S. Tobin, "Disengagement and Patterns of Aging," in *Middle Age and Aging*, ed. Bernice Neugarten (Chicago: University of Chicago Press, 1968), p. 161.

[6] Ernest W. Burgess, "Social Relations, Activities, and Personal Adjustment," *American Journal of Sociology*, 59 (1953–1954), 352–60.

[7] Havighurst, Neugarten, and Tobin, "Disengagement and Patterns of Aging," p. 161.

[8] Sheldon S. Tobin and Bernice L. Neugarten, "Life Satisfaction and Social Interaction in the Aging," *Journal of Gerontology*, 16 (1961), 344–46.

[9] Idris W. Evans and Arnold S. Brown, *Aging in Montana: A Survey of the Needs and Problems of Older Americans* (Helena: Montana Commission on Aging, 1970), pp. 6–8.

[10] Elizabeth Moen, "The Reluctance of the Elderly to Accept Help," *Social Problems*, 25, no. 3 (February 1978), 293–303.

[11] Robert C. Atchley, *The Social Forces in Later Life* (Belmont, Calif.: Wadsworth, 1980), p. 188.

[12] Elaine Cumming and William B. Henry, *Growing Old: The Process of Disengagement* (New York: Basic Books, 1961), pp. 210–18.

[13] Arnold S. Brown, "Satisfying Relationships for the Elderly and Their Patterns of Disengagement," *The Gerontologist*, 14, no. 3 (June 1974), 258–62.

[14] Margot Tallmer and Burnard Kutner, "Disengagement and Morale," *The Gerontologist*, 10 (1970), 99–108.

[15] Maddox and Campbell, "Scope, Concepts, and Methods," p. 5.

[16] Andrei Simic, "Aging in the United States and Yugoslavia: Contrasting Models of Intergenerational Relationships," *Anthropological Quarterly*, 50 (1977), 53–63.

[17] Sylvia Vatuk, "Withdrawal and Disengagement as a Cultural Response to Aging in India," in *Aging in Culture and Society*, ed. Christine Fry (Brooklyn, N.Y.: J. F. Bergin, 1980), pp. 126–48.

[18] Arnold M. Rose, "A Current Theoretical Issue in Social Gerontology," in *Older People and Their Social World*, eds. Arnold M. Rose and Warren A. Peterson (Philadelphia: F. A. Davis, 1965), pp. 359–66.

[19] Helena Znaniecki Lopata, "The Life Cycle of the Social Role of the Housewife," *Sociology and Social Research*, 51 (1966), 5–22.

[20] Irving Rosow, *Socialization to Old Age* (Berkeley, Calif.: University of California Press, 1974), pp. 162–72.

[21] Ernest W. Burgess, *Aging in Western Societies* (Chicago: University of Chicago Press, 1960), pp. 352–60.

[22] Havighurst, Neugarten, and Tobin, "Disengagement and Patterns of Aging," pp. 162–172.

[23] George L. Maddox, "Fact and Artifact: Evidence Bearing on Disengagement Theory," in *Normal Aging*, ed. Erdman Palmore (Durham, N.C.: Duke University Press, 1970), pp. 324–26.

[24] Rose, "A Current Theoretical Issue," pp. 359–66.

[25] Robert C. Atchley, *Social Forces and Aging: An Introduction to Social Gerontology* (Belmont, Calif.: Wadsworth, 1985), p. 118.

[26] Vatuk, "Withdrawal and Disengagement," pp. 126–48.

[27] Deborah Davis-Friedmann, *Long Lives: Chinese Elderly and the Communist Revolution* (Cambridge: Harvard University Press, 1983), pp. 80–84.

[28] Marjorie M. Schweitzer, "The Elders: Cultural Dimensions of Aging in Two American Indian Communities," in *Growing Old in Different Societies: Cross-Cultural Perspectives*, ed. Jay Sokolovsky (Belmont, Calif.: Wadsworth, 1983), pp. 168–78.

[29] Richard Videbeck and Alan B. Knox, "Alternative Participatory Responses to Aging," in *Older People and Their Social World*, eds. Arnold M. Rose and Warren A. Peterson (Philadelphia: F. A. Davis, 1965), pp. 37–48.

[30] Herbert C. Covey, "A Reconceptualization of Continuity Theory: Some Preliminary Thoughts," *The Gerontologist*, 21, no. 6 (December 1981), 628–33.

[31] Tallmer and Kutner, "Disengagement and Morale," pp. 99–108.

[32] Brown, "Satisfying Relationships," pp. 258–62.

[33] Victor M. Marshall, "No Exit: A Symbolic Interactionist Perspective on Aging," *International Journal of Aging and Human Development*, 9 (1978–1979), 345–58.

[34] Jack Zusman, "Some Explanations of the Changing Appearance of Psychotic Patients: Antecedents of the Social Breakdown Syndrome Concept," *The Milbank Memorial Fund Quarterly*, 44 no. 1, pt. 2 (January 1966), 363–88.

[35] Joseph A. Kuypers and Vern L. Bengtson, "Social Breakdown and Competence: A Model of Normal Aging," *Human Development*, 16 (1973), 181–201.

[36] Georgia M. Barrow, *Aging, the Individual, and Society* (St. Paul, Minn.: West, 1986), p. 83.

[37] Kuypers and Bengtson, "Social Breakdown and Competence," pp. 181–201.

[38] Linda K. George, *Role Transitions in Later Life* (Monterey, Calif.: Brooks/Cole, 1980), pp. 41–43.

[39] Arnold M. Rose, "The Subculture of the Aging: A Framework for Research in Social Gerontology," in *Older People and Their Social World*, eds. Arnold M. Rose and Warren A. Peterson (Philadelphia: F. A. Davis, 1965), pp. 3–16.

[40] Rosow, *Socialization to Old Age*, pp. 162–72.

[41] Martha Baum and Rainer C. Baum, *Growing Old: A Societal Perspective* (Englewood Cliffs, N.J.: Prentice-Hall, 1980), p. 82.

[42] Charles F. Longino, Jr., Kent A. McClelland, and Warren A. Peterson, "The Aged Subculture Hypothesis: Social Integration, Gerontophilia and Self-Conception," *Journal of Gerontology*, 35, no. 5 (September 1980), 758–67.

[43] Richard A. Kalish, *Late Adulthood: Perspectives on Human Development* (Monterey, Calif.: Brooks/Cole, 1982), pp. 111–12.

[44] Bernard Kutner, "The Hospital Environment," *Social Sciences and Medicine,* 4, suppl. 1 (1970), 9–12.

[45] *Gray Panthers Pamphlet,* Philadelphia: Gray Panthers, 3700 Chestnut Street, Philadelphia, Penn., 19104 (1974).

[46] Barrow, *Aging, the Individual, and Society,* pp. 26–43.

[47] Alex Comfort, "Age Prejudice in America," *Social Policy,* 17 (November–December 1976), 3–8.

[48] Matilda White Riley, "Social Gerontology and the Age Stratification of Society," *Gerontologist,* 11, no. 2 (Summer 1971), 79–87.

[49] Ibid.

[50] Ibid.

[51] Peter Yin and Kwok Hung Lai, "A Reconceptualization of Age Stratification in China," *Journal of Gerontology,* 38, no. 5 (September 1983), 608–13.

[52] Donald O. Cowgill, "Aging and Modernization: A Revision of the Theory" (1974) in *Aging in America: Readings in Social Gerontology,* eds. Cary S. Kart and Barbara B. Manard (Sherman Oaks, Calif.: Alfred, 1981), pp. 111–32.

[53] Yin and Lai, "A Reconceptualization of Age Stratification," pp. 608–613.

[54] Donald O. Cowgill and Lowell Holmes, *Aging and Modernization* (New York: Appleton-Century-Crofts, 1972).

[55] Donald O. Cowgill, "Aging and Modernization: A Revision," pp. 111–32.

[56] W. Andrew Achenbaum, *Shades of Gray: Old Age, American Values, and Federal Policies Since 1920* (Boston: Little, Brown, 1983), p. 15.

[57] Erdman B. Palmore and Frank Whittington, "Trends in the Relative Status of the Aged," *Social Forces,* 50 (September 1971), 84–91.

[58] Cowgill, "Aging and Modernization; A Revision," pp. 111–32.

[59] Judith A. Roth, "Timetables and the Lifecourse in Post-Industrial Society," in *Work and Lifecourse in Japan,* ed. David W. Plath (Albany, N.Y.: State University of New York Press, 1983), pp. 248–59.

[60] Ruth Campbell and Elaine M. Brody, "Women's Changing Roles and Help to the Elderly: Attitudes of Women in the United States and Japan," *The Gerontologist,* 25, no. 6 (December 1985), 584–92.

[61] Erdman B. Palmore, "The Status and Integration of the Aged in Japanese Society," *Journal of Gerontology,* 30, no. 2 (March 1975), 199–208.

[62] Lowell Holmes and Ellen Rhoads, "Aging and Change in Samoa," in *Growing Old in Different Societies,* ed. Jay Sokolovsky (Belmont, Calif.: Wadsworth, 1983), pp. 119–29.

[63] Erdman B. Palmore and Kenneth Manton, "Modernization and Status of the Age: International Correlations," *Journal of Gerontology,* 29, no. 2 (March 1974), 205–10.

6

The Aged in Changing Living Situations

INTRODUCTION

The well-being of the elderly is the paramount concern of gerontologists today. The concern is not only that they should receive the kind of care that allows them to live as long as possible, but also that their lives continue to be meaningful, personally satisfying, and worth living. It is obvious that the situations or conditions of their daily lives are central to their sense of well-being.

As we begin to analyze the living situations of the aged, we are struck with the fact that there is much cross-cultural variation. Even more striking is the realization that living situations of the aged have changed and are apparently still in the process of changing. Their lives as individuals change as they adjust to different stages of the life cycle, and their life-styles in general have tended to change over time. It is interesting to note further that the two types of changes seem to be interrelated. That is, the fact that living situations change over the life course is itself part of the social changes that are taking place. It is as important for us to understand the characteristics of those changes as it is for us to understand the present living conditions of the aged. Understanding what factors have contributed to the changes and what the processes of change have been give us clues about the adequacy of present conditions.

A deep concern for independence tends to be the most important factor influencing both the changes that have taken place and the present choices that people make about their living situations. This, then, will be the focus of analysis in this chapter. We will examine the possible sources of the desire for independence, the extent to which it prevails cross-culturally, and the potential consequences.

There are essentially five types of living situations that have tended to be prevalent among elderly populations. These situations have tended to reflect certain societal changes, and all forms still exist and seem to be prevalent in given cultures. Furthermore, the rates of changes from one living situation to another differ from culture to culture.

EXTENDED-FAMILY HOUSEHOLDS

Historically and cross-culturally, the most prevalent situation in which elderly people have lived has undoubtedly been in three-generation households. There have been times in the history of almost all economically stable societies when most of the elderly lived with their extended families. Entire extended families have often lived under one roof.

This living situation persists for most of the aged today in most Oriental countries,[1,2] in Eastern European countries,[3] to some degree among Native American tribes,[4] and in many developing countries of the world. This type of living situation is relatively rare, however, in the United States and in Western European countries.

This kind of arrangement tends to prevail in some cultures because of (1) religious/ideological traditions, (2) certain social and economic structures, (3) practical realities, or (4) a combination of these factors. This pattern existed in the past in Western societies when the family was the basic social and economic structure. Those living within a household did not share only living quarters and family solidarity; they also shared economic goals and responsibilities, and much of the stability of the society depended on how they lived their lives. Zimmerman described this type of family as the "domestic family,"[5] and elderly people were very much a part of this kind of structure. In fact, they often controlled how the families functioned.[6] For them, social or economic dependence was not an issue they had to face. Instead, they—especially older men—were in control. Age seniority was a fact of life.

The pattern of Japanese and Chinese elderly living with their adult children has continued largely because of the strong cultural traditionals of filial piety in both of those countries. These traditions have religious as well as cultural connotations and contain two-fold expectations with regard to aged family members. First, the aged are respected and venerated. Second, because of that veneration, families (particularly children) are expected to provide whatever care their elderly members need in their old age.[7]

It is noteworthy that even though most Japanese elderly still live with the families of their adult children, there is the beginning of a trend away from that pattern. Also, more and more adult children are expressing feelings of being burdened by having to care for their elderly parents in addition to working and raising their own children. Increasing numbers of elderly are having to live separately from their children and grandchildren.[8]

Analysis of intergenerational households in China is somewhat complicated by the Communist takeover in that country. Davis-Friedmann points out that many of the actions of the Chinese Communist party leaders after they took over power in 1949 served to undermine the patriarchal authority of Chinese elders. Young people were provided jobs by the government and gained economic independence from their families. Marriage laws encouraged young people to ignore the wishes of their families in the choice of mates. Expectations were that the traditions of intergenerational households would be destroyed as a result. Ironically, that did not happen, partly because the long tradition of filial piety was too culturally entrenched to be destroyed. More important, as Davis-Friedmann found, "the traditional living arrangements of the elderly are compatible with the Communist revolution."[9]

That point needs clarification. At present, although three-generational households are similar in composition to what they have always been—elderly parents living with the eldest son and his family—the structure of authority and responsibility is very different. It is in essence a cooperative arrangement between somewhat equal partners. Neither father nor son owns the home and household finances and domestic duties tend to be approximately equally shared. This emphasis is the direct result of, and is compatible with, Communist ideals. In a country in which poverty has been widespread, it is also something of an economic necessity. Then too, the fact that there is a serious lack of housing in China also influences the continuation of the traditional three-generational households in that country. Lack of housing is also said to be the main reason that the aged in Eastern Europe continue to live in households with their children.[10] Practicality and necessity may be more important than tradition in the continuation of this practice.

Despite all of this, however, there are some reasons to believe that the prevalence of three-generation households may decline in China in the future. For one thing, Davis-Friedmann reports that there are already cases of elderly parents being rejected as household members by their adult children.[11] Also, this author was informed by a Chinese official of sentiments among some Chinese elderly, who are becoming relatively more affluent than most, that they would prefer to live in households separate from their children. It may well be that these tendencies will grow if the present emphasis on economic reforms continues and the society as a whole becomes increasingly affluent. In fact, Zeng Yi reported in 1986 that nuclear families versus three-generation families are gaining proportionately in China.[12]

The tendency on the part of Oriental elderly people not to live in extended family situations is even more pronounced among those who migrate to the West. Koh and Bell interviewed a sample of Korean elderly who had migrated to the United States between 1972 and 1982, for example. They found that a large percentage of them had opted not to live with or become overly dependent upon their adult children, even though most of them could not speak English. The investigators concluded that these people, who were still very much steeped in their traditional Oriental culture, had nevertheless "accepted a pattern of co-existence more characteristic of the United States than of Korea."[13]

It would seem, then, that there are signs of potential change even in those societies in which the majority of elderly people live with their families. In the industrially developed nations of the West, this pattern has already been abandoned. An important question is why this life-style is being rejected. Probably the most prevalent explanation is that it is due to the dynamic influence of modernization processes and economic development. The essence of this argument is that these processes tend to provide younger people with the necessary educational skills to enable them to become economically and socially independent from their families. Thus the aged end up becoming dependent upon their children instead of the other way around, an intolerable situation for both young and old.

This has been a convincing argument in a world currently focused on the importance of modernization. Fischer has provided a quite different and perhaps more profound explanation.[14] He makes the point that a "revolution in age relations" began in the United States long before the era of modernization. The first signs of this revolution began to appear in the United States in about 1750, according to Fischer. Therefore, there must be some other explanation. His contention is that the changes in intergenerational relationships were not the product of economic development at all, but were the result of a whole new set of values that severely challenged the existing social and political structure as well as the economic structure. Specifically, the radical belief in "equality" and individual "liberty" revolutionized the daily lives of Americans in the mid-nineteenth century. As Fischer explains it, "the growth of those ideas in Anglo-America was caused primarily by the interaction of English Protestant ideas with the American environment."[15] The vast untapped resources in the United States provided practical opportunities for the young to be liberated from the traditional authority of the aged and to claim equality with them.

According to Fischer, these values have spread throughout the world and with them the revolution in age relations. It is important to realize that belief in these revolutionary ideas has tended to influence the aged as well as younger people. It is thus very important to the elderly that they remain independent. Consequently, they are probably even more apt than are young adults to reject the three-generation household today as a viable living situation.

EXTENDED-FAMILY INTERDEPENDENCY

The pattern of multigenerational housing has been overwhelmingly rejected in Western Europe and in the United States. It has been rejected by both the aged and their families. Almost the only exceptions to that trend occur when lack of family finances make other options impossible and when the elderly person's need for care becomes critical and families feel obligated to provide it. These exceptions would tend to pertain especially to those elderly people who become widowed. To the extent that it still exists, then, it is practiced, not by preference, but as a result of practical necessity.

The movement away from multigenerational households made the development of other options necessary. The most prevalent option could be characterized as just one step removed. Contrary to the rather common notion that families tend to abandon their elderly members, as a whole, neither younger nor elderly family members have ever declared total independence from each other. They simply prefer not to live together, in order to avoid what could become daily dependence. Consequently, the most prevalent kind of living situation that the aged choose is to live in their own private homes, separate from but near their families. This was the life-style pattern found to exist in selected European countries and in the United States by a group of researchers.[16] They characterized this kind of choice as "intimacy at a distance,"[17] indicating that while elderly people and their families wanted to avoid becoming dependent upon one another, they still prized continued and regular intrafamily relationship.

The data show that there was more to the continued family relationship than the need for intimacy, however. Also found were very prevalent mutual helping patterns between the aged and their adult children. They tended to help one another with a number of needs, including finances and domestic tasks.[18] Therefore, this life-style might be best conceptualized as a living situation in which family members are able to avoid total dependency within the family and move instead to family interdependency. Obviously neither the older nor younger adults want to give up the privileges of family membership; they merely want a change in those relationships. In a national survey of the attitudes of both young adults and the aged, Okrahu found more acceptance of the idea of multigenerational residence in 1983 than there had been in 1973.[19] The change toward more acceptance of that idea was greater among the younger adults than among the aged, however. These data by no means indicate the beginning of a return to three-generation household living for the aged. Respondents were not asked whether they were willing to live in multigenerational living situations; they were asked only whether they thought it was a good idea. Neither were they asked to distinguish between types of multigenerational residences. Probably the most that can be made of these data is that increasing numbers of people may be willing to consider that kind of living arrangement in a time when adequate care for the elderly is increasingly costly and unavailable, but only if and when necessary. Past evidence has shown that most elderly people still cling to their children and grandchildren more than anyone else for their ultimate care and security.[20]

Living in their own private homes is not only by far the life-style that most of the aged prefer; it is also probably the one that is the most feasible for them. In the United States, far more of the aged than any other age group are homeowners (more than 65 percent, compared to 40 percent for those under 35). Furthermore, as many as 84 percent of the elderly homeowners actually own their homes outright.[21] Most of these homes have been the places of residence of the elderly who own them for many years and are located in communities that they consider their own. This kind of living situation, then, symbolizes their sense of life's accomplishments, a deep sense of security, and a sense of continued independence.

Nevertheless, there are a number of problems associated with this kind of living situation. First, because most of the houses that older people own are old, they are often in need of major repairs that are difficult for the aged themselves to make. Second, because their houses were typically purchased at a stage in life when their families were growing, they are often too large for elderly couples or single individuals. Third, elderly people living in single-family dwellings often face the danger of eventually becoming severely isolated. The older they become, the more likely they are to become widowed and to live alone, and the less able they will be to leave their homes to interact with others. At the same time, they will have an increasing need for assistance in daily living. Many who remain in their homes also live in small communities in which the availability of such help is extremely limited. They must rely on the help of just one or two other people—usually family members—or they are forced to enter a long-term care institution. Ironically, the most popular life-style choice among the aged often eventually places them in the very kind of dependency that they have tried to avoid by making that choice.

INDEPENDENT LIVING

A sizable minority of the aged in the modern world strongly value their right to remain independent. These are people who not only choose to live in their own private dwellings, but who also tend to refuse to relate to anyone else upon whom they might become even partly dependent. They typically refuse even the kinds of assistance, from either families or community agencies, that they badly need.

Independent elderly people are found in a variety of living situations. Many live either as couples or alone in their own homes in extreme isolation from both their families and others in their communities. Many live in isolated rural areas, often in primitive living quarters that require heavy labor to maintain. Others live in rented rooms in rundown inner-city hotels, and some are among the growing number of homeless living on the streets of our large cities. Ironically, the older these people become, the more adamant they become about refusing help.

This pattern is found even among those whom Frankfather labeled "confused." In discussing the plight of those who live on city streets, Frankfather said that professionals who deal with them tend to assume that their pitiful situation is due to their having been abandoned by their families.[22] In examining their patterns of behavior, however, we find that their condition is at least partly the product of their continued struggle for independence. In a study of homeless and hotel-dwelling elderly men on the New York City Bowery, for example, Cohen and Sokolovsky found that the one characteristic that distinguished them from other elderly men was their "sociability." They tended to be exceptionally socially isolated, and they related to others, if at all, "with adherence to a strict norm of reciprocity."[23] The case of Charles E. Perkins in Fairfax, Virginia, illustrates the plight of the elderly in their continued struggle for independence. He had been a highly intelligent biochemist, but at 89 he became confused. He challenged the right of law enforcement and welfare personnel to place him in institutional confinement and won. Nevertheless, he finally ended up in a state hospital geriatric ward, where he was forced to interact with others who had mental illnesses far more serious than his.[24]

We in the United States tend to admire the tenaciousness of elderly people who try to maintain their independence. It is generally not a realistic stance on their part, however. They tend to become increasingly isolated and have less capacity to care for themselves as they age. They also tend to neglect their own health and well-being by way of declaring their independence. Thus, the need for care becomes acute earlier than necessary, and they tend to be institutionalized prematurely more than do other elderly people. The lesson that these people do not seem to learn is that total independence is impossible, and attempts to live that way are ultimately defeating. Sadly, we as a society have not found practical ways of avoiding the negative consequences of emphasizing the extremes of both independence and dependence.

PEER-GROUP INTERDEPENDENCY

There is no doubt that the family has long been the social group to which elderly people have been oriented and from which they have gained their identities and sense of security. As we have seen, families are generally still viewed as vital to them. However, the spread of the values of equality and individual liberty and the focus on the importance of independence for the aged have placed important qualifications on their total reliance on family relationships. Most elderly would be willing to settle for interdependent relationships with members of their families, but that kind of relationship cannot always be worked out with family members. Interdependency can work only in communities of equals, and relationships between parents and their children do not tend to be equal.

Fischer makes the point that among those who believe in equality and individual liberty, the establishment of communities is possible, but only with those who are "roughly alike."[25] This finding would indicate that, in their common goal of maintaining as much independence as possible for as long as possible, the aged might well increasingly turn to each other. In fact, peer-group participation is increasing among the aged in all parts of the world today.

This pattern of interaction began in the United States in the early part of this century with the development of such groups as the "Townsend movement." Urbanized elderly who shared the common plight of unemployment came together as political advocates to attempt to solve their economic problems. While this did not represent a holistic, interdependent life-style, it served as the beginning of peer-group interdependency.

In the early 1960s, Rose predicted a fully developed "subculture of aging." He believed that as the aged population grew, they would increasingly interact with one another. This interaction pattern would develop partly because of the cohort affinities that elderly people would feel for each other and partly because they were being systematically neglected by the rest of society. Out of these peer-group interactions, he said, an age-group consciousness, as well as group values and norms, would take form.[26] Others have argued that this would never happen because of the great tendency on the part of those who are aging to resist being identified as old. Resistance to old-age identity does not necessarily preclude a sense of affiliation with one's peer group, however. Even critics of Rose's predictions acknowledge the increased peer-group interactions that are taking place. Communities of the aged in which interdependent relationships exist have materialized out of their interactions.

Elderly peer groups have taken a number of forms in recent years. One form in the United States has been in response to government-sponsored organizations. Local senior citizens' centers have been organized in local communities across the nation through the planning efforts of the federal, state, and local agencies on aging. Elderly people are brought together daily at these centers for a meal, recreation, and informal interaction.

Although these centers are professionally administered by local agencies, the government requires that local councils on aging, made up primarily of elderly participants, serve in an advisory capacity to provide input on the centers' operation. These councils often have policy-making power over their local programs.

Similar councils on aging serve as advisory bodies to regional, state, and federal planning agencies. Members of these councils are elected by local bodies, and they often have a great deal of power as direct representatives of the elderly people who have elected them. There are limits to the independence this system allows elderly people to have, however, since it is greatly dependent upon federal funding. Yet it provides abundant opportunities for the elderly to interact with one another and offers potential for them to develop interdependent relationships.

Another form of peer groups among the aged is the autonomous advocacy group, made up of, and run by, the aged themselves. There are at least three such groups in the United States that are well known and nation wide: the Gray Panthers, the National Council of Senior Citizens (NCSC), and the American Association of Retired Persons (AARP). All of these groups are effective advocates, but of the three, the AARP is the best illustration of an interacting, interdependent group. The Gray Panthers and the NCSC have somewhat fixed points of view, are dominated by strong leaders, have members who share the same viewpoints, and promote only limited interaction among elderly people. In contrast, the AARP emphasizes local interactive chapters and, in addition to its advocacy work, promotes a variety of activities among its members. This serves as a very practical interdependent peer group for thousands of elderly Americans, and its advocacy work is largely a product of that interdependency.

There are also local "grassroots" advocacy groups that serve as interactional interdependent peer groups. In a study of the development of community service programs for the aged, it was discovered that local advocacy groups provided the necessary impetus. In communities in which programs were developed, local elderly people had first informally gathered on the basis of their common interests. They had then become organized in order to act on their common needs, and they advocated for outside assistance in developing programs to meet their needs.[27] This is an effective type of interactional, interdependent peer group that has largely escaped our attention until now.

Probably the most obvious form of interdependent peer group interaction is that found in retirement communities and age-concentrated public housing. It is noteworthy that the demand for both of these situations—the latter a living situation used predominantly by the elderly poor and the former used by those who are more affluent—has been increasing among the aged population. Both of these types of living situations have been investigated recently to determine the extent to which they fit Rose's description of the subculture of the aging.[28,29] Only limited support for the subculture hypothesis as a whole was found in these studies. Longino and colleagues, for example, found that those who live in retirement communities tend to represent a retreatist life-style, rather than the activist life-style that Rose had predicted. What is more important to our analysis of peer group interdependency, however, is the fact that significantly more age-peer social relationships were found among those in both public housing and retirement housing than would have been true in integrated living situations. Apparently, elderly people tend to interact more with their peers than with others, and it is in the context of interaction that interdependent relationships become established.

Still another illustration of an interactional interdependent peer group is to be found in a very unlikely setting—among single room occupants (SROs) of old inner-city hotels (mostly elderly men). As previously noted, these people tend to be much more isolated than most other elderly people. It has been found, though, that their isolation is by no means complete. They participate in identifiable social networks on at least a limited basis. These networks are typically made up of the occupants themselves in the hotels in which they live. A pattern of interdependency is found among network participants. While this kind of interdependency is limited in scope (the amount of interaction is minimal), it represents virtually the only interaction these people have and the only source of assistance in daily living to which they are willing to turn.[30-33] Peer-group interdependency is clearly a type of interaction to which elderly people from virtually all walks of life are turning.

DEPENDENT LIVING

A fifth type of situation in which elderly people in today's world live is generally conceptualized as dependent living. Two basic questions must be answered in order to analyze this type of living situation. First, how do we define dependency? Second, what particular situations can be treated as dependent?

Investigators of the issue of dependency among the elderly population have tended to apply two basic definitions of dependency. Probably the most prevalent is a functional definition. Various scales have been devised that attempt to measure the functioning of individuals in society, based on sets of criteria considered to be normal. Four areas of functioning have been highlighted for analysis: (1) *economic dependency*, which occurs when the older person is no longer a wage earner; (2) *physical dependency*, which occurs as individuals lose the capacity to control their bodily functions and physical environment; (3) *social dependency*, which arises as an elderly person loses meaningful others; and (4) *mental dependency*, which occurs as individuals lose the capacity to make decisions for themselves or to solve their own problems.[34]

Many of these investigators have focused on just one of these forms of functioning—usually on physical functioning—in order to assess the level and types of care that individuals need and the kind of care facilities that may be appropriate for them. These are valuable assessments, but they tend to overestimate the extent of dependency. Kalish, for example, makes the very important point that for individuals to be dependent in terms of one type of functioning does not imply that they are also dependent in other ways; yet they are often treated as though that were the case. He suggests that "help with one kind of dependency tends to alleviate problems with other kinds of dependency."[35]

A definition that captures the essence of dependency is that which focuses on the extent to which individuals have decision-making control over their own lives and their environment. Obviously, this necessitates that their mental capacities are intact, but an even more important issue is the amount of control over their daily lives that others may impose on them. Since the large majority of the aged do not in fact lose their mental capabilities, it is fair to ask why it is ever necessary to exert total control over them.

An important component of this analysis, then, is to examine the living situations that tend to be categorized as dependent living. Institutional living is the most obvious of these. To a large degree, institutionalization has become the most prominent symbol of the dependent life-style for the aged in the Western world. Nursing homes in the United States have come under severe criticism in the media in recent years because of the failure of many of them to provide adequate care. More important to elderly people themselves, though, is that becoming institutionalized represents total and permanent dependency and the loss of control of any part of their lives.

It is assumed that the way in which nursing homes are managed and the manner in which care is provided serves to foster dependent attitudes and behavior patterns among residents. A number of British nursing homes with different management styles were studied in order to test that assumption. The institutions differed in the amount of freedom of action that they allowed their patients to have. It was discovered that the level of dependency was just as great in the institutions allowing some freedom of action as in those with strict controls over patient's activities. The investigator indicated, however, that the differences between the institutions' management styles were probably not great enough to make any significant impact on the dependency problem. He concluded that "some radical departure from current residential practice is required in order to improve the well-being of residents."[36]

Approximately 5 percent of those 65 and over in the United States live in institutions, and assessments indicate that many of them could remain in their own homes if some assistance were available to them. The most prominent sentiment today is that institutionalization ought to be avoided by the aged for as long as possible. However, two very important factors related to dependency tend to be ignored in the prevailing negative attitudes about institutions and positive attitudes about residential living on the part of the aged. On the one hand, as previously noted, remaining in one's own home can create as much dependency as institutional living can. On the other hand, it is clearly possible for forms of interdependency to be created and put into practice even in institutions.

The latter point was illustrated by a program developed and administered by Kutner in the 1960s. This program consisted of helping terminally ill, institutionalized elderly patients to (1) become sensitized to the institutional environment in which they lived; (2) identify problems related to that kind of environment; and (3) initiate problem-solving processes in cooperation with institutional staff. The patients themselves were often able to help execute the problem-solving plans and even to take charge of the processes involved. They found, in fact, that in some cases the patients, working together, were able to take care of problems without staff assistance. As a result of this program, life in an institution was literally transformed from one of total dependency, in which some patients had to some degree even lost their interactional skills, to one of vital interdependency with their fellow-patients and even with the institutional staff.[37]

CONCLUSION

Totally dependent living is necessary for only relatively few elderly people. It obviously cannot be avoided on the part of those who suffer from severe dementia. Otherwise, however, dependent living is purely a matter of individual choice, institutional policy, or socially imposed control over the daily lives of elderly people. Furthermore, it is difficult to imagine how unnecessary dependency on the part of elderly people benefits anyone.

Neither is an extreme emphasis on independence a realistic or desirable option. The elderly among us ought to be not only allowed but encouraged to develop interdependent life-styles. Given present myths about aging, perhaps the most realistic form of interdependency is with age-related peers. The potential for intergenerational interdependent relationships is just as prevalent and desirable and ought also to be a goal toward which we move.

NOTES

[1] Deborah Davis-Friedmann, *Long Lives: Chinese Elderly and the Communist Revolution* (Cambridge, Mass.: Harvard University Press, 1983), pp. 34–46.

[2] Erdman B. Palmore and Daisaku Maeda, *The Honorable Elders Revisited* (Durham, N.C.: Duke University Press, 1985), pp. 33–42.

[3] Ethel Shanas, "Family-Kin Networks and Aging in Cross-Cultural Perspective," in *The Family: Functions, Conflicts, and Symbols*, eds. Peter J. Stein, Judith Richman, and Natalie Hannon (Reading, Mass.: Addison-Wesley, 1977), pp. 300–307.

[4] Arnold S. Brown, "Report on Navajo Elder Abuse" (unpublished research report submitted to the Navajo Office on Aging, Window Rock, Arizona, Fall 1986).

[5] Gerald R. Leslie and Sheila K. Korman, *The Family in Social Context* (New York: Oxford University Press, 1985), pp. 192–94.

[6] Gail P. Fullerton, *Survival in Marriage: Introduction to Family Interaction, Conflicts, and Alternatives* (Hinsdale, Ill.: Dryden Press, 1977), pp. 4–11.

[7] Gino K. Piovesana, "The Aged in Chinese and Japanese Cultures," in *Dimensions of Aging: Readings*, eds. Jon Hendricks and C. Davis Hendricks (Cambridge, Mass.: Winthrop, 1979), pp. 13–20.

[8] "The Japanese-Style Welfare System," *Japan Quarterly*, 30 (July–September 1983), 327–30.

[9] Davis-Friedmann, *Long Lives*, pp. 34–35.

[10] Shanas, "Family-Kin Networks and Aging," pp. 300–307.

[11] Davis-Friedmann, *Long Lives*, pp. 43–44.

[12] Zeng Yi, "Changes in Family Structure in China: A Simulation Study," *Population and Development Review*, 12, no. 4 (December 1986), 675–703.

[13] James Y. Koh and William C. Bell, "Korean Elders in the United States: Intergenerational Relations and Living Arrangements," *The Gerontologist*, 27, no. 1 (February 1987), 66–71.

[14] David Hackett Fischer, *Growing Old In America* (New York: Oxford University Press, 1978), pp. 72–112.

[15] Ibid., p. 109.

[16] Ethel Shanas et al., *Old People in Three Industrial Societies* (New York: Atherton Press, 1968), pp. 192–97.

[17] Shanas, "Family-Kin Networks and Aging," pp. 300–307.

[18] Shanas et al., *Old People in Three Industrial Societies,* pp. 217–25.

[19] Ishmael O. Okrahu, "Age and Attitudes Toward Intergenerational Residence, 1973–1983," *Journal of Gerontology,* 42, no. 3 (May 1987), 280–87.

[20] Arnold S. Brown, "Satisfying Relationships for the Elderly and Their Patterns of Disengagement," *The Gerontologist,* 14, no. 3 (June 1974), 258–62.

[21] M. Powell Lawton, *Environment and Aging* (Monterey, Calif.: Brooks/Cole, 1980), p. 54.

[22] Dwight Frankfather, *The Aged in the Community: Managing Senility and Deviance* (New York: Praeger, 1977), pp. 27–34.

[23] Carl I. Cohen and Jay Sokolovsky, "Toward a Concept of Homelessness Among Aged Men," *Journal of Gerontology,* 38, no. 1 (January 1983), 81–89.

[24] Thomas Grubisich, "Aged Wanderer Baffles State," in *Human Services for Older Adults: Concepts and Skills,* eds. Anita S. Harbert and Leon H. Ginsburg (Belmont, Calif.: Wadsworth, 1979), pp. 224–27.

[25] Fischer, *Growing Old in America,* p. 111.

[26] Arnold M. Rose and Warren A. Peterson, *Older People and Their Social World,* (Philadelphia: F. A. Davis, 1965), pp. 3–16.

[27] Arnold S. Brown, "Grassroots Advocacy for the Elderly in Small Rural Communities," *The Gerontologist,* 25, no. 4 (August 1985), 417–23.

[28] Charles F. Longino, Jr., Kent A. McClelland, and Warren A. Peterson, "The Aged Subculture Hypothesis: Social Integration, Gerontophilia and Self-Conception," *Journal of Gerontology,* 35, no. 5 (September 1980), 758–67.

[29] Gregory A. Hinrichsen, "The Impact of Age-Concentrated, Publicly Assisted Housing on Older People's Social and Emotional Well-Being," *Journal of Gerontology,* 40, no. 6 (November 1985), 758–60.

[30] Rosemary Erickson and Kevin Eckert, "The Elderly Poor in Downtown San Diego Hotels," *The Gerontologist,* 17, no. 5, pt. 1 (October 1977), 440–46.

[31] Carl I. Cohen and Jay Sokolovsky, "Social Engagement Versus Isolation: The Case of the Aged in SRO Hotels," *The Gerontologist,* 20, no. 1 (February 1980), 36–44.

[32] Cohen and Sokolovsky, "Toward a Concept of Homelessness," pp. 81–89.

[33] Carl I. Cohen, Jeanne Teresi, and Douglas Holmes, "Social Networks and Adaptation," *The Gerontologist,* 25, no. 3 (June 1985), 297–304.

[34] Richard A. Kalish, *Late Adulthood: Perspectives on Human Development* (Monterey, Calif.: Brooks/Cole, 1982), pp. 111–12.

[35] Ibid., pp. 111.

[36] Tim Booth, "Institutional Regimes and Induced Dependency in Homes for the Aged," *The Gerontologist,* 26, no. 4 (August 1986), 418–23.

[37] Bernard Kutner, "The Hospital Environment," *Social Sciences and Medicine,* 4, suppl. 1 (1970), 9–12.

7

The Elderly in the Family

INTRODUCTION

Change has characterized not only the living situations of elderly people, but also the way in which they fit into their families. The family itself has changed in its interactions with other social institutions, particularly the economic and political ones. The foundations upon which the family rests, its structure and definition, and the kinds of relationships that exist among its members have all undergone basic changes.

There are obviously fundamental cross-cultural differences in the family and in how the aged fit into it. The ways in which the family has changed within cultures is also different from one culture to another. In the context of change, the family has at times appeared to be an extremely fragile institution. Some analysts have even predicted its eventual demise. Surprisingly, though, it has continued to survive as a vital institution in all of its cultural forms.

The elderly member's place in the family in part reflects the changes that have taken place in the family as an institution. What is often overlooked, but is perhaps just as important, is the fact that the elderly have themselves contributed to and influenced the transformation of the family.

In this chapter we will examine how elderly people tend to fit into their families in light of the many changes. Particular attention will be paid to the roles and relationships that elderly people tend to have within their families, and to the cross-cultural differences in these relationships.

THE CHANGING FAMILY

Zimmerman has provided an informative analysis of changes in the family in the Western world over a number of centuries.[1] According to the analysis, throughout the centuries of ancient and medieval history, the family served both as the seat of political power and as the primary unit of production. These were the times in Western civilization of the "trustee family." Each generation of family members gained identity and social status by serving as trustees of family power and traditions and passing them on to the next generation. Whole societies were dependent upon their large, multigenerational, extended-family systems. An inevitable part of the trustee family, however, was the frequently severe abuse of power. Eventually, two strong institutions—the Christian church and nationalism as a political system—developed to challenge the abuses of power and the trustee family itself. In competition with both of these institutions (which often worked together), families lost their authority as political entities.

According to Zimmerman, the trustee family was eventually replaced by the "domestic family." In its competitive interaction with the increasingly powerful religious and new political institutions, the family was not destroyed, but was transformed and survived in a still vital form. The domestic family was characterized as an autonomous, self-contained, economically and socially interdependent unit. While this type of family no longer had political power, societies still depended upon it for the socialization and integration of its citizens. The needs of the family unit were more important than the rights of individuals, but the family was still the source of individuals' identity and social status. The family as a kinship system, rather than conjugal relationships, was the foundation of the strength of the family.

Elderly people tended to have positions of importance in the domestic family. By and large, they owned and controlled the economic (productive) enterprises in which the family was involved. They also served as authoritative heads of households. As long as Western cultures in the modern era remained primarily agrarian, the domestic family remained dominant and the aged continued to be very well integrated into the family system.

As societies became industrialized, the family found itself in competition with two new developments that brought about still another form of family. Corporations began to form and to compete with family units as the primary production units upon which the economies of modern societies depended. At the same time, individualism began to take the place of loyalty and commitment to family as the dominant motivating force. As a result, the family lost both its economic function and much of its control over its members, and was transformed into what Zimmerman called the "atomistic family." He characterized this type of family as oriented to the needs and aspirations of individuals. The rights of individuals took precedence over the rights of the family as a unit. Families now existed only to serve their individual members.

The nuclear family is the most prominent form of this type of family, and the basis of its strength is the conjugal (marriage) relationship rather than the kinship system. The family exists and serves the needs of its individual members only as long as the conjugal relationship exists. The irony is that the maintenance of the conjugal relationship itself depends upon the extent to which it satisfies the needs and aspirations of the individual marriage partners. These kinds of families do not survive from generation to generation. Instead, the survival of the family as a functional social institution depends upon its being re-created, unit by unit, with each generation. Zimmerman saw this type of family as inevitably self-destructive because self-interest cannot continue over the long haul to create the kind of family solidarity upon which individuals want to depend in order to satisfy their own needs.

The question for our analysis is how elderly people fit into the atomistic family. Like other individual family members, they would be expected to look to their families for the satisfaction of their felt needs. Logically, however, they could not expect much from their extended families since the nuclear family is the dominant family form. Their greatest source of satisfaction would seem to be the continuance of their own conjugal relationships into old age. The extent to which this is true today will be examined later.

A similar description of changing family patterns in the modern era has more recently been offered by Fullerton.[2] She explains that only 100 years ago, economic production in the United States was family-dominated. Virtually all families served as economic units, mostly in the form of family farms which they owned and operated. That, probably more than anything else, gave family members common identities, life goals, and a sense of security. Division of labor between men and women and between young and old was pronounced, but everyone in the family had a role to perform and a common stake in the success of the family business. The division of labor was not between production and domestic responsibilities; instead, all of the adult roles were blends of both of those types of family responsibilities. Elderly people did not retire from productive roles, but simply took on less strenuous work without relinquishing either their share of family responsibilities or their share of the family benefits.

According to this analysis, changes in family roles and relationships accompanied industrialization. Production moved from the home to the factory, and workers had to leave home and family behind in order to participate in productive work. It was this situation that brought about the division of labor within the family between the provider role for men, the domestic role for women, and virtually no family roles for the aged. In addition, workers now became paid employees, subject to being laid off and retired, especially as they became older. Thus, they were more and more frequently left with neither productive nor domestic family roles.

It would be a mistake to conclude from this analysis that elderly people were better off in the time of the domestic family or in the preindustrial era. In fact, those times were harsh, most elderly people worked hard throughout their lives, many were poor, and many workers died young.[3] Neither should we conclude that individuals were passive recipients of the forces of change. Families were made up of individuals, young and old, who were active participants making deliberate choices about such vital matters as working, moving to new communities, getting married, having children, retiring, and living separately from family members. These choices directly affected family roles and relationships and the positions of families in their communities. Together these choices created the changes in families discussed here. Members of today's elderly population were among the active participants. It is not our purpose to pass judgment about whether the changes were good or bad, however. This analysis simply helps us to understand both the processes that have created the changes and the fact that change is a dynamic process in which we ourselves are involved.

Changes in the family have also taken place and continue to take place in societies with cultures very different from our own. Although the processes of change are based on quite different premises and involve very different players, some are as drastic and far-reaching as those in the West. This is true, for example, in both China and Japan, two Oriental societies which are themselves very diverse from each other.

Families in both China and Japan have been steeped in the tradition of filial piety for centuries. This tradition specified the positions to be held by elderly people and the ways in which they were to be treated within the family. In addition, as explained in Chapter 6, it was part of the religious belief system of these societies as well. It was the foundation of their tradition of ancestor worship. According to this tradition, elderly family members held positions of authority, were treated with great respect, and were expected to be taken care of by their families in old age.

Although filial piety was a well-established tradition in China, it applied almost exclusively to those in the upper class. In a practical sense, poor families had too few resources to make it work.[4] Their whole lives were spent in hard labor in order to survive. The few who lived into old age also had to labor as long as physically possible. The tradition applied primarily to men, even in the upper class. While elderly women were cared for by their families, their authority in the family was mostly over daughters and daughters-in-law. They were subject to and controlled by their husbands, as symbolized by the traditional binding of their feet.

Casual observation of the Chinese family today seems to indicate that the filial piety tradition is still intact. As noted in Chapter 6, almost all elderly people live with the families of their adult children (usually their eldest sons), and it is stipulated in the national constitution that families are legally responsible to take care of their elderly members. In fact, though, great changes in the family have taken place during the years of Communist rule in that country, and the elderly member's place in the family is only partly influenced by the tradition of filial piety.

Communism in China quite effectively challenged the authority of aged males over their family members and the religious beliefs on which that authority rested. Children were free to marry whomever they chose, and women were liberated from slavery to their husbands. Employment opportunities were separated from family control.[5] Although poverty still exists, the poor now receive basic benefits from the government or their local work units. Thus, the patterns of family roles and relationships between older and younger family members that have developed since 1949 have actually changed from the ancient traditions. They conform more to the ideals of Communism than to the traditions of filial piety.

This point is illustrated by the roles and relationships found in the three-generation households of today. The fact that most elderly people live with their eldest sons and their families is undoubtedly due to the influence of tradition. In direct contrast to tradition, though, is the fact, mentioned in Chapter 6, that the authority structure of those households belongs to neither the elderly parents nor their adult children. Instead it is a shared or cooperative authority and an arrangement of mutual benefit to everyone in the household.[6] This practice applies broadly to the entire population. That kind of emphasis represents a substantial change in the place of the aged in the Chinese family.

Changes away from the oriental tradition of filial piety are also taking place in Japan, but because of very different influences. Japan has undergone the same modernization and economic development that has taken place in the Western world, but even more rapidly and intensely. These processes have also affected families and the position of the elderly in those families. Changes in the Japanese family are nevertheless different from those that have taken place in the West.

The filial piety tradition in Japan was somewhat different from that in China. While its basic orientation was familial, it also applied to larger communal structures. As Piovesana explains, the family in China was basically a self-contained unit, somewhat independent of larger social structures. Therefore, the tradition of filial piety applied only to family relationships. In Japan, the family was part of the larger social structure (that is, politics and the military). Thus loyalty to political and military leaders was a requirement of the tradition of filial piety in that country.[7] As Japan became industrialized and large corporations developed and grew during the era since World War II, then, it is not surprising that they have been organized to include the tradition of filial piety as part of their management–worker relationships. In effect, corporations have been conceived of as large families, and workers have been treated as family members. As part of this arrangement, corporate heads have given their employees life-time guarantees of social and economic security. Even though the immediate families are still expected to provide care to their elderly members, they are thus relieved of much of what is expected from the filial piety tradition in Japan. That has affected the kinds of roles and relationships that exist between the generations of the family.

MARITAL ROLES AND RELATIONSHIPS

For the vast majority of elderly people, the marital relationship is the most vital aspect of family life. Almost two-fifths of the women and over two-thirds of the men over 65 years old in the United States are married and living with their spouses. Most of these couples have lived together for many years, and a major part of their social lives has been oriented to marriage, regardless of the quality of their marital relationships.

Evidence indicates that how couples divide their family responsibilities and define their respective roles tends to change throughout the course of their marriages. Marriages tend to begin on an egalitarian basis but move toward greater differentiation. This pattern tends to be reversed again in the later years of marriages, mainly as a result of the empty nest and retirement experiences.[8,9] Marital adjustment and satisfaction through the course of marriage has been an important area of research in recent years. In a cross-sectional comparison of couples at eight stages of married life, Rollins and Feldman examined a number of facets of marital adjustment.[10] Couples in the study were asked to indicate the extent to which they: (1) felt that their marriages were going well; (2) had negative feelings as a result of interactions with their spouses; (3) enjoyed having positive companionship experiences with their spouses; and (4) felt satisfied with their present marital relationships. The stages of the family life cycle included in the study were (1) beginning families (without children); (2) child-bearing families; (3) families with preschool children; (4) families with school-age children; (5) families with teenagers; (6) families as launching centers; (7) families in the middle years; and (8) aging families.

The findings showed that the older the couples, the more both spouses said that their marriages were consistently going well. More aging families felt that way than any of the others. Elderly men were even more positive about their marriages than their wives. Compared with those at other stages of the family life cycle, elderly couples reported the fewest negative feelings from interactions with their spouses and the greatest levels of marital satisfaction. As many as 82 percent of the elderly wives and 66 percent of the elderly husbands said that their marriages were "very satisfying" (Figure 7-1).

Other studies on marital relationships show similar high levels of marital satisfaction among elderly couples in the United States and elsewhere.[11-16] Some have suggested that this simply may be because elderly couples represent successful marriages that have survived into old age. The unsuccessful marriages that have ended in earlier divorces are never included. Gilford found evidence, however, that marital satisfaction among aged couples does not

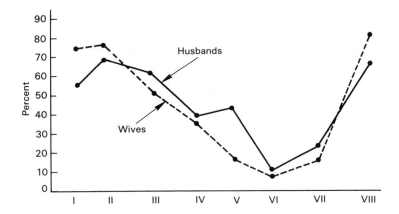

FIGURE 7–1 Percentage of Individuals in Each Stage of the Family Life Cycle Reporting That Their Present Stage Is Very Satisfying (*Source:* B. C. Rollins and H. Feldman, "Marital Satisfaction over the Family Life Cycle," *Journal of Marriage and the Family*, 32, no. 6 (February 1970), 20–28.) Copyrighted 1970 by the National Council on Family Relations, 1910 West Country Road B, Suite 147, St. Paul, MN 55113. Reprinted by permission.

represent just the continuation of previously successful marriages. Instead, there is much potential for marital satisfaction to develop in the context of elderly marriages themselves.[17]

In contrast to these positive findings on the marital relationships of elderly couples, Rollins and Feldman found that levels of positive companionship among the elderly were lower than those at any of the other family life cycle stages. Only 36 percent of the elderly wives and 32 percent of the elderly husbands reported such experiences at least once per day (Figure 7-2). This raises the question of what the basis of marital satisfaction is for elderly couples.

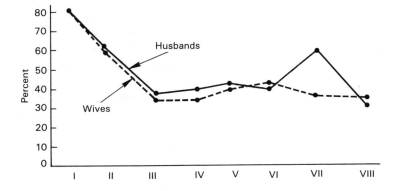

FIGURE 7–2 Percentage of Individuals in Each Stage of the Family Life Cycle Reporting "Positive Companionship" Experiences with Their Spouse at Least "Once a Day" (*Source:* B. C. Rollins and H. Feldman, "Marital Satisfaction Over the Family Life Cycle," *Journal of Marriage and the Family*, 32, no. 6 (February 1970), 20–28.) Copyrighted 1970 by the National Council on Family Relations, 1910 West Country Road B, Suite 147, St. Paul, MN 55113. Reprinted by permission.

Rollins and Feldman did not address that issue, but subsequent studies have identified four basic reasons that elderly couples give for their positive feelings about their marriages. Ironically, one of the reasons given was companionship. Stinnet and colleagues found that companionship, seen by both husbands and wives, was the most rewarding aspect of their marriages.[18] This finding would seem to conflict with that of Rollins and Feldman. It may simply help to explain the previous finding, however. While Rollins and Feldman focus on the frequency of companionship experiences, the Stinnet data emphasized the quality of marital companionship. Elderly couples may not be as concerned about the number of events that they share as they are about the meanings of what they do together.

Another aspect of marital life that has been identified by elderly couples is that of intimacy.[19-21] Stinnet and colleagues found that being in love was seen by those in their sample as the most important factor in achieving marital success. Most couples also remain sexually active throughout their lives. In addition, intimacy among elderly couples includes showing mutual affection, respect, and trust. They gain much satisfaction from freely and openly sharing feelings, ideas, and opinions. For many older people, especially men, their mates are their only confidants.[22]

The third reason for marital satisfaction among the aged, very much related to intimacy, is the sense of *belonging* that being married provides. Families, and particularly marriages, apparently become an increasingly important source of identity and of the sense of being important to others as we become older. This would be particularly vital in retirement, with the loss of an active work role.

Still another source of marital satisfaction for elderly couples is interdependency. The sharing of household responsibilities and income are often mentioned as part of their interdependency.[23-25] An even more vital aspect of their interdependence, though, is their reliance on each other for the care that they may need in their later years. Spouses are by far the most frequent caregivers for elderly people, and the knowledge that care by someone as intimate as a spouse is available would provide individuals with a great sense of security and satisfaction.

Not all elderly couples are satisfied with their marriages, of course. Factors that tend to be related the most to lack of marital success among the aged are chronic health conditions, lack of mutual interests and values, and lack of companionship.[26-28] It is noteworthy that retirement is hardly ever related to marital problems.[29]

Cowgill makes the point that very little attention has been paid to the marital relationships of elderly people in societies other than Western societies.[30] This does not mean that marriages are unimportant to families in other societies. It does mean, however, that family solidarity in other cultures is not as vitally dependent upon the kinds of relationships married couples have. Likewise, elderly people in non-Western societies tend to be integrated into family life regardless of their marital relationships. Because of these differences, then, attention to marital adjustment and satisfaction as an important aspect of family life for elderly people is mostly a phenomenon of the Western world.

EXTENDED-FAMILY ROLES AND RELATIONSHIPS

In the past, the extended family was the most important social context within which the aged were provided with meaningful roles and relationships. During the post–World War II era, students of the family predicted that the extended family would soon cease to exist as a functioning entity in the modern world.[31] This has not happened. Instead, the extended family itself has substantively changed and remains vital to elderly people. Extended family roles and relationships differ among cultures, but there are similarities as well.

In Western cultures, there has been a move away from the traditional extended family, a kinship system in which there was complete economic interdependence and a daily exchange of goods and services. In its place we have adopted what has come to be called the "modified extended family." This is a kinship system in which economic resources are controlled by independent nuclear family units, but goods and services are freely and regularly shared and emotional support is provided.[32,33]

If the modified extended family actually exists in Western societies today, then the aged should have solid family roles and relationships beyond their marriages. During the early post–World War II era in the United States and Europe, it was thought by many that this was not the case and that elderly people were being abandoned by their families. A comprehensive study of the aged in the United States, Great Britain, and Denmark in the mid-1960s, however, clearly showed that almost all elderly people do in fact benefit extensively from a number of types of relationships within the modified extended family.[34]

Because the modified extended family is composed of relatively independent individuals and nuclear family units, it is by nature a voluntary system. Important areas of inquiry, therefore, are (1) what prompts the on-going relationships between elderly people and their family members; (2) whom the relationships tend to be with; and (3) what the nature of those relationships tends to be.

One study indicates that many patterns of interaction between the aged and others outside their immediate households are very much related to how satisfied the elderly are in relating to those other people.[35] Four types of relationships were compared in this study to determine if and when the elderly tended to disengage from each. These included (1) group relationships; (2) relationships with friends and neighbors; (3) extended-family relationships (any family members other than descendants of the elderly people); and (4) immediate family relationships (direct descendants, including sons- and daughters-in-law). It was found that those who expressed some level of dissatisfaction with the first three types of relationships had a distinct tendency to disengage from people in those categories. There were no associations between those specific disengagement patterns and overall disengagement, however. As they gave up one kind of relationship, they tended to develop others to take the place of those that were lost. It is important to note that those in the sample treated extended-family relationships very similarly to relationships outside their families. They were given up just as readily when they were no longer personally satisfying.

Relationships with their immediate-family members tended to be quite the opposite, however. The distinct pattern in that case was that they did not disengage from their children, sons- and daughters-in-law, or grandchildren, regardless of how satisfying or dissatisfying those relationships might have been. It is interesting that those who expressed less than total satisfaction with immediate-family members tended to demonstrate overall disengagement patterns. It was as though, having withdrawn from most other types of people, they were finally clinging to those relationships that were the most vital to them. Apparently, then, of all extended-family members, descendants are preferred over all others. It is not that other types of family relationships and friendships are unimportant to the aged. As noted in Chapter 6, age-peer friendships help provide much of the meaning and purpose of their lives in old age. This would be true of family and nonfamily relationships alike. These types of relationships do, nevertheless, tend to be less permanent than those with one's descendants. Elderly parent–adult children relationships are quite complex. They involve elements of both personal intimacy and role performances on the part of the both parties. These relationships are often beset with problems. Nevertheless, they have remained persistent over time and across a variety of cultures.

Relational characteristics between elderly people and their adult children were identified in the cross-cultural study on aging conducted by Shanas and her colleagues in the 1960s.[36] One of those characteristics was that elderly people tended to live in close enough proximity to at least one of their children to have contact with them at least once a week. Data from a study of three other very different countries (Poland, Yugoslavia, and Israel) conducted at about the same time showed similar patterns.[37] A more recent study of weekly contacts between the aged and their adult children in Sweden showed that this interactional pattern still persists today.[38] This has been found to be true even for the elderly who live in retirement communities.[39]

Children have clearly been, and continue to be, an important source of intimacy for elderly people, even though those in most Western countries prefer to maintain an element of independence between themselves and their children. Some types of elderly parent–adult children relationships are more important than others. Beckman and Houser studied the other side of this issue—elderly people who have no children with whom to relate. They found that the widowed who were childless had lower feelings of well-being than the widowed with children, particularly if they were in poor health and were socially isolated. This was also more true for Jewish and Catholic widows than Protestants.[40] It is reported that the mother–daughter relationship tends to be closer and to be characterized by more frequent contact than those of either mothers and sons, fathers and sons, or fathers and daughters.[41,42]

There is much more to elderly parent–adult children relationships than affection and intimacy, however. Bengtson, Orlander, and Haddad theorized that intergenerational family solidarity or the lack of it was based on three basic elements of compatibility: continuous association or interaction, degree of consensus about values, and affection.[43] In a recent study of intergenerational solidarity, though, almost no support was found for that theory.[44] Helping behavior, especially by females, rather than either consensus or affection, provided the basis for continued interaction and solidarity. Thus, contacts between elderly people and their adult children involve not only affective relationships but role obligations and responsibilities as well.

Most elderly people and their children readily accept the fact that they have role obligations toward one another and are willing to perform those helping roles. They also understand that the substance of their roles is to provide help when it is needed. Almost never do the parties involved understand the specific duties involved or have a consensus about who is to do what and when, however. Parent–child relationships may be well understood when children are young, but they become more complicated when both are adults and when parents are in the process of becoming old. Typically, these role obligations must be negotiated in the context of interaction. In all likelihood, role negotiations make up a good part of the interactions between elderly people and their children, and these negotiations are subject to a great deal of misunderstanding and conflict. Interactions are complicated by the fact that what is being negotiated is not just what kinds of help to give to whom at what time, but also who has the power to control the helping processes. Quite often this involves role reversal—a process that neither the elderly parents nor their adult children find desirable.

Evidence of the problematic aspects of elderly parent–adult children relationships was found in a study of the association between intergenerational solidarity and life satisfaction and depression among older Mexican Americans.[45] It was found, contrary to the investigators' expectations, that affection toward them had nothing to do with the extent to which the elderly respondents associated with their children. Association with their children was, in fact, positively associated with depression. At the heart of this relational problem was the extent to which the elderly tended to receive more help from their children than they gave to them.

There are indications that the problematic aspects of elderly parent–adult children relationships may be even more pronounced in Japan than in America. Campbell and Brody studied the attitudes of women in those two countries related to their roles in helping elderly family members. They found that the women of all ages in both countries uniformly agreed that caring for the aged is a family responsibility. However, Japanese women reported fewer positive experiences with older family members than American women did. In contrast to the American women, they also said that old people in Japan are too powerful.[46] Perhaps the lack of positive experiences and the negative attitudes about power in old age among Japanese women caregivers results from role negotiations that typically take place in intense household settings.

In the People's Republic of China, the most problematic intergenerational role negotiations have been between mothers-in-law and daughters-in-law, since elderly parents typically live with sons rather than daughters. This problem is still somewhat prevalent but may be less so today than in the past, because fairly well-defined and extensive interdependent helping roles characterize their intergenerational relationships within common households. It is well understood today, for example, that both men and women will have jobs and that their retired parents will assume the child-rearing responsibilities while the children's parents are at work. Having in-laws to care for their children is generally viewed as a sign of privilege.[47] Through these cooperative efforts, more income is available to maintain the household, and both young and old benefit. Davis-Friedmann reports that power within today's Chinese households is determined not by age or tradition, but by who is able to earn the highest income.[48]

Much of the literature on relationships between elderly parents and their children treats the helping process as a one-way phenomenon—adult children helping their elderly parents. As the findings from the 1968 cross-cultural study of the aged demonstrated, however, that is only one part of the helping process. Shanas and colleagues noted substantial helping behavior in both directions. As Table 7-1 shows, more of the Danish elderly provided help to their children than received help from them, although there were fewer helping relationships in that country than in either the United States or Great Britain. In all three countries, helping relationships were reciprocal. While this makes elderly people more equal partners in the parent–child relationships than is generally assumed, it undoubtedly serves to complicate the process of role negotiation.

TABLE 7–1   Proportion of Older Men and Women Giving Help to and Receiving Help from Children

Helping Patterns	Denmark			Britain			United States		
	Men	Women	All	Men	Women	All	Men	Women	All
Gave help	24	32	28	40	48	44	59	60	60
Received help	17	21	19	53	63	59	61	75	69

Source: E. Shanas et al., *Old People in Three Industrial Societies* (New York: Atherton Press, 1968), pp. 203–6.

The caregiver role is an important aspect of the helping process in which many adult children engage in behalf of their aged parents. This is a role that not only must be negotiated but is also problematic in terms of what it requires in performance. It has been discovered that at least 75 percent of the care that elderly long-term care recipients receive in the United States is being provided by informal caregivers.[49-51] Most of these are family members, primarily spouses and daughters of the care recipients. The evidence also indicates that the majority of informal caregivers have had no training in, and therefore lack the skills needed for, caregiving.[52] While family members generally accept the responsibilities of this role without reservations,[53,54] many become somewhat overwhelmed by what is required in the actual performance of the caregiver role. They often feel frustrated at being unable to do all that needs to be done, heavily burdened by the constancy of the role in competition with other role responsibilities, and guilty about feeling burdened. When these feelings on the part of caregivers are combined with the sense of dependency that elderly parents tend to feel toward their caregiver daughters, caregiving situations can easily threaten parent–child relationships. When elderly parents suddenly become dependent upon their children due to unanticipated physical or mental impairments, even neglect and abuse of elderly parents by their children can result.[55] Affection between parents and children has often been seen as a key to successful caregiving, but Jarret has suggested that a sense of obligation, somewhat apart from affection, is a more reasonable basis for caregiving.[56]

The relationships between elderly parents and their adult children are obviously vital to elderly people. They are neither consistently negative nor consistently positive but can potentially be both. They involve extremely complex and dynamic processes that can easily result, alternatively, in great personal satisfaction and in frustration.

Elderly persons' positions as grandparents constitute another area of growing interest concerning their place in the family. Limited analysis has been done in this area, and almost all of the existing data was collected during the 1970s and 1980s, with virtually no cross-cultural comparisons included. There are also major disagreements in the literature about the nature of this particular family relationship. Partly at issue are (1) the extent to which grandparents tend to interact with their grandchildren; (2) the importance to them of being a grandparent; (3) the nature of grandparents' relationships with their grandchildren; and (4) the kinds of role expectations or performances connected to being grandparents.

The role of the grandparent has changed quite drastically in recent times. As Troll points out, the image of grandparents as old people confined to a rocking chair no longer fits reality. Instead, they are active, middle-aged people.[57] More and more typically, both grandmothers and grandfathers work, and many engage in active community roles.

Available statistics show that American grandparents tend to interact with their grandchildren regularly and often, even though very few live in the same households. Troll and co-workers report, for example, that nearly half of American grandparents see at least one of their grandchildren each day and that such interactions are more frequent among blacks than whites.[58]

Cherlin and Furstenberg also found that grandparents see grandchildren who live near them often even when the grandparents and the children's parents don't get along well.[59] It has been discovered, too, that there tend to be more interactions between grandmothers and granddaughters than between grandfathers and grandsons, perhaps because elderly women have more to share with their granddaughters than elderly men have with their grandsons.[60] Interaction with grandchildren tends to be very dependent upon proximity of living, however.

There is some disagreement in the literature about how important relationships with grandchildren are to the aged and about how the aged tend to relate to their grandchildren. The amount of interaction would indicate that they want to have those kinds of interactions, but the question is whether or not they are seen as vital relationships to the elderly. On the one hand, Kornhaber has accused grandparents of living by a norm of noninvolvement and therefore abdicating their responsibility to help their grandchildren in ways that they uniquely could.[61] On the other hand, Cherlin and Furstenberg present evidence that, although they tend not to interfere when life for their grandchildren is going well, grandparents have a strong sense of obligation to help in times of crisis. For example, when and if their parents get divorced, many grandparents (men as well as women) take their grandchildren into their homes.[62] Thomas also presents evidence that especially the relatively young grandparents readily discipline, care for, help, and offer advice to their grandchildren.[63] There are indications, too, that grandchildren and grandparents deliberately try to influence each other, and both are at least somewhat successful.[64]

Others characterize grandparent–grandchildren relationships as "ambiguous,"[65] "peripheral,"[66] and "free of normative guidelines."[67] Wood reports that while grandparents may personally enjoy interacting with their grandchildren, few see those relationships as vital. Research findings show that their level of involvement is unrelated to either life satisfaction or the condition of their mental health.[68]

There is much ambiguity in the literature about whether or not grandparenthood today constitutes an identifiable role. Based on their analysis of grandparents helping their grandchildren in times of crisis, Cherlin and Furstenberg conclude that being a grandparent is a deeply meaningful role.[69] Neugarten and Weinstein studied grandparents in the 1960s and reported that they had discovered five basic role models among grandparents: (1) *formal grandparents*, who show interest but whose involvement is limited; (2) *fun-seekers*, who informally share leisure activities; (3) *parent surrogates*, who take on child-rearing responsibilities; (4) *reservoirs of family wisdom*, who serve as authority figures in the family; and (5) *distant figures*, who visit occasionally but are formal and remote.[70] By and large, however, these categorizations describe the extent and kind of interactional involvement more than they represent defined roles. Parent surrogate could be considered a role, but, according to Neugarten and Weinstein, relatively few American grandparents practice that role, and even fewer prefer it as a grandparenting style.

Many grandparents may interact with their grandchildren in accordance with some selectively defined role, but there is certainly no normatively prescribed role to which grandparents are expected to adhere. Many simply prefer to maintain informal and expressive relationships with their grandchildren rather than perform some instrumental role. As George concludes, "normative guidelines are so few and so vague that individuals pursue the style of relationship they find the most comfortable."[71]

In contrast to grandparenting in the United States, grandparents in China are oriented almost exclusively to role performance. While much affection may indeed be involved in the grandparent–grandchild relationship, their interactions take place in the context of grandparents' serving as caretakers of their grandchildren, a role they share equally with the children's parents.[72]

CONCLUSION

It is clear that the family is vital to the aged. The older they become, the more that is true. In a real sense, elderly people depend upon their families for their social and psychological well-being and survival.

Some of the behavioral tendencies of elderly people would seem to indicate that families are less important to them than was true in the past. Their preferences to live separately from other family members and their increasing tendency to choose age-segregated living situations and daily interaction with nonfamily age peers would seem to be evidence that families are of decreasing importance to the aged.

Evidence indicates, however, that while they increasingly rely on interactions with others for meaning in their daily lives, those relationships tend to be much less vital to the aged than family relationships. We in modern Western societies have modified the extended family, not because it is less important to us, but simply to maintain elements of independence between the generations within the family.

In analyzing the place of the aged in the family, it is important to distinguish between family relationships that provide them with needed affection and emotional support and those that represent meaningful roles within the family. In Western societies there tends to be a great deal of confusion about those two aspects of family relationships. Many family interactions between the elderly and other family members include elements of both affection and role performance or negotiation. Probably for that reason, the aged tend to declare a certain amount of independence from those of younger generations.

In contrast, the elderly in Oriental societies tend to emphasize well-defined family roles for their aged. Therefore, they have much less need to live separately from younger generations. Their attention is centered on the performance of those roles rather than on their needs for emotional support. While emotional support may be as important to their elderly as to ours, they may think of it as simply a by-product of their role performance within the family.

We have seen in this chapter that relationships between elderly people and various family members have different degrees of value for elderly members. It is clear that marital relationships have priority. Most elderly couples have successful marriages which provide them with the kinds of intimacy they want and need and with a great deal of social and economic security. Elderly people treat their relationships with their adult children as vital, even though they may be plagued with elements of conflict over the continuing processes of parent–child and authority negotiations. For most elderly people, relationships with siblings and other extended-family members are apparently similar to those with close friends: They are important as long as they are satisfying but are expendable when they are not satisfying.

Relationships with grandchildren have much symbolic and affective meaning for the aged. Grandparents in the modern era, though, tend to have very little, if any, authority over the lives of their grandchildren, and relationships with them tend not to be as socially or psychologically vital to them as other family relationships. In Oriental societies, grandchildren are much more a part of the daily lives of elderly people.

NOTES

[1] Gerald R. Leslie and Sheila K. Korman, *The Family in Social Context* (New York: Oxford University Press, 1985), pp. 192–94.

[2] Gail P. Fullerton, *Survival in Marriage: Introduction to Family Interaction, Conflicts, and Alternatives* (Hinsdale, Ill.: Dryden Press, 1977), pp. 4–34.

[3] David Hackett Fischer, *Growing Old in America* (New York: Oxford University Press, 1978), pp. 59–73.

[4] Myrna Lewis, "Aging in the People's Republic of China," *International Journal of Aging and Human Development*, 15, no. 2 (1982), 79–105.

[5] Deborah Davis-Friedman, *Long Lives: Chinese Elderly and the Communist Revolution* (Cambridge, Mass.: Harvard University Press, 1983), p. 34.

[6] F. Butterfield, *China Alive in the Bitter Sea* (New York: Times Books, 1982), p. 219.

[7] Gino K. Piovesana, "The Aged in Chinese and Japanese Cultures," in *Dimensions of Aging: Readings*, eds. Jon Hendricks and C. Davis Hendricks (Cambridge, Mass.: Winthrop, 1979), pp. 13–20.

[8] Lillian E. Troll, *Early and Middle Adulthood* (Monterey, Calif.: Brooks/Cole, 1985), pp. 109–19.

[9] Robert C. Atchley, *Aging: Continuity and Change* (Belmont, Calif.: Wadsworth, 1987), p. 185.

[10] Boyd C. Rollins and H. Feldman, "Marital Satisfaction Over the Family Life Cycle," *Journal of Marriage and the Family*, 32, no. 1 (February 1970), 20–28.

[11] Wesley R. Burr, "Satisfaction with Various Aspects of Marriage Over the Life Cycle: A Random Middle Class Sample," *Journal of Marriage and the Family*, 32, no. 1 (February 1970), 29–37.

[12] Nick Stinnet, Janet Collins, and James E. Montgomery, "Marital Need Satisfaction of Older Husbands and Wives," *Journal of Marriage and the Family,* 32 (August 1970), 428–34.

[13] Nick Stinnet, Linda M. Carter, and James E. Montgomery, "Older Persons' Perceptions of Their Marriages," *Journal of Marriage and the Family,* 34 (November 1972), 665–70.

[14] Robert C. Atchley and Sheila J. Miller, "Retirement and Couples," *Generations,* 7, no. 2 (Winter 1982), 28–29, 36.

[15] Rosalie Gilford, "Marriage in Later Life," *Generations,* 10, no. 4 (Summer 1986), 16–20.

[16] Kyriakos S. Markides and S. Hoppe, "Marital Satisfaction in Three Generations of Mexican Americans," *Social Science Quarterly,* 66 (March 1985), 147–54.

[17] Rosalie Gilford, "Contrasts in Marital Satisfaction Through Old Age: An Exchange Theory Analysis," *Journal of Gerontology,* 39, no. 3 (May 1984), 325–33.

[18] Stinnet, Carter, and Montgomery, "Older Persons' Perceptions of Their Marriages," pp. 665–70.

[19] Ibid.

[20] Gilford, "Marriage in Later Life," pp. 16–20.

[21] Atchley, *Aging: Continuity and Change,* pp. 189–91.

[22] Marjorie F. Lowenthal and Betsy Robinson, "Social Networks and Isolation," in *Handbook on Aging and the Social Sciences,* eds. Robert H. Binstock and Ethel Shanas (New York: Van Nostrand Reinhold, 1976), pp. 432–56.

[23] Atchley, *Aging: Continuity and Change,* p. 191.

[24] Gilford, "Marriage in Later Life," pp. 16–20.

[25] Yael Kremer, "Parenthood and Marital Roles Performance Among Retired Workers: Comparison between Pre- and Post-retirement Period," *Aging and Society,* 5, no. 4 (1985), 449–60.

[26] Atchley, *Aging: Continuity and Change,* pp. 185–86.

[27] Stinnet, Carter, and Montgomery, "Older Persons' Perceptions of Their Marriages," pp. 665–70.

[28] Gilford, "Marriage in Later Life," pp. 16–20.

[29] Atchley and Miller, "Retirement and Couples," pp. 28–29, 36.

[30] Donald O. Cowgill, *Aging Around the World* (Belmont, Calif.: Wadsworth, 1986), pp. 80–81.

[31] William J. Goode, *World Revolution and Family Patterns* (Glencoe, Ill.: Free Press, 1963), pp. 179–95.

[32] J. Ross Eshleman, *The Family: An Introduction* (Boston, Mass.: Allyn and Bacon, 1985), pp. 88–89.

[33] Leslie and Korman, *The Family in Social Context,* pp. 233–38.

[34] Ethel Shanas et al., *Old People in Three Industrial Societies* (New York: Atherton Press, 1968), pp. 132–257.

[35] Arnold S. Brown, "Satisfying Relationships for the Elderly and Their Patterns of Disengagement," *The Gerontologist,* 14, no. 3 (June 1974), 258–62.

[36] Shanas et al., *Old People in Three Industrial Societies,* pp. 195–206.

[37] Ethel Shanas, "Family-Kin Networks and Aging in Cross-Cultural Perspective," in *The Family: Functions, Conflicts, and Symbols,* eds. Peter J. Stein, Judith Richman, and Natalie Hannon (Reading, Mass.: Addison-Wesley, 1977), pp. 300–307.

[38] Gerdt Sundstrom, "Intergenerational Mobility and the Relationship Between Adults and Their Aging Parents in Sweden," *The Gerontologist,* 26, no. 4 (August 1986), 367–71.

[39] Michael Baker, "The 1982 Sun City Long Term Care Survey: A Statistical Profile of Resident Characteristics, Attitudes, and References" (unpublished research report from the Arizona Long Term Care Gerontology Center, Tucson, Arizona, 1983), pp. 66–67.

[40] Linda J. Beckman and Betty B. Houser, "The Consequences of Childlessness on the Social Psychological Well-Being of Older Women," *Journal of Gerontology,* 37, no. 2 (March 1982), 243–50.

[41] Majda Thurnber, "Family Patterns Vary Among US Ethnic Groups," *Generations,* 7, no. 2 (Winter, 1982), 8–9, 38.

[42] Lillian E. Troll, "Parents and Children," *Generations,* 10, no. 4 (Summer 1986), 23–25.

[43] Vern L. Bengtson, E. B. Orlander, and A. A. Haddad, "The 'Generation Gap' and Aging Family Members: Toward a Conceptual Model," in *Time, Roles, and the Self in Old Age,* ed. J. F. Gubrium (New York: Human Sciences Press, 1976), p. 257.

[44] Maxine P. Atkinson, Vira R. Kivett, and Richard T. Campbell, "Intergenerational Solidarity: An Examination of a Theoretical Model," *Journal of Gerontology,* 41, no. 3 (May 1986), 408–16.

[45] Kyriakos S. Markides and Neal Krause, "Intergenerational Solidarity and Psychological Well-Being among Older Mexican Americans: A Three-Generations Study," in *Journal of Gerontology,* 40, no. 3 (May 1985), 390–92.

[46] Ruth Campbell and Elaine M. Brody, "Women's Changing Roles and Help to the Elderly: Attitudes of Women in the United States and Japan," *The Gerontologist,* 25, no. 6 (December 1985), 584–92.

[47] Davis-Friedmann, *Long Lives,* p. 21.

[48] Ibid., p. 80.

[49] Marjorie H.Cantor, "Strain Among Caregivers: A Study of Experience in the United States." *The Gerontologist,* 23, no. 6 (December 1983), 597–604.

[50] Vida Goldstein, Gretchen Regnery, and Edward Wellin, "Caretaker Role Fatigue," *Nursing Outlook,* 29, no. 1 (January 1981), 24–30.

[51] Laurence G. Branch and Alan M. Jette, "Elders' Use of Informal Long-Term Care Assistance," *The Gerontologist,* 23, no. 1 (February 1983), 51–56.

[52] Beth J. Soldo and Jaana Myllyluoma, "Caregivers Who Live with Dependent Elderly," *The Gerontologist,* 23, no. 6 (December 1983), 605–11.

[53] Troll, "Parents and Children," pp. 23–25.

[54] Campbell and Brody, "Women's Changing Roles," pp. 584–92.

[55] Arnold S. Brown, "Report on Navajo Elder Abuse," (unpublished research report submitted to the Navajo Office on Aging, Window Rock, Arizona, Fall 1986), pp. 10–12.

[56] William Jarrett, "Caregiving Within Kinship Systems: Is Affection Really Necessary?" *The Gerontologist,* 25, no. 1 (February 1985), 5–10.

[57] Troll, *Early and Middle Adulthood,* p. 148.

[58] Lillian E. Troll, Sheila J. Miller, and Robert C. Atchley, *Families in Later Life* (Belmont, Calif.: Wadsworth, 1979), p. 109.

[59] Andrew Cherlin and Frank F. Furstenberg, "Grandparents and Family Crisis," *Generations,* 10, no. 4 (Summer 1986), 26–28.

[60] Troll, Miller, and Atchley, *Families in Later Life,* pp. 113–14.

[61] A. Kornhaber, "Grandparenthood and the 'New Social Contract,'" in *Grandparenthood,* eds. Vern L. Bengston and J. F. Robertson (New York: Anchor Press/Doubleday, 1985), pp. 97–116.

[62] Cherlin and Furstenberg, "Grandparents and Family Crisis," pp. 26–28.

[63] Jeanne L. Thomas, "Age and Sex Differences in Perceptions of Grandparenting," *Journal of Gerontology,* 41, no. 3 (May 1986), 417–23.

[64] Vivian Wood, "Grandparenthood: An Ambiguous Role," *Generations,* 7, no. 2 (Winter 1982), 22–23, 35.

[65] Ibid.

[66] Troll, Miller, and Atchley, *Families in Later Life,* p. 113.

[67] Linda K. George, *Role Transitions in Later Life* (Monterey, Calif.: Brooks/Cole, 1980), p. 88.

[68] Wood, "Grandparenthood," pp. 22–23, 35.

[69] Cherlin and Furstenberg, "Grandparents and Family Crisis," pp. 26–28.

[70] Bernice L. Neugarten and Karol K. Weinstein, "The Changing American Grandparent," *Journal of Marriage and the Family,* 26 (1964), 199–204.

[71] George, *Role Transitions in Later Life,* p. 88.

[72] Davis-Friedmann, *Long Lives,* p. 83.

8

Patterns of Participation of the Aged in the Community

INTRODUCTION

Throughout the 1960s and early 1970s in the United States, a movement took place that came to be labeled "the quest for community." It began among college-aged people but eventually involved people of all ages in some way or another. In essence, it was a response to the growth of large and powerful corporate and governmental structure during the post–World War II period. Big business and big government were perceived as impersonal machines that were taking over the personal lives of individuals. People came to feel as though they were cogs in the wheels used to run the machines of business and government; they felt that they had no control over their own destinies or even their daily lives.[1,2]

Mead had used the concept of the *generalized other* to represent the norms and understanding of society as a whole. His assumption was that all individuals have the ability to understand this kind of societal perspective and to take it into account as they decide how to act and interact. As society became increasingly complex and came to be defined as a *mass society*, however, it became more and more impossible to comprehend. The emphasis thus shifted to the concept of *reference groups* that individuals could define and to which they could actually relate.[3]

The quest for community was manifested in two major emphases. One was the search by individuals to restore personal relationships to their daily experiences. A distinction had been made between primary (personal and intimate) and secondary (impersonal and instrumental) relationships, with an increasing sense that more and more of life was being dominated by secondary relationships. This prompted a deep desire to reemphasize primary groups and reestablish the personal aspects of life.

The second emphasis in the quest-for-community movement was the insistence that individuals and groups of individuals had the right to self-expression and self-determination. There was the overwhelming sense that the power over individuals' daily lives, and even over their final destinies, increasingly rested with large, impersonal forces controlled by a few powerful people.[4]

Even in local communities and bureaucratic structures, power was perceived as being in the hands of small, elite groups who were unaccountable to anyone but themselves.[5] Much of the revolutionary activity of the 1960s constituted a struggle by individuals and groups for power over their personal lives and their communities as well as over national events. Thus, while it was in part a quest for a sense of community, it was, ironically, also a struggle for individual rights.

As a result of this movement, many types of communal, voluntary, and special-interest groups were formed, some spontaneously and others through a deliberate planning process. Many people, young and old, joined communes and friendship clubs in which they could establish somewhat permanent and intimate ties with others in order to satisfy their desire for more personal relationships. Others became part of voluntary associations and action groups in an attempt to influence public policy and bring about needed social reform. Grassroots community action and development projects were organized and implemented across the country. People in small towns and urban neighborhoods met, organized into task forces, and worked together for change.

Another result of this movement was that new meanings were added to the concept of community. A community was no longer just a local geographical gathering of individuals and families organized with governmental and institutional entities for their common protection and welfare; more important, it became defined as any group in which individuals felt that they belonged and through which their individual rights would be enhanced. We now have medical, academic, environmental, retirement, and many other communities whose members relate to one another, not so much out of a sense of commitment to their group, but because of a common individual interest that they happen to share. It has been suggested that groups based on self-interest alone last only as long as members continue to have common interests. Kanter observed, for example, that communes quickly cease to exist unless members develop a sense of commitment to the community itself, separate from their own individual goals.[6] At best, with the major emphasis being placed on individual rights in the quest for community, we end up with a segmented society made up of many different groups with conflicting values and interests. Age has come to be one of the major factors that has divided us into distinct groups.

Participation in community, then, has largely come to mean the extent to which individuals participate in one or another of the various types of groups. Particularly important to assess with regard to the aged are groups and relationships in which they participate in order to enhance their personal and social lives, and community action groups and efforts in which they become involved in order to bring about what they see as needed change.

PERSONAL-ENHANCEMENT GROUPS AND RELATIONSHIPS

Having and relating to friends is obviously an important part of the social lives of elderly people. To be sure, as was noted in Chapter 7, relationships with family members are generally viewed by the elderly as more permanent and ultimately more reliable in times of crisis and for need fulfillment than are friendships. Friends are important to them, however, in helping them to find meaning in their daily lives. In this respect, as was also noted in Chapter 7, elderly people tend to very much prefer having friends among their age peers. Friendships among cohorts with whom they share common values and experiences would understandably provide them with the greatest satisfaction in their search for life enhancement.

The distinction between friends and neighbors is an important one. The elderly do not, of course, consider all of their neighbors as friends, nor do neighbors as a whole relate to elderly people indiscriminately. Cantor has optimistically suggested that friends and neighbors can be counted upon to offer needed support to elderly people when family members are not available.[7] O'Bryant found, however, that neighbors do not necessarily tend to provide support to those with the least family support. She compared the amount of support offered by neighbors to three types of widowed elderly people: (1) those with children living in their communities, (2) those with children but none in their communities, and (3) those with no children. Ironically, of the three types of widows, neighbors tended to give the least assistance to those with no children.[8] In all probability, neighbors are more inclined to respond more to the elderly people who are socially active than to respond according to their level of needs, and, as O'Bryant suggests, having had children may have helped them to be more socially active in their neighborhoods. As important as some neighbors are to some elderly in particular situations, they cannot always be depended upon to offer assistance, even when it is needed.

Nevertheless, friends are generally chosen by the aged from among their neighbors. Lawton points out that proximity is one of the most important determinants of the establishment of active friendships among the aged.[9]

Friendships among old people often form into friendship networks composed largely of age peers. Substantial research has been done on the importance of social networks of the aged. This research tends to focus on two basis questions: (1) Do they tend to provide needed support to those involved? and (2) Do they contribute to the overall sense of well-being of those involved?

It has been discovered that social networks in at least some situations do, in fact, provide support to old people with special needs. A group of investigators studied elderly residents in a number of single-room occupancy hotels in Manhattan to determine the extent to which social networks existed there, and, if they did, whether or not members of those networks tended to help one another when needs arose.[10] They found that even in an environment in which social interaction tends to be limited, social networks not only exist, but they help individuals in two important ways. To some degree they contribute directly to meeting needs, and they help individuals cope with their problems. An earlier, similar study, however, showed that network interventions into people's problems are not always effective.[11] Many individuals had needs that were too immediate and they were too distrustful of others to rely on network responses. Many also cared more about their privacy than about being helped by friends in the network.

The amount of support that individuals receive from social networks in these types of settings also depends greatly on the network members' attitudes about helping their friends. In a study of relationships among older residents in retirement housing, Goodman identified three types of helping neighbors: (1) high helpers (willing to help anyone without regard to reciprocation); (2) mutual helpers (willing to help based on reciprocal exchange); and (3) neighborhood isolates (the disengaged who did not participate in the helping processes).[12]

Ironically, as was found to be true in traditional neighborhoods, those with the most need for assistance seem to be the most ignored by the social networks in public housing for the aged. Paris found that those who were the most isolated in planned housing projects tended to be those who were the most chronically ill. Whatever support network they had was composed of people from outside the projects.[13] Sheehan also found that the frail elderly living in public housing did not tend to be supported by the existing informal network of residents. Her data indicated that the attitudes and behaviors of both the frail and the healthy residents tended to keep them from interacting with each other. The frail elderly often deny that they have needs and distance themselves socially from in-housing neighbors as a mechanism for maintaining that denial. Healthy residents tend to ignore their frail neighbors out of the fear that interaction with them will sap too much of their energy. Thus they tend to confine their interactions to those who can reciprocate.[14]

Ward reports that there is very little evidence to show that social networks contribute to the general well-being of those in old age.[15] Rook reports that, in fact, interactions with friends often have more negative results than positive. Some interactions are downright unpleasant and even cause stress. In a study of elderly widows, she found that friends and relatives had made life more difficult for over two-thirds of the respondents.[16]

Ward makes the point, though, that social support of the aged is not static but dynamic, and in order to understand the importance of support networks, we need to examine those dynamic processes and not just note whether or not they exist.[17] For example, widowhood is often very socially disruptive, and few peers who have not experienced it are able to comprehend or relate to the problems involved.[18]

There is no doubt that individual friendships and those found within social networks among the aged are valuable sources both of practical assistance and of a sense of well-being for many of those who participate. Not all age-peer relationships are positive or beneficial, however. Old people are probably more diverse than any other age group. They differ in terms of their past experiences as well as their present living conditions. Those differences as well as others influence the extent to which peer group interactions are or are not rewarding. An especially important factor that seems to influence whether or not elderly people will have positive interaction with one another is the extent to which those interactions are potentially reciprocal and thus preserve the common desire for elements of independence in their lives.

Participation in voluntary community groups is another important source through which elderly people look for meaningful and satisfying personal relationships. It is true, as reported in Chapter 7, that older people have a tendency to become dissatisfied with groups in general and to disengage from those types of social relationships.[19] There is, however, a growing tendency for them to join and actively participate in various types of age-specific groups in which they can interact with others on the basis of shared values and interdependent relationships.

A 1969 survey of the aged in Montana identified a number of types of community organizations in which elderly people were members.[20] These organizations included lodges, church-related groups, and professional groups in which they shared membership with adults of all ages. With the exception of the church groups, participation in these organizations decrease with age. The other major type of organization that was identified in the survey was specifically for senior citizens. Some of these were small clubs that met weekly. More important, there were also 14 senior citizens' centers in the state at the time, with a total membership of 6,750. With the exception of the religious groups, rates of attendance in the age-specific groups were generally higher than in the integrated groups.

It has consistently been found that, as a whole, the aged in the United States participate more in religious groups and activities than in any other type of group activity in the general community. Evidence shows, however, that church attendance itself has not consistently been associated with life satisfaction or personal adjustment. This does not mean, of course, that religious involvement is not important to those who participate. The fact is that religious groups are quite different from other groups to which elderly people tend to belong. Church memberships are often made up of very diverse types of people with many different views. The purpose of participation in them is not merely to have compatible and satisfying interactions, but to worship, learn spiritual truth, and share in the mission of the group. Controversy, and even conflict, are not at all uncommon in church meetings, and conflict can be expected to be negatively related to such things as morale and life satisfaction. Probably the most comforting aspect of religious participation is the beliefs that result. Indeed, Haitsma found that intrinsic religious orientation among the elderly was related to their level of life satisfaction.[21]

There has been a growing demand for senior citizens' centers in the United States since their inception in the early 1960s. Krout reports that by the late 1970s there were about 5,000 centers nationwide, and by 1985 the number had grown to about 10,000.[22]

Nevertheless, it has been found that even senior citizens' centers with elaborate activity and meals programs attract only a minority of the elderly in their communities. For example, it was found that in 1975, only 18 percent of elderly Americans participated in seniors' centers.[23] Program planners and administrators have viewed this as an outreach problem. What has often been overlooked, though, is the fact that the elderly population is a diverse group in many more ways than just age, and that those who differ typically choose not to interact with one another on a daily basis.

This reluctance to participate is understandable when we realize that individuals are recruited on the basis of how the program is supposed to benefit them, and that becomes their main motivation to participate. Thus, individuals of different socioeconomic, racial, and ethnic backgrounds, and with different health conditions, often do not feel personally rewarded by interacting with one another. It has been found that individual centers tend to attract mostly one type of elderly people or another. Some tend to serve one type and others serve other types of senior citizens, but few, if any, serve more than one or two types of populations. Even in homogeneous communities, differences between individuals keep some elderly people from participating in center activities. Participants were compared to nonparticipants in a study in a Burbank, California, center. They differ in three respects: (1) level of activity, (2) mental condition, and (3) physical condition.[24]

From the viewpoint of professional planners, senior citizens' centers are multipurpose agencies providing a variety of services to all elderly people with unmet needs.[25] From that viewpoint, discrimination against the elderly at centers is unacceptable. By and large, the senior citizens themselves see the centers as opportunities to interact and share experiences with those they consider to be their peers. This distinction is evident in a study of five senior citizens' centers in Crawford County, Arkansas, a predominantly rural, low-income county. To the obvious disappointment of the service provider–oriented investigators, those with the greatest need were not primarily the ones who participated in the centers' programs. Instead, participants tended to be those who were relatively healthy and already active.[26]

The choices that the elderly make to live in retirement homes and communities and age-segregated housing also reflect their desire to establish a sense of community with their peers. There are, of course, a number of practical reasons that such choices are made, such as economics and safety, but the desire to live in an environment in which elderly individuals can regularly interact with their peers seems clearly to be part of those choices. For example, senior citizens' housing projects have been constructed with government subsidies for the primary purpose of providing affordable housing for the elderly poor, yet Varady found that the most economically needy are not the ones who tend to apply or even express interest in such housing. It is noteworthy that black elderly, who tend to be disproportionately represented among the poor, did not tend to be interested because they tend to be more integrated into their extended families than others. The Varady study does not deal with specific motivations for applying for public housing, but the primary motivation clearly was not economic need.[27]

Another possible alternative motivation is the desire on the part of the elderly to live close to and interact with peers. Further evidence of the importance of peer relationships to the aged is provided in a study by Longina, McClelland, and Peterson of why retirement-community residents prefer age-based interaction and housing.[28] They found what they labeled a "retreatist" style of life among the residents. One of the major aspects of that style, as they expressed it, was "the warm companionship of those like themselves" that they enjoyed in retirement communities.

It is important to note that little or no cross-cultural literature is available about such variables as individual life satisfaction and its relationship to friendships or group involvement. That may simply be an oversight by investigators. More likely, though, it means that those types of data are unimportant to the aged in many other parts of the world. People of most other non-Western countries do not seem to be engaged in the search for personal identity and a sense of community as we in the West seem to be. In other cultures, being part of a community may be taken for granted, and personal identity is seen as a natural consequence of community integration.

In Communist China, for example, communities, not individuals, are emphasized as the more important part of society. People are identified and treated as members of communes or organized neighborhoods.[29] Regardless of how individuals feel about this, it nevertheless provides them with a sense of where they belong and who they are. They are also dependent upon their communities for their daily welfare. In that kind of social context, the pursuit of individual identities and interests simply is not culturally appropriate.

In a different way, the Japanese elderly are also, to a great extent, oriented to culturally defined groups rather than to individuals. They not only tend to be integrated into their extended families, but many have been given lifetime identities by the companies for which they work.[30] A good part of their social contacts are presumably oriented to those groups. Again, membership in these groups has, at least until recently, provided individuals with welfare, identity, and a sense of belonging.

Data on the relationship between interpersonal involvement and personal feelings of life satisfaction among the elderly is also largely missing from some culturally unique minority groups in the United States. The Navajo Indian tribe is an example. Many senior citizens' centers have now been developed across the reservations, and the Navajo elderly readily participate. For most of them, however, involvement is not motivated by a desire to interact with their age peers as a way of improving their own sense of well-being apart from their families. At least for the most traditional Navajo elders, families have always been the source of personal identity and social well-being. The centers simply provide them with needed services and a supplementary source of social contact. The maintenance of these cultural traditions by the Navajo elderly was discovered in a recent study of elder abuse on the reservation.[31]

COMMUNITY ACTION GROUPS AND EFFORTS

An increasing amount of the involvement of elderly people in community groups today is motivated not only by the need for meaningful interaction, but also by what is perceived as the need for action. According to some analysts, older people have been ineffective and reluctant political activists. It is true that many of them would not choose to be involved in politics as such, but increasing numbers of them are realizing that some of their needs could be met by community-based programs. They are often willing to join groups that work to initiate those programs and to bring about change. This kind of community involvement has largely been ignored in the gerontological literature and unrecognized in modern societies that tend to view the aged as dependent.

The processes by which elderly people become involved in community action were discovered in a study of how programs for the aged in small communities are developed.[32] It was found that these programs became reality mostly by the actions, not of professional planners, as might be expected, but of groups of elderly people themselves, almost none of whom would have identified themselves as political activists. Several stages were found to characterize the way in which these groups became involved in this particular form of community action. The first stage in the process was just *getting together*. It turned out that this was a very dynamic event. In the small towns under study, elderly folks had known one another for years, but coming together as cohorts of elderly people prompted a keen awareness of their common interests.

The second stage was that of *getting organized*. Without that formalization step, such groups either eventually disbanded or remained casual friendship groups. In becoming organized, the groups chose leaders and began to think in terms of what the group should be doing and what activities they could plan. Long-range goal setting and planning was not involved, however. At this stage, groups simply planned those activities in which they as group members were interested and that they could achieve with their own resources. They were generally not yet ready to engage in community action projects.

The third stage can be characterized as that of *identifying needs.* Typically, this was not a process in which the group members deliberately engaged. Instead, as they interacted with one another and tried to recruit other elderly people into their groups, unmet needs among the aged in their communities became apparent. With the recognition of needs, the desire typically grew within the groups to do something about them. It was at this point that the groups began to become oriented to community action.

The final stage in this process was *seeking outside help.* Groups soon understood that developing programs to meet the needs of a whole segment of the communities' populations required resources beyond what those in the groups could provide. The search for help typically took them to town and county governments and eventually to Area Agencies on Aging.

Another form of community involvement typical of many aged in the United States today follows almost naturally from involvement in the local grassroots groups just described. As local service programs are developed from Area Agency on Aging funds, and as staff are hired to administer the programs, advisory councils on aging are required to advise the administrative staff. Members of the local groups of aged are usually asked to serve in that capacity. Although their role is advisory, members of these councils are able to exert a great deal of influence over the policies and operations of such programs. Some individuals have been thrust into new careers in their retirement years by serving on regional, state, and even national councils on aging.

It is important to realize that, contrary to the rather common myth that they are relatively uninvolved in their communities, involvement among the aged is actually quite substantial. More of their participation than we might suppose involves action to bring about change. Much of their community participation, however, as we have seen, is oriented to their own concerns. In that sense, though, they are not very different from the rest of the population in the growing trend toward powerful special-interest groups.

Community involvement by the aged in the People's Republic of China, by comparison, is very different from that in the United States. It is true that in large urgan neighborhoods, some elderly can be observed getting together at neighborhood centers for recreational activities similar to those at seniors' centers in the United States.[33] This clearly does not represent a predominant type of community participation for elderly Chinese, however. Rather, their community participation generally involves performing important community leadership roles. Some of these roles, in fact, provide them with a great deal of influence and even power within their communities.[34] According to Lewis, more elderly women than men serve as community leaders.[35] Lewis has identified a number of community roles that retired people tend to perform, including dispute settlement, work consultant, neighborhood cleanup, child care, neighborhood study groups, health and welfare service provision, community watching, and mentoring. These are roles that they are uniquely qualified to perform for two basic reasons: (1) Because they are retired, they are more consistently available within the neighborhoods; and (2) they often have years of work experience to qualify them for particular assignments.

It is important to realize that neighborhoods in Chinese cities are organized into a system of committees that manage the neighborhoods and offer various types of services to neighborhood residents. To a large extent, retired people make up those committees.

The role of mentor is a particularly vital one at present. Yin and Lai point out that children and adolescents were denied formal educational opportunities during the Cultural Revolution and have thus moved into young adulthood with educational deficits. Today's elderly people were relatively well educated, especially in Communist doctrine and the history of the revolution.[36] Thus they can now uniquely serve as effective mentors. This role may well be the most socially vital of them all. Obviously, the participation of elderly Chinese in these roles involves them directly in the mainstream of society. That involvement is probably the major source of their maintenance of social status.

THE AGED AS STUDENTS

Active academic involvement is a rapidly growing type of community participation on the part of older people today. This is a phenomenon found in both the United States and China, and the different emphases in this kind of activity in the two countries further illustrate their different life-styles.

Many services that are available to the elderly population have been initiated by others. In contrast, educational opportunities for the aged have generally developed as a result of the demands made by elderly people who are relatively well educated and who value further education. Those who lack formal education rarely participate.

Two different approaches to providing education for elderly students have emerged in the United States. Some elderly students prefer to enroll as regular students at colleges and universities. They share classes with students of all ages. An important part of the learning process, according to them, is the intergenerational interaction in which they become involved.

The second approach to education for the aged in the United States is best illustrated by the Elder Hostel Program. Elder Hostel is a nationwide program that offers classes exclusively for older students on many college and university campuses across the country. This program offers at least two attractive opportunities: (1) the chance to learn and (2) the chance to interact with other elderly people on an academic level.

In China, Shandung Province founded "The Old People's University of Shandung Province" in 1983 at the Red Cross University in Jinan. The emphasis in this program, in contrast to education for the aged in the United States, is on completing an established curriculum. The basic intent is not so much to enable individual students to pursue their own academic interests, but to better prepare the aged to live in their retirement years in ways that benefit society as a whole.[37] The subject of the aged as students is discussed further in Chapter 12.

CONCLUSION

Participation in community activities on the part of the aged is substantial in both the United States and the People's Republic of China. The patterns of participation are quite different between the two countries, however.

The search for community and personal satisfaction has provided the basic orientation of those in the United States. Their basic motivation for community involvement has been to gain a sense of self-fulfillment. The important focuses of community involvement have been on pursuing friendships among like-minded age peers, joining groups that provide personal relationships and meaningful recreational opportunities, and moving to retirement communities where they can live near age peers. Many elderly Americans have also participated in community action efforts that focus on meeting the needs of their own population. Elderly Americans are rapidly becoming interested in education, with an emphasis, again, on individual self-interest. It is obvious in all of this that elderly Americans fit very nicely into the overall American culture, which places great value on the pursuit of self-interest.

In contrast, community involvement among the Chinese elderly is clearly focused on maintaining their integration into the community. Community participation, in fact, provides them with opportunities to exert influence and power over others. Opportunities to interact exclusively with peers may represent enjoyable experiences but are by no means central to their community activities. The emphasis of their educational program also reflects the importance of community integration rather than the pursuit of personal interests. This, too, is consistent with the culture of which they are a part.

NOTES

[1] Maurice R. Stein, *The Eclipse of Community* (New York: Harper & Row, Pub., 1960), pp. 275–303.

[2] Irwin T. Sanders, *The Community* (New York: Ronald Press, 1975), pp. 3–19.

[3] John P. Hewitt, *Self and Society: A Symbolic Interactionist Social Psychology* (Boston: Allyn & Bacon, 1984), pp. 84, 129–32.

[4] C. Wright Mills, *The Power Elite* (New York: Oxford University Press, 1956).

[5] Floyd Hunter, *Community Power Structure* (Chapel Hill, N.C.: University of North Carolina Press, 1953).

[6] Rosabeth Moss Kanter, *Commitment and Community* (Cambridge, Mass.: Harvard University Press, 1972), pp. 61–74.

[7] Marjorie Cantor, "Neighbors and Friends: An Overlooked Resource in the Informal Support System," *Research on Aging*, 1 (1979), 434–63.

[8] Shirley L. O'Bryant, "Neighbors' Support of Older Widows Who Live Alone in Their Own Homes," *The Gerontologist* 25, no. 3 (June 1985), 305–10.

[9] M. Powell Lawton, *Environment and Aging* (Monterey, Calif.: Brooks/Cole, 1980), p. 40.

[10] Carl I. Cohen, Jeanne Teresi, and Douglas Holmes, "Social Networks and Adaptation," *The Gerontologist*, 25, no. 3 (June 1985), 297–304.

[11] Carl I. Cohen and Arlene Adler, "Network Interventions: Do They Work?" *The Gerontologist*, 24, no. 1 (February 1984), 16–22.

[12] Catherine Chase Goodman, "Natural Helping Among Older Adults," *The Gerontologist*, 24, no. 2 (April 1984), 138–43.

[13] Mary Ann Parris Stephens and Murray D. Bernstein, "Social Support and Well-Being Among Residents of Planned Housing," *The Gerontologist*, 24, no. 2 (April 1984), 144–48.

[14] Nancy W. Sheehan, "Informal Support Among the Elderly in Public Senior Housing," *The Gerontologist*, 26, no. 2 (April 1986), 171–75.

[15] Russell A. Ward, "Informal Networks and Well-Being in Later Life: A Research Agenda," *The Gerontologist*, 25, no. 1 (February 1985), 55–61.

[16] Karen Rook, "The Negative Side of Social Interaction: Impact on Psychological Well-Being," *Journal of Personality and Social Psychology*, 46, no. 5 (1984), 1097–1108.

[17] Ward, "Informal Networks and Well-Being," p. 60.

[18] Arnold S. Brown, "Socially Disruptive Events and Morale Among the Elderly" (unpublished paper presented at the Gerontological Society 27th Annual Meeting in Portland, Oregon, October 1974). Abstract printed in *The Gerontologist*, 14, no. 5 (October 1974), p. 72.

[19] Arnold S. Brown, "Satisfying Relationships for the Elderly and Their Patterns of Disengagement," *The Gerontologist*, 14, no. 3 (June 1974), 258–62.

[20] Idris W. Evans and Arnold S. Brown, *Aging in Montana: A Survey of the Needs and Problems of Older Americans* (Helena: Montana Commission on Aging, 1970), pp. 3–10.

[21] Kim Van Haitsma, "Intrinsic Religious Orientation: Implications in the Study of Religiosity and Personal Adjustment in the Aged," *The Journal of Social Psychology*, 126, no. 5 (1986), 685–87.

[22] John A. Krout, "Senior Center Linkages in the Community," *The Gerontologist*, 26, no. 5 (October 1986), 510–15.

[23] Ibid., p. 510.

[24] Anne M. Hanssen et al., "Correlates of Senior Center Participation," *The Gerontologist*, 18, no. 2 (April 1978), 193–99.

[25] David Guttman and Phyllis R. Miller, "Perspectives on the Provision of Social Services in Senior Citizen Centers," *The Gerontologist*, 12, no. 4 (Winter 1972), 403–6.

[26] Mary Jo Schneider, Diana D. Chapman, and Donald E. Voth, "Senior Center Participation: A Two-Stage Approach to Impact Evaluation," *The Gerontologist*, 25, no. 2 (April 1985), 194–200.

[27] David P. Varady, "Determinants of Interest in Senior Citizen Housing Among the Community Resident Elderly," *The Gerontologist*, 24, no. 4 (August 1984), 392–95.

[28] Charles F. Longino, Jr., Kent A. McClelland, and Warren A. Peterson, "The Aged Subculture Hypothesis: Social Interaction, Gerontophilia and Self-Conception," *Journal of Gerontology*, 35, no. 5 (September 1980), 758–67.

[29] Myrna Lewis, "Aging in the People's Republic of China," *International Journal of Aging and Human Development*, 15, no. 2 (1982), 79–105.

[30] "The Japanese-Style Welfare System," *Japan Quarterly*, 30 (July–September 1983), 327–30.

[31] Arnold S. Brown, "Report on Navajo Elder Abuse" (unpublished research report submitted to the Navajo Office on Aging, Window Rock, Arizona, Fall 1986).

[32] Arnold S. Brown, "Grassroots Advocacy for the Elderly in Small Rural Communities," *The Gerontologist*, 25, no. 4 (August 1985), 417–23.

[33] An observation made by this author in Shanghai as a member of an American Gerontology team, sponsored by People to People, International, June 1984.

[34] Judith Treas, "Socialist Organization and Economic Development in China: Latent Consequences for the Aged," *The Gerontologist*, 19, no. 1 (February 1979), 34–43.

[35] Lewis, "Aging in the People's Republic of China," pp. 79–105.

[36] Peter Yin and Kowk Hung Lai, "A Reconceptualization of Age Stratification in China," *Journal of Gerontology*, 38, no. 5 (September 1983), 608–13.

[37] Li Heng, "A Brief Introduction of the Red Cross Old People's University of Shandung Province" (unpublished paper presented at meeting of an American Gerontology team, sponsored by People to People, International, at Jinan Red Cross University, June 9, 1984).

9

Old Age as a Social Problem

INTRODUCTION

In recent years, the problems usually associated with aging have tended to increase, and growing old itself has become defined as a social problem that requires collective social action.[1-8] Social policies on aging have emerged in the United States and in the other industrialized societies as direct results of that kind of view of aging. We must examine how growing old became defined as a social problem and how social policies on aging resulted from those definitions if we are to have a comprehensive understanding of what it is like to be old in modern societies.

SOCIAL PROBLEMS DEFINED

Sociologists generally agree that no social problems can be considered such by virtue of the existence of an adverse condition alone, not even when the condition severely affects great numbers of individuals. Many individuals may suffer with similar "private troubles" and not have their condition considered a "public issue."[9] It is only when a given condition becomes defined as such through collective action that it becomes a social problem. Thus, in order for a social problem to exist, as one author puts it, "a significant number of people—or a number of significant people—must agree" that a condition violates an accepted value and that it should be eliminated.[10]

Wright and Weiss contend that defining a social problem is a group process involving five major elements.[11] First, there must be an "observable set of conditions—something that can be seen, reported, and discussed." Second, there must be a "subjective analysis of the conditions." This involves what Bell describes as "a naming process"[12] and what Tallman sees as "perception."[13] Third, the condition must be seen as solvable, which involves the belief that something can and should be done to alleviate the problem. Fourth, there must be active involvement of persons who are able to influence others—those with credibility and political power. Finally, organized efforts to solve the problem must take place.

Tallman believes that a social problem emerges when a condition is perceived as unjustly or unfairly victimizing a given segment of the population, and when the fault is seen as lodged in part of the "social structure."[14] As Wright and Weiss put it, the social structure is "the breeding ground of social problems."[15] Therefore, according to Tallman, solutions demand changes in the social structure, and these demands bring conflict between the forces for change and the powers that tend to resist change.[16] Inevitably, it is out of the struggle between these two forces that solutions are or are not found. The political and governmental structures are particularly challenged by the emergence of social problems.[17] We generally look to those in politics and government to deal with the conflicts related to given problems and to make the changes needed to solve the problems that have been identified.

According to this perspective, each social problem has a developmental history. Part of that history is the formation of social policies related to the particular social problem. In order to adequately understand this aspect of the aging process, therefore, it is necessary to review the history of how aging has become defined as a social problem, how policies on aging have emerged, and how the aged have been affected in various cultural settings.

FACTORS IN DEFINING OLD AGE AS A SOCIAL PROBLEM

Growing old has never been without its problems in any society throughout history. It is true that being old has been defined in many societies as a position of privilege and respect, but the aged have always been plagued with at least the potential problems of becoming physically and mentally incapacitated. In some cultures, the aged with these problems have been quite severely rejected, primarily because those societies lacked the resources necessary to care for them.[18] Until very recently, however, only the debilitating experiences often related to old age, and not becoming old itself, were defined as problems. Furthermore, even the age-related debilitating experiences were seen as problems only to the elderly individuals who experienced them, and not to the elderly population as a whole. Therefore, the responsibilities for the care of these individuals fell not to the society as a whole, but to the families and perhaps the local communities of those unfortunate individuals.

With the many social changes accompanying the industrialization process throughout the Western world in particular, however, problems of growing old have increasingly taken on social and economic as well as physiological and psychological dimensions. Consequently, growing old itself has progressively been defined as a social problem. The first stages of this defining process began in the latter part of the nineteenth century in Europe and the United States.[19] Since the 1930s and 1940s, however, a number of factors have served to define the aged as an identifiable group and being old as a social problem that needs the attention and collective action of societies in many parts of the world.

Dominant Social Values as a Factor

Defining old age as a social problem rests in part on a set of values that has dominated the attitudes, aspirations, and behaviors of Western cultures for many years. The problem is that those categorized as old have increasingly been considered unable to measure up to dominant societal values.

Sociologists generally agree that one of the most dominant values in modern industrialized societies is the work ethic, with its emphasis on independent productivity and achievement.[20,21] At the turn of the century, the German sociologist Max Weber explained that this value had a strong religious basis as well as a social one. It was his contention that the "protestant ethic," as he termed it, was the foundation on which the whole capitalist economic system was built.[22] Although the validity of this value may be effectively challenged in the future, as some have recently suggested,[23] it, more than any other, has until now been the value that has defined the status and worth of individuals in modern Western societies. It is certainly true that at times and for many industrial laborers in the past, work has been viewed more as a struggle to survive than as a privilege.[24] Nevertheless, it has consistently been true in the industrialized West that if individuals, for whatever reason, fail to achieve by performing some form of productive role, they have lacked status and have tended to be labeled and treated as socially unworthy.[25]

A second prominent value in Western cultures emphasizes that those who are relatively well off ought to act benevolently and do what they can to help the poor who are unable to provide for their own needs. Although this has seldom, if ever, been a formalized or socially mandated obligation of the rich,[26] it has been emphasized as a religious duty that has influenced national policies toward the poor. It has resulted in elaborate welfare institutions designed to help those unable to achieve independently.

The consequences of societal responses to this combination of values have been that nonachievers not only lack status and social worth, but are also seen as dependent burdens to the societies in which they live. The situation for nonachievers is complicated by their tendency to internalize the labels of being dependent and unworthy and to continue to act accordingly. Perceived dependency and lack of self-worth tend to perpetuate themselves.[27,28]

In the Western world, the elderly, more than any other identifiable group, tend to be labeled as dependent and as nonachievers.[29,30] While it is expected that younger nonachievers will be trained to take on productive roles some time in the future, the aged are viewed as permanent nonachievers and social dependents.[31]

Indications are that elderly people today are beginning to question the application of these traditional social values to their situations.[32] Neither do they tend to internalize the labels of being dependent and unworthy to any significant extent.[33] Nevertheless, the dominant social values of achievement and independence have historically provided the framework for defining old age as a social problem in Western societies.

A comparison of Western and Oriental cultures with regard to the influence of values on treatment of the aged reveals both similarities and differences. The People's Republic of China, for example, is not only an Oriental society but has very different ideological and political bases. Nevertheless, a set of values similar to that in the West seems to be at work there, but with somewhat different results.

The importance of work was a major tenet of the Chinese communist revolution under the leadership of Mao Tse Tung. It was seen not merely as the means of producing needed goods and services and of stimulating the economy; labor was also central to the Communist ideologies of preventing alienation between humans and of building human character. During Mao Tse Tung's reign, production units were formed, everyone was placed in a production unit, and every able-bodied person was assigned a job within the production unit. All physically able citizens were not only expected but were required to work. Elderly people were expected to work along with middle-aged and younger adults.[34]

With such a strong emphasis on work, it would be expected that retirement would be discouraged except for the physically incapable. We might also expect that those who were retired, for whatever reason, would experience the same kind of loss of status as has tended to be true in Western societies. Ironically, however, retirement for able-bodied elderly people began in China as early as the 1950s and has now become a widespread policy throughout the country, with no apparent loss of status.[35,36]

The idea that those without adequate resources to care for their own needs ought to be cared for has also been an important value in Communist China. The guiding philosophy that everyone should be "eating from the same big pot" has been practiced throughout China since 1949.[37] Welfare, in fact, is available not only to people in emergency situations but to all citizens throughout their lives.[38] Most of the care for elderly people who need it is provided by their families, according to cultural tradition and as a requirement of the national constitution. For elderly people without families to care for them, the constitution guarantees basic provisions through what have been called "the five guarantees": (1) *food,* including fuel, cooking utensils, and pocket money; (2) *clothing,* including bedding; (3) *housing,* including furniture and home repairs; (4) *medical treatment;* and (5) *burial.*[39,40] Under the Chinese socialist system, then, welfare is viewed not as an act of benevolence to the poor on the part of those who are not poor, but as a right for everyone. Thus, it obviously does not carry the stigma of unworthiness for recipients that it does in Western capitalist societies. Partly for that reason, Chinese elderly tend to retain social status, even though they generally do not participate in economically productive work. With the new economic reforms now being established in China, however, something of a shift in values is taking place. According to Vice-Premier Tian Jiyun, the reforms call for less emphasis on the egalitarian idea of "eating from the same big pot" and increased emphasis on the more competitive idea of "to each according to his work."[41] This inevitably raises the question of whether the relatively high social status that elderly people now enjoy will be maintained under Chinese socialism.

Indications are that both the work ethic and the benevolency norm are also applicable to the aged in Japan, another, but very different, Oriental society. Japan today is a democratic country with a totally capitalistic economy. In that context, even though it does not have the religious base that it once had in the West, the work ethic seems to be as strongly imbedded in Japan today as in any other modernized, industrialized nation, if not more so.[42] By the early 1970s, Japanese workers were being described as "workaholics," and today even their so-called leisure activities tend to be oriented to their work obligations.[43] A Japanese person's occupation is probably as important to his or her personal identity, social status, and sense of self-worth as it is to any of us in any Western society. Yet many employers in Japan expect people to retire at relatively early ages.[44,45]

Providing care for those who need it, particularly for the elderly, is also very much a part of the tradition of Japanese culture, and that tradition has apparently been maintained in the modernized Japan. Although government welfare provisions for the elderly are not yet as well developed in that country as they are in most of the Western industrialized nations, life-long care for the aged is said to be provided by the corporations for which most people work. The tradition of filial piety, of families being responsible for the care of their elderly members, has been taken over by some employers. Japanese workers, therefore, are said not only to have their specific welfare needs taken care of, but also to have life-long security as part of their work commitments. This system of care for the aged has been noted to reflect commitment to the elderly that is unique in modernized societies. It is also a system in which the elderly enjoy relatively high social status and the respect of the rest of the population, even in retirement, despite the value of work in their society.

Such an analysis has been seriously questioned in recent years, however.

As Maeda points out, retirement pensions tend to be so low that a majority of retirees must try to find other jobs, most of which offer lower pay and lower social status than those from which they retired.[46] It has also been noted that the adult children of the aged increasingly view their sense of duty to their elderly parents as a burden that they are less and less willing to bear.

Societal values differ somewhat from one culture to another, to be sure, as do the ways in which they affect the treatment and perception of elderly members. An important question to ask, however, is whether or not those differences will persist in the future. Some evidence seems to indicate that as nations become more economically industrialized, their cultural values may tend to become increasingly similar, and those values may eventually result in a view of old age as a social problem.

Public Provision of Services as a Factor

In virtually all societies, caring for the aged has traditionally been a private matter, with families shouldering most of the responsibility. Increasingly, however, in economically developing as well as developed nations, the aged as a group are being highlighted as having financial, physical, and social needs great enough to require a public response. This has led many national governments to adopt policies of service provision specifically targeted to the elderly. It is especially in this sense that old age is being treated as a social problem. It is important to note, however, that the public provision of services is not just a sign that old age is being viewed as a social problem; it also contributes to such a perception, as the following analysis will show.

The passage of the Social Security Act in 1935 in the United States clearly contributed to the view of old age as a social problem. In the early years of this century, there was a growing recognition that poverty was a serious problem among the elderly, and a political movement developed to make special economic provisions for them. A major focus of that movement was the Townsend Plan in the 1930s. A group of elderly people in southern California, led by Dr. Francis Townsend, proposed that every elderly citizen be guaranteed a monthly income of $200.[47] A congressional bill to that effect failed, but the proposal was significant in the development of an awareness of the growing economic needs of the elderly. This early movement culminated, during the Great Depression, in the passage of the Social Security Act of 1935.[48]

The Social Security program was initially very weak, and it did little to solve the problems of the growing number of elderly citizens who were living in poverty in the days of the Great Depression.[49] It was passed not merely as a benevolent act toward the elderly poor, but also to eliminate as many elderly people as possible from the work force in order to reduce, as cheaply as possible, the alarmingly high unemployment rate. It was also used by the New Deal administration as the first, precedent-setting step toward passage of legislation in behalf of all the unemployed.[50]

While it did little to solve the economic problems of the elderly in that day, the passage of Social Security legislation did significantly contribute to the process of defining old age as a social problem. First, it began the process of official societal acceptance of the responsibility for the care of the elderly. Although Social Security was not originally designed to deal with all elderly people, it has increasingly taken on that characteristic. Second, it made retirement conceptually synonymous with old age.[51] Third, it provided a working social definition of who in society would be identified and treated as old. The aged became an identifiable and socially visible group that included all of those who were over age 65 and retired. As a group, they were beginning to be seen as having special needs.

The phenomenon of public provision of services for the aged has become a pattern in many other nations throughout the world, largely for the same reasons and with very similar results. As previously noted, public provision of services in the People's Republic of China is not confined to the elderly but is universally applied, and that would seem to prevent the elderly from being stigmatized. Yet, increasingly and in a number of ways, the aged are being singled out for special attention. As the birth rate decreases and life expectancy increases, the aged population is growing rapidly both in sheer numbers and in proportion to the rest of the population.[52,53] They are protected by the constitutionally provided "five guarantees," as previously noted. Great numbers are allowed to retire on relatively good-sized pensions, and both the number of retired and the amounts of their pensions are rising.[54] More government-supported homes for the especially needy aged are being built in both rural and urban areas across the country.[55] These changes have led Du Renzhi to the following conclusions: (1) The society at large will have to take over the burden of looking after the aged in the next twenty years; and (2) there is a growing lack of understanding of old age in China on the part of the masses.[56]

From all indications in the early 1970s, Japan was avoiding the necessity of public provisions for the aged and thus also avoiding the perception of old age as a social problem. The tradition of family support was working well in that a large majority of elderly people lived with their adult children rather than relying on publicly supported homes for the aged. Most elderly opted to remain on the job as long as possible, thus remaining productive in high-status positions and avoiding publicly supported financial benefits. The retirement support that was needed was being provided by corporations in their promises of lifetime commitments to all of their employees. This "Japanese-style welfare system" seemed to work so well that it was adopted by the government in 1980.[57]

In recent years, however, the Japanese have become painfully aware that they have the fastest growing aged population in the world and that this is already beginning to undermine their reliance on their nonpublic welfare system. Furthermore, it is projected that the problems of that system will rapidly worsen in the future. Public services have already begun to be provided, especially in the form of free health services for those 65 and over and increases in pension benefits provided by the National Pension Plan.[58–60] Ironically, the more their traditional system fails and the more they move to publicly supported services, the less the elderly are favored in the work place and the more old age is being defined as a social problem.

Post–World War II Retirement as a Factor

During World War II, in which all of the world's major countries were involved, it is safe to assume that none of the nations of the world considered old age a social problem. All able-bodied workers, including the elderly, were needed and used in their country's war efforts. For the relatively short period of the war, therefore, a view of old age as a social problem was deferred. In the post–World War II era, however, being old once again became a social problem, and with much more intensity than ever before.

In the United States, a number of key social and economic factors contributed to the dramatic development of the view that the elderly constituted a social problem. One of those factors was the almost universal establishment of mandatory retirement by employers across the United States within less than a decade after the war. Following the war, the job market was flooded by young men returning to civilian life from the armed forces. With a shift away from a war economy, fewer jobs were available for a dramatically increased work force. It became necessary to eliminate people from the work force if the United States was not to be faced again with the disastrously high unemployment rates of the Great Depression. Sentiment was high that the United States owed jobs to its fighting men. Sentiment also dictated that, because the elderly had faithfully worked hard in the war effort, they deserved to be allowed to rest and take it easy.

Retraining was increasingly necessary for workers in the developing peace-time technological industries, and it made sense to retrain young adults rather than the elderly, for two important reasons. First, the young were seen as more effective and efficient at highly technological tasks. Second, with retirement having already been institutionalized and with Social Security benefits available, mandatory retirement policies provided the simplest way of easing the keen competition for jobs. With almost no voices of opposition, mandatory retirement policies spread among employers, including the federal government. By 1960, nearly 70 percent of U.S. citizens over 65 were retired.[61]

Primarily as a direct result of these policies, the aged increasingly became perceived as financially dependent, as having lost their major life roles, and as socially disengaging or withdrawing at alarming rates.[62] In the eyes of much of the American public, these became problems that the vast majority of the elderly shared and over which they had no control. The aged seemed incapable of charting the course of their own destiny. They were seemingly unable to cope with the rapid social and economic changes that were eliminating them from productive participation in society's mainstream. It seemed clear that they needed the helpful intervention of the nation as a whole to provide the resources necessary for their survival. Mandatory retirement was thus a key contributor to the process of defining old age as a social problem in the United States.

In neither China nor Japan were the patterns of retirement as rapidly established as in the United States. Only recently has retirement become widespread throughout China, and even at present the Chinese tend to take a more positive than negative view of those who are retired because many of them are performing social roles and making financial contributions that are seen as vital to their families and communities.[63] It is also apparent that the Chinese population is still young enough and the size of the younger work force is still large enough to easily support the retired population.[64] Nevertheless, it is projected that families will soon begin to feel the burden of caring for their elderly members and that the nation as a whole will begin to be burdened with the economic support of its aged, as a result of the strictly imposed population-control policy in China. It is likely that, at least in the future, retirement policies in China will contribute to the notion of old age as a social problem in that country also.[65]

The Japanese are having to face the fact that they are rapidly becoming an old population; as a result, old age is becoming a social problem. Although mandatory retirement is not a widespread policy in Japan, the pattern of retirement at relatively young ages is well established, and more and more of those who reach retirement age are retiring. As that trend continues, the burden of support for the retired population is increasingly being felt by both the private and public sectors of their society, and old age is rapidly coming to be perceived as a social problem.[66-68]

Changing Family Roles as a Factor

Another factor contributing to the defining of old age as a social problem is the changing patterns of family roles and relationships. Extended-family relationships have retained their importance to people in the United States.[69-71] Research has revealed, contrary to modern myth, that the elderly in modern Western societies do in fact tend to remain in close and regular relationship with members of their families. Most, for example, live in close proximity to at least one of their adult children and have regular weekly and even daily contacts with them; some even tend to have reciprocal helping relationships.[72,73] Nevertheless, an overwhelming majority of elderly parents in the Western world live separately from their adult children and their grandchildren and avoid interfering in the family lives of their adult children.[74,75] As a result, the elderly are left with diminished family roles.[76]

While the roles of parent and grandparent are important to many of the elderly,[77] those roles tend to lack substance or authority beyond informal friendships and occasional helping relationships with adult children and grandchildren.[78-80] Of particular importance are the facts that the housewife role tends to diminish and even disappear for elderly women,[81] that the head-of-household status for elderly men tends to diminish,[82] and that the tendency for older persons to live alone in increased isolation has become a distinct pattern.[83]

As an awareness has developed of the loss of family roles and relationships and the tendency toward isolation, families of the elderly have increasingly been accused of abandoning their elderly members and leaving their care to the society at large. Although this generally has not been found to be true, the prevalence of the social myth has contributed greatly to the definition of old age as a time of special need and thus as a problem that the entire society needed to address.

Family roles and relationships of the aged in Oriental societies are quite different from those in the Western part of the world. Distinct remnants of the filial piety traditions, which dictate that it is the duty of family members to respect and care for their elderly members, still exist in both China and Japan. In fact, as previously noted, this tradition has been incorporated into the present Chinese constitution and has been made part of the law.[84] Where once the tradition applied mostly to the privileged classes, it is now applied to all Chinese families.[85] From a practical perspective, virtually all elderly Chinese who have children live in the same household with one of them, usually the oldest son. This practice is actually much more than simply a way for families to meet their obligation to care for their elderly members, however. It amounts to the mutual sharing of economic and social responsibilities.[86] Elderly parents and the adult children with whom they live typically contribute part of their incomes (pensions and wages) to the economic maintenance of the household. Elderly parents, both men and women, also typically contribute major efforts to the care and rearing of their grandchildren, as well as to the necessary housekeeping. Because both husbands and wives among Chinese young couples typically work full-time, the roles that elderly people play within the family and their contributions to the Chinese households are substantial. Because of these contributions, made in their early retirement years, the care they receive in their later years is more reciprocal than a one-way obligation. As Davis-Friedmann puts it, "Chinese personal relationships are saturated with the obligations to reciprocate."[87]

As positive as this may be, however, future projections indicate that changes now taking place in China may soon result in changes in the family roles of the aged. The warning is already being issued that, with most couples being allowed to have only one child, the burden of caring for the aged will soon be too much for young families to bear.[88,89] Thus, changing family roles will undoubtedly contribute to the designation of old age as a social problem in China, as has been the case in the United States and elsewhere.

Elderly Japanese still live with their adult children in most families in Japan.[90] It is clear, however, that the trend is already moving away from this cultural tradition, and it is increasingly being seen by many younger adults as a burden that they can no longer afford to carry.[91,92] The tradition itself is beginning to contribute to the perception of old age as a social problem in Japan.

Life Expectancy and Changing Health Problems as Factors

Two other factors contributing to the definition of old age as a social problem in recent years are the increasing life expectancy and the resulting changing health problems of the aged. Technological advances in disease control and health maintenance in this century have substantially raised the life expectancy in many countries around the world. For example, the life expectancy increased from 42.9 years in 1900 to 73.3 years in 1978 in the United States; from 46.9 years for males and 49.6 years for females to 73.6 years for males and 79 years for females in 1980 in Japan; and from 35 years in 1949 to 69 years in 1980 in China.[93] Consequently, the number of people reaching old age has dramatically increased. In addition, recently declining fertility rates have drastically increased the proportion of the total population who are elderly in all three of these countries.

The fact that increased numbers of people are living into old age indicates that they have survived the many acute health problems (temporary and short-term illnesses such as flu or pneumonia) that once took the lives of many at relatively younger ages. As a result, increased numbers of elderly people are suffering from chronic diseases (long-term illnesses that tend to produce permanent impairments).[94,95] Particularly in the United States, this has served to refocus much of the health care for the elderly from rehabilitative to long-term care. Although the percentage of elderly people with severe chronic health problems is relatively small, it is large enough to make them quite visible. Those suffering from chronic health problems are particularly visible because many are institutionalized in nursing homes, where the media have portrayed them as pathetically helpless. Thus the general image of the elderly as physically dependent has resulted.[96]

The image of the aged as sick and physically helpless is not yet nearly as prominent in China. This is primarily due to three factors: (1) With a lower life expectancy, not nearly as many elderly people survive to ages at which chronic health problems become severely debilitating; (2) the emphasis in the Chinese healthcare system is more on preventive measures and less on the extensive rehabilitative and life-saving methods that characterize Western medicine; and (3) much of the care of elderly Chinese who are impaired is provided in their homes by family members and neighborhood health care paraprofessionals ("barefoot doctors"). Consequently, although Chinese people tend not to live as long as Americans, they tend to remain relatively healthy and physically functional. Thus, they often avoid developing crippling chronic problems in their later years, and they almost never end up in institutions for the severely physically impaired.

Different types of institutions are available for the aged in Japan, depending upon the levels of care they need.[97] Because of the prevailing tendency for the aged to live with their adult children, however, only 1.4 percent of them are institutionalized.[98] Thus, although the Japanese population is aging rapidly, a trend which may soon result in the institutionalization of many more elderly people, the public image of the aged in general still seems to be that they are integrated into family life rather than that they are physically impaired and helpless.[99]

The Aging Network as a Factor

Taken together, the previously outlined factors have logically served to create the public image in the United States that the elderly are dependent, helpless, and even incompetent.[100] They have been retired partly because they have been characterized as less competent than younger workers. They have been eliminated from productive roles in society and left with few, if any, socially useful roles to perform. Many have been forced into financial dependence upon those still working, and the elderly as a group have been seen as economic burdens to the rest of the population. More and more of them have been found to be physically dependent, in need of long-term care, and confined to institutions, where their visibility has created the image of helplessness. Their increasing numbers have made them even more visible in their dependent situations, and they have become defined as people whose special needs are extensive enough to demand the attention of the entire society.

Public concern for the elderly in this country grew rapidly throughout the 1950s, and defining their specific needs and providing services to meet those needs became political issues. As early as 1950, the Truman administration organized and held a National Conference on Aging as part of a push to establish a national health program. Just a decade later, a full-fledged White House Conference on Aging was held to discuss the special needs of the aged and to recommend congressional action in their behalf.

As a result of this kind of political activity in behalf of the elderly in the United States, the Older Americans Act was passed in 1965. One provision of the Older Americans Act was the establishment of a federal bureaucracy (the Administration on Aging) with a vast planning and service-delivery network. It was the responsibility of this "aging network" to plan and implement social-service programs for all of the elderly in every local community across the country.

One of the network's primary goals has been to help solve the problem of dependency among the aged, but at least one analyst today claims that it has instead served to perpetuate dependency and contribute to the definition of old age as a social problem.[101] For one thing, the planning perspective of those in the network has largely been that old people are dependent and relatively helpless. As Hudson puts it, it was "the widely held belief that most older persons were impoverished or ill for reasons which were no fault of their own."[102] From this perspective, it was appropriate for the planners and providers in the network to assume a paternalistic attitude and approach to their work. Without a doubt, this approach has served to perpetuate the image of the elderly as dependent. Another part of the problem is what Estes describes as a tendency for agencies to serve as agents of social control. Although their work is defined in terms of "helping," they also exert power over the lives of those being served. Estes contends that "the help rendered may be given from the purest and most benevolent of motives, yet the very fact of being helped degrades."[103] The aging network itself can thus be seen as still another factor contributing to the continued definition of old age as a social problem.

Those serving the elderly populations in China and Japan have apparently not been organized as elaborately or with the same attitudes as the U.S. "aging network." It is also true that the view of old age as a time of dependency and helplessness, and thus as a social problem, is not nearly as well developed in either of those countries as it is in the United States. This is true for at least three basic reasons. First, both of these Oriental societies still place great emphasis upon their traditions of filial piety and, to a large extent, rely upon families to care for the aged who need special care. Second, as compared with the United States, the percentages of their populations who are old are still small enough to be less of a burden to younger adults. Third, more of the aged in China and Japan either remain in the work force or fill societally vital roles in retirement than is true in this country.

Nevertheless, there are clear indications that the social-problem percentage of old age is developing in both of these Oriental societies due to processes that are very similar to those that have taken place in the United States. This is especially true in Japan, where the elderly population is growing more rapidly than in any other nation in the world and the sense of burden of their care is being felt and expressed. As these trends continue, the view of the aged as dependent is bound to increase. Although these trends are not as far advanced in China as they are in either Japan or the United States, the signs of their deveopment are being recognized. The question of whether either of these societies will be able to avoid the view of old age as a time of helplessness and dependency remains to be answered.

CONCLUSION

Few would suggest that all elderly people are totally dependent, incompetent, or in dire need of special services. When individuals are defined and treated as part of a group so labeled, however, they are considered part of the social problem. As a result, they may internalize the labels applied to them.[104]

As our analysis in this chapter shows, the chronology of events affecting the aged, especially in the three decades following World War II and particularly in the United States but to some extent in other very different societies, have fully developed and perpetuated the definition of old age as a social problem. This lends support to the theory that modernization leads to the loss of status for the aged. It also highlights another variable that is ignored by that theory but that also contributes to the view of old age as a time of dependency and loss of social status—namely, the proportionate growth of the elderly population. The more the population of a society ages, the greater the society's sense of burden; and the more dependent and helpless the elderly seem, the greater their loss of status.

It is apparent from this analysis that the social problem of old age as it has been defined has not been solved. Although the attempted solutions may have improved the quality of life for many elderly people,[105] they have also served to perpetuate the public perception that to be old in modern society is to be dependent, helpless, and in need of special services.

The social-problem perception of old age raises two important questions. First, to what extent is the view of old people as a burden to the rest of the society a valid one? Second, if such a view is not valid, is it possible to change it, or is the loss of status for the aged inevitable in modern societies, as Cowgill and Holmes have implied? The answer to the first question is clearly, no, since the percentages of old people with severe physical and mental impairment are relatively small in all societies. Even very old people have many competencies for which they are seldom credited. The latter question as yet has no definite solution, but the most promising seems to be for the aged themselves to advocate in their own behalf. It may be that only they will be able to (1) advocate for a greater voice in their own destinies, (2) demonstrate their remaining competencies, and (3) claim new or restored social statuses.

There is a growing recognition among those responsible for policy formation that past social policy has failed to solve the social problems associated with being old. As a result, a redefinition of the problem and new directions in the social policy of aging are being called for. A key question to be raised is whether the redefinitions, the new policies being proposed, and attempts at self-advocacy on the part of the elderly will diminish or improve the quality of life for the aged.

NOTES

[1] David Hackett Fischer, *Growing Old in America* (New York: Oxford University Press, 1978), pp. 157–95.

[2] Martha Baum and Rainer C. Baum, *Growing Old: A Societal Perspective* (Englewood Cliffs, N.J.: Prentice-Hall, 1980), p. 3.

[3] Burton Wright and John P. Weiss, *Social Problems* (Boston: Little, Brown, 1980), pp. 204–30.

[4] Elizabeth S. Johnson and John B. Williamson, *Growing Old: The Social Problems of Aging* (New York: Holt, Rinehart and Winston, 1980).

[5] Mildred M. Seltzer, Sherry Corbett, and Robert C. Atchley, eds., *Social Problems of the Aging* (Belmont, Calif.: Wadsworth, 1978), pp. 4–19.

[6] Robert R. Bell, *Contemporary Social Problems* (Homewood, Ill.: Dorsey Press, 1981), pp. 271–98.

[7] Joan W. Moore and Burton M. Moore, *Social Problems* (Englewood Cliffs, N.J.: Prentice-Hall, 1982), pp. 143–49.

[8] Zena Smith Blau, *Aging in a Changing Society* (New York: Franklin Watts, 1981), p. 9.

[9] C. Wright Mills, *The Sociological Imagination* (New York: Oxford University Press, 1959), pp. 1–18.

[10] Joseph Julian, *Social Problems* (Englewood Cliffs, N.J.: Prentice-Hall, 1980), p. 3.

[11] Wright and Weiss, *Social Problems*, pp. 6–16.

[12] Bell, *Contemporary Social Problems*, pp. 8–10.

[13] Irving Tallman, *Passion, Action, and Politics* (San Francisco: W. H. Freeman & Company Publishers, 1976), pp. 27–29.

[14] Ibid., pp. 27–28.

[15] Wright and Weiss, *Social Problems*, pp. 30–56.

[16] Tallman, *Passion, Action, and Politics*, p. 200.

[17] Ibid., pp. 224–30.

[18] Baum and Baum, *Growing Old: A Societal Perspective*, pp. 106–7.

[19] Fischer, *Growing Old in America*, pp. 158–61.

[20] Neil J. Smelser, *Sociology* (Englewood Cliffs, N.J.: Prentice-Hall, 1981), pp. 187–88.

[21] Thomas M. Kando, *Leisure and Popular Culture in Transition* (Saint Louis, Mo.: C. V. Mosby, 1975), pp. 8–15.

[22] Max Weber, *The Protestant Ethic and the Spirit of Capitalism*, trans. Talcott Parsons (New York: Scribner's, 1958), pp. 53–54.

[23] Russell A. Ward, *The Aging Experience: An Introduction to Social Gerontology* (New York: Harper & Row, Pub., 1984), pp. 364–65.

[24] Reinhard Bendix, *Work and Authority in Industry* (Berkeley, Calif.: University of California Press, 1956), pp. 73–74.

[25] Ruby Neuhaus and Robert H. Neuhaus, *Successful Aging* (New York: John Wiley, 1982), p. 150.

[26] Bendix, *Work and Authority in Industry*, p. 76.

[27] Joseph A. Kuypers and Vern L. Bengtson, "Social Breakdown and Competence: A Model of Normal Aging," *Human Development*, 16 (1973), 181–201.

[28] Carroll L. Estes, *The Aging Enterprise* (San Francisco: Jossey-Bass, 1979), p. 13.

[29] Ward, *The Aging Experience*, pp. 364–65.

[30] Seymour B. Sarason, *Work, Aging, and Social Change* (New York: Free Press, 1977), p. 264.

[31] Ibid., pp. 264–65.

[32] Ward, *The Aging Experience*, pp. 365–66.

[33] Linda K. George, *Role Transitions in Later Life* (Monterey, Calif.: Brooks/Cole, 1980), p. 43.

[34] Myrna Lewis, "Aging in the People's Republic of China," *International Journal of Aging and Human Development*, 15, no. 1 (1982), 79–105.

[35] Ibid.

[36] "Growing Old in China," *Beijing Review*, 43 (October 26, 1981), 22–28.

[37] Jiyun Tian, "Will Reform Lead to Capitalism?" *Beijing Review*, 29 (February 3, 1986), 15–17.

[38] Bong-ho Mok, "In the Service of Socialism: Social Welfare in China," *Social Work*, 28, no. 4 (July–August 1983), 269–72.

[39] "Growing Old in China," pp. 22–28.

[40] Bong-ho Mok, "In the Service of Socialism," pp. 269–72.

[41] Jiyun Tian, "Will Reform Lead to Capitalism?" pp. 15–17.

[42] Barbara Casassus, "The Fight to Weave Silver Threads into a Golden Age," *Far Eastern Economic Review*, 130 (December 19, 1986), 74–75.

[43] Bruce Roscoe, "The Search for an Antidote to Workaholism," *Far Eastern Economic Review*, 130 (December 19, 1985), 76–78.

[44] Casassus, "The Fight to Weave Silver Threads," pp. 74–75.

[45] Daisaku Maeda, "Japan," in *International Handbook on Aging: Contemporary Developments and Research*, ed. Erdman Palmore (Westport, Conn.: Greenwood Press, 1980), pp. 253–70.

[46] Ibid.

[47] Fischer, *Growing Old in America*, pp. 180–81.

[48] Ibid., p. 182.

[49] Ibid., pp. 183–84.

[50] Robert B. Hudson, "The 'Graying' of the Federal Budget and its Consequences for Old-Age Policy," in *The Aging in Politics*, ed. Robert B. Hudson (Springfield, Ill.: Chas. C Thomas, 1981), pp. 261–81.

[51] Arnold M. Rose, "A Current Theoretical Issue in Social Gerontology," in *Older People in Their Social World*, eds. Arnold M. Rose and Warren A. Peterson (Philadelphia: F. A. Davis, 1965), pp. 359–66.

[52] "Forecasting on the Aging Population," *Beijing Review*, 27 (March 10, 1986), 25–34.

[53] Zhou Shujun, "Prospects for China's Population in 2000," *Beijing Review*, 27 (April 2, 1984), 20–23.

[54] "Growing Old in China," pp. 22–28.

[55] Du Renzhi, "Old People in China: Hopes and Problems," *Beijing Review*, 27 (April 16, 1984), 31–34.

[56] Ibid.

[57] "The Japanese-Style Welfare System," *Japan Quarterly*, 30 (July–September 1983), 327–30.

[58] Maeda, "Japan," pp. 253–70.

[59] "The Japanese-Style Welfare System," pp. 327–30.

[60] Hashimoto Shiro, "Population Trends in Japan," *Japan Quarterly*, 30 (April–May 1983), 194–200.

[61] Robert C. Atchley, *The Sociology of Retirement* (New York: Wiley, 1976), p. 17.

[62] Rose, "A Current Theoretical Issue," pp. 359–66.

[63] Deborah Davis-Friedmann, *Long Lives: Chinese Elderly and the Communist Revolution* (Cambridge, Mass.: Harvard University Press, 1983), pp. 21–27.

[64] "Forecasting on the Aging Population," pp. 25–34.

[65] Du Renzhi, "Old People in China," pp. 31–34.

[66] Casassus, "The Fight to Weave Silver Threads," pp. 74–75.

[67] Shiro, "Population Trends in Japan," pp. 194–200.

[68] "The Japanese-Style Welfare System," pp. 327–30.

[69] Arnold S. Brown, "Satisfying Relationships for the Elderly and Their Patterns of Disengagement," *The Gerontologist*, 14, no. 3 (June 1974), 258–62.

[70] Ethel Shanas, "Family-Kin Networks and Aging in Cross-Cultural Perspective," in *The Family: Functions, Conflicts, and Symbols*, eds. Peter J. Stein, Judith Richman, and Natalie Hannon (Reading, Mass.: Addison-Wesley, 1977), p. 309.

[71] Lillian E. Troll, Sheila J. Miller, and Robert C. Atchley, *Families in Later Life* (Belmont, Calif.: Wadsworth, 1979), pp. 8–10.

[72] Ethel Shanas, "Family Help Patterns and Social Class in Three Countries," *Journal of Marriage and the Family*, 29 (1967), 257–66.

[73] Troll, Miller, and Atchley, *Families in Later Life*, pp. 84–92.

[74] Shanas, "Family-Kin Networks," pp. 300–309.

[75] Troll, Miller, and Atchley, *Families in Later Life*, pp. 84–85.

[76] J. Ross Eshleman, *The Family: An Introduction* (Boston: Allyn & Bacon, 1985), pp. 537–38.

[77] Brown, "Satisfying Relationships," pp. 258–62.

[78] Bernice Neugarten and Karol K. Weinstein, "The Changing American Grandparent," *Journal of Marriage and the Family,* 26 (1964), 199–204.

[79] George, *Role Transitions in Later Life,* pp. 84–88.

[80] Troll, Miller, and Atchley, *Families in Later Life,* pp. 110–19.

[81] Helena Z. Lopata, "The Life Cycle of the Social Role of the Housewife," *Sociology and Social Research,* 51 (1966), 5–22.

[82] Mark Hutter, *The Changing Family* (New York: Wiley, 1988), pp. 431–32.

[83] Arlie Hochschild, "Communal Living in Old Age," in *The Family: Functions, Conflicts, and Symbols,* eds. Peter J. Stein, Judith Richman, and Natalie Hannon (Menlo Park, Calif.: Addison-Wesley, 1977), pp. 404–9.

[84] "Old Customs Enriched with New Content," *Beijing Review,* 24 (October 26, 1981), 23.

[85] F. Butterfield, *China Alive in the Bitter Sea* (New York: Times Books, 1982), pp. 217–18.

[86] Ibid., p. 219.

[87] Davis-Freidmann, *Long Lives,* p. 10.

[88] Du Renzhi, "Old People in China," pp. 31–34.

[89] Zhou Shujun, "Prospects for China's Population," pp. 20–23.

[90] Maeda, "Japan," pp. 253–70.

[91] "The Japanese-Style Welfare System," pp. 327–30.

[92] Shiro, "Population Trends in Japan," pp. 194–200.

[93] Statistical Reference Index 1987 Annual, World Demographic Topics, series #R8750-2.

[94] Tom Hickey, *Health and Aging* (Monterey, Calif.: Brooks/Cole, 1980), pp. 2–3.

[95] Molly S. Wantz and John E. Gay, *The Aging Process: A Health Perspective* (Cambridge, Mass.: Winthrop, 1981), p. 81.

[96] Hickey, *Health and Aging,* pp. 92–95.

[97] Erdman Palmore, "What Can the USA Learn from Japan about Aging?" *The Gerontologist,* 15, no. 1 (1975), 64–67.

[98] Maeda, "Japan," pp. 253–70.

[99] Erdman Palmore, "The Status and Integration of the Aged in Japanese Society," *Journal of Gerontology,* 30, no. 2 (March 1975), 199–208.

[100] Kuypers and Bengtson, "Social Breakdown and Competence," pp. 181–201.

[101] Estes, *The Aging Enterprise,* pp. 2–3.

[102] Hudson, "The 'Graying' of the Federal Budget," pp. 261–81.

[103] Estes, *The Aging Enterprise,* p. 25.

[104] Ibid.

[105] Alvin Rubuska and Bruce Jacobs, "Aging and Public Policy: Rethinking Issues and Programs," *Grants Magazine,* 3 (1980), 152–56.

10

Political Advocacy by and in Behalf of the Aged

INTRODUCTION

With the definition of old age as a time of life characterized by unique needs has come the recognition that advocacy is also necessary. Meeting the needs of elderly people depends to a large extent upon advocacy activities that take place in their behalf. Various types of advocacy structures and processes have been developed and put to work at all levels of government (national, state, provincial, local, and so on) and have often quite drastically influenced the social and cultural lives of old people.

Advocacy has become so vital to the elderly that it has become defined as one of their basic needs in some societies. It became a factor in the development of a basic social policy of aging and an important component of the social policy of aging that was developed in the United States, for instance.[1,2]

In this chapter, we will review what is meant by advocacy for the aged, identify the advocacy structures and processes that have been used, and analyze their appropriateness and effectiveness from various cultural perspectives. We will also analyze the ways in which advocacy activities have influenced societal responses to the needs of the older population, the changes in the social lives of the aged that have resulted, and the potential results of future trends in advocacy.

THE MEANING OF ADVOCACY

The definitions that some authors have given to advocacy as an ideal concept are helpful in providing a meaningful basis for analyzing the quality of advocacy in behalf of the aged. Fritz states that advocacy in general involves the "marshalling of resources for the benefit of a clientele constituency."[3] In his definition, Berger indicates that advocacy involves the political power of special-interest groups. He says, "advocacy activities are designed to enable special-interest groups to acquire and use power effectively to produce desired changes in society."[4] Lauffer defines advocacy more in terms of specific end products, which are "efforts to represent the interests of specific populations, to reallocate resources in their favor, or to provide services for them."[5]

These definitions of advocacy raise a number of questions that are important in analyzing advocacy activities in behalf of the elderly. It is important to ask the following questions about advocacy: by what authority? with what accountability? by whom? for whom? by what means? toward what ends? and with what results?

Lauffer recognizes potential problems regarding the answers to some of these questions. He draws a distinction between legal and social advocacy, in terms of the focus of authority and accountability of those doing the advocating.[6] He points out that the authority of *legal* advocacy is prescribed by law and is an integral part of the legal system, and that, by legal definition, accountability is directed to those individuals or groups that constitute the clientele. It is primarily *social* advocacy that relates to the sociology of aging, and this is not nearly as clearly defined in terms of either authority or accountability. The authority of social advocacy may come from such a variety of sources as legislative mandate (as in the case of the Older Americans Act), the specified purposes and goals of local organizations or agencies, and the will of groups of aged themselves. Regardless of the source of the authority, however, social advocacy invariably takes place in the political arena and is very much oriented to what is politically acceptable and feasible. Because of that, ironically, social advocacy is often oriented as much to the politics of social control and the ideological and survival concerns of organizations, agencies, and programs as to the interests and needs of the client populations.

If the questions of authority and accountability cannot be clearly answered or taken at face value when dealing with social advocacy, neither can the questions of who is doing the advocating, by what means, for whom, and to what ends. The latter questions logically follow from those of authority and accountability and require careful analysis.

THE DEVELOPMENT OF THE NEED FOR ADVOCACY FOR THE AGED

It may be asked why advocacy for the elderly is necessary in today's societies. In part the assumption that elderly people need advocates is undoubtedly the product of the mythical but prevailing attitude on the part of youth-oriented societies that old people are incapable of caring for themselves and of living relatively independent lives.[7] There is much evidence of the prevalence of such an attitude in the dominant American culture.[8,9] It does not tend to prevail in some ethnic groups in the United States, however, and certainly not in Oriental societies. Youth bias, then, cannot fully explain why advocacy has become necessary for elderly people in this day and age. From the perspective of many elderly people, in fact, part of the defined need for advocacy is to combat the myths of aging.[10]

Two basic factors help to explain why advocacy for elderly persons seems to be necessary today. First, there is a growing tendency in many countries to define old people as a group with special unmet needs.[11] Second, the peculiar characteristics of the institutional structures that we create to attempt to meet those needs make advocacy necessary.

In the United States, defining the elderly population as a group with special unmet needs began with the emergence of industrialized job-related poverty, especially among elderly workers, in the early part of the twentieth century. Pay was insufficient to allow industrial workers to save for old age, and elderly workers were more vulnerable than others to losing their jobs. This led to a widespread movement for the establishiment of pension plans to provide for their economic needs.[12] For the first time in history, it was becoming apparent that elderly people constituted a group with a common unmet need that neither they themselves, their families, nor their communities had the resources to meet.

The definition of the aged as a population with special unmet needs grew in more recent years to include an array of need areas. Besides the recognition that economic poverty was still very prevalent, the delegates to the 1961 and 1971 White House conferences on aging identified the following need areas: physical and mental health, housing and environment, nutrition, education, employment, retirement roles and activities, transportation, and spiritual well-being.[13] Virtually all aspects of the lives of the aged were seen as being inadequately addressed by local community institutions. Conference delegates, contending that meeting these needs was the responsibility of the nation as a whole, called for a "national policy on aging."[14–16]

With the passage of the Social Security Act in 1935, the Older Americans Act in 1965, and the numerous revisions of these pieces of legislation, provision for the many perceived unmet needs of the elderly increasingly became the responsibility of the federal government. However, it is one thing to establish policy and say that the federal government is responsible and quite another for the federal government to carry out those responsibilties effectively. Two basic practical problems have progressively hampered the efforts of the federal government to fulfill its defined responsibility to elderly people: (1) mustering and coordinating the necessary resources to do the job, and (2) locating and reaching all of the eligible elderly constituents.

Some analysts rather cynically conclude that the intent behind any social-service legislation is to provide merely enough services to diffuse complaints and never to provide universal coverage or total need fulfillment.[17] Regardless of the intent, however, it has been impossible to fulfill either of those goals given the limited amount of money allocated to support programs for elderly people and the kind of benefit-delivery systems that have been created.[18,19]

The legislation that was passed in behalf of the aged in this country entitled them to participate in programs designed to meet their special unmet needs. It did not guarantee that all of them would receive the benefits that were available, however. Instead, what could be characterized as an "eligibility-claims" benefit-provision system was created. This system has required that those who need and want to receive any of the available benefits must prove eligibility, claim the right to participate, and go through a complex program-planning process in order to avail themselves of the benefits.

Several prevailing characteristics of the elderly population, especially among those with the greatest levels of unmet needs, make such a system functionally inadequate. Many tend to be unaware of available benefits. Most tend to under define their own needs relative to their conditions and functioning abilities and relative to the living conditions of others. Many lack the knowledge, skills, and power to plan programs and make the necessary claims for benefits.[20] Many are also reluctant to make such claims because of the fear of the "welfare" stigma and the label of being "dependent" which they perceive as the price of receiving "government handouts."[21] With this combination of situational factors, advocacy for the aged has become necessary for a variety of purposes: to influence social policy; to acquire, coordinate, and consolidate the resources necessary to meet the defined needs of the aged; and to implement existing program benefits on as equitable a basis as possible.

An analysis of how advocacy has become important for the elderly in a culturally different group within the United States shows that, although the circumstances may be different, the end results tend to be similar. For example, the Navajo elderly are the recipients of many of the same programs that apply to the rest of the American aged, but the processes of defining needs and the implementation of the programs to serve them have been quite different. In the past, and still to some extent today, Navajo families cared for and helped their aging parents until they finally passed on. Government aging services were historically of little concern to them. Due to a short life expectancy among the Navajos in the past, few elders reached an age at which support services were needed. Life expectancy has increased with the eradication of communicable diseases, however, and a great many more Navajo people are living to become old and are experiencing many of the same aging problems as others.[22]

A major difference between Navajo and Anglo elderly is that, culturally, Navajos are still very much attached to the land on which they live. Thus, while a large percentage of them have lived and still live in severe poverty, their poverty is not the result of being forced into unemployment. It has been the land, not employer policies, with which they have had to struggle for economic survival. Therefore, the definition of their unmet needs was related not so much to their financial stiuation as to the issues of health care in old age and the many cultural changes that tended to leave them without the traditional support structures that would once have been available to them.

In 1980, the first nationwide research effort to document the needs of older Indians was conducted. It was found that the major services needed in Arizona included transportation, home health, homemaker services, residential repair, information and referral, outreach, and escort services.[23] As their numbers increased and the traditional family support systems disappeared, professional and formalized provider systems began to be developed in response to these defined needs. Needless to say, they, even more so than their Anglo counterparts, were ill-equipped to cope with or use those formal systems. Thus, the need for advocates in behalf of the Navajos has been even more acute than for other elderly Americans.

ADVOCACY AS INFLUENCING SOCIAL POLICY AND PUBLIC OPINION

Advocating for the purpose of influencing public opinion and social policy in behalf of elderly people has involved very different processes from one culture to another. As would be expected, the results are also different but have some similarities. By comparing US advocacy efforts with those in the People's Republic of China, we will gain a sense of some of those cross-cultural differences and similarities. In analyzing the efforts that have been made in this regard, it is important to look at who the advocates have been, what ends they have pursued, and what the results have been. Especially, we should understand the extend to which the elderly themselves have been involved, whether their own perceived needs have been addressed, and what the impacts have been for them.

In the United States, this kind of advocacy is clearly a twentieth-century phenomenon. As noted in Chapter 9, efforts to influence public opinion and policy in behalf of the aged began in the 1920s as groups of elderly people in urban areas became organized to make the public aware that increasing numbers of them were unemployed and living in poverty, with little or no chance of improving their economic conditions. The Townsend movement, which originated in Long Beach, California, and spread across the country, was the classic example of these early efforts at advocacy. This group proposed that the federal government establish the policy of subsidizing all unemployed US citizens over 60 years old in the amount of $200 per month,[24,25] an astounding proposal for that time.

Although the Townsend movement was popular among the urban elderly, its influence on policy is questionable. The monthly income proposal was never acted on by Congress.[26] It was considered far too radical and expensive to be taken seriously. Most political analysts agree that the power of the "Townsendites" to influence subsequent policies was quite minimal. They had some influence on the development of private and state pensions,[27] and they claimed to have had a direct influence on the passage of the Social Security Act in 1935.[28] Other more important issues undoubtedly helped to bring that legislation to reality, however, and it did almost nothing to alleviate poverty among elderly recipients,[29] the major goal of the Townsend movement. Because of the lack of continuous leadership and the lack of a political power structure, what influence these groups did have was only temporary. In the absence of the leaders who initiated them, the groups went out of existence.

What might be considered more effective policy-related advocacy began to emerge shortly after World War II, especially with the development of the tradition of holding White House conferences on aging every ten years. This tradition grew out of the National Conference on Aging held in August of 1950. Pratt points out that this conference was called because of two concerns. First, professionals, particularly those in the area of health care, were increasingly requesting help with the unique problems of providing care for their elderly patients. Second, the older population was seen by the Truman administration as a politically ideal group to serve as a first-stage target in establishing a national health plan, to which that administration was committed.[30] It is significant that no input or delegate representation from the elderly population itself was sought for this conference. Instead, local nongovernment and volunteer workers with the aged were invited as delegates.[31] Although no policy recommendations were made, the pattern of having people other than the aged serve as advocates in matters of aging was established, and White House conferences became a tradition.

Delegates to the 1961 and 1971 White House Conferences on Aging were selected on the basis of state representation and representation of a number of newly formed age-related special-interest organizations. The organizations that were represented included such groups as the National Council of Senior Citizens (NCSC), the American Association of Retired Persons (AARP), the National Association of Retired Teachers (NART), the National Council on Aging, and the Senate Subcommittee on Aging. Only a few such groups had been formed by 1961, and their influence was limited. They had become more influential by 1971, but it is noteworthy that, with the exception of AARP and NART, none of the groups was exclusively made up of elderly people and some had no elderly members at all. Even the AARP and NART memberships were by no means representative of the total elderly population. No care was taken at either the 1961 or 1971 conferences to ensure that any elderly people would be present. Pratt points out that "there was no 'gray lobby' as such" at the 1961 conference.[32] The same could be said of the 1971 conference.

Delegates at both the 1961 and the 1971 White House conferences claimed to speak for the aged. They outlined what they saw as unmet needs among the aged and recommended that a national policy on aging be established, focused particularly on providing special health care, nutrition, and social- and support-service programs. Clearly, a pattern of relying on special-interest groups to advocate for social policy on aging had been established. This pattern continued and even expanded throughout the 1960s and 1970s as more and more age-related special-interest groups came into existence.

Particularly significant were groups comprised of members of specific racial and ethnic minority groups and professionals working in the ever-expanding "aging network." These included such organizations as the National Center for Black Aged, the National Indian Council on Aging, the Association of National Pro Personae Mayores, the National Association of State Units on Aging, the National Association of Area Agencies, the National Association of Nutrition Directors, the American Association of Homes for the Aging, the National Institute of Senior Centers, the Gerontological Society, the Western Gerontological Society (now the American Society of Aging), and the Association for Gerontology in Higher Education. Obviously, these organizations were formed for the sole purpose of advocating for policy from the persepctive of quite specific special interests. As Estes points out, "the agencies created, nurtured, and legitimated by the Older Americans Act . . . have become the focus of government policy for the aged."[33]

Perhaps interest-group advocacy was the only feasible approach. Berger has contended that senior citizens as a group are "disenfranchised," live in "relative isolation," do not widely subscribe to advocating techniques, and do not even "recognize that they share common problems and needs"[34] It is doubtful that many aged people today would agree with that description of their conditions. Nevertheless, it is important to understand the policy-related problems of that advocacy approach.

One clear problem has to do with the special or vested interests of the groups advocating for policies on aging. At least part of the their concern has to do with the continued existence of the groups themselves. As Estes points out, the agencies in the aging network "have taken on a momentum of their own, demonstrating the primacy of organizations' tendencies toward survival, maintenance, and enhancement." Consequently, she contends, "the needs of the aged are replaced by the needs of the agencies formed to serve the aged, and this transposition turns the solution into the problem."[35]

Another, perhaps more serious consequence of the special–interest group advocacy approach, is its almost exclusive emphasis on the definition of the aged as people with unmet needs. Virtually all of the age-related legislation that has been passed (the Social Security Act, the Older Americans Act, and the Medicare revision of the Social Security Act), and the agencies and programs that have resulted from those congressional acts, are products of advocacy that may not represent, as Estes puts it, "the interests of the aged, as perceived by the aged themselves."[36] There have been both positive and negative consequences of this. On the positive side, many practical benefits have been provided to the aged that are vital to many of them. The negative consequences have been that the needs-oriented advocacy has led to needs-oriented policy and practice, by and large ignoring the value of older people to society. The needs of the aged (not the importance of their social contributions) are, ironically, the major emphasis in the implementation even of such volunteer programs as the Retired Senior Volunteer Program (RSVP) and Service Corps of Retired Executives (SCORE). The emphasis on needs has in turn helped to create a prevailing public perception of the aged as an almost exclusively dependent, societally burdensome population characterized by irreversible physical and mental deterioration. This emphasis has undoubtedly caused many of the aged themselves to share this perception of themselves and to become segregated and isolated from the rest of society.[37,38]

In a real sense, even the critics of existing policies on aging and their negative consequences end up contributing to them. By offering her own policy-on-aging recommendations, for example, Estes assumes that the aged are still dependent on someone else to advocate for them and to some extent presumes to speak for them. Some of what she recommends may in fact represent neither "the interests of the aged, as perceived by the aged themselves" nor what would be politically most feasible for them. For example, she advocates for "policies to facilitate intergenerational bonding and support" and the "adoption of universalist policies and principles that would not place the aged in a separate (and potentially unequal) status but that would instead eradicate the structural segregation of aging policies from those of other groups in society."[39] Implied in this seems to be the same assumption that others have made in the past—that the aged do not have the political power or skills to advocate for themselves separately from other dependent, needs-oriented groups. Perhaps also implied is the idea that assigning a separate status to the aged with regard to policy is wrong. It is not at all clear that either of those positions are shared by many of the aged themselves.

The effective involvement of the elderly in policy-related advocacy has, in fact, dramatically increased since the late 1970s. This has taken place at both state and federal levels. Two events that took place in the state of Arizona serve to illustrate this phenomenon at the state level. The first of these was related to the issue of age-segregated housing in the Phoenix area. After the age-restrictive policies in the many retirement communities and housing projects had been declared unconstitutional by the Arizona courts in 1973, the elderly residents formed a lobbying group and succeeded in having a state law passed to reinstate those policies.[40] This illustrates that, in fact, the aged themselves are quite capable of acting as their own policy advocates. Still, the case by no means represents all elderly people nor even a trend toward advocacy. A second event in Arizona—a series of advocating activities that led to the passage of the Arizona Older Americans Act in 1980—is much more representative. It is very significant that it was almost exclusively retired people, advocating in their own behalf, who initiated the idea of state support for programs on aging and worked for the passage of the act. The movement began when a retired member of a regional council on aging from a small rural community recognized the potential political power of the retired people in the state and initiated a petition calling for funding from the state government for aging programs. As the petition was circulated and signed by more and more senior citizens throughout the state, enthusiasm grew about the possibility of the passage of a comprehensive Older Americans Act for Arizona. A statewide planning and advocacy group was formed under the auspices of the Governor's Advisory Council on Aging, a well-organized advocacy group made up primarily of retired people. The group wrote the law and lobbied for its passage in the state legislature. The law passed easily even though no such law had ever before even been considered in Arizona.

Advocacy activities by the elderly have also increased dramatically at the national level. This is probably best illustrated by the events of the 1981 White House Conference on Aging. For the first time in the history of White House Conferences on Aging, regulations stipulated that a majority of delegates would be chosen from among the elderly. Then, at the conference itself, the claim of the traditional age-related groups that they spoke for elderly people was effectively challenged by those representing the Reagan administration at the conference, and the influence of special-interest groups was clearly diminished. The elderly delegates themselves stood squarely behind such elderly spokesmen as Representative Claude Pepper (not even an official delegate) and Charles Schottland (retired delegate from Arizona), who fought for issues that were universally vital to elderly people, especially the continuation of Social Security benefits and adequate health care. It has clearly been the overwhelmingly strong voice of the elderly themselves, and not the voices of others who claim to speak for them, that has thus far made it politically unfeasible for anyone in the political arena to drastically change or reduce Social Security benefits, even in times when the national economy is in crisis and most social programs are being cut.

A look at advocating in behalf of the special needs of the elderly in China reveals a quite different set of circumstances. Singling out the aged as a group with special needs began at a grassroots level having to do primarily with the issues of work, retirement, and care for the aged who needed it. During the reign of Mao Tse Tung, everyone who was able, no matter how old, was expected to work. Not to work was to deny the ideals of the Communist ideology. Practically, however, a large labor surplus has existed in China for many years, and retirement for the aged has emerged as a need. As explained by Mr. Wang, an official of the Chinese Association of Science and Technology, the initial impetus for this came from the aged themselves and their families.[41]

Following the end of the Cultural Revolution, growing numbers of elderly workers and their families began to make requests to the production units to which they belonged that the elderly members be allowed to do less work and even to retire. Agreements were often made between family members and production unit officials that the younger workers in the families would do the work that normally would have been done by their elderly relatives, and that the elderly relatives would continue to receive a percentage of their salaries. In a situation of surplus labor and large families, this plan placed little or no burden on family members. In fact, since both fathers and mothers had work assignments outside the home, having retired elderly grandparents available to help with child care and home maintenance was distinctly beneficial to families. Because of the time that retired persons have available to them, they have also been able to help their families take advantage of the free-enterprise opportunities allowed by the new economic reforms underway in China today. Elderly people and their families, in effect, initiated a retirement system that became general policy first within production units and eventually across much of the nation.

The care of elderly people without families became a concern of local production units in the early days of the Communist revolution. Leaders of local communes advocated for such care even before the entire country became Communist. Special homes for such people were established in some communes even before 1949. Now many such homes exist throughout the country, and the care of the elderly without families has become a constitutional guarantee.[42]

To a large extent, the Chinese aged themselves have had a major voice in defining their own needs, have acted as their own advocates, and have been able to influence policy in their own favor. According to the Chinese traditions of filial piety, perhaps this is not surprising. Nevertheless, it seems to be an outstanding accomplishment in a country that has been dominated by an ideology (communism) that, as such, offers no special place of honor to the aged, and that is controlled by a totalitarian regime in which policy is set at the top levels of the political structure and imposed on the populace. According to Yin and Lai, though, elderly people were honored and powerful because of Chinese traditions, and they have managed to retain much of their power and influence even under communism. As they analyze it, the Cultural Revolution, during which many elderly people suffered severely, ironically served to restore them to positions of authority in the society. The circumstances were that younger adults, who seemed to be gaining control during the Cultural Revolution, in fact failed to become educated and trained for positions of power. When the Cultural Revolution was over, the country once again had to turn to the aged for direction.[43] It remains to be seen how long the authority of the aged will last in the current period of economic reform and modernization.

ADVOCACY TO ACQUIRE, COORDINATE, AND CONSOLIDATE RESOURCES

The acquisition of resources to meet the needs of the elderly has been a particular problem in the United States, especially in the way the Older Americans Act was outlined and implemented. Social Security and Medicare never claimed to meet the total financial and health needs of retired people,[44,45] but no such disclaimer accompanied the Older Americans Act. In passing the Older Americans Act in 1965, Congress made the federal government responsible for the overall welfare of the aged in the United States.[46] To fulfill that responsibility, two things were necessary: (1) the planning and implementation of programs and (2) the acquisition of the resources necessary to implement such programs. The dilemma has been that the first requirement is dependent upon the second, and the federal government has always been unwilling or unable to allocate enough funds to provide adequate resources for the programs promised in the Older Americans Act.[47]

In order to resolve the dilemma of having accepted the responsibility but not providing the necessary resources, Congress created an agency, the Administration on Aging, with a dual mandate: (1) to plan and implement needs-providing programs, and (2) to advocate for resources.[48] While the original Older Americans Act did not use the term *advocacy,* one of the functions it assigned to the Administration on Aging (AoA) was to "stimulate more effective use of existing resources and available services for the aged and aging."[49]

Fritz points out that, while the AoA's planning responsibilities have been thoroughly outlined and strongly emphasized throughout the history of that organization, its advocacy function has not been clearly defined. One implication of this responsibility, however, was that the AoA would have the authority to review all programs related to the aged being planned by other federal agencies and to coordinate interagency implementation efforts. In addition, a limited amount of effort has been made by AoA officials to coordinate efforts with nongovernment age-related groups.[50]

The need for advocacy was given special emphasis at the 1971 White House Conference and consequently in the 1973 and 1978 revisions of the Older Americans Act. The result was that not only the AoA but all of the agencies throughout the aging network were mandated to perform advocacy activities.[51] The 1973 Older Americans Act revisions called for the establishment of substate Area Agencies on Aging (AAAs), and part of their function was to advocate for the acquisition of local resources. As Fritz explains it, with regard to the AAA's working with local organizations, "AoA could learn about other federal programs and inform area agencies about opportunities for tapping into these resources and thereby articulate and respond to the needs of older persons at the local levels."[52]

Some analysts contend that those advocacy efforts that have been made by AoA and the aging network to acquire and coordinate resources have been spasmodic, unsystematic, and relatively ineffective. Fritz cites several reasons for this. For one, AoA is located at too low a level of the federal bureaucratic structure to have the authority to function as an interagency coordinating agency. In addition, the advocacy role was too poorly defined for agency personnel to know how to perform it in any practical way. Whether and how to act as advocates largely depended upon the interests and whims of the individuals working in AoA at any given time. Furthermore, advocacy work has had to compete with program-planning activities within the network, and it has consistently been given second priority. Network personnel no doubt see their responsibilities for planning, implementing, monitoring, and maintaining programs as sufficiently time-consuming to justify their positions. It may also be that planning and advocacy are perceived as somewhat incompatible roles for an agency to perform.[53]

This set of circumstances raises the question of how seriously the federal government has taken the advocacy role. Perhaps it is unrealistic to expect federal agencies to perform such a role effectively. According to Spector and Kitsuse, the best that can be expected of government agencies is that they provide a high enough level of services to diffuse complaints, not that they actually solve problems.[54] Agencies tend to become at least as concerned about their own existences as they are about the welfare of their client groups.[55] It is up to individuals and groups that are independent of official government agencies, such as elderly people themselves, to advocate effectively for resource acquisition.

In fairness to Congress, they recognized the importance of this kind of advocating by mandating the advisory council on aging structures at each level of agency activities (project, county, region, state, and federal). By federal regulation, these councils are made up of a majority of elderly members in order to provide the opportunity for the aged to do their own advocating. Ironically, however, councils on aging have generally been dependent for their resources upon the agencies that they advise, and they have largely been co-opted into program planning and maintenance efforts by those agencies. Thus they have not been given much incentive to advocate for resources.[56]

From the perspective of agencies, it would be somewhat risky to support truly independent groups of senior citizens engaged in resource-acquisition advocacy.[57] It is too likely that the advocacy would be directed back to the agencies providing the support rather than elsewhere. Consequently, advocacy to acquire needed resources, no matter to whom the job has fallen, has been only minimally successful.

ADVOCACY TO IMPLEMENT PROGRAM BENEFITS EQUITABLY

One of the basic concerns in the provision of services for the welfare of the elderly is that services be provided on an equitable basis to those who need and want them. There have been problems with this kind of advocacy for the aged in very different cultural settings.

In the United States, the history of service provision by the AoA and the whole aging network has been one of systems themselves creating inequities. Great numbers of eligible and particularly needy individuals have not been served, not because of the choices of those individuals, but because the needed services were not available. Whole neighborhoods, communities, and geographical areas have been denied service programs that were readily available in other similar areas. A large part of the problem, however, is clearly that the lack of accessibility to services is attributable to the ways in which service programs have been planned and implemented.

The system of service provision that has been created for the aged almost automatically leads to an inequity of services. For individuals to receive any of the variety of potentially available services under the Older Americans Act, local agencies must be organized and must follow a very complex and technical planning process (according to elaborate federal guidelines) in order to create the necessary service programs. Without the existence of these organizations and their successful planning efforts in local communities, no services are even available to elderly people who may need them. Even within neighborhoods and communities where service programs have been organized and supported by Older Americans Act funds, there is by no means equal access to services. Accessibility, especially for those with the greatest needs, depends to a great extent upon the kind and extent of support services that are provided (transportation, information and referral, and outreach). Very clearly, whether or not given neighborhoods and communities have services to offer their elderly people and whether those elderly people have access to the services depend on effective advocates. For services to be made available on an equitable basis, a system of advocacy is necessary that can potentially reach all communities and all elderly individuals.

This problem was recognized in the 1973 revision of the Older Americans Act. That revision mandated that all states be divided into planning districts and that an area agency on aging be formed in each planning district. In addition to being responsible for helping to plan and monitor programs, AAA staff members were expected to advocate for the potential elderly recipients throughout their respective areas. As previously noted, the Older Americans Act revisions also mandated the creation of a system of advisory councils, made up of a majority of elderly members, in each area. These included (1) project councils, advisory to local program staff; (2) county councils, responsible to advocate for the elderly in communities in their respective counties; and (3) regional councils, advisory to AAA staff. Theoretically, as previously noted, these councils gave elderly people the opportunity to advocate in their own behalf for equal access to services as well as for needed resources.[58] It is important, though, to ask about the extent to which this system has actually given the aged a voice, and about whether it has made service provision more equitable.

Some analysts contend that, since the councils are only advisory, they constitute mere tokenism as far as the involvement of elderly persons is concerned.[59] Their control or even influence over program development and over the population they reach greatly depends upon the extent to which staff members are willing to allow such control or influence. Funding for council activities typically comes from the agencies they advise, and thus they are very dependent upon those agencies. In discussing the mandated advocacy role of AAA advisory councils, Cohn points out that "the extent of the advocacy function is not delineated; the legislation does not legitimatize 'protest' activities," and that the activities in which councils engage "are 'reactive' kinds of activities, critiquing and responding to programs and plans already in effect rather than initiating and formulating programs."[60] Providing services to elderly persons in neighborhoods and communities that lack service programs does not seem to be a practical function of the advisory council advocacy system.

In a study of advocacy for the aged in the rural area of northern Arizona, it was discovered that there were definite limits to any attempts to provide services equitably in rural communities.[61] Members of county councils either did not understand their equitable-oriented advocacy role or were frustrated with trying to make it functional. Those who understood it and took it seriously reported two problems connected to that kind of advocacy work. First, travel funds needed to reach unreached communities were not available. Funds for county council activities were controlled by the AAA, and the AAA's first priority was for council members to travel to meetings in support of existing programs. Second, the few attempts that were made either by council members or by AAA staff to reach communities without programs were often met with indifference and even opposition on the part of leaders in those communities.

It is noteworthy that no county or regional council members represented communities in the region that lacked service programs. Therefore, neither AAA staff nor council members had much incentive to advocate for equitable access to services on the part of the aged in communities without programs. Instead, their first priority was to maintain and improve existing programs. This is not to say that no new programs were started in new communities in the region. New programs did emerge, but not as a result of the system of advocacy mandated by the Older Americans Act. Neither did the emergence of new programs guarantee equitable access.[62]

The northern Arizona advocacy study revealed that program development and the provision of services in given communities came as a result of a localized, grassroots advocacy process. Local leaders recognized the needs of the aged in their communities and persistently helped the aged themselves to organize in order to meet those needs. From the perspective of the AAA and the larger aging network, then, the development of new programs is not the result of mandated advocacy on their part. Rather it is their response to the grassroots advocacy emanating from local neighborhoods and communities. Thus, advocacy to provide equitable access to services has by no means yet been accomplished. The official system of advocacy has not functioned as it was expected to function to make services equitably accessible to the needy aged.

Similar grassroots advocacy processes to provide the elderly with needed services seem to have been operating in the two other cultural situations that we have been examining in this chapter. Advocacy for the aged among the Navajos began in the early 1970s when a small group of elderly people organized themselves into the Navajo Council on Aging and began investigating sources to fund and develop programs to serve the Navajo elderly population. They were encouraged and helped by a young Volunteers in Service to America (VISTA) worker, then serving on the reservation, who knew where to go and how to proceed.

At first the Navajo Council on Aging was an autonomous group with no attachment to any official tribal organization. Acting largely on their own, the council members acquired funding to develop and staff a number of service programs for the aged in selected chapters of the reservation (regions into which the Navajo Reservation is divided). The need for coordination of existing programs and for systematic planning for more programs soon became apparent. The result was the establishment of the Office of Aging Services, located in the Division of Health Improvement Services of the Navajo tribal government. Tribal government eventually took over the official responsibility for aging services among the Navajos, and the Council on Aging became merely an advisory group.

For a time, the Office of Aging staff and the Council on Aging worked closely together to advocate for program expansion and the acquisition of new programs that would be culturally compatible. Within less than a decade, two nursing homes were built and became operational on the reservation, nutrition sites were opened in 36 of the 60 chapters across the reservation, meals-on-wheels programs were functioning in a number of places, two experimental group homes were opened to provide temporary respite care for elders with special healthcare needs in the chapter where they were located, and a home healthcare program was planned in one selected area of the reservation. A system of support from a combination of four federal agencies (AoA, the Bureau of Indian Affairs, Indian Health Service, and ACTION) and the Navajo Tribal Council was established.

Despite this initial success, however, there are clear limitations to the advocacy processes for Navajo aged, similar to those for other aged Americans. Although the initial advocacy efforts were made by the elderly themselves, that aspect of their work has subsequently diminished as their role became advisory. The responsibility to advocate for all Navajo elderly has largely become the responsibility of the Office of Aging staff, but they now have many existing programs to maintain in a time when federal support for social services is declining. Thus, many Navajo elderly still have no access to services that they badly need because no services exist in many of the chapters.[63]

As explained earlier, advocacy in behalf of the elderly in China began with the elderly people themselves, their families, and production unit officials at the grassroots level, and spread to have influence on national policy. However, these advocacy efforts have not been successful in providing equal access to the benefits that are available to many of the aged in that country. According to the present Chinese constitution, care of all elderly people is not only promised but guaranteed. Still, no national commitment of resources has been made to support that guarantee, except to those who have worked directly for the government. Instead, the national government has expected that families of the aged or the production units to which they belonged, or both, would provide the resources for their care. How to make those provisions has been left up to families and local production units. Until recently, the poorer production units, especially in rural areas, often simply did not have the resources to provide the kinds of social and health services available to those in more wealthy production units. The individualization of production in recent years raises further questions about how services will be provided.

The Chinese national government has a relatively generous retirement policy for government workers, is now boasting about its widespread practice throughout the nation, and is beginning to advocate for it as a nationwide policy.[64] Nevertheless, it has never become a mandated policy of the national government and has not been established at all in some financially poor production units in rural areas. A structure of gerontology committees has been formed throughout China at national, provincial, and city levels to advocate and plan for needed services for the aged. Yet not only are services still not offered equitably to all aged, but no plans have been proposed as a means of doing so.[65]

CONCLUSION

With the emergence of the definition of the aged as "dependent" has come the growing assumption that they need someone to advocate for them. This assumption has been prevalent in countries with very different cultural backgrounds and political structures. Informal grassroots systems of advocacy involving the elderly themselves, as well as formal systems involving government and agency personnel, have been at work in behalf of the elderly population. In the United States, the very legislation that was passed to provide special services for the aged has also mandated a system of advocacy to be carried out in conjunction with the planning and service-provision systems. However, these advocacy systems have historically been relatively ineffective in actually representing the needs of the all of the elderly and in meeting the needs as defined by the aged themselves.

In the United States, for example, age-related special-interest groups have claimed to advocate for the aged in terms of influencing policy, but they have often advocated as much for their own vested interests as for the actual needs of the aged as they themselves might define them. That kind of advocating has, in fact, tended to perpetuate the view of the aged as dependent and helpless.

The legislatively mandated system of advocacy in which federal, state, and area agencies and their advisory councils have been expected to acquire and coordinate needed resources and equitably provide services to the aged has by no means functioned as expected. While the aging network has planned and delivered many vital services to elderly people, it has done little to muster additional resources beyond those provided by the Older Americans Act itself. Neither has it delivered services on an equitable basis.

In fairness to those in the aging network, it is probably unreasonable to expect them to fulfill such a role. Their advocacy roles have not been well defined. They have not been given an adequate power base within bureaucratic structures to be able to function as advocates. In addition, it seems clear that the planning and service-provision roles are somewhat incompatible with the advocacy role. Effective advocates must be independent of the service-providing agencies.

Logically, it would seem that the aged themselves ought to act as their own advocates. They have not had great success at this in the past, however, at least in the United States. Many of them have not understood how to advocate, nor have they even had the desire to be involved in advocacy activities. Furthermore, with the great economic and social divergence among their population, they have lacked group consensus about their needs. Given their social positions of economic dependency, they have also lacked the political power to advocate effectively for themselves.

Recent indications are, however, that they may well become their own effective advocates in the future. Although needs issues of the past may not be the ones that the aged themselves would emphasize, they are nevertheless beginning to recognize that there are issues that touch them all. With the formation of large, independent groups made up almost exclusively of elderly members, they are finding that they now have great political power, and they are beginning to advocate quite successfully in their own behalf.

As the aged take over their own advocacy, a substantial shift will undoubtedly take place in how their needs are defined and what concerns will emerge as policy issues. Much less emphasis will be placed on dependency-building, stereotyping, needs-providing issues. Much more emphasis will be placed on their capabilities and potential contributions to society, and on the provision of opportunities to perform meaningfully productive roles, both in and outside of retirement. This is an emphasis already being made by such groups as the Gray Panthers.[66]

Increasing demands will also almost certainly be made in the future for the rights of the aged themselves to plan and control their own activities and destinies, in terms of such matters as financial stability, social activities, health care, and retirement. In addition, the elderly are increasingly recognizing the importance of advocating to combat the stigmas and myths of aging. Self-advocacy on the part of the elderly themselves will almost certainly result in a dramatic change in our social policies on aging, in the rest of society's view of them, and in the roles and relationships they enjoy.

In China, as compared with the United States, elderly people have enjoyed relatively greater social and political power and have thus been considerably more successfully involved in defining their own needs and in influencing policy. Navajo elderly have also been successfully involved in advocating for themselves, at least initially and in terms of acquiring services that were previously nonexistent. Neither the Chinese nor Navajo self-advocacy efforts have yet succeeded in creating equitable systems of service provision, however.

As a whole, much has been accomplished due to advocating efforts on behalf of elderly people in the world today. Much also remains to be accomplished.

NOTES

[1] *Guide to AoA Programs,* Publication No. (OHDS) 80-20176 (US Department of Health and Human Services, 1980), pp. 3–5.

[2] Dan Fritz, "The Administration on Aging as an Advocate: Progress, Problems, and Perspectives," *The Gerontologist,* 19, no. 2 (April 1979), 141–50.

[3] Ibid.

[4] M. Berger, "An Orienting Perspective on Advocacy," in *Advocacy and Age,* ed. Paul A. Kerschner (Los Angeles: University of Southern California Press, 1976), pp. 2–13.

[5] Armand Lauffer, *Social Planning at the Community Level,* (Englewood Cliffs, N.J.: Prentice-Hall, 1978), p. 289.

[6] Ibid.

[7] Joseph A. Kuypers and Vern L. Bengtson, "Social Breakdown and Competence: A Model of Normal Aging," *Human Development,* 16 (1973), 181–201.

[8] Russell A. Ward, *The Aging Experience: An Introduction to Social Gerontology* (New York: Harper & Row, Pub., 1984), pp. 118–31.

[9] D. G. McTavish, "Perceptions of Old People: A Review of Research Methodologies and Findings," *The Gerontologist,* 11, no. 2 (Summer 1971), 90–101.

[10] Georgia M. Barrow, *Aging, The Individual, and Society* (St. Paul, Minn.: West, 1986), pp. 33–41.

[11] Berger, "An Orienting Perspective on Advocacy," pp. 2–13.

[12] David Hackett Fischer, *Growing Old in America* (New York: Oxford University Press, 1978), pp. 157–82.

[13] Louis Lowy, *Social Policies and Programs on Aging* (Lexington, Mass.: Lexington, 1980), pp. 31–32.

[14] Robert C. Atchley, *Social Forces and Aging: An Introduction to Social Gerontology* (Belmont, Calif.: Wadsworth, 1985), pp. 361–64.

[15] Lowy, *Social Policies and Programs on Aging,* p. 31.

[16] US Subcommittee on Aging of the Committee on Labor and Public Welfare and the Special Committee on Aging, United States Senate, *Post–White House Conference on Aging Report,* 1973 (Washington, D.C.: US Government Printing Office, 1973), p. 153.

[17] M. Spector and J. I. Kitsuse, "Social Problems: A Reformulation," *Social Problems,* 21 (1973), 145–59.

[18] B. Cohen, "Older Americans Act Funding Inadequate to Provide Full Range of Services," *Network,* 1977, p. 8.

[19] James H. Schulz, "The Future of Social Security and Private Pensions or Does Social Security Have a Future?" *Generations,* 4, no. 1 (May 1980), 21–23.

[20] Lowy, *Social Policies and Programs on Aging,* p. 193.

[21] Elizabeth Moen, "The Reluctance of the Elderly to Accept Help," *Social Problems,* 25, no. 3 (February 1978), 293–303.

[22] Arnold S. Brown and Thomas Timmreck, "Summary Report of a Survey of the Navajo Nation Long Term Care and Aging Policy" (unpublished paper submitted to the Arizona Long Term Care Gerontology Center, the University of Arizona, Tucson, Arizona, 1984).

[23] National Indian Council on Aging, *American Indian Elderly: A National Profile* (Albuquerque, N. Mex.: Cordova Printing, 1981), pp. 14–28.

[24] Fischer, *Growing Old in America*, pp. 180–81.

[25] Lowy, *Social Policies and Programs on Aging*, pp. 190–91.

[26] Ibid., p. 191.

[27] Fischer, *Growing Old in America*, 182.

[28] Lowy, *Social Policies and Programs on Aging*, p. 191.

[29] Fischer, *Growing Old in America*, p. 183.

[30] J. J. Pratt, "Symbolic Politics and the White House Conference on Aging," *Society* (July–August 1978), pp. 67–72.

[31] Ibid.

[32] Ibid.

[33] Carroll L. Estes, *The Aging Enterprise* (San Francisco: Jossey-Bass, 1979), pp. 73–74.

[34] Berger, "An Orienting Perspective on Advocacy," pp. 2–13.

[35] Estes, *The Aging Enterprise*, p. 74.

[36] Ibid.

[37] Alex Comfort, *A Good Age* (New York: Crown, 1976), pp. 28–30.

[38] Estes, *The Aging Enterprise*, pp. 227–28.

[39] Ibid., p. 241.

[40] William A. Anderson and Norma D. Anderson, "The Politics of Age Exclusion: The Adults-Only Movement in Arizona," *The Gerontologist*, 18, no. 1 (February 1978), 6–12.

[41] Arnold S. Brown, "Social Policy of Aging in Mainland China" (unpublished report of an informal study of the social policy on aging in China, Summer of 1984).

[42] Ibid.

[43] Peter Yin and Kwok Hung Lai, "A Reconceptualization of Age Stratification in China," *Journal of Gerontology*, 38, no. 5 (September 1983), 608–13.

[44] Lowy, *Social Policies and Programs on Aging*, p. 35.

[45] Ward, *The Aging Experience*, pp. 161, 314.

[46] Donald E. Gelfand and Jody K. Olsen, *The Aging Network: Programs and Services* (New York: Springer, 1980), p. 243.

[47] Atchley, *Social Forces and Aging*, p. 330.

[48] Fritz, "The Administration on Aging as an Advocate," pp. 141–50.

[49] Robert Binstock, *Planning Background Issues: White House Conference on Aging Report* (Washington, D.C.: US Government Printing Office, 1971), p. 8.

[50] Fritz, "The Administration on Aging as an Advocate," pp. 142–46.

[51] *Guide to AoA Programs*, pp. 3–5.

[52] Fritz, "The Administration on Aging as an Advocate," pp. 142–46.

[53] Ibid.

[54] Spector and Kitsuse, "Social Problems," pp. 145–59.

[55] Robert B. Hudson, "The 'Graying' of the Federal Budget and its Consequences for Old-Age Policy," in *The Aging in Politics: Process and Policy*, ed. Robert B. Hudson (Springfield, Ill.: Chas. C Thomas, 1981), pp. 261–81.

[56] J. Cohn, "Advocacy and Planning: Its Strength, Potential, and Future," in *Advocacy and Age*, ed. Paul A. Kerschner (Los Angeles: University of Southern California Press, 1976), pp. 74–76.

[57] Ibid.

[58] Ibid.

[59] Ibid.

[60] Ibid.

[61] Arnold S. Brown, "Grassroots Advocacy for the Elderly In Small Rural Communities," *The Gerontologist*, 25, no. 4 (August 1985), 417–23.

[62] Ibid.

[63] Brown and Timmreck, "Summary Report of a Survey."

[64] "Growing Old in China," *Beijing Review*, 43 (October 26, 1981), 22–28.

[65] Brown, "Social Policy of Aging in Mainland China."

[66] Christina Long, "Gray Panthers: Some Grassroots Projects," *Generations*, 6, no. 2 (Winter 1981), 28–29.

11

The Extent of Economic Dependency Among the Aged

INTRODUCTION

It is generally assumed in the modern world today that elderly people are economically dependent and are an unfair burden on younger workers. Those over 65 and under 16 years old are compared with those 16 through 65 by economists and demographers to analyze what they term the *dependency ratio* of a given population, for example. The idea behind this concept is that children, youth, and old people are being totally supported by young and middle-aged adults, and that this is placing an increasing and unfair burden on the rest of the population.[1]

To analyze the extent of economic dependency among the aged, we first need to understand what is meant by economics, how the economic system is assumed to work, and how the notion of old-age dependency emerged. We will also see how the notion of economic dependency of the aged is being avoided in other nations.

ECONOMICS AND THE ECONOMIC SYSTEMS

We have a tendency today to think of money whenever economics is discussed. Money does not define economics, however. In essence, economics has to do with the production, distribution, and consumption of goods and services by given societies. Money is involved merely as the basic tool to facilitate those processes in today's complex societies.

Historically, human labor has been needed to produce and distribute necessary goods and services. In fact, in the hunting, fishing, and agricultural societies, in which the level of technology has been limited or nonexistent, all of the available human labor has been needed for these purposes. The very survival of many such societies is constantly threatened if enough human labor is not available. Therefore, in these kinds of societies, those unable to do the work required in the productive or distributive processes become dependent upon those who can and do perform those kinds of tasks.

The burden of dependency of those unable to perform physical labor, especially the aged, has been found to be too great for some hunting and fishing societies living in particularly harsh environments. Sharp reports, for example, that old age in the Chipewyan tribe in the subartic area of northern Canada is despised and feared. If the aged are no longer able to hunt, they are left out of social life, feel useless and powerless, and are sometimes even abandoned. Subsistence for the Chipewyan is so precious that the tribe simply cannot support those aged who become economically dependent.[2]

Sheehan compared the place of the aged in three types of "traditional" societies located in various parts of the world: (1) those that were geographically unstable (seminomadic); (2) tribes that lived in relatively permanent villages; and (3) those living in peasant communities and engaged in agriculture. His data showed that the status of the aged in the geographically unstable societies largely depended on each individual's ability to continue to contribute to the group's survival. Among the relatively stable tribes, older people typically had positions of importance, but priority was still given to younger members of the tribes. Among the agricultural peasant groups, older people were held in high esteem.[3]

In agricultural societies, production has developed beyond the level of simply subsistence, and the accumulation of family assets becomes possible. A division of labor is typically worked out, with management positions becoming important. Land ownership also develops, with owners holding positions of control over others. Far from being treated as dependent, the aged in these types of societies tend to continue to participate in the productive processes throughout their lives, with increasingly important and powerful positions. They often own the land and manage production while younger family members provide the hard labor. As Williamson and his colleagues explain, "The institution of property rights gave the elderly considerable control over those who were younger; particularly their children."[4] Fischer reports that land owndership contributed greatly to the veneration and economic power of the aged in the United States from colonial days at least through the eighteenth century.[5] Actually, remnants of economic power among the aged in rural parts of the United States have survived to the present day.

Production and distribution of goods and services in hunting, fishing, and agricultural societies is controlled and carried out by family or kinship units. In these kinds of situations, the economic security of older people depends primarily on whether or not the accumulation of resources is possible. As we have seen, that is clearly most possible in those societies in which agriculture has been developed. Even then, however, old age itself does not guarantee economic security. That comes only to those who are able to acquire and control resources within their families and communities. It is just that economic power among older people is most possible in agricultural settings.

The economic status of the aged is strengthened not merely because they are able to control economic resources, but also because they tend to continue participating in production. While the work they do tends to be less physically demanding as they age, they nevertheless continue to contribute vital efforts to production. Thus, the work ethic is upheld as much by elderly family members as others, and human labor continues to be emphasized as the most important determinant of economic status.

Much has been made of the loss of productive roles experienced by the aged in industrialized societies. It is assumed that economic status declines and economic dependency sets in as a result of their retirement from those active roles. It is assumed that, because they are retired, the aged make no contributions to the productive processes of society and that their dependency is the burden of those who remain in the work force. This kind of analysis is based on the notion that human labor is still the primary factor that makes production possible. To assess the validity of this notion, we must examine the economic system prevalent in the industrialized world.

Two factors about modern economics are important in analyzing the economic status of the aged today. One is the importance of technology in the actual production processes, and the other is the importance of capital in the capitalist system that dominates production today.

It is obvious that the functions of modern economic systems are extremely complex. In agrarian societies, both production and distribution are relatively simple processes. In some cases distribution is nonexistent; families tend to be economically autonomous, producing what they themselves consume. In contrast, distribution is as vital as production in industrialized societies, and both of these processes are extremely complex. It is not at all uncommon, for example, for many goods to be shipped thousands of miles from where they are produced to potential consumer markets through a complex system of wholesale and retail companies. Adding to the complexity of this kind of system is the fact that both production and distribution depend upon increasingly sophisticated technology.

There are two important things to consider with regard to the development of the technology involved in modern economics. First, it is eliminating much of the need for human labor in the production and distribution of goods and services. Machines are now available not only for those tasks that once required manual labor, but for mental tasks as well. Second, technology requires money.

Relying on labor-saving technology is generally more profitable for businesses than relying on human labor. Machines are faster and more efficient. Nevertheless, acquiring the needed machinery requires initial capital. The need for capital, then, is a vital part of the modern economic system.

The use of technology and the need for capital in modern economic systems are both important to understand if we are to get a true picture of the extent to which the aged are economically dependent in the industrial world today. The specific issues are (1) the extent to which their elimination from the work force actually creates an economic burden of dependency for those in the work force, on the one hand, and may enhance the economic situation for those in the work place, on the other hand, and (2) the extent to which and the ways in which the aged may actually contribute positively to today's economic conditions. These are issues that are largely ignored in today's gerontological literature.

DEVELOPMENT OF FINANCIAL SUPPORT FOR THE AGED
IN THE UNITED STATES

As the United States moved into the twentieth century, the last areas of the great western frontier were being settled. For over 200 years, the frontier movement had been a major source of economic development. As land for new frontiers diminished, though, economic expansion moved in a very different direction. The nation rapidly became industrialized. With an abundance of natural resources and the growing technology to transform those resources into usable products, factories were built and an ever-expanding array of goods were produced. Jobs in the city factories were readily available to individuals who chose to leave the drudgery of farm work. Jobs in industry became an increasingly attractive alternative to that of eking out a living on small acreages of farmland, especially to young adults. Pay tended to be better, the working hours were fewer, the chances for advancement were greater, and the living conditions in the cities were far less primitive and harsh.[6]

Ironically, although industrialization greatly benefitted the rest of the American population economically, it had a negative effect on many elderly people. They no longer owned or controlled their work situations. Instead, their economic conditions depended entirely upon their being employed by others (usually large corporations). Whether or not they were employed and continued to be employed as they aged was controlled by employers whose primary concern was to produce as many goods as possible in order to make as much profit as possible. Employers tended to assume that older workers were not as efficient or productive as younger workers.[7] Thus, increasing numbers of elderly people became unemployed, especially during the 1920s. At the very time when much of the rest of the society enjoyed relative economic prosperity, increasing numbers of old people were experiencing poverty. The older they were, the poorer they tended to be.[8] Fischer reports that 23 percent of elderly Americans were economically dependent in 1910; by 1922, that figure had risen to 33 percent, and it was as high as 40 percent by 1930.[9]

Attempts to provide financial support for the elderly poor in the United States began with the development of pension plans by a few states as a result of pressure from a number of grassroots organizations. By 1933, most states had enacted at least modest pension plans despite the opposition of conservative politicians and judges.[10] With the advent of the Great Depression in the 1930s, however, state pensions did almost nothing to stop the spread of poverty among the aged. Finally, in 1935, Congress passed the Social Security Act, part of which was the establishment of a social insurance program that became the backbone of financial support for older people in this country.

It is important to examine the political motivation of the passage of this piece of legislation and the principles on which it was structured in order to understand its effect on the economic status of elderly people today. Part of the motivation for passing Social Security, to be sure, was to alleviate at least some of the economic woes of poverty-stricken, unemployed older workers. Politicians in the era of President Roosevelt's New Deal could no longer be insensitive to that kind of problem. An even more pressing problem in the depths of the Great Depression, though, was the fact that nearly one-fourth of the entire American work force was unemployed, and the economic structure of the nation was threatened with collapse. Young adults by the hundreds of thousands needed work in order to provide food and shelter for their families. Social Security was one of many pieces of legislation to help overcome the economic crisis that was crippling society. It would eliminate many older people from the unemployment lists as cheaply as possible. The initial benefits were by no means sufficient to lift any older people out of poverty. It would, however, give them a small monthly income and take them out of competition for the few precious jobs that were available or that were being created. As Schulz explains, "Old age pensions were provided to help the elderly financially but also to encourage them to leave or remain out of the work force."[11]

That this was initially, and has remained, a basic reason for the establishment of Social Security becomes apparent when we examine the principles on which the program was built. Those principles also show us the place that elderly people have in financing the program.

The old-age pension part of the Social Security law was based on six principles, as outlined by Schulz.[12] First, participation in the program was compulsory. With only a few exceptions, such as those who were self-employed, all American workers were required to contribute to the Social Security fund out of their monthly pay checks. By paying into the fund, they were eligible to receive retirement benefits from it when they retired. This principle does not mean that retirement itself was compulsory. The Social

Security program has never made retirement mandatory for anyone, even though one of the purposes of the law was clearly to encourage retirement from the work force.

The second principle of Social Security was that it was an *earnings-related system*. This program has often been referred to as a type of welfare for the aged. This principle clearly shows that assumption to be false. No one receives retirement benefits from the program except those who have first paid into it and their dependents, and each person contributes an amount based on earned wages. Subsequently, the amount received in benefits upon retirement is based on salary earned while working.

The third principle stated that Social Security would simply be *a floor of protection*. The intention was not to cover all of the financial needs of retired individuals. Workers were expected to prepare financially for their retirement years beyond the benefits they would be eligible to receive from Social Security. Given the level of poverty among the elderly and even among younger workers in 1935, this was certainly an unrealistic expectation. Nevertheless, it was all that could be hoped for at the time from a political perspective. As Fischer observes, "the astonishing fact about Social Security was not that it was passed in so conservative a form, but rather that it was passed at all in so conservative a nation."[13]

The fourth principle of Social Security was that the funds for the program were to come from *contributions* made by the workers themselves. Again, this was meant to be not a welfare program, but a social insurance program. Eligibility based on need has never been a part of Social Security. Instead, participants have earned the right to receive benefits because of having contributed as workers.

The program's fifth principle was what has been called *social adequacy*. Lower-income workers were to be somewhat favored. Therefore, a minimum income benefit was set, and salaries above a certain amount were neither subject to Social Security taxation nor considered in determining benefits.

The last principle on which Social Security was based was that a *retirement test* would be required before individuals could receive the income benefits for which they were eligible. It was clear from this that one of the major purposes of the program was to remove the aged from, and keep them out of, the work force. Although the retirement test has been somewhat liberalized since the 1930s, it has always been strictly followed. It is important to note that there are no restrictions on the amount of income individuals are allowed to earn in retirement as long as that income is not earned from employment. They may, for example, earn substantial incomes through investments, and those with money typically do. This very pointedly illustrates the fact that the modern economic system needs capital more than it needs workers in order to function.

In addition to the Old Age Insurance (OAI) pension program, the Social Security Act of 1935 also established Old Age Assistance (OAA), a welfare program for the elderly poor. Under OAA, states received federal grants to provide income assistance to their elderly poor. Within broad federal guidelines, states were allowed to set their own standards for eligibility and amount of assistance. Consequently, there was a great lack of uniformity from state to state as to who received the benefits and how adequate they were. Thus, in the 1974 Social Security Act revisions, the OAA program was changed to the Supplemental Security Income (SSI) program. Under this new program, eligibility criteria were set and a nationwide formula for benefits was standardized. Administration of the program was assigned to the Social Security Administration. In essence, SSI specified a minimal guaranteed income for all elderly Americans. If they have no other source of income, the total specified amount is provided from SSI funds. If individuals receive small amounts of income from other sources, then SSI will make up the balance in order to bring their total incomes up to the specified amount. That amount does not lift recipients out of poverty, however.

Many people confuse the SSI and OAI programs. They are, however, quite different. SSI is a welfare program funded out of the general federal budget (not from the Social Security retirement fund). In contrast, OAI is a social insurance program, the benefits of which are reserved for those who have participated by contributing to the fund. About the only similarities between the two programs are that (1) both target elderly people, and (2) both are administered by the Social Security Administration.

An increasing amount of financial support for the older population today is coming from private pension programs. Pension programs are provided by private employers, government agencies, labor unions, and professional groups as part of the benefit packages for their worker constituents. Employers have developed pension programs and even make contributions to pension funds in behalf of their employees as a way of influencing them to continue working with them.[14]

Typically, a percentage of employees' regular pay checks is placed in pension funds that are reserved for them. Records are kept of the amounts that individuals or their employers, or both, have paid into the fund. The accumulated funds plus the interest they earn throughout individuals' working years become available to them as retirement incomes.

At retirement, individuals typically have three types of options for receiving the money they have accrued. First, most programs usually give individuals the option of taking their pension funds out in one lump sum. Almost no one chooses this option for the simple reason that the tax rate on that much money makes it prohibitive. A second option is to divide the available money over a fixed number of years and take it out in monthly payments. This type of option involves the risk that a person may live beyond the fixed number of years, during which no pension income will be available to them. A third option for individual retirees is to settle for somewhat lower monthly incomes, but with the promise that they will continue to receive monthly checks for the rest of their lives. This option represents no risk to the fund itself since monthly payments are set on the basis of the interest being earned on those funds. The total amount of individually accrued funds remains available to the program for investment.

Except in the case of the first option, funds accrued to individuals still in the pension fund at the time of their death do not become part of those individuals' estates. Instead, they become the property of the on-going funds and continue to be available as a source of income for whatever entity is sponsoring the program (insurance companies, banks, employer organizations, unions, professional groups, and so on).

For a number of years, there were serious problems with many private pension programs in the United States. Some were too small and too poorly managed to guarantee their continued existence. There were no eligibility standards or controls. Consequently, many workers who had paid into pension funds for years found upon retirement either that no funds were available for their pensions or that they were not eligible to receive them. In 1974, Congress passed the Employment Retirement Income Security Act (ERISA) to insure against those kinds of injustices. Among other provisions, this legislation (1) outlined vesting programs (specifications of when participants have been in the plan long enough to receive full benefits) to be followed by all pension plans; (2) required that certain funding standards be set to guard against the fund's unnecessarily going bankrupt; (3) required annual reporting to participants; and (4) established the Guaranty Benefit Corporation with a government-controlled fund to guarantee benefits if a pension fund went bankrupt.[15] This has not only made it possible for employees to plan for their retirements with much greater confidence, but it has increased the amount of money accumulated in pension funds across the country. Olson reports that by 1979, 40 percent of the women and 55 percent of the men working in the private sector in the United States were covered by private pensions.[16] She also reports that the amount of money in pension funds has increased enormously in the past two or three decades. For example, between 1960 and 1980, the amount accrued in retirement funds grew from $73 billion, representing 4 percent of outstanding stock in the United States, to $653 billion, representing between 20 and 25 percent of total stocks of companies listed on the New York and American exchanges. She concludes that "rather than assuring adequate retirement income and economic security for the vast majority of older people, a major goal of private, state, and local trusts is capital formation."[17] Clearly, then, elderly people are making a major economic contribution through the provision of needed capital funds.

Despite a number of improvements in providing financial support for older people in the United States in recent years, the adequacy of that support remains in question. On the one hand, a number of cross-sectional studies have reported that the financial condition of the elderly population in general has improved in recent years. Harris studied the income statistics of elderly people between 1945 and 1980 and concluded that there were no declines throughout that period. In fact, he reported improvements of incomes of the aged relative to others, especially between 1967 and 1977. He attributes these statistics to improvements in Social Security and pension fund benefits.[18] Similarly, Moon looked at changes in income levels of the aged compared to others in the United States between 1980 and 1984. She found the elderly suffered far less of a decrease in income benefits than did other groups. She also assumed that this was due to improvements in Social Security.[19]

On the other hand, recent studies of the economic conditions of specific groups of older people and longitudinal studies of the economics of old age reveal a much less optimistic picture. The rates of poverty among minority elderly people are much higher than those of the white majority. In 1977, for example, only 11.9 percent of elderly whites were poverty stricken, compared with 21.9 percent of Hispanics and 36.3 percent of blacks.[20]

Poverty has also been found to be much more prevalent among elderly women, especially widows, than among men. Warlick has provided evidence for her statement that poverty in old age "has become and will continue to be largely a woman's problem." She found that the basic reason for the relative deprivation of elderly women in this country is that when they become widowed, the retirement systems upon which they must rely for income fail to provide the necessary support. As she points out, "Social Security benefits are reduced," and "private pensions may cease altogether."[21] Another study of changes in the incomes of older women from 1960 to 1980 found that, in absolute terms, older women tended to have higher incomes in 1980 than in 1960. More important, though, the drop in incomes that the elderly women tended to experience in 1980 as they moved into old age was much greater than they had been in 1960. In terms of the living standards represented by their incomes, elderly women today are not really any better off than they were in 1960.[22]

It has long been recognized that widowhood is closely associated with poverty among elderly people. It has generally been assumed that women are financially hurt but that men are not. A recent study has shown that this assumption tends to be misleading, however. Zick and Smith conducted a longitudinal study of financial changes that a group of nonpoor elderly couples experienced over a 12-year period. They found that those in the sample who tended to suffer severe economic losses were those who became widowed. Nearly half of those who experienced the loss of a spouse during the 12-year period spent at least one year out of the first five years of widowhood in poverty. Surprisingly, widowers and widows suffered similar financial losses. Neither group recovered those losses quickly.[23] The study provides no evidence of why the widowed experience such financial losses. One possible explanation that tends to be ignored in the literature on widows is the cost of caregiving that often precedes the loss of one's spouse, in terms of such aspects as loss of jobs and medical treatment. Regardless of the costs of widowhood, though, financial losses are apparently as much related to the processes of becoming widowed as they are to the differential treatment between males and females.

Furthermore, it has been discovered that poverty is still much more related to old age in general than much of the cross-sectional data on poverty rates would indicate. Evidence of this was provided by a longitudinal study of the changing income patterns of a nationwide sample of over 4,000 elderly heads of households. Respondents were interviewed every two years over a 10-year period between 1968 and 1978. It was found, once again, that women tended to be plunged into poverty with the loss of their husbands. As many as 80 percent of them also eventually escaped from poverty during the ten years, however. It was discovered, too, that poverty was by no means confined to widowhood. Couples often experienced it just before one of them became widowed. In addition, even among the continuously married couples, as many as 20.9 percent of them experienced at least one episode of poverty during the 10-year study period. The overall conclusions from the study were that (1) there is considerable movement in and out of poverty among the elderly, including both couples and those who are widowed; and (2) while most people do eventually escape from poverty, that escape tends to be temporary.[24]

Obviously, the risks of poverty among the aged in the United States are much greater than annual poverty-rate statistics would lead us to believe. In addition, Uehara and colleagues have found that, even though the actual cash benefits to elderly welfare recipients were not cut as much as were benefits for others on welfare in the 1980s, they endured even more cutbacks in terms of other benefits, such as food stamps and health care.[25]

ECONOMICS OF AGING IN OTHER CULTURES

That old people are dependent is by no means a universally shared belief. Neither is the discrepancy between the financial situations of elderly men and women universal.

With regard to sexual equality of financial resources of the aged, a comparative study of ten different nations between 1960 and 1980 was conducted. It was found that the financial situation of both men and women improved over the 20-year period. In five of those countries (Australia, West Germany, the Netherlands, New Zealand, and the United Kingdom), there was absolute financial parity between men and women; but in the other five (Finland, France, Switzerland, Sweden, and the United States), men improved much more than women.[26] Parity is generally achieved by establishing pension benefits on the basis of either flat rates for retirees or rates that reflect a share of material economic growth. The countries that favor men tend to base pensions, at least in part, on the work histories of retirees. These systems have generally provided increased benefits for both men and women but have benefited men much more than women because of disparities in employee salaries. These disparities were not reflective of either the adequacy of old people's incomes or the extent to which they were financially independent, however.

In 1976, Pendrell noted that early retirement was becoming a pattern not only in the United States but throughout the world. This, she contended, would mean mounting social costs that would alarm economists and government workers of the nations of the world.[27] This type of analysis reflects the rather common notion, which has prevailed in the United States for some time, that equates pensions for the aged with economic dependency. Many gerontologists have also made this assumption. Pendrell quoted Cottrell as saying, for example, that "business is simply not going to take adequate care of most of the aging," when reflecting on the inadequacy of the incomes of most elderly Americans in the 1960s.

Undoubtedly, the dependency perspective is largely determined by the cultural contexts in which the provision of financial support for the aged takes place. It also depends upon the extent to which the provision of financial old-age benefits are personalized or collectivized.

The elderly in Japan represent an informative study in this respect. On the one hand, as explained in Chapter 9, the claim has been made that employers provide their workers with lifetime economic security. If that were true, workers would tend to stay with their employers throughout their careers and would enjoy economic security in old age. Indeed, Palmore and Maeda report that the average family income for households headed by persons 65 and over in 1955 amounted to 90 percent of the average of all Japanese households in 1982. They also report that more elderly people in Japan than in any other industrial nation claim to have adequate incomes.[28]

On the other hand, Levine reports findings to show that lifetime relationships with employers are actually not typical of Japanese workers. They seem to have little or no reluctance to change jobs in order to pursue new career opportunities. Lifetime relationships may once have been a cultural ideal, but they are no longer widely practiced.[29] Furthermore, the relative financial well-being of elderly people's households in Japan is undoubtedly due to the fact that many of the elderly remain employed. In 1981, over half of those 65 to 69 years old, and almost 40 percent of those 70 to 74 were still in the work force. As many as 18 percent of even those 80 and over were still working.[30] For those who live on pensions, the wage-replacement value of those pensions averaged only 41 percent, about the same as it is for retirees in the United States and less than it is for those in West Germany.[31] Palmore and Maeda also report that a shift has been occurring among the Japanese elderly away from the idea that economic security is a family responsibility and toward a dependency on social security, pensions, and savings.[32] Concepts of economic dependency among the aged, similar to those in the United States, seem to be developing in Japan.

An analysis of the economic situation of the aged in the People's Republic of China provides important insights. A combination of the influences of Oriental traditions and socialism have served to create a rather unique economic situation for the older population. As Treas points out, there have been forces in that country since the Communist takeover in 1949 that have increased the power and prestige of younger people. Laws have been passed and official practices established to eliminate the filial piety traditions and to undermine the economic authority of the elderly within families. The whole Cultural Revolution, much of which was aimed at the final elimination of traditional authority, was carried out by youth.[33] Nevertheless, elderly people in China today tend to retire at ages 55 or 60 with pensions that equal from 70 to 90 percent of their employment wages. Furthermore, their retirement benefits are viewed neither as burdens on the younger, employed population nor as symbols of dependency.

There are three basic reasons that the Chinese elderly have not been viewed as economically dependent, as those in industrialized nations tend to be. First, they typically contribute financially to their families on an approximately equal basis with their adult children. Their retirement income, from which they contribute to household maintenance, is often equal to the salaries of the adult children with whom they live. In most households in which the elderly live, four salaries are contributed to the costs of those households. Younger couples who live with elderly parents therefore tend to be financially better off than those who do not.[34]

The second reason that the aged in China have not generally been viewed as dependent is related to the way in which retirement benefits have been financed. They have not been provided out of funds that come from taxes on individual workers' incomes, as is the case in many capitalist countries. Neither have they come from the national government. Instead, they were paid out of profits made by the collective production units to which workers belong. Therefore, younger workers have perceived no sense of burden, since their work-related incomes were not directly involved and many of them directly benefited from their parents' retirement pensions.[35] The ways in which this system may change as a result of economic reforms in that country remain to be seen.

The third reason that the elderly in China are not considered economically dependent is related to the economic reforms being instituted in that country today. Families in urban areas are now allowed to develop small businesses, and those in rural areas are permitted to farm plots of land for their own profit. These businesses and farms tend to be cooperative intergenerational family ventures. Retired family members often do much of the work of the family businesses while younger adults are at their jobs.

Although the elderly in China tend to retire from paid jobs at relatively young ages and receive relatively generous financial benefits, they are not generally viewed as dependent. They make direct and obvious economic contributions to their families and, in turn, to their communities. In addition, they are eliminated from an increasingly competitive labor force.

The financial situation of still another, very unique cultural group provides further insights about the relative dependence of elderly people. Native Americans in the United States are often lumped together as one of many minority groups, but each of the native American tribes has a unique culture. An analysis of the elderly in the largest of these tribal groups, the Navajos, in terms of both their minority status and their cultural traditions, provides us with some valuable information.

Culturally, the kinship system has been the center of their social and economic lives. Family and clan relationships were built around the sharing of available resources and around mutual obligations to care for one another. These traditions of sharing and family interdependence are still quite prevalent today, particularly among the older members of the tribe.

The Navajos also have some of the same minority-group characteristics as other minorities. The younger generation has increasingly become dependent upon jobs for financial support, and relatively few jobs are available to them on the reservation. Consequently, the unemployment and poverty rates among them are extremely high. Many younger adults have little or no sources of income.

As a twist of fate, many elderly Navajos are eligible to receive minimum amounts of income in the form of either Social Security or SSI benefits. Those small amounts of monthly income give them something important to share with their needy family members. As Foner explains, "In poor communities where cash is hard to come by, old-age pensioners provide a steady source of income for their households, sometimes becoming the mainstay of their domestic economy."[36]

There is a tendency on the part of some service workers to define this as exploitation on the part of the family members involved. In a 1986 survey of Navajo elder abuse, however, every one of the elderly people who admitted that some of their money had gone to family members said that they had voluntarily shared what they had. They insisted that that was what they wanted to do and should do. The family members who received the help often provided the elderly people with needed care. The survey showed, in fact, that, by and large, Navajo families respond in whatever ways they can when their elderly members need care.[37]

Although the majority of Navajo elderly fall below the poverty line, they are not viewed as economically dependent by either their families or the tribe. Instead, they are seen as financially independent and even as making important financial contributions to their families. The relationships are generally characterized by mutual dependency or interdependency.

CONCLUSION

Four basic issues have been dealt with in this chapter: (1) the financial well-being of elderly people; (2) the sources of their financial support; (3) the public view of their economic dependence or independence; and (4) their financial contributions to the economies of the nations in which they live. There are major cross-cultural differences regarding each of these concerns.

Ironically, the financial situation of the elderly, relative to others in their societies, is better in the poorer of the cultural groups we have examined. It is also in those cultural groups that elderly people are recognized as making important economic contributions and are not defined as economically dependent and burdensome.

In the highly industrialized and economically affluent societies, the tendency is to fund old-age support from taxes on individual salaries and to politicize the processes of providing pensions. One of the consequences of this tendency has been to define the older population as a burden and to provide inadequate support.

The problem is that much of the rationale for defining the elderly as economically dependent and burdensome is based on false assumptions. Sheppard and Rix, for example, make the case that as the American population grows older, it will be increasingly impossible for the nation to support older people in retirement.[38] Despite these kinds of arguments, there is still a distinct tendency for employers in this country to encourage early retirement because they see it as economically beneficial. The policy also continues to be favored by younger workers seeking jobs and fighting for promotions. In fact, even as the older population continues to grow, the competition for jobs also seems to be increasing.

Three important factors are ignored in the argument that old people are an economically dependent and burdensome part of the population. First, with an increasingly technologically based system of production less, not more, human labor is needed. Elderly people are simply not needed in the work force. In fact, their continued participation in it tends to stifle the economic advancement of younger adults.

Second, modern production companies need capital far more than they need labor. As we have seen, the aged are making a major contribution to this aspect of the overall economy in the form of pension funds. This in itself ought to be enough for the rest of society to recognize that older people are not economically dependent and burdensome.

Third, the highly productive units of modern societies badly need markets. Consumer markets are probably the greatest source of stimulation to the economy. Obviously, consumerism is an important part of retirement today. Leisure among the retired populations of the world has created large and vital consumer markets.

NOTES

[1] Harold L. Sheppard and Sara E. Rix,*The Graying of Working America: The Coming Crisis in Retirement-Age Policy* (New York: Free Press, 1977), pp.13–35.

[2] Henry S. Sharp, "Old Age Among the Chipewyan," in *Other Ways of Growing Old: Anthropological Perspectives,* ed. P. T. Amoss and S. Harrell (Stanford, Calif.: Stanford University Press, 1981), pp. 99–109.

[3] Tom Sheehan, "Senior Esteem as a Factor of Socioeconomic Complexity," *The Gerontologist,* 16, no. 5 (October 1976), 433–40.

[4] John B. Williamson, Linda Evans, and Lawrence A. Powell, *The Politics of Aging: Power and Policy* (Springfield, Ill.: Chas. C Thomas, 1982), p. 5.

[5] David Hackett Fischer, *Growing Old in America* (New York: Oxford University Press, 1978), pp. 52–58.

[6] W. Andrew Achenbaum, *Shades of Gray: Old Age, American Values, and Federal Policies Since 1920* (Boston: Little, Brown, 1983), pp. 9–10.

[7] Laura K. Olson, *The Political Economy of Aging: The State, Private Power, and Social Welfare* (New York: Columbia University Press, 1982), pp. 33–34.

[8] W. Andrew Achenbaum, "The Obsolescence of Old Age," in *Dimensions of Aging: Readings,* eds. Jon Hendricks and C. Davis Hendricks (Cambridge, Mass.: Winthrop, 1979), pp. 21–37.

[9] Fischer, *Growing Old in America,* p. 174.

[10] Ibid., pp. 175–176.

[11] James H. Schulz, *The Economics of Aging* (Belmont, Calif.: Wadsworth, 1980), p. 93.

[12] Ibid., pp. 94–95.

[13] Fischer, *Growing Old in America,* p. 184.

[14] Olson, *The Political Economy of Aging,* p. 82.

[15] Ibid., p. 5.

[16] Ibid., p. 81.

[17] Ibid., p. 100.

[18] Richard Harris, "Recent Trends in the Relative Economic Status of Older Adults," *Journal of Gerontology,* 41, no. 3. (May 1986), 401–7.

[19] Marilyn Moon, "Impact of the Reagan Years on the Distribution of Income of the Elderly," *The Gerontologist,* 26, no. 1 (February 1986), 32–37.

[20] Jacquelyne J. Jackson, *Minorities and Aging* (Belmont, Calif.: Wadsworth, 1980), p. 144.

[21] Jennifer L. Warlick, "Why is Poverty After 65 a Woman's Problem?" *Journal of Gerontology,* 40, no. 6 (November 1985), 751–57.

[22] Peter Uhlenberg and Anne P. Salmon, "Change in Relative Income of Older Women, 1960–1980," *The Gerontologist,* 26, no. 2 (April 1986), 164–70.

[23] Cathleen D. Zick and Ken R. Smith, "Immediate and Delayed Effects of Widowhood on Poverty: Patterns from the 1970s," *The Gerontologist,* 26, no. 6 (December 1986), 669–75.

[24] Karen C. Holden, Richard V. Burkhauser, and Daniel A. Meyers, "Income Transitions at Older Stages of Life: The Dynamics of Poverty," *The Gerontologist,* 26, no. 3 (June 1986), 292–97.

[25] Edwina S. Uehara, Scott Geron, and Sandra K. Beeman, "The Elderly Poor in the Reagan Era," *The Gerontologist,* 26, no. 1 (February 1986), 48–55.

[26] Martin B. Tracy and Roxanne L. Ward, "Trends in Old-Age Pensions for Women: Benefit Levels in Ten Nations, 1960–1980," *The Gerontologist,* 26, no. 3 (June 1986), 286–91.

[27] Nan Pendrell, "Old Age Around the World," *Social Policy,* 7, no. 3. (1976), 107–10.

[28] Erdman B. Palmore and Daisaku Maeda, *The Honorable Elders Revisited* (Durham, N.C.: Duke University Press, 1985), pp. 71–76.

[29] Solomon B. Levine, "Careers and Mobility in Japan's Labor Market," in *Work and Lifecourse in Japan,* ed. David W. Plath (Albany, N.Y.: State University of New York, 1983), pp. 18–33.

[30] Palmore and Maeda, *The Honorable Elders,* p. 50.

[31] Ibid., p. 78.

[32] Ibid., pp. 74–75.

[33] Judith Treas, "Socialist Organization and Economic Development in China: Latent Consequences for the Aged," *The Gerontologist,* 19, no. 1 (February 1979), 34–43.

[34] Ibid.

[35] Arnold S. Brown, "Social Policy of Aging in Mainland China," (unpublished report of an informal study of the social policy on aging in China, Summer 1984).

[36] Nancy Foner, *Ages in Conflict* (New York: Columbia University Press, 1984), p. 218.

[37] Arnold S. Brown, "Report on Navajo Elder Abuse," (unpublished research report submitted to the Navajo Office on Aging, Window Rock, Arizona, Fall 1986), pp. 14–15.

[38] Sheppard and Rix, *The Graying of Working America*, pp. 13–35.

12

Retirement as a Social Institution

INTRODUCTION

Retirement is rapidly becoming an institutionalized part of the modern world. More and more people in many societies are moving into retirement, and it is increasingly accepted as an inevitable part of the life cycle. Furthermore, in contrast to common misconceptions, a fairly large majority of people today actually look forward to it and enjoy it. Then, too, it serves a fairly well-defined societal need in those societies in which it is practiced.

Retirement is a concept that requires definition. There is a great deal of confusion in the gerontological literature about how to define it, depending upon the perspective from which it is discussed. Part of the definitional confusion has to do with the relationship of retirement to three other concepts: (1) work, (2) leisure, and (3) volunteerism. Retirement must be defined and discussed in terms of not only *from* what, but also *to* what people retire.

Part of the definitional problem is also how those concepts relate to one another in the context of old-age experiences. A historical analysis of each of these concepts and their relationship to one another will help us to understand more about the meaning of retirement to the elderly. Just as important, it may provide us with some insights about potential future meanings of retirement.

CHANGING CONCEPTS OF WORK AND THEIR EFFECT
ON THE AGED

Work and its effect on peoples' lives, especially during the twentieth century, is central to the meaning of retirement. Work has always been, and still is, a vital part of the daily lives of people of all cultures. Yet what is considered work and how individuals experience the world of work has changed quite drastically.

Work is often equated with activity—keeping busy physically or mentally. That kind of definition does not capture the essence of what work is all about, however. Work has economic, social, psychological, and even religious significance.

First and foremost, work has been an economic necessity throughout history. Primitive and modern societies alike have depended upon the physical and mental efforts of their members to produce goods and services for their survival. Work, then, is not merely human activity, but activity that has productive purpose and is conducted with an economic obligation.

Marx contended that economics was the basis of all human life, and that workers were the most vital part of economics. He referred to economics as the ship of life and all other aspects of life as merely the superstructure, built on top of and totally dependent upon the economic structures. In the final analysis, it is economics that determines human values, beliefs, and norms.

As important as economics may be to our lives, however, it is by no means the only reason that work has been important to the human experience. Weber challenged Marx's ideas. His contention was that religious beliefs, more than economic significance, gave meaning to work, at least in that particular time and place. According to Weber, the theological perspective of Protestant Christianity had come to determine European attitudes about work. For most Europeans, work amounted to nothing less than a calling by God. In that context, more than anything, work was the symbol of their commitment to God and of their faithfulness to that calling. Their success in their work was a sign that God had indeed called them and was blessing them. That they also produced necessary goods and services for secular societies in which they lived was of only secondary importance to them.

From the perspective of what Weber termed "the Protestant ethic," as well as from an economic perspective, it was important that everyone worked. Pursuit of their Christian calling was as vital to the Protestant Christians' sense of religious well-being and relationships with God as worship or any other part of their religious lives.

Much of this particular religious connotation of work has been lost today. Nevertheless, its influence is still felt. The work ethic remains very much intact. In effect it says that work, for its own sake, is important, regardless of its social or economic utility. A general norm seems to exist that, regardless of the kind of work people do, it is important that they work. As Morse and Weiss discovered in a 1950s study on the function and meaning of work, "for many individuals, commitment to working is much deeper than commitment to their particular jobs."[1]

The Marxist idea of work was not religious, but it was certainly ideological. It was an integral part not just of economics in general, but of a particular economic philosophy. The idea was that everyone should work not merely to produce needed goods and services but because the division between workers and capitalists was wrong. That kind of division caused alienation among individuals and within society as a whole and created inevitable and serious social conflict. The economic structure in China under Mao Tse Tung illustrates this philosophy. Everyone belonged to work units and everyone who was able worked, regardless of whether that much labor was really needed. Technology that would have advanced productivity and stimulated economic growth was never allowed to develop under Mao because it was important that everyone work.

Very closely associated with the religious and ideological orientation of work is the social psychological significance of work. Due to its religious importance in some societies and because of its economic importance in all societies, work is generally an important part of most societal value sytems.

From the societal perspective, work is part of the behavior expected of all able-bodied individuals. Some form of sanctions tend to be applied to those who fail to comply with that expectation, and rewards are given to those who comply. The division of labor is one of the most important parts of the social structure.

From an individual perspective, work is a major source of social status, power, and prestige, as well as a means of making a living in order to provide for self and family. It typically becomes not merely a social obligation but also a major life orientation—a career. It provides individuals with a sense of belonging, a personal identity, and a sense of purpose. Working is often thought of as a right that individuals do not want to lose. For some the loss of the right to work represents the loss of self.

Retirement, then, would seem to be a major adjustment problem for people in most societies. Indeed some studies show that to be true. A study in Great Britain in 1977 of the attitudes of men and women, aged 50 to 72, revealed that as many as 65 percent of them were either unhappy or ambivalent about the prospect of retiring.[2] In China today, in an era of economic reform, women are expected to retire five years earlier than men. This is a country in which work outside the home was not even available to women before 1949. Yet many Chinese women today are protesting the expectation that they will retire earlier than men. Sixty-two percent of the women questioned about this in a survey said that they wanted to postpone their retirements.[3]

In the United States, retirement has become quite widely accepted. Yet even among fairly well-adjusted retirees, Ekerdt observed that the work ethic directly influences their behavior patterns. While their lives may no longer be directly controlled by the work ethic, they tend to act on the basis of something very much akin to it—namely, "the busy ethic."[4] This behavioral approach to retirement has a number of purposes, according to Ekerdt. First, it makes retirement more closely fit mainstream social values. Second, it symbolically defends against the appearance of aging. Third, it tends to legitimize leisure activities in retirement.

There can be little doubt that work has been a vital part of the human experience, both from an individual and societal perspective. It has always been so for men, and it has become increasingly so for women. This raises an important question about the acceptance of retirement: How is it possible to reconcile work and retirement, either conceptually or experientially? Part of the answer to that dilemma has to do with the changing nature of work.

Two historical technological developments related to economics have brought about drastic changes in how humans perform their work and in what work means to them. Agricultural technology made it possible to produce more goods and services with less work than was possible in hunting and gathering societies. Families were able to settle into stabilized communities. A division of labor became possible, and specialties in work began to develop.

Societies were now lifted a step above simple survival. Few able-bodied persons were exempted from the need to work. Yet certain types of work required little physical strength, and some luxuries became possible. It was also possible to incorporate limited amounts of pleasurable activities, unrelated to work, into the life-styles of families and communities. Leisure as a reward for work became part of the orientation of life.

Agricultural technology by no means diminished the importance of work for individuals or societies. In fact, it made it possible for elderly people to continue to work and enjoy long careers even after hard physical labor was no longer possible. It also introduced leisure as an integral part of life, albeit on a very limited basis. As Miller has explained, "The preindustrial culture based on an agricultural economy and rural in character . . . did not separate work and leisure, nor did the demands of labor segment the life of the person into a world of work and another of the family."[5]

Industrial technology is the second development that has tended to change the nature and meaning of work. With industrialization, both the place of work and the types of work have changed. The place of work moved away from the home setting to the office, the factory, and the marketplace. The type of work changed progressively from hard, unskilled labor toward that demanding the technical skills needed to run the increasingly sophisticated industrial machinery. The division of labor increased dramatically, with specialization being more strictly defined in narrower terms. Training and education became increasingly necessary in order to perform the specialized labor, and further technology soon made existing specialities obsolete.

Where, when, and how individuals worked was controlled, not by the workers themselves, but by bosses and corporate managers. Thus workers could no longer plan and implement productive processes from beginning to end.

Instead, they tended to be confined to just one aspect of those processes, and work became extremely routinized.

Kando describes the way in which industrialization changed the nature of work as follows:

> Scientific technology led to the Industrial Revolution. During the successive stages of a revolution that has yet to be concluded, handcraft was first superceded by mechanical production of commodities; subsequently machines were built that built other machines; finally machines were built to regulate themselves. As mechanization, automation, and finally cybernation succeeded each other, man's role could be expected to be reduced, or elevated, to that of decision maker rather than operator.[6]

Work in industrial settings has become extremely monotonous and competitive, even in the service industries. Labor unions have been formed to make jobs more secure and to improve working conditions, but they have done nothing to alleviate the problems of either the monotony of work or the competition for jobs. Both of these problems at least potentially undermine the meaning and importance of work to individuals. Competition inevitably informs workers that their skills are no longer necessary in the production of goods and services. The meaning of work, then, is confined to one or more of the following: (1) the intrinsic value of the particular job to the individual; (2) its value as a means of providing for self and family; or (3) its value as a means of keeping active. If there is no intrinsic value to the work one does, and if there are other, more challenging ways of providing for self and family and of keeping busy, we in the modern world would presumably be inclined to opt for the alternatives. Given the competition involved in training for and acquiring jobs, it is little wonder that retirement is attractive to elderly people in today's industrial and postindustrial world. Older adults seldom have the advantage in training and job competition.

THE EMERGENCE OF RETIREMENT POLICIES AND SYSTEMS

What is retirement and what does it mean to elderly people who retire? First, the emergence of and the institutionalization of retirement in the world today is very much related to the changing nature of work. Specifically, retirement policies have been developed by employers as the most feasible means of solving today's labor-related problems. More than anything else, therefore, retirement means the separation of individuals and groups from the labor force. That was the basis on which the initial retirement policies were set, and it remains the rationale for their continuation today. To be sure, retirement holds other, more subjective, meanings for those who anticipate and experience it, but those meanings are generally by-products of its relationship to the labor force. According to that kind of definition, those who are still part of the official labor force are not retired, while those outside that group can rightfully be considered retired. It is from that perspective that we will begin our analysis of the emergence of retirement. From there we will look at what else it has become.

Retirement is often treated from what Graebner terms "the mythology of individual responsibility." It is as though the aged initiated it and continue to support it for the benefits it offers them. He points out that its real beginnings and its actual economic functions have largely been ignored. The result has been "a form of blaming the victim."[7] This approach is well illustrated by the emphasis in recent literature on the concept of the dependency ratio and the great economic burden that it is said to represent. Sheppard and Rix argue about the burden of the dependency of older people in the United States,[8] and Rix and Fisher give it an international focus.[9] Ironically, the basis for these analyses is not actual finances but the demographics of aging—the ratio of those over 65 to those 16 to 64—and the assumption that that defines economic dependency.

In fact, retirement policies were developed precisely for the benefit of economics and were initiated by those in charge of the corporate structures. As Graebner explains, "The history of retirement reflects the changing methodologies of American capitalism in the nineteenth and twentieth centuries."[10] Before corporations controlled the productive process and the labor on which they depended, retirement was not a well-developed concept. There was an informal expectation that older workers would voluntarily retire, or at least take on less demanding types of jobs, when they could no longer perform the work that was required. No mandatory retirement policies existed, however.

By 1885, corporations had become the basic economic units, and retirement policies began to emerge, with the agreement of leaders in both business and labor. According to Graebner, this was very much related to the problems of an increasing labor surplus and the assumption that young people were more efficient workers. As he puts it, "For business, retirement meant reduced unemployment, lower rates of turnover, a younger, more efficient, and more conservative work force; for labor, it was in part a way of transferring work from one generation to another in industries with a surplus of workers."[11] Similarly, in studying retirement in Great Britain, Parker concluded that it is "not something that has been fashioned by human aspirations. It is closely associated with the growth of bureaucracy, government organizations, and large companies which have their own reasons for 'retiring' older employees."[12]

An important component of the rationale for retiring older workers has been the assumption that they are less efficient than younger workers. Yet in periods when labor for industry was in short supply, the push for retirement policies was eased and older workers were, in fact, encouraged to remain at work. During World War II, for example, elderly workers staffed defense factories and the production of military supplies flourished. After the war, when there was once again an abundance of workers, strict mandatory policies were put in place and older workers were once again labeled as less efficient. Graebner contends that retirement policies and age discrimination emerged at the same time, not by coincidence, but because retirement was the easiest means available to deal with the problem of surplus labor. It was both impersonal and gave the appearance of being egalitarian.[13]

Early in the process of setting retirement policies, pensions were developed to legitimize them. Weak and inadequate as many of them were, they provided incentives for individual workers to retire, and they promised retirees financial support. Some were private pensions, provided by employers, and others were public, provided by government entities. The types of financial support (private pensions, public pensions, publicly provided old-age assistance) have been related to society's defining the aged as economically dependent. As in the United States, government support for the aged in Great Britain has come from both contributory pension programs and noncontributory old-age assistance. Even though both government support and private pensions were provided as an incentive to retire, government support, especially in the form of old-age assistance, as Parker puts it, "brought an abrupt transition from independence to dependence" on the part of those in retirement.[14]

A slightly different pattern has taken place among elderly workers in modern, industrialized Japan. The larger firms in particular have promised their workers pensions to support them throughout their lives and have tended to set mandatory retirement policies at relatively young ages, typically 60 years of age for men and 55 for women. According to Maeda, the problem is that the pensions are seldom enough for retirees to live on, and pensioners are therefore forced to find other, lower-paying jobs.[15] It is ironic also that, as Cowgill has observed, people in developing nations are asked to retire at even earlier ages than in developed nations.[16]

It would seem, from this historical analysis of retirement, that elderly workers are being victimized and that they might therefore be expected to resist retirement policies. Evidence that this may be true comes from the struggle to pass antimandatory retirement legislation in the United States in the 1970s. The fact that legislation was passed in 1978 to severely restrict mandatory retirement policies before the age of 70 would seem to indicate something of a victory for resistance to retirement. Graebner provides quite a different interpretation of what was behind that legislation, however. He makes the point that it was passed "only when influential elements within American capitalism had concluded that retirement as then constituted was unduly costly as well as inefficient in allocating labor."[17] It might be more correct to assume that such legislation became possible when government officials began to see the elderly as dependent and too costly to support. Furthermore, there are indications that very few elderly people actively supported the bill. Most supported it in principle, but left it to key political figures like Claude Pepper to fight for it.

Ironically, indications are that older workers, instead of opposing the retirement systems that seem to have been imposed on them, have largely accepted them. They have generally welcomed the pension plans and supported the reality of retirement.[18] Maeda reports that the same is true in Japan.[19] The question of why this is true leads us to an examination of the subjective meaning of retirement.

SUBJECTIVE MEANING OF RETIREMENT

What has the institution of retirement come to mean to elderly people them-selves? Why have they retired? What have their attitudes been as they have faced retirement and after they have retired?

Most elderly people, in fact, choose to retire.[20] An important question, though, is, why? Some benevolent reasons are often overlooked. In the early days, when retirement was just beginning to be considered, no substantial financial support systems had been established and poverty was typical among retirees. Yet even then, many elderly people were willing to sacrifice their own jobs in favor of younger workers.[21] The struggle of the Townsend movement in the 1920s, for example, was not to restore lost job opportunities, but to gain financial support in retirement.

Motivation to retire can be analyzed from two perspectives: (1) objective factors that correlate with their retirement patterns and (2) the reasons they themselves give for retiring. We will look at data from both of these perspectives.

Palmore and a group of associates recently reviewed and compared a number of longitudinal studies on retirement that had been conducted in the 1960s and 1970s. Their analyses provide us with many insights about both the causes and the consequences of retirement. The group found five major factors that had been emphasized as potential predictors of retirement: (1) demographic characteristics, such as age, marital status, and number of dependents; (2) socioeconomic status; (3) health; (4) job characteristics; and (5) attitudes toward work and retirement.

Data from these studies indicated that of those five variables, by far the strongest predictors of retirement were socioeconomic status and job characteristics. Contrary to findings from some cross-sectional studies, though, health and attitudinal variables were relatively unimportant as predictors of retirement at age 65. Instead, poor health was found to be a major reason for early retirement.[22] Those with poor health not only tended to retire early, but they also tended to have poorer attitudes about retirement. Thus, poor health is not a result of retirement, as is often assumed.[23] Instead, when retirees have poor health, it has typically been a precondition of, and even a reason for, their retirement. The negative attitudes about retirement associated with early retirement also tend to be more a result of the poor health than of retirement itself. It has often been supposed that having to retire is causally linked to acquiring health problems and even dying. As Robinson and her colleagues point out, these suppositions are based on clinical impressions without solid evidence of real causal relationships, but they have nevertheless had an influence on some key aging issues.[24] Longitudinal studies, such as those reviewed by Palmore and co-workers, are therefore important in that they clearly show that the causal link tends to be in the opposite direction. Keith also discovered, in a longitudinal study on retirement among unmarried elderly people, that poor health was especially hard on those who had never been married. Because they tended to lack adequate family support groups, health problems threatened their ability to maintain a semblance of independence.[25]

As noted, socioeconomic status and job characteristics turned out to be the strongest predictors of retirement in the longitudinal studies. Specifically, those with greater socioeconomic resources in their work situations generally tended to be more reluctant to retire. This very much depended upon the kinds of jobs they held, however. Not surprisingly, individuals tended to more regularly retire if retirement was mandatory or if they had pensions than if those conditions did not exist. Kilty and Behling found, also, that characteristics of the jobs themselves were important predictors of retirement. They studied retirement patterns among four types of professional workers: (1) attorneys, (2) social workers, (3) high school teachers, and (4) college professors.[26] Although all of these workers had professional careers, their retirement patterns tended to be quite different. Lawyers tended to be the least positive about the prospects of retirement and the most apt to want to postpone it. Most high school teachers said that they would be ready to retire at relatively young ages. Social workers and college professors tended to be more reluctant than high school teachers to retire early. These differences were largely related to a form of alienation from work. Although none of these workers were dissatisfied with their careers, those who had put in many years in the same job routines had tended to become disenchanted with their work. High school teachers were much more apt to have accumulated many years of work at earlier ages than the other professionals.

Decisions about whether and when to retire are much more dynamic processes than much of the research literature would indicate, however. Important interactional negotiating patterns are involved, as are the influences of such variables as types of jobs. Data from the longitudinal Normative Aging Study begun in 1963 in Boston show, for example, that the ages at which men preferred to retire and the ages at which they planned to retire differed.[27] Five age-level worker cohorts said that they would prefer to retire at earlier ages than they actually planned to retire. Furthermore, the older the cohorts, the higher they set both their preferred and planned retirement ages and the closer together those two ages became.

Further analysis of the data from the Normative Aging Study revealed that part of the dynamic involved in retirement decisions was what was labeled "preretirement involvement behavior." It was discovered that the closer men came to the time when retirement tended to be expected of particular worker cohorts, the more frequently they talked to wives, relatives, friends, and co-workers about retirement, and the more they read about it.[28] Presumably, these kinds of involvements tend to influence individuals to reconcile their preferences about retirement with the practical considerations. They also probably tend to influence attitudes about retirement. These kinds of interactional patterns seem to have become fairly well established for those facing retirement and constitute what has come to be thought of as "anticipatory retirement."

How retirement tends to turn out is another important aspect of the institution of retirement. What happens to retirees in terms of personal economics might seem to be a key to other considerations. In that regard, it has long been recognized that, on the average, the incomes of retirees are drastically cut. Conclusions drawn from cross-sectional studies on retirement income have been that incomes are cut in half, on the average, when people retire. Those kinds of data are misleading, however, because the incomes of given cohorts of retirees are compared to other cohorts rather than to their own preretirement incomes. Longitudinal studies, which compare individuals' own incomes before and after retirement, reveal that the actual average loss of income due to retirement amounts to only about one-fourth.[29] In China today, retirement benefits range from 60 to 90 percent of preretirement wages.[30]

Questions about the adequacy of retirement income remain. The cross-sectional studies show that the retirement income improves for each succeeding generation of retirees. Thus, the older people become, the less income they will have, relative to others who retire later. Retirees' financial status relates to more than just what they made before they retired, of course. It was found in one study, for example, that, because of such income support mechanisms as Social Security, SSI, and food stamps, the incomes of the elderly poor tended to improve, while the incomes of those who had enjoyed middle-level and relatively high salaries tended to decline. The relatively wealthy were able to maintain quite comfortable and satisfying lives, while the financially marginal, whose incomes had been insufficient to allow them to save for their retirements, were hurt the most. They had the benefits of neither life savings nor of government subsidies. The conclusion from these findings was that retirement has an income-leveling effect.[31]

The social and psychological adjustments that people make in their retirement years have been a major concern of gerontologists. Much of the attention paid to this concern has focused on satisfaction among the elderly with life in general and with various aspects of being retired.

In this regard, Davies likens the experiences of retirees to those of younger people who are being relegated to positions of permanent unemployment due to technological developments. He depicts the experiences of both the unemployed and retirees as characterized by alienation, lack of direction, economic dependence on the general public, and aimless expenditure of time.[32] His contention is that, in order for these people to positiviely adjust to their nonproductive situations, society would have to redefine the importance of the work ethic.

There are indications that the experiences of semipermanent unemployment are, indeed, socially and psychologically devastating. In a study of unemployed professional men, Powell and Driscoll found that long periods of unemployment caused respondents to become cynical, to lose confidence in their professional competence, and to develop feelings of malaise.[33] There is little evidence that these experiences are typical of those in retirement, however.

Adjustment to retirement has not been nearly as negative as it was thought to be even in the early days of mandatory retirement in the United States (in the 1950s and 1960s). It is true that high percentages of retirees expressed negative feelings about retirement in a 1960s international survey. Retired men in the United States, Great Britain, and Denmark were asked, among other questions, what they liked about retirement. Sizable percentages, especially in Denmark, answered "nothing." It was also found, however, that many of them, particularly in Denmark, also answered "nothing" to the quesiton of what they missed about their work. Furthermore, many of the negative feelings about retirement were expressed by those with relatively poor health.[34] Few negative attitudes about retirement have been found in subsequent surveys.[35] As Cowgill suggested, retirement has been the most difficult for the first cohorts of retirees.[36]

Indications of the high level of adjustment to retirement in more recent years were found in the National Longitudinal Surveys in the United States. The 1976 part of that survey, based on a sample of both black and white males, revealed high levels of satisfaction with a number of aspects of aging.[37] As many as 89 percent of the whites and 84 percent of the blacks expressed some level of happiness with retirement in general. Nearly half of the blacks (47 percent) and slightly more than half of the whites (51 percent) said they were "very happy." Health was found to be the least satisfying of any of the factors under study, which included housing, area of residence, standard of living, and leisure activities. It is especially noteworthy that a slightly higher percentage of the healthy retirees than those in the sample who had not yet retired reported being very happy with life in general.

To be sure, some experiences that elderly people have tend to be related to low levels of life satisfaction or morale. It was noted many years ago, for example, that disengagement was associated with lack of life satisfaction.[38] It was generally assumed, therefore, that disengagement was a cause of low morale.[39] A later study compared disengagement related to widowhood and disengagement related to retirement. It was discovered that while disengagement related to widowhood was associated with substantial loss of morale, that related to retirement was almost totally unrelated to morale.[40] It was concluded from this study that the elderly experience loss of morale when events in their lives are socially disruptive. While little can be done to prepare for becoming widowed, retirement can now be anticipated, planned, and adapted to with relative ease.

One's social contacts and interactions appear to be key factors in determining successful adjustment to retirement. Much has been made of the impact of retirees' attitudes about work and retirement on whether or not they make satisfactory adjustments. Foner and Schwab suggest that thinking about when to retire and having positive preretirement attitudes may influence adjustment to retirement even more than actual planning for it.[41] The question that arises, though, is what the sources of the preretirement attitudes are. Sheley found that attitudes about work and retirement among those living in retirement communities tended to be especially conducive to positive adjustments in retirement.

This was true because the retirement-community dwellers lived in an atmo-sphere in which emphasis on work is largely missing and a sense of belonging exists for those who are retired.[42]

Adjustment to retirement is not automatic, nor is it instantaneous. Retire-ment represents change, regardless of whether major losses are involved, and regardless of whether those changes are welcome. Ekerdt and his colleagues investigated differences in overall life satisfaction among men who had been retired for various lengths of time. Those retired for less than 6 months were compared to those retired for 7 to 12, 13 to 18, 19 to 24, 25 to 30, and 31 to 36 months. It was found that life satisfaction tended to be high for those retired 6 months or less but diminished for subsequent cohorts. The lowest measure of life satisfaction was found among those retired between 13 and 18 months, but it tended to increase among those retired longer than 18 months. The investigators concluded that adjustment to retirement typically involves a letdown period but tends, overall, to be a positive life experience.[43]

SOCIAL ROLES IN RETIREMENT

Social status in modern societies is described by sociologists as *achieved* rather than *ascribed*. That is, we gain our sense of identity not by virtue of the family or clan into which we are born, but by virtue of the positions we come to hold and the roles we play due to our own efforts. Therefore, an analysis of roles in retirement is important to our understanding of retirement.

In 1960, Burgess described retirement as a "roleless role,"[44] because it appeared in those days that, while elderly people were being forced to retire, they were given no meaningful roles to perform. This was a reasonable perception to have of retired people at that time. The aged could be observed daily gathered in city parks, hotel lobbies, local barber shops, and the like, with nothing apparent to do that would be meaningful to them.

Rosow provided a comprehensive explanation for this phenomenon. He contended that the problem was that modern society was failing to provide the aged with adequate socialization into retirement and old age.[45] He explained that socialization for those at younger ages typically involves assigning social positions (mostly in the form of well-defined occupations), prescribing the roles related to those positions, and providing rewards for performing the roles. In contrast, while elderly people are assigned the position of retired persons, no roles are specified for them, nor are they rewarded for becoming retired. Instead, they experience a major loss of status. Disengagement would thus be a typical repsonse on the part of older persons.

This is obviously a basically negative perspective of retirement roles. It depicts socialization as a process that is controlled and implemented by society. Thus, as Davies implied, any improvement of the lives of people in retirement would depend upon a major shift in societal value of work.[46]

While this perspective provides a good introduction to the concept of retirement roles, it has severe limitations. From the perspective of retired people themselves, for example, retirement is generally not perceived as a negative experience, as we have already noted. In addition, this perspective overlooks the fact that roles are generally acquired and assumed not so much from set prescriptions imposed by society, but from a negotiating process, through individuals' interactions with the social entities of which they are part.[47]

Even from the perspective of societal expectations of retirement, it is not fair to assume that retirees are expected to disengage and do nothing. Instead, it was precisely that apparent tendency among those in retirement that became disturbing to the American public in the 1960s. It is probably more accurate to say that society provides those in retirement with freedom from the social obligations of previous roles. In the context of that freedom, the societal expectation is that they will negotiate their own roles. In that sense, disengagement may be tolerated but is certainly not encouraged.

This does not mean that each individual retiree necessarily defines a unique role or that there are no roles common to retired people in general. It is the nature of the role-negotiating process that common role patterns will emerge. We can rightfully expect that retirement roles are indeed being negotiated, that they will be substantially different from preretirement roles, and that they will be adopted by many of those in the retired population.

What, then, characterizes emerging retirement roles? There is much disagreement in the gerontological literature about this. The main issue of disagreement is whether leisure constitutes a viable role for the elderly and whether, in fact, they are even willing to adopt it.

Gerontologists often discuss the question of whether leisure is a viable role for the aged today. The problem in these discussions, however, has been the definition of leisure. Leisure has been viewed simply as the negative side, or absence, of work. Much emphasis, for example, has been placed on "free time,"[48] and on what people with time on their hands do with that time. Rosow defined leisure negatively, as a reward for work, and he therefore contended that it could never be a viable role for retired people.[49]

In some societies in the past, leisure was given a positive definition. The classical Greek definition of leisure, for example, was that it consisted of the cultivation of self. It was viewed as a viable role for the privileged class, and it called for such pursuits as meditation and the development of true spiritual freedom.[50] Freedom is a central part of most definitions of leisure. It is noteworthy that probably the one aspect that retirees most often say that they enjoy about retirement is the freedom that it offers them. By this they do not mean simply "free time," but freedom from the obligations of the work from which they have retired, which many refer to as "the rat race," and freedom to pursue their own interests and preferred associations.[51]

In analyses of leisure among retirees, the focus is often on the kinds of activities in which they engage. In that sense, it has been noted that retirees often simply engage in activities similar to those that they engaged in in their work, and that is seen as evidence of their continuing orientation to the work ethic.[52] What is missing in this analysis is that even though the activities may be similar, when they are done as leisure they are done from the perspective of freedom from the social obligation of work and of the pursuit of individual interests.

This perspective on retirement is increasingly found among retirees today. There is also evidence that it is not confined to those in higher socioeconomic classes. In one study it was found, to the surprise of the investigator, that both retired professionals and individuals who had worked as day laborers saw retirement as a positive experience because of the freedom it offered them, provided there were opportunities for them to pursue their individual interests.[53]

Three specific types of roles are rapidly emerging among retired people today that fit under the umbrella of leisure: (1) volunteer,[54] (2) student, and (3) pursuer of arts and crafts. Among these three types of roles there is great potential for the aged to make creative contributions to the cultures of which they are a part.

Elderly volunteers are quickly becoming seen by governments as valuable community resources, and increasing resources are being offered toward their support and recognition. Some of these roles represent social needs that the elderly are better able to fulfill than other people. Two examples, one from China and the other from the United States, will illustrate how vital these kinds of roles are to communities as well as to the elderly participants.

In the People's Republic of China, women, particularly those in urban areas, normally retire at age 55. At that time, many of them volunteer to work in various types of community services.[55] They somewhat uniquely have the time and skills to perform these types of roles. Many of these women become members of neighborhood committees that serve as both welfare and social-control agents. These roles are vital to the community and are meaningful to those who fill them.[56]

One of many similar volunteer roles that have been developed exclusively for the aged in the United States is that of "senior companion." It functions under a program sponsored by the federal government. Senior companions are recruited from among able-bodied, low-income elderly, most of whom have become relatively isolated. They serve as companions to other frail elderly people to help them with activities of daily living. Those who serve the homebound make particularly important contributions. The record of their work reveals that lives have literally been saved and that many elderly have been kept from being prematurely institutionalized. Senior companions almost universally testify that their roles have provided them with new leases on life.

Still another of what might be categorized as a volunteer role for the elderly comes from a very traditional culture. As a participant observer, Schweitzer analyzed what old age was like among the Oto-Missouri and Ioway Indian tribes in Oklahoma.[57] She found, in contrast to the prevailing negative definitions of aging in the dominant American culture, that the prevailing definition of old age in these tribes continued to be positive. What provided that basically positive definition was the "functional" roles that those tribes reserved for their elderly members. Based on their knowledge of "tribal ways and traditions," elders of the tribes served as "ritual specialists" and "religious specialists" in tribal ceremonies, and as teachers of tribal traditions. These are not required roles for all who are old, but they represent positions of honor, prestige, and power in these tribes.

Volunteerism indeed provides new and vital roles for the elderly in today's world. Many of these roles resemble work roles in that they contribute to societal productivity. Yet because they are voluntary, they also offer the freedom that characterizes leisure roles. Their value to those who perform them is primarily that of self-improvement and secondarily that of productivity.

Volunteerism is apparently not a role that is universally enjoyed by retired people in all cultures. Cowgill reports, for example, that volunteers are neither respected nor treated with dignity or appreciation in Sweden. Although some who are retired do volunteer work, they typically complain that they are given tasks that are menial, inconsequential, and boring.[58]

The second rapidly emerging role among elderly people today is that of student. This role is so new that it is only now beginning to be discussed in the gerontological literature. Interest in education among the aged population was, from all appearances, almost nonexistent any place in the world in the early 1970s. As late as 1978, in his article "An Overview of Gerontology Education," Peterson ignored this aspect of age-related education in favor of education for professionals serving elderly people.[59] Since then, the demand for educational opportunities among older adults has mushroomed in at least two very different cultures.

The forms that this phenomenon has taken illustrate why it is fair to identify it as an important leisure role for older adults. With few exceptions, older adults are clamoring for educational opportunities, not for the purpose of meeting the requirements for a degree or learning a marketable skill, but merely to learn and share the learning process with other students. The only instrumental goal they may have is to learn to cope psychologically, socially, economically, and politically as older adults.

In the United States, the primary structure of older-adult education is epitomized by the Elder Hostel program. Administered by a nationwide private organization, week-long educational programs exclusively for elderly people are offered at many colleges and universities across the country. Classes included in each program are selected purely on the basis of student interest, with no attempt to develop any kind of comprehensive curriculum. Participants in each week's program are treated as cohort groups. As a rule, all participants attend all of the courses being offered each day. Courses are not offered for credit since the students enroll simply to learn and to share what they learn with their fellow students. The program has become quite popular and is well attended.

As explained in Chapter 8, in the People's Republic of China a program called "the Old People's University" was begun in 1983 at the Red Cross University in Jinan, sponsored jointly by that university and Shandung Province. It is administered by a president, 7 full-time staff members, and 8 part-time vice presidents. During the first year of operation, there were 48 part-time volunteer teachers in the program. Some 37 of the teachers were professors at the university, and the others were recruited from the community.

The guiding principle of the program is that of "taking good care of the old people to improve their health and to prolong their lives and providing a chance for them to study to increase their knowledge to enable them to continue to serve for the society."[60] To accomplish these goals, a full two-year curriculum has been developed. The curriculum includes courses on health care and physical exercise; courses in such academic areas as history, geography, philosophy, and literature; and creative-expression courses such as calligraphy, painting, photography, gardening, and music. Although courses are not for credit in the usual sense, elderly students who complete the two-year program receive a certificate of recognition from the university. During the first year of operation (1983 to 1984) a total of 980 students were enrolled. The majority were between 60 and 69 years old; the oldest student was 86. Those from other parts of China live at the university along with other regular students.

The third type of leisure role that has emerged among the elderly today is that of pursuers of arts and crafts. Those involved in this type of role range from those who take courses on various kinds of crafts at senior citizens' centers and do crafts as hobbies, to those who are or become accomplished artists. There are those among the accomplished artists who did not discover their artistic abilities until after they retired and began to pursue art as an area of personal interest. As previously noted, art classes are part of the curriculum at the Old People's University in Jinan, China. This author had the privilege of observing displays of sculpture that some of these elderly students had done at the Red Cross University in Jinan in 1984.

Admittedly, by no means all elderly people have taken on leisure roles. There are those who do indeed experience a net loss of roles as they age, and who disengage from active social participation. This is particularly true of those who have the least amount of formal education and who have particularly low incomes.

Nevertheless, it is significant that the number of elderly people who are opting for one or more of the leisure roles is rapidly growing. Increasing numbers are becoming active volunteers. This type of role is involving many poor and uneducated elderly people, especially through federally mandated programs.

It is important to understand that these roles are largely leisure roles, in the classical sense, in that they are freely chosen by individuals for the primary goal of self-improvement. Precisely because they are leisure roles, they carry great potential for creativity and innovation. In addition, individuals who are involved make vital contributions to their communities that all too often go unrecognized or unappreciated.

CONCLUSION

Retirement is becoming an increasingly well-established social institution. It exists with basic systems of support in the developed nations of the world. It is also quickly becoming an established part of society in most of the developing nations. Only in those areas where the environments tend to be harsh and economic conditions are still undeveloped is it mostly nonexistent.

The institution of retirement has become possible in today's world largely because of the changing nature and meaning of work. Throughout much of history, work, in the form of productive human labor, was economically necessary, and had religious and ideological meaning. It was also a primary source of individual identity and self-worth. With the great advancements in technological development in the modern era, however, machines have rendered much of human labor not only unnecessary but obsolete. Much of the work that is still needed has become routine, tedious, and even boring. To be sure, work remains important for its intrinsic value and as a means of making a living. It has largely lost its religious and ideological meaning, and most jobs have become extremely competitive. Only the highly trained and skilled are able to compete.

In the modern technological world, retirement began, not as a system of support benefits for an indulgent older population, as we might be led to believe, but as an economic necessity. It has been imposed on the aged population by the executives of corporations and employment organizations as the easiest way of dealing with the problem of surplus labor.

The argument that older workers are less efficient and competent than younger workers has never been substantiated. It has largely been used as a rationale to legitimize mandatory retirement policies. In cases in which surplus labor is not an issue and older workers are employed, for example, no such complaints are given.

Ironically, retirement has also become not only accepted but welcomed by the world's older populations. It is true that many of those among the early cohorts of people upon whom mandatory retirement policies were imposed had serious adjustment problems. It is also true that a minority of people with poor health, financial difficulties, and strong orientations to the work ethic still have adjustment problems. Most who are retired today, though, express much satisfaction about both retirement and life in general.

Part of the subjective meaning of retirement has to do with the growing role opportunities available to retirees. Contrary to the many arguments against leisure as being meaningful to retired people, the classic definition of leisure is precisely the orientation that most elderly people adopt in accepting retirement roles. They are free from productive obligations, and they take on roles primarily for their own self-improvement. Analyzing leisure simply in terms of specific activities misses that important point. Activities are leisure activities, not by virtue of the types of activities they are, but by virtue of how they are approached.

Leisure for those in retirement is becoming a way of life for both rich and poor. Volunteer programs of various kinds today have made this possible. Such programs as the Senior Companion Program in the United States, which is specifically designed for the elderly poor, illustrate that point. Creative activities in the forms of education and artistic work are also increasing among those in retirement. These roles are not only meaningful to those who adopt them, but they are also beginning to provide the aged with new and important identities.

In conclusion, retirement is not only a firmly established social institution, but it may well be one of the most valuable social inventions of the modern era. Admittedly, associated problems such as poor health, poverty, and adjustment difficulties remain. Still, a leisure class that is free from productive obligations and is oriented to self-improvement can prove to be socially valuable. As the ancient Greek philosophers, who were part of a privileged leisure class, demonstrated, these kinds of leisure activities have the potential to add significantly to the world's body of knowledge and to contribute to artistic beauty. While this kind of potential is now only beginning, these kinds of accomplishments will almost certainly multiply as the educational level of the retired population increases.

NOTES

[1] Nancy C. Morse and Robert S. Weiss, "The Function and Meaning of Work and the Job," *American Sociological Review*, 20, no. 2 (1955), 191–98.

[2] Stanley Parker, *Work and Retirement* (London: George Allen and Unwin, 1982), p. 67.

[3] "Should Women Retire Earlier Than Men?" *Beijing Review*, 29, no. 17 (April 28, 1986), 9–10.

[4] David J. Ekerdt, "The Busy Ethic: Moral Continuity Between Work and Retirement," *The Gerontologist*, 26, no. 3 (June 1986), 239–44.

[5] Stephen J. Miller, "The Social Dilemma of the Aging Leisure Participant" in *Older People and Their Social World*, eds. Arnold M. Rose and Warren A. Peterson (Philadelphia: F. A. Davis, 1965), pp. 77–92.

[6] Thomas M. Kando, *Leisure and Popular Culture in Transition* (Saint Louis, Mo.: C. V. Mosby, 1975), p. 4.

[7] William Graebner, *A History of Retirement: The Meaning of an American Institution, 1885–1978* (New Haven, Conn.: Yale University Press, 1980), pp. 234–36.

[8] Harold L. Sheppard and Sara E. Rix, *The Graying of Working America: The Coming Crisis in Retirement-Age Policy* (New York: Free Press, 1977), pp. 135–55.

[9] Sara E. Rix and Paul Fisher, *Retirement-Age Policy: An International Perspective* (New York: Pergamon Press, 1982), pp. 18–28.

[10] Graebner, *A History of Retirement*, p. 13.

[11] Ibid.

[12] Parker, *Work and Retirement*, p. 19.

[13] Graebner, *A History of Retirement*, p. 53.

[14] Parker, *Work and Retirement*, p. 17.

[15] Daisaku Maeda, "Japan," in *International Handbook on Aging: Contemporary Developments and Research*, ed. Erdman Palmore (Westport, Conn.: Greenwood Press, 1980), pp. 253–70.

[16] Donald O. Cowgill, *Aging Around the World* (Belmont, Calif.: Wadsworth, 1986), p. 125.

[17] Graebner, *A History of Retirement*, p. 270.

[18] Ibid., p. 267.

[19] Maeda, "Japan," p. 253–70.

[20] Erdman B. Palmore et al., *Retirement: Causes and Consequences* (New York: Springer, 1985), p. 36.

[21] Graebner, *A History of Retirement*, p. 266.

[22] Palmore et al., *Retirement*, pp. 23–36.

[23] David J. Ekerdt, "Why the Notion Persists that Retirement Harms Health," *The Gerontologist*, 27, no. 4 (August 1987), 454–57.

[24] Pauline K. Robinson, Sally Coberly, and Carolyn E. Paul, "Work and Retirement," in *Handbook of Aging and the Social Sciences*, eds. Robert H. Binstock and Ethel Shanas (New York: Van Nostrand Reinhold, 1985), pp. 503–27.

[25] Pat Keith, "Work, Retirement, and Well-Being Among Unmarried Men and Women," *The Gerontologist*, 25, no. 4 (August 1985), 410–16.

[26] Keith M. Kilty and John H. Behling, "Predicting the Retirement Intentions and Attitudes of Professional Workers," *Journal of Gerontology*, 40, no. 2 (March 1985), 219–27.

[27] David J. Ekerdt, Raymond Bosse, and John M. Mogey, "Concurrent Change and Planned and Preferred Age for Retirement," *Journal of Gerontology*, 35, no. 2 (March 1980), 232–40.

[28] Linda Evans, David J. Ekerdt, and Raymond Bosse, "Proximity to Retirement and Anticipatory Involvement: Findings from the Normative Aging Study," *Journal of Gerontology*, 40, no. 3 (May 1985), 368–74.

[29] Palmore et al., *Retirement*, p. 47.

[30] "Growing Old in China," *Beijing Review*, 43 (October 26, 1981), 22–23.

[31] Gerda G. Fillenbaum, Linda George, and Erdman B. Palmore, "Determinants and Consequences of Retirement Among Men of Different Races and Economic Levels," *Journal of Gerontology*, 40, no. 1 (January 1985), 85–94.

[32] Christopher S. Davies, "The Throwaway Culture: Job Detachment and Rejection," *The Gerontologist*, 25, No. 3 (June 1985), 228–31.

[33] Douglas H. Powell and Paul F. Driscoll, "Middle-Class Professionals Face Unemployment," in *Socialization and the Life Cycle*, ed. Peter I. Rose (New York: St. Martin's Press, 1979), pp. 309–19.

[34] Ethel Shanas et al., *Old People in Three Industrial Societies* (New York: Atherton Press, 1968), pp. 330–40.

[35] Robert C. Atchley, *Social Forces and Aging: An Introduction to Social Gerontology* (Belmont, Calif.: Wadsworth, 1985), p. 201.

[36] Cowgill, *Aging Around the World*, p. 129.

[37] Herbert S. Parnes and Gilbert Nestel, "The Retirement Experience," in *Work and Retirement: A Longitudinal Study of Men*, ed. Herbert S. Parnes (Cambridge, Mass.: MIT Press, 1981), pp. 155–97.

[38] Robert J. Havighurst, Bernice Neugarten, and Sheldon S. Tobin, "Disengagement and Patterns of Aging," in *Middle Age and Aging*, ed. Bernice Neugarten (Chicago: University of Chicago Press, 1968), pp. 162–72.

[39] George L. Maddox, "Fact and Artifact: Evidence Bearing on Disengagement Theory," in *Normal Aging*, ed. Erdman Palmore (Durham, N.C.: Duke University Press, 1970), pp. 324–26.

[40] Arnold S. Brown, "Socially Disruptive Events and Morale Among the Elderly" (unpub-

lished paper presented at the Gerontological Society 27th Annual Meeting in Portland, Oregon, October 1974), Abstract printed in *The Gerontologist*, 14, no. 5, pt. 2 (October 1974), 72.

[41] Anne Foner and Karen Schwab, *Aging and Retirement* (Monterey, Calif.: Brooks/Cole, 1981), p. 61.

[42] Joseph F. Sheley, "Mutuality and Retirement Community Success: An Interactionist Perspective in Gerontological Literature," *International Journal on Aging and Human Development*, 5, no. 1 (1974), 71–77.

[43] David J. Ekerdt, Raymond Bosse, and Sue Lewkoff, "An Empirical Test for Phases of Retirement: Findings from the Normative Aging Study," *Journal of Gerontology*, 40, no. 1 (January 1985), 95–101.

[44] Ernest W. Burgess, *Aging in Western Societies* (Chicago: University of Chicago Press, 1960), pp. 352–60.

[45] Irving Rosow, *Socialization to Old Age* (Berkeley, Calif.: University of California Press, 1974), pp. 162–72.

[46] Davies, "The Throwaway Culture," pp. 228–31.

[47] Robert H. Lauer and Warren H. Handel, *Social Psychology: The Theory and Application of Symbolic Interactionism* (Englewood Cliffs, N.J.: Prentice-Hall, 1983), pp. 314–17.

[48] Harold Cox, *Later Life: The Realities of Aging* (Englewood Cliffs, N.J.: Prentice-Hall, 1984), p. 207.

[49] Irving Rosow, "Retirement, Leisure, and Social Status," in *Duke University Council on Aging and Human Development*, (Durham, N.C.: Duke University Press, 1968), pp. 249–57.

[50] Kando, *Leisure and Popular Culture in Transition*, pp. 19–24.

[51] Arnold S. Brown, "The Elderly Widowed and Their Patterns of Social Participation and Disengagement," (unpublished doctoral thesis, University of Montana, 1972), pp. 91–94.

[52] Parker, *Work and Retirement*, pp. 138–45.

[53] Idris W. Evans and Arnold S. Brown, *Aging in Montana: A Survey of the Needs and Problems of Older Americans* (Helena, Mont.: Montana Commission on Aging, 1970), pp. 27–28.

[54] Claude Pepper, "Senior Volunteerism: Alive and Well in the 80s," *Generations*, 5, no. 4 (Summer 1981), 6–7.

[55] Myrna Lewis, "Aging in the People's Republic of China," *International Journal of Aging and Development* 15, no. 2 (1982), 79–105.

[56] Judith Treas, "Social Organization and Economic Development in China: Latent Consequences for the Aged," *The Gerontologist* 19, no. 1 (February 1979), 34–43.

[57] Marjorie M. Schweitzer, "The Elders: Cultural Dimensions of Aging in Two American Indian Communities," in *Growing Old in Different Societies: Cross-Cultural Perspectives*, ed. Jay Sokolovsky (Belmont, Calif.: Wadsworth, 1983), pp. 168–78.

[58] Cowgill, *Aging Around the World*, p. 131.

[59] David A. Peterson, "An Overview of Gerontology Education," in *Gerontology in Higher Education: Perspectives and Issues*, eds. Mildred Seltzer, Harvey Sterns, and Tom Hickey (Belmont, Calif.: Wadsworth, 1978), pp. 14–26.

[60] Li Heng, "A Brief Introduction of the Red Cross Old People's University of Shandung Province," (unpublished paper presented at a meeting of an American gerontology team, sponsored by People to People, International, at Jinan Red Cross University, June 9, 1984).

13

Health and Health Care for the Aged

INTRODUCTION

In the mid-1960s, Rose predicted that good physical and mental health was becoming a major component of the value system of the rapidly growing elderly population. Everyone wants to be healthy, but for elderly people, health is also an important symbol of social status. It is often more important, in fact, than such traditional social status symbols as income and occupation. This would be true, according to Rose, especially among those elderly people who become part of the "subculture of the aging" that he said was developing.[1]

Indeed, the maintenance and restoration of health has become one of the highest-priority concerns of elderly people today. It is one of a very few subjects about which virtually all of the aged tend to agree. Rich and poor alike see health care as a common need. Consequently, health care for the retired population has become one of the major expenditures of individual elderly people and of the governments of the industrialized world.

Given the vital nature of this topic to the aged, it is important to explore the answers to a number of questions. First, what, precisely, do we mean by health, and how has it become so vital to the aged? How is it related to aging, to illness or disease, and to everyday living? What are the basic types of health problems with which the aged must deal? What are the processes in which they must become involved in the pursuit of their own health status? How do these processes compare cross-culturally? What are the typically positive and negative consequences to the lives of the elderly in their pursuit of good health? We will deal with these kinds of issues in this chapter.

CHANGES IN THE HEALTH PROBLEMS OF THE AGED

In the past, before science had been extensively applied to the problems of health, the health problems of elderly people were not very different from those of any other age group. In those times, few people lived into their 60s. Many died in early childhood. Most others died either in adolescence or as relatively young adults of accidents, communicable diseases, or any number of other acute ailments. Individuals were susceptible to any of these kinds of often fatal problems throughout their lives. Many people at every age level suffered from them. Those who lived longer than others did so primarily because they had been fortunate enough to have escaped health-related problems or were strong enough to overcome them.

Infectious diseases posed the most serious threat to health. Epidemics of such diseases as cholera, yellow fever, and smallpox took many lives in countries that were becoming industrialized and urbanized as late as the latter part of the nineteenth century.[2]

In the past, health status was typically thought of quite differently than it is today. Science had not yet been applied to providing practical remedies for illness. As Carlson points out, "Medical practice was largely an art."[3] Thus, many perceived health and health problems from a religious perspective. It was a matter of individuals' relationships with God and God's benevolence toward them. For many others, good health was simply a matter of good luck, and most families used home remedies to treat illness. Carlson also points out that homeopathic medicine was practiced in the past.[4] That is, health problems were treated by attempting to stimulate the body's capacity to recover. As we will see later, that is the basic difference between Oriental and Western approaches to medicine.

Those few who lived to be very old were indeed plagued with mental and physical problems that were different from those of the rest of the population. Those problems were not even viewed as health problems that called for remedies, however. Instead, they were thought to be simply the natural consequences of old age.

Dramatic changes have come about during the twentieth century, especially in the Western industrialized world, in people's orientation to health and the conditions of their health. These changes have had a major impact on the lives of elderly people. It was essentially the application of modern science to solve the problems related to health that brought about the changes. Modern science transferred the focus of health maintenance from a religious or fateful

orientation to an almost total en...   ...ase concept. DuBois, for
example, has said that it is unrealis...   ...alth as the absence of
disease. A healthy society, he believes, ...ccessfully adapts to
diseases."[5] This concept has been so all-enc...   ...at it has also been
widely applied to such areas as mental disorders, c...   ...riminal behavior,
and the debilitating problems of old age.[6]

At the heart of the meaning of the disease concept is causation. Diseases are not matters of religion or fate. Neither do they need to be fatal when acquired. Instead they have causes that, if discovered, can be eliminated through specified treatments. Thus, the diseases themselves can be cured and their debilitating effects corrected through technology. Scientific advancements have been made, then, in three basic areas: (1) the study and discovery of the causes of diseases, (2) the creation of treatment and disease-control methods, and (3) the development of corrective and lifesaving technologies.

Particular attention was paid, in the latter part of the nineteenth and the early part of the twentieth centuries, to the causes of contagious diseases that had taken the lives of people of all ages. The discovery of bacteria as the cause of these diseases and the reason for their contagiousness was a particularly important scientific breakthrough. Knowledge of the causes of diseases led to (1) the establishment of public health programs that effectively controlled the contagion processes, (2) the development of immunization procedures that virtually eliminated a number of diseases, and (3) the discovery of treatments that helped to cure many diseases. In addition, a great deal of progress was made in developing many forms of technology that would correct the debilitating effects of many accidents and diseases and replace the functions of a number of the vital organs of the body.

The scientific use of the disease concept has, thus, had a dramatic effect on the maintenance of physical health and the preservation of life. Consequently, that concept has been widely applied to other human conditions and problems. Of particular importance to our analysis of the health of the elderly are the mental disorders and long-term physical problems typically found among the aged. These problems become defined as diseases rather than as the inevitable results of aging itself. Even though the causes of most of these ailments have not yet been established, and thus no cures have been developed, it has become something of a matter of scientific faith that the causes and cures will eventually come.

As a result of this kind of scientific perspective, a distinction has been made between two very different types of diseases: acute and chronic. This distinction has very important practical implications for health and health care among the aged. *Acute* diseases have been defined as "physical conditions with a specific onset and limited duration," and *chronic* diseases as "conditions that persist over time."[7] Another distinction between them today is that acute illnesses tend to be curable while chronic problems tend to be incurable. In the past, however, the acute more than the chronic diseases were the ones that were fatal. The speed with which they develop and their durations are the most important distinctions between them. Chronic problems are long term and often even permanent conditions with which the elderly especially must live.[8]

The important consequences of the scientific successes in the field of health care are that increasing numbers of people have survived the danger of infant mortality, avoided fatal involvement with infectious diseases, avoided or survived other acute illnesses, and lived safely into old age. The longer they live, however, the more apt they are to acquire chronic problems that require some level of long-term care. In old age, the incidence of acute problems usually diminishes and the probability of acquiring chronic problems grows. Thus, in contrast to the past, the health problems of the aged today tend to be quite different from those of the rest of the population. That is a fact that the present healthcare system has thus far tended to ignore, as we will discuss later.

DEVELOPMENT OF HEALTHCARE SYSTEMS

Few would argue with the observation that an elaborate and effective healthcare system has been put in place in this country. It is also true that important components of that system have been targeted toward the aged. The health of millions of people has been preserved even into old age, and many lives have been saved as a direct result of the application of our system of health care. Some would argue that it is a system that is second to none in the world in terms of the benefits it offers, especially to the older population.

Despite its many, often spectacular, accomplishments, some analysts are challenging such an optimistic assessment of the U.S. healthcare sytem today. Critics contend that it has serious limitations in terms of the care it provides those of all ages and older people in particular.

In order to gain a true picture of our healthcare system, we must analyze it from at least three perspectives: (1) the economic perspective, (2) the political perspective, and (3) the medical perspective. As we will see, it has been developed not merely to provide consumers with the best medical care available, but also to comply with political and economic demands.

It is somewhat ironic and puzzling that health care in the United States has always been offered from an economic as well as a medical basis. While other service-providing institutions, such as education, law enforcement, and welfare, have operated on the basis of public support, health care has largely functioned on the basis of private enterprise. Individual practitioners and service providers in the system (physicians, hospitals, and so on) have generally been motivated by profit.

In the era of our history when the United States was essentially an agrarian society, the healthcare system was rather simple. Families served as the basic economic production unit, and maintaining health was largely a family concern. Ailments were treated with home remedies, and families were responsible for the care of their older members. To the extent that they were available, physician and hospital services were used in cases of emergency on a fee-for-service basis.

As the United States became industrialized and urbanized, health maintenance was not only an individual and family concern. Employers became increasingly dependent upon a healthy work force in order to compete in the marketplace. They therefore began to work to mold the healthcare system to meet their needs. According to Estes and her colleagues, those in the private sector have even influenced the way in which health is defined today. They point out that although it would be in individuals' best interest to define health in terms of their ability to control their own destiny, those concerned about economics have influenced it to be defined in functional terms, or in terms of individuals' capacities to produce.[9] Maintaining people's physical and mental functional capabilities has thus become one of the main goals of the modern healthcare system, with little or no attention being paid to health needs as individual consumers might define them.

The healthcare system that has emerged as a result of the political influences of the medical profession and industry has been labeled a "medical industrial complex."[10] Two major emphases have characterized this system. First, care is provided in the context of what has been called the "medical-engineering model of health and illness," or the medical model. This model focuses almost exclusively on the biological causes of diseases and functional disability. Ignored is the relationship between health and the social, environmental, and intellectual aspects of life.[11]

The second characteristic of the modern healthcare system is the economic commercialization of health care. A number of analysts contend that health care has moved from the simple fee-for-service system of the past to a system that is controlled primarily by business and government policies for the purpose of making money. Iglehart accuses business and government of beginning "to look at medical care as more nearly an economic product than a social good."[12] Carlson points out that allocations for purposes of health care are almost exclusively allocated for "a medical care system focused on the agents of disease." He believes that the decisions for these kinds of allocations are made "far more for political, social, and economic reasons than therapeutic ones."[13]

The presently existing healthcare system is the result of negotiations that have been carried out in the political arena since World War II. Those negotiations were rife with conflict between those representing the medical community and those adovcating for a publicly supported national healthcare system. A national, publicly supported and administered healthcare program, as most European countries had adopted, would have taken the control of health care away from those in the medical profession. The legislation that resulted not only allowed those in the medical profession to continue to define and control health care, but helped it to become a lucrative business enterprise. The emergent system clearly serves both medical and business interests in a collaborative way.

As previously explained, the basic orientation of the medical model of health has been on the control and cure of disease. Of central importance to that orientation are hospitals, where the latest medical technology is available and healthcare professionals are able to control the treatment process. This concept of health care was greatly affirmed and supported by the federal government with the passage of the Hill-Burton Hospital Survey and Construction Act of 1946. Substantial subsidies were provided to the private sector for the construction of hospitals and nursing homes across the country.[14] The act also provided the major impetus for the establishment of health care as a private business enterprise.[15] The medical model has also been boosted by the biomedical research financed through federal grants from the National Institutes of Health; such research has concentrated most exclusively on what makes people sick rather than on why they may remain healthy.[16]

Due to the effective lobbying efforts of those in the medical professions, especially members of the American Medical Association, the goal of labor organizations and others to form a publicly supported and administered national healthcare system was never realized. Instead, private health insurance companies were created to provide financial services to unions and businesses for compulsory healthcare coverage for their workers. Services were provided by established healthcare systems. Thus, still another health-related business enterprise was created that provided substantial support to modern medicine and the professionals in it.

As the foregoing discussion indicates, the primary focus of the healthcare system that emerged in the United States following World War II was on those in the work force. It was in the best interests of both business and labor that industrial workers remain as physically and mentally functional as possible. Two overlapping segments of the American population, both of which were growing in numbers and in political importance, were left out, however. The poor and the aged had little or no promise of adequate healthcare coverage. In the War on Poverty era of the 1950s and '60s, though, a great deal of sentiment existed to provide needed services to both of those populations. Politicians favoring a national healthcare system pushed for special healthcare legislation for the poor and the aged as a first step toward national health care for everyone. Consequently, the 1965 revisions of Social Security included Medicaid for the poor and Medicare for the aged.

Both of these pieces of legislation were vehemently opposed by those in the medical profession. Ironically, however, they, more than any other health-related entities, have helped to create a healthcare system that serves the interests of both business and professional medicine. Both programs are designed to pay for healthcare services according to funding criteria set by the government. Once again, the actual provision of services is left to health professionals, who are reimbursed by annual allocations made for the programs.

Medicare is a national health insurance program for Americans 65 years of age and older. The bias toward workers in building a system of health care, discussed earlier, is also demonstrated in this law. Eligibility to receive benefits is limited to participants in the Social Security retirement program. Others who are 65 and over must pay monthly premiums in order to participate. It was not designed as a welfare program but as an "earned right" for years of productive work.[17] As such, it also serves as an added incentive for individuals to retire and leave the work force.

The Medicare program is divided into two parts, one compulsory and the other voluntary. Part A, the compulsory component, is the hospital insurance program, the benefits of which are paid for out of a Social Security Administration fund created for that purpose out of worker payroll taxes. The amount of hospital costs that are covered under Part A, however, are limited by a designated "deductible," which participants themselves must pay for each incident of hospital care before they are allowed to receive Medicare coverage.

Part B is a supplementary medical insurance program to cover 80-percent of physicians' fees and certain other designated out-of-hospital medical costs. This part of the Medicare program is also subject to an annual "deductible," which participants themselves must pay. This part of the program is voluntary and is financed by monthly premiums that participants must pay.

Medicaid provides funds to states to help them cover the healthcare costs of their poor, many of whom are also elderly. Individual states have the option to participate in the program or not. If they choose to participate, they must provide a certain percentage of the program costs with state funds, based on their per capita income levels. Within federal guidelines, states may set eligibility standards and determine how the money will be spent. It is up to participant states to administer this program within their borders. Needless to say, coverage under Medicaid varies greatly from state to state. Generally, though, it is the major source of public funding for long-term care in this country.[18] Some support is given to provide in-home medical care, but much more goes for institutional, nursing home care. Thus, to a large extent, Medicaid has helped to build the nursing home industry as a sizable business enterprise in the United States.

PRESENT CONDITIONS OF HEALTH AND HEALTH CARE FOR THE AGED

The life expectancy of elderly Americans has increased dramatically in this century and continues to increase. That means that the very old constitute an ever-increasing percentage of the population. It might be expected, therefore, that an increasing percentage of the elderly would be functionally disabled and institutionalized. Instead, the percentage of them who are institutionalized remains about the same, which means that the health status of elderly Americans has improved, largely as a result of the many medical achievements made in recent years.

Nevertheless, there are serious problems related to the present healthcare system in this country in terms of the adequacy with which it serves the health needs of the aged. Part of the problem is related to the medical model on which the existing system is based. As previously explained, the medical model basically defines health problems in terms of diseases which require advanced professional knowledge to understand. A further assumption of this model is that the best treatments and corrective measures are those that are technologically developed external to the body. From this perspective, then, the diagnostic and treatment processes for health care must be controlled and administered by medical specialists. Furthermore, for these processes to be effective, they must be carried out in the most technologically advanced settings—namely, physicians' offices and hospitals.

As valid as many of the basic assumptions of this model may be, Carlson criticizes it for essentially ignoring other health-related factors. For example, there are aspects of modern life that are unrelated to disease, but that directly affect health. Stresses that are not yet understood or even identified, certain life-styles and environmental conditions, and the loss of social support groups may all directly affect health. Yet they receive little or no attention in either medical research or practice.[19]

Probably the most severe criticism that can be leveled against the medical model, however, is that it tends to create and foster dependency among the client populations. To be sure, this is not serious when acute problems, typical of younger people, are being diagnosed and treated. In that case the dependency period is short, and it tends to be reassuring to clients that competent professionals are diagnosing and treating the problem. For those with chronic problems for which there are few, if any, promises of cure, however, dependencies tend to become long term and even permanent and often lead to a sense of hopelessness for elderly clients.

It might seem that the great advancements in spectacular, life-saving technology would represent renewed hope. In fact, that kind of technology often has precisely the opposite effect. For many, technology represents the ultimate form of dependency and indignity. Increasing numbers, in fact, are willing to die rather than experience that kind of indignity.

Medical sociologists have analyzed some of the negative effects of the sense of dependency that elderly people with chronic problems tend to experience. These analysts have long recognized a quite well-established behavior pattern related to acute illness, which they have identified as the "sick role."[20] This is a socially sanctioned set of behaviors typical of those who recognize some kind of physical or mental problem. At that point, individuals are expected to take time out of their normal activities, seek help with their problems (typically from physicians), and do what is necessary to get well and return to normal functioning. Assuming the sick role helps to alleviate the psychological stress that is often related to illness. In that sense, the sick role constitutes something of a coping response to illness for many people.[21]

For people with chronic illness, however, taking on the sick role is an entirely different matter. For them, the sick role typically becomes transformed into an "at-risk role."[22] The sick role is socially acceptable in the case of acute health problems because these kinds of problems are temporary. The sick-role behavior pattern has become quite clearly institutionalized, with well-established resolutions to the problems. In contrast, chronic problems are long term, behaviors connected to them have not been institutionalized, and there are no resolutions. To take on the sick role on a permanent basis in response to chronic problems is not socially acceptable. Chronic patients tend to receive inconsistent social support from both their families and health practitioners. Elderly people with serious chronic problems are therefore said to be socially at risk. Instead of being expected to eagerly seek medical help, they could well be expected to avoid seeking help.

In a study of patients with chronic multiple sclerosis, Stewart and Sullivan discovered a number of negative results stemming from being caught in a relatively permanent sick-role performance. They found (1) a tendency to avoid medical treatments even for other acute ailments, (2) a great deal of conflict between patients and medical professionals, (3) a tendency for patients to reject physicians' diagnoses, and (4) a great deal of emotional stress on the part of patients, which often led to a variety of psychosomatic symptoms.[23]

In addition to the problem of dependency-building, the program designed exclusively for the aged largely fails to cover their most salient healthcare needs. The Medicare legislation was passed by Congress as a health insurance program specifically to cover the costs of elderly persons' medical needs, over the vehement objections of those in the medical professions. It is therefore ironic that, while the professional and economic interests of the medical community were carefully safeguarded, the worst healthcare problems of older people were not even addressed in the program's structure. Medical professionals were allowed to maintain control over the diagnostic and treatment processes while long-term care needs were systematically ignored.

Specifically, while Medicare takes care of acute ailments quite adequately, it barely begins to cover chronic problems. This is clearly illustrated by Part A of the Medicare provisions.[24] Medical coverage for each ailment requiring hospitalization decreases the longer the problem lasts. For the first 60 days of hospitalization, Medicare covers all hospital costs, less the amount of the deductible ($540 in 1988). Then, on the 61st day of hospitalization, elderly patients must begin to pay as much as $123 per day; and on the 91st day, twice that much ($246 per day). If their hospitalization lasts beyond 150 days, they are forced to bear the total cost of their care for the duration of their hospitalization.

Most elderly long-term patients are transferred from hospitals to skilled nursing homes as soon as possible if they need institutional care beyond 60 days. The problem with this, though, is that Medicare will support their stay in nursing homes for even fewer days than in hospitals. They are supported fully for only the first 20 days in skilled nursing facilities. For 80 days after that, they are individually charged as much as $61.50 per day, and they must cover the total costs of their care beyond 100 days.

Medicare will now fully support, on an indefinite basis, whatever medical services are needed by homebound elderly long-term patients. It will not cover any of the support services these people typically need in order to live at home, however. The program simply is not designed to meet the long-term care needs of the many elderly who suffer from chronic diseases. A bill to provide for the long-term care needs of the aged was voted down by Congress in June 1988.

Another part of the problem related to the healthcare system on which elderly Americans must depend is an economic one. As we have seen, the system has been developed to foster profit-making businesses that are expected to provide the needed health benefits. As Estes and colleagues put it, "The goals of the health service industry are not only to improve the health status of the population and to protect a plurality of vested interests, but also, and more importantly, to strengthen and preserve the private sector in different ways."[25]

From a business perspective, those services that require the most advanced scientific technology and professional knowledge legitimize the highest charges and are therefore the most profitable. Therefore, if we insist that our healthcare system operate from a private-sector, business-oriented model, we have to expect that it will follow those healthcare procedures that will be the most profitable. It should not be surprising when businesses indeed act like businesses.

Medical research and practice has focused on increasingly sophisticated, technological, lifesaving techniques, not merely to advance medicine and save lives, but to make more money. A point in all of this that many in the medical profession choose to ignore is that the medical services that cost the most serve only an extremely small minority, and the extent to which the quality of even their lives is improved is being seriously questioned today.

The result of this approach has been an enormous escalation of the costs of health care in recent years. Costs have increased at such an accelerated rate that many in government have become alarmed about whether or not Medicare and Medicaid will be able to continue to bear the costs of supporting the elderly to the extent that they have in the past. Cost-cutting measures are being sought for both programs today.

One way of cutting costs in recent years is to turn to home health, on the assumption that it will be cheaper to provide services to people in their own homes than in expensive institutions. The accuracy of this assumption has not yet been established, but it is noteworthy that, for home health to gain Medicare approval, it must be delivered by "Medicare certified home health agencies."[26] Increasing numbers of such agencies are also profit-making businesses.

Another clear trend in the Medicare program is the shifting of more and more of the costs to individual clients who are eligible for coverage under that program. One method that has been used has been to raise the deductible amount under Part A, which represents the amount that elderly patients must

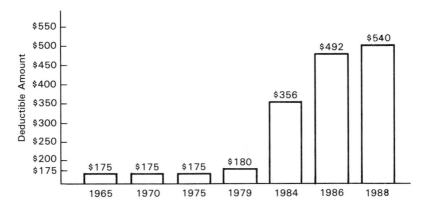

FIGURE 13-1   Increase In Medicare, Part A, Deductible, 1965–1988 (*Source:* compiled from publications from Health Care Financing Administration, US Department of Health and Human Services.)

pay out of their own pockets, each time they are hospitalized. As Figure 13-1 shows, that amount has increased by 209 percent since 1965, and by as much as 206 percent during the nine-year period between 1979 and 1988.

Still another cost-cutting measure has been the development, under Medicare, of *diagnostic-related groups* (DRGs). Under this policy, hospitals are reimbursed for services by Medicare, not on the basis of "reasonable costs" (as they were before), but on the basis of flat fees established by the government for each type of service. In cases in which allowable fees do not cover the actual costs, hospitals are expected to absorb the difference. Critics of this approach contend that the policy simply invites hospitals to discharge patients prematurely and endanger their lives.[27]

The cost of all forms of health care is becoming prohibitively high for increasing numbers of elderly Americans, particularly for those with debilitating chronic conditions. Coverage of institutionalized care on an extended long-term basis is only available under Medicaid, to those living in poverty. Consequently, many aged who require full-time skilled care quickly use up what financial resources they have and are forced into poverty in order to get the care they need. This situation compounds their condition of dependency. Sometimes almost overnight they move from a situation of relatively secure independence into a permanent condition of both financial and physical dependency. Supplemental, private, long-term care insurance policies are available to guard against this type of eventuality, but most of them have a number of exclusions and many elderly simply cannot afford the high monthly premiums.[28] One study indicates, for example, that only about 50 percent of those 65 and over can afford to insure their health with private programs. Many of them can only do it if they spend their assets.[29]

The healthcare system that has unfolded in the United States during the post–World War II years has served both the medical community and the business world well. Many profitable private-sector businesses have been created and sustained from the expenditure of public funds. Likewise, the program has continued to allow medical professionals to control both the definition and practice of health care. It has also supplied physicians, hospitals, and nursing homes with an ever-increasing and virtually certain client constituency.

At the same time, however, the existing system has failed to serve the elderly population either adequately or appropriately. It has failed to address the most prevalent health problems of older people and has tended to place them into situations of permanent dependency.

HEALTH AND HEALTH CARE IN OTHER CULTURES

Cultures differ greatly in their definitions of health and illness, the health status of their aged, and the types of healthcare systems they have. With more and more cross-cultural interactions with regard to matters of health and health care, however, cross-cultural accommodations are beginning to be made.

The definition of health is basic to other differences that exist between cultures. In that respect, societies might be divided between those that emphasize "traditional" and those that emphasize "modern" definitions of health. A number of societies are influenced by a combination of both definitions. As previously discussed, the modern medical model most basically defines both physical and mental health from the perspective of diseases. While other environmental factors, such as accidents and stress, can impede one's physical and mental conditions, the most essential definition of health is the absence, or at least the effective treatment, of disease. As we have seen, this model has largely determined how individuals' health conditons are assessed and how they will be treated in the United States. The influence of this perspective is spreading to other parts of the world as well.

Nevertheless, traditional definitions still exist and are even dominant in some societies. Indications are that there may also be a resurgence of this type of definition throughout the world. While traditional definitions differ somewhat from culture to culture, they all tend to define health from what has come to be called a *holistic* approach.[30] Health is seen as much more than the process of the body's being invaded by harmful and destructive matter from the outside. Instead, it is a matter of how the total body functions in a state of equilibrium and harmoniously relates to its environment. One's state of health, therefore, cannot be determined merely by diagnosing the presence or absence of specified diseases, but more adequately by assessing all of the elements of life (social, psychological, economic, political, and spiritual, as well as biological and mental).

This essentially captures the meaning of health for the people of two separate and quite different cultures that we will examine here: the Navajos and the Chinese. To the Navajo people, health has a distinct spiritual or religious connotation. Their traditional religious belief is that they as humans have emerged out of the earth and that their health is dependent upon living close to and in constant harmony with the earth. Being ill means being out of harmony with nature as a whole. Treatment is therefore placed in the hands of medicine men, who are also religious practitioners. Their job is to restore individuals to a proper state of harmony with the natural environment through ceremonies that symbolize that process. As Sandner discovered, those who are believers are often, indeed, cured of their ailments,[31] although there is little empirical evidence to indicate the extent to which that process is effective or which kinds of illnesses it best serves. Limited as this may seem to us as an effective healing process, it nevertheless focuses our attention on at least two important elements of life obviously important to health and well-being: the spiritual component of life and our relationship with the rest of nature. Traditional medicine is still especially important to elderly Navajos, who are still oriented to the traditional culture.

Modern medicine is also prevalent in the Navajo Nation, provided by the Indian Health Service, an agency of the US federal government. Therefore, in essence, they have two quite separate healthcare systems. Many elderly Navajos use both systems, and yet there are only minimal attempts to establish working relationships between the two systems, and little has been done to discover a way in which they may be compatible or complementary. Many still go to medicine men, not only because they believe in them but also because they are much more immediately accessible. This would be particularly true of the elderly who live in isolated areas.

In contrast to the rest of Americans, Navajos living on the reservation (as well as all native American tribes in the US) enjoy health care that is provided through a publicly supported system. Health care provided by the Indian Health Service without charge to individuals is part of the agreements made with Indian tribes in treaties between them and the US goverment.

Provision of health services needed by elderly Navajos is basically ignored by Indian Health Services, however. That agency does not provide for long-term care, for example. In an attempt to provide for that special need among their elderly people, therefore, the tribal government has opted for a system of care similar to that in the rest of the country. In part, they have contracted with private nursing homes off the reservation to provide the skilled care needed by some of their aged. They have also contracted with a private company to build and operate three nursing homes on the reservation.

This kind of program is even more devastating to the Navajo aged than it is to white Americans. It creates the same type of dependency in their daily lives. In addition, it is much more culturally incompatible for them than for other Americans. It removes them from their extended families, upon whom they have traditionally depended for their security. It also separates them from the land that is culturally vital to their sense of well-being.

Two special programs have recently been developed under tribal sponsorship to provide alternatives to institutionalization for those with long-term care needs. One is a home health program and the other is a group home health program in which those in temporary need of continuous care may live for a limited time. Neither of these programs has been developed across the reservation. Many Navajo elderly long-term care patients still become institutionalized either on or off the reservation.[32]

In no other place in the world today is traditional medicine more alive than in the People's Republic of China. It is not based on superstition or ancient religious beliefs, as is often supposed, but on a well-developed theory of natural phenomena. Health is defined in terms of how the human body is structured and is affected by the forces of the natural environment, including the whole cosmos.[33]

The theory on which traditional Chinese medicine is based says that all natural phenomena is composed of and functions in terms of opposite forces: *yin*, which is basically a positive force, and *yang*, which is basically a negative force. All of nature is made up of and subject to these forces. According to this theory, the human body is divided into identifiable functions and has an elaborate system of conduits, along which energy moves throughout the body, and sensitivity points along those conduits.

Humans can be negatively as well as positively affected by the natural forces around or within them. The most appropriate treatments for mental or physical problems, therefore, are those that come from nature itself and that focus on the sensitivity points of the body. Medicines used consist of carefully selected herbs. Two treatments widely used in Chinese traditional medicine are massage and acupuncture. Many in Western medicine have very little respect for Chinese medicine because they contend that it has no established scientific basis. Porkert disagrees, noting that, "the traditional medical practices of Chinese medicine continue to stand up remarkably well in the diagnosis and treatment of certain types of disease."[34] In fact, he suggests that it may offer better rational diagnoses and therapies than Western medicine for some functional diseases for which the record of effective treatment in the West is poor. It is noteworthy that the Chinese elderly prefer the treaments of traditional medicine for chronic ailments.

Western medicine has also made its way to China and is now practiced widely there. The two types of approaches to medicine, according to Porkert, are potentially not only compatible but complementary.[35] Western medicine tends to be more effective with acute dieases, for example. Yet the practitioners of the two approaches have little recognition or respect for each other. In some places in China they are not even practiced in the same hospitals. Also, the diagnoses of some problems that have been identified in one are changed to fit the cultural definitions of the other, and the practices originated in one are given different rationales before they are used in the other. On the one hand, for example, Kleinman found that the emotional problem neurasthenia has been found to be quite prevalent in China today but has been diagnosed as a physical disease there.[36] On the other hand, Wolfe reports that before medical doctors would approve the practice of acupuncture in the United States, they had to find some logical scientific explanation for it, even though it has clearly been an effective treatment in China for centuries.[37] There is one exception to the lack of coordination between the two models. Acupuncture is now used by many surgeons in China to provide anesthesia.

The healthcare system in China differs from the system in the United States in three basic ways: (1) the manner in which it is financially supported, (2) the kinds of care that are administered, and (3) how and to whom it is delivered. Improving and maintaining the health of all Chinese citizens, regardless of age, has always been a very high priority of the Communist government.[38] Health care became established under a system of public support soon after the People's Republic of China was founded in 1949. A few years later it was stipulated as a right for elderly people in the "five guarantees" promised to them in the national constitution.[39]

This does not mean that a national healthcare system was established and funded by the national government. Neither does it mean that all citizens enjoyed equal coverage. The national government has provided health care to those who fought in the revolution and those who worked for the government. Otherwise, the government has mandated that local work units build and support their own systems of health care. The level of health care provided by each brigade or commune has depended upon their financial capability.

Nevertheless, some level of health care has been available to all Chinese. Much of the care provided in rural areas is administered by "barefoot doctors," who are somewhat equivalent to paramedics in the United States. Their training is minimal and mostly concentrated on traditional medicine. They also rely to some extent on the knowledge they gain from their experiences caring for their local clients. They are, in fact, often trusted more than better-trained medical people because they have a keener understanding of the local people and the environments in which they live.[40]

Even though health care is not equally available to all Chinese on a daily basis, it is available for those with critical ailments. As Lewis points out, "If the ailment is complicated, confusing, or requires more sophisticated treatment, the person is sent on to the next level of care."[41]

Geriatrics has not been developed as a medical specialty among medical professionals in China. Part of the reason for that is that health practitioners have paid much more attention to preventing the onslaught of debilitating ailments than to developing and using lifesaving technology.[42] Major efforts have been made to overcome the problems of hunger and malnutrition. Beyond that, regular exercise among the aged is encouraged and has become a part of the way of life for a large percentage of them. It has been estimated by the Secretary General of the Chinese National Gerontology Committee, Yu Guanghan, that at least 40 percent of the nation's aged participate daily in organized exercise programs.[43] Also, as was previously noted, the treatments of Chinese traditional medicine tend to be relatively effective in treating the chronic problems of the aged.

What are the consequences of these quite different emphases on health care in China compared to the United States? On the one hand, few Chinese people live to advanced ages. As noted in Chapter 2, the life expectancy in China is significantly lower than that in the United States. On the other hand, as a whole, Chinese elderly people who are fortunate enough to have great longevity appear to be healthier than their counterparts in this country. For example, as Lewis points out, there are no long-term care institutions such as our nursing homes,[44] and it is rare to find any public place in China where the aged are permanently bedridden. There are frail and chronically ill elderly in China, but they tend to remain in their homes and to be cared for by their families until they die. That may place a heavy burden on families, yet it is precisely the kind of situation for which more and more American elderly are advocating.

TRENDS IN HEALTH CARE FOR THE AGED

It is not the purpose here to attempt to predict what health care for the aged will be like in the future, either in terms of specifics or even in terms of general directions. Even if human behavior itself were subject to that kind of prediction, the personal, professional, and political issues involved in health care for the aged are far too complex to warrant such an attempt. Instead, we will simply explore the beginnings of a number of trends that could well influence the future of this vital gerontological issue.

The rising cost of health care in the United States has prompted a number of potentially innovative approaches to improving and maintaining the health of elderly people. For one thing, some attempts are being made at prevention. Some senior citizens' centers and individual volunteers, for example, sponsor exercise programs and conduct health fairs and other types of programs to assess the health status of elderly people and to provide opportunities for them to have assessments of various aspects of their health. Valuable as these efforts are, however, they are not mandated by any authoritative agencies and they do not, as yet, seem to represent a major, growing trend.

Nutrition programs, on the other hand, are widespread, and have become a central and permanent part of Older American Act programs across the country. These programs typically provide hot, nutritiously approved meals to millions of elderly Americans, including the homebound, on a daily basis. The importance of this emphasis to the maintenance of health, if not the prevention of illness, is recognized by virtually everyone concerned about aging. The social relationships resulting from the meals programs are another valuable benefit that undoubtedly also contributes to the health of the elderly participants.

An emphasis on home health care has been growing in recent years in response to public criticisms of the costs and quality of care in many nursing homes. The basic assumption has been that home healthcare costs less than institutional care and that the quality of care is as good if not better than that provided in institutions. As previously noted, Medicare now provides for home health coverage, but only for those services that are delivered by health professionals from Medicare-certified home health agencies. These services, of course, represent only a small percentage of those provided in institutions. If the costs of such services as meals, housekeeping, and assistance with personal care were added to the more specifically defined health services, home healthcare might well be as costly as institutional care. All of these kinds of services are often necessary on a daily basis to enable elderly long-term care patients to remain at home, but housekeeping and personal care assistance are rarely, if ever, provided by home health agencies. In some communities, publicly supported social-service agencies provide some homemaker services to elderly clients, but the amount they are able to provide is limited and often does not meet the need.

The great bulk of care received by elderly people is, in fact, provided by informal caregivers. It has been found that over 80 percent of all care for the aged comes from the elderly person's own natural support systems (family members, neighbors, and friends).[45] Most of this kind of care comes from female family members, typically the wives and daughters of those receiving the care. Not surprisingly, the pattern of families caring for their elderly members has been found to be prevalent in such diverse cultural groups as the Navajo tribe in North America[46] and the Japanese. It may be surprising to learn, however, that the commitment to caregiving on the part of American women is as great as among Japanese women.[47] When it is called for, working daughters provide care to their elderly parents as readily as do nonworkers.[48]

The problems that informal caregivers in the United States encounter are numerous. Research indicates that the majority of informal caregivers have had no training in this kind of very demanding work. They tend to lack knowledge about outside help and worry about how to obtain it when and if it is needed.[49] It is reported that spouses, who are the most committed caregivers and tend to provide the most consistent care of all of the caregiver types, also tend to be the highest risk group of all caregivers in terms of developing debilitating health problems of their own.[50] According to Soldo and Myllyluoma, caregiving efforts on the part of family members are often "last ditch" efforts to prevent their family members from having to be institutionalized.[51] Maeda reports similar caregiver problems in Japan.[52]

The question of the feasibility of creating liaisons between informal caregivers and health professional groups to improve the care they provide and to more effectively use that source of care has been discussed. On the one hand, some see this as an exploitation of families' resources.[53] On the other hand, it could be thought of as support for an existing system of care in need of help. At least one attempt has been made, in a small, rural Arizona community, to organize the informal caregivers into a cooperative group and to provide them with training in effective caregiving. Participants were taught the needed caregiver skills, informed about potential sources of outside help, and encouraged to provide one another with mutual support. As a first effort, it was quite effective in helping those in the group to be better caregivers.[54] The potential of this kind of program for cutting costs and providing quality care for long-term care elderly patients is great, but it would need the endorsement, and perhaps the sponsorship, of the medical profession. That kind of sponsorship may not be politically possible in the United States today.

A great deal of concern has been expressed about "cost-containment" of medical expenditures for the aged in the United States in recent years. It has become a political issue among gerontology planners, policymakers, and the aged themselves.

There have been two basic responses to the cost-containment issue. One has been for the government to set specific amounts that they will reimburse elderly people for each medical service under Medicare and Medicaid. The hope is that hospitals and physicians will charge patients only the amount of the reimbursement figure, but they are not obligated to do so. Insurance companies have begun to follow a similar cost-containment policy. If the fees being charged are more than the insurance coverage allows, the elderly patients are obligated to pay the balance. Some hospitals have been accused of discharging elderly patients prematurely as a way of complying with this policy and ensuring that they still make a profit.

Another response to the cost-containment issue has been the formation of health maintenance organizations (HMOs). Those participating in an HMO pay a set annual fee to, and sign a contract with, the organization, which guarantees that all of their health needs for the year will be taken care of by the HMO medical staff. The claim made by HMO staff is that that kind of system cuts costs while making it possible for participants to practice preventive medicine. The rationale is that under this system, physicians have no incentive to perform unneeded medical procedures since they would have to pay for such procedures. Furthermore, checkups are encouraged because they often help to prevent the need for more expensive remediation.

The major problem associated with HMOs, however, is that there is no guarantee that patients who require health care will receive prompt or adequate attention. The legitimacy of that concern was demonstrated in a study in the early 1980s comparing Medicare-eligible cancer patients who enrolled in HMOs with those who were treated under the fee-for-service system. The data revealed that there was a significantly longer period of time between being diagnosed as having cancer and the beginning of treatment for HMO patients than those not participating in HMOs.[55] Among a significant number of physicians, the profit-making incentive would seem to take some precedence over that of providing care, even for patients who most vitally need to be treated. HMOs may indeed cut costs, but whether they ensure quality care is in question.

Cost-containment efforts will undoubtedly continue, but those efforts are also likely to be scrutinized in terms of the adequacy of the care they provide. It ought to be clear that, as long as a medical industrial complex is allowed to control whatever healthcare programs we create for the elderly population, cost containment and quality of care will be in continuous tension. With profit as a major reason for providing services, we cannot expect to be able to cut costs without also sacrificing services.

Another trend today is a set of challenges to the prevalence of the medical model of health. Central to that challenge is the idea that emphasis ought to be placed on holistic medicine. The notion behind this concept is that poor health cannot be explained with a narrow focus on biological disease processes and specific physiological functions. To get at the problems involved, close attention must be paid to all aspects of people's lives and the environments in which they live. Treatments that are prescribed must take all aspects of life into account and must consider the relationship between human life and the environment, as much of the cross-cultural data indicate. A change in life-style or attitude may be as crucial, or more so, to improved health as taking medicine. As Teegarden, a physician, explains, "Rather than focusing only on the malfunctioning body part, it also explores the broader dimensions of the patient's life—physical, nutritional, environmental, emotional, spiritual, and life-style."[56] Teegarden contends that medical practitioners and the public as a whole are moving toward this kind of perspective of health and health care. Indeed, something of a movement is under way to promote the holistic approach to medicine. Heading that movement is the American Holistic Medical Association.

This movement is not only based on the belief that the holistic model results in better health than the medical model; it also represents a challenge to what is seen as too great a reliance on the medical model. Its proponents basically reject "lifesaving technology" in favor of "health-preserving technology" for elderly patients, for example. On the one hand, the net effect of lifesaving technology has often been to sustain people's lives "in a miserable, unhealthy state." On the other hand, life-preserving technology promises longevity on the basis of "prolonged and productive involvement in family and community affairs . . . , and an enduring sense of meaning and purpose of life itself."[57]

The holistic approach does not deny the validity of the specific practices of the medical approach. Rather, the challenge is to the attitude that the biochemical approach either has all of the answers to existing health problems or that no answers are available. That medical practitioners ought to control all diagnostic and treatment processes is also being challenged. From the holistic perspective, other practitioners (such as social workers, religious counselors, nutritionists, and educators) and especially patients themselves and their families have the right to control much of the treatment processes for the restoration and maintenance of health. One does not need an appointment with or a prescription from a physician, for example, to engage in such vital "medicine" as regular physical activity and to learn that it improves circulation, helps get rid of toxic substances, and burns off excess body fat.[58]

The basic concepts and tools are readily available to apply the holistic-medicine model to aging in a very realistic and practical way. Three such concepts, representing steps that can be taken, are particularly important in this effort.

The first step in applying holistic medicine to the aged is health assessment. From the holistic perspective, this involves much more than determining which particular ailments the patient may or may not have. Instead, as in the case of the "Older-American Resources Survey" (OARS), developed at Duke University in the early 1970s, their social, mental, economic, and environmental situations, as well as their physical conditions, are assessed. In addition, an account is taken of the resources that are already available to them.[59]

The second step in applying holistic medicine to the aged is the development of a case-management program. This means (1) determining individuals' needs in order to restore and maintain their lives at maximum functional levels, (2) identifying the resources already available to them, and others that are needed, and (3) assigning responsibility to appropriate people in applying resources to the needs. Central to case management is that the elderly themselves are the most important players in defining their own needs and taking on as much of the responsibility to help themselves as possible.

The third step in applying the holistic approach to the health of the aged is to base caregiving on the principle of reciprocity or interdependency. The assumption here is that most elderly people with healthcare needs also possess talents that can potentially be used to benefit others who are younger (for example, retired teachers can serve as tutors to young students, even from a sick bed). To match young and old in reciprocating helping relationships helps to keep elderly patients in a useful, productive mode, which is an important component of a healthy life.

CONCLUSION

Holistic medicine is a concept in which increasing numbers of people believe. It represents a growing movement. To some extent it has been and continues to be applied to the health care of the elderly population.

Ironically, though, it has not tended to influence the policies that are being set regarding health care for the aged. Medicare and Medicaid legislation, in all of their revisions since 1965, have continued to favor practices prescribed and controlled by those still very much oriented to the medical model.

For an answer to the question of why the medical model continues to dominate policy decisions about health care for the aged, we must turn to the economics and politics involved. Making policy decisions is not so much based on ethical considerations as it is determined by a political process that is very much influenced by the vested interests of those with economic and political power. The truth of the matter is that it is in the best economic interest of both medical professionals and those in the business end of health care for the medical model to remain dominant. This so-called medical industrial complex constitutes an effective lobby in favor of their own interests.

Innovative ideas and demonstrations about how holistic medicine would improve the healthcare system indeed provide definitive and rational bases for change. Cross-cultural data also strengthen that rationale. Vital as the new ideas may be for the future well-being of elderly people, however, they will only be translated into actual policy through the political processes. That will necessitate the formation of coalitions of those willing and able to advocate for the kinds of change needed. At present there are few indications that such a coalition is forming. It remains to be seen whether the pressures of such issues as healthcare costs and dependency among the aged will prompt the necessary political activity to bring the needed changes.

NOTES

[1] Arnold M. Rose, "Subculture of the Aging: A Framework for Research in Social Gerontology," in *Older People and Their Social World,* eds. Arnold M. Rose and Warren A. Peterson (Philadelphia: F. A. Davis, 1965), pp. 3–16.

[2] Rick Carlson, "Health Promotion and Disease Prevention," *Generations,* 7, no. 3 (Spring 1983), 10–12, 72.

[3] Ibid, pp. 10–12.

[4] Ibid.

[5] René Dubos, *Man Adapting* (New Haven, Conn.: Yale University Press, 1965), pp. 344–51.

[6] David Mechanic, *Medical Sociology* (New York: Free Press, 1978), pp. 99–105.

[7] Tom Hickey, *Health and Aging* (Monterey, Calif.: Brooks/Cole, 1980), p. 175.

[8] Nancy Eustis, Jay Greenburg, and Sharon Patten, *Long-Term Care for Older Persons: A Policy Perspective* (Monterey, Calif.: Brooks/Cole, 1984), p. 7.

[9] Carroll Estes et al., *Political Economy, Health, and Aging* (Boston: Little, Brown, 1984), pp. 17–18.

[10] Arnold S. Relman, "The New Medical-Industrial Complex," in *Dominant Issues in Medical Sociology,* ed. Howard D. Schwartz (New York: Random House, 1987), pp. 597–608.

[11] Estes et al., *Political Economy, Health, and Aging,* p. 18.

[12] J. K. Iglehart, "Health Care and American Business," *The New England Journal of Medicine,* 306, no. 2 (January 1982), 120–24.

[13] Carlson, "Health Promotion and Disease Prevention," pp. 10–12, 72.

[14] Eustis Greenburg, and Patten, *Long-Term Care for Older Persons,* pp. 17–18.

[15] Estes et al., *Political Economy, Health, and Aging,* pp. 18, 60.

[16] Carlson, "Health Promotion and Disease Prevention," pp. 10–12, 72.

[17] Estes et al., *Political Economy, Health, and Aging,* p. 50.

[18] Donald E. Gelfand and Jody K. Olsen, *The Aging Network: Programs and Services* (New York: Springer, 1980), pp. 56–58.

[19] Carlson, "Health Promotion and Disease Prevention," p. 10.

[20] Mechanic, *Medical Sociology,* pp. 84–89.

[21] Ibid, pp. 266–67.

[22] Hickey, *Health and Aging,* pp. 92–96.

[23] David C. Stewart and Thomas J. Sullivan, "Illness Behavior and the Sick Role in Chronic Disease: The Case of Multiple Sclerosis," in *Dominant Issues in Medical Sociology,* ed. Howard D. Schwartz (New York: Random House, 1987), pp. 40–51.

[24] US Department of Health and Human Services, Health Care Financing Administration, "Guide to Health Insurance for People with Medicare" (Washington, D.C.: Publication No. HCFA 02110, 1986), pp. 10–11.

[25] Estes et al., *Political Economy, Health, and Aging*, pp. 61–62.

[26] US Department of Health and Human Services, "Guide to Health Insurance for People with Medicare," p. 19.

[27] Danielle A. Dolenc and Charles J. Dougherty, "DRGs: The Counterrevolution in Financing Health Care," *Hastings Center Report*, 15, no. 3 (June 1985), 19–29.

[28] Joshua M. Weiner, Deborah A. Ehrenworth, and Denise A. Spence, "Private Long-Term Care Insurance: Cost, Coverage, and Restrictions," *The Gerontologist*, 27, no. 4 (August 1987), 487–93.

[29] Marc A. Cohen, "The Financial Capacity of the Elderly to Insure for Long-Term Care," *The Gerontologist*, 27, no. 4 (August 1987), 494–502.

[30] David S. Sobel, *Ways of Health: Holistic Approaches to Ancient and Contemporary Medicine* (New York: Harcourt Brace Jovanovich, Inc., 1979), pp. 15–19.

[31] Donald F. Sandner, "Navajo Indian Medicine and Medicine Men," in *Ways of Health: Holistic Approaches to Ancient and Contemporary Medicine*, ed. David S. Sobel (New York: Harcourt Brace Jovanovich, 1979), pp. 117–46.

[32] This discussion of the Navajo healthcare systems is based on observation by this author during ten years of involvement with the Navajo Office on Aging at Window Rock, Arizona.

[33] Manfred Porkert, "Chinese Medicine: A Traditional Healing Science," in *Ways of Health: Holistic Approaches to Ancient and Contemporary Medicine*, ed. David S. Sobel (New York: Harcourt Brace Jovanovich, Inc., 1979), pp. 147–72.

[34] Ibid., p. 166.

[35] Ibid.

[36] Arthur Kleinman, "Social Origins of Distress and Disease: Depression, Neurasthenia, and Pain in Modern China," *Current Anthropology*, 27, no. 5 (December 1986), 499–509.

[37] Paul R. Wolfe, "The Maintenance of Professional Authority: Acupuncture and the American Physician," in *Dominant Issues in Medical Sociology*, ed. Howard D. Schwartz (New York: Random House, 1987), pp. 580–94.

[38] Myrna Lewis, "Aging in the People's Republic of China," *International Journal of Aging and Human Development*, 15, no. 2 (1982), 79–105.

[39] "Growing Old in China," *Beijing Review*, 43 (October 26, 1981), 22–28.

[40] From lectures by Dr. Jing-Fang Li given at Northern Arizona University during the summer of 1986.

[41] Lewis, "Aging in the People's Republic of China," p. 98.

[42] Ibid., p. 96.

[43] From a lecture given by Yu Guanghan in Beijing, June 14, 1984.

[44] Lewis, "Aging in the People's Republic of China," pp. 98–99.

[45] Marjorie H. Cantor, "Strain Among Caregivers: A Study of Experience in the United States," *The Gerontologist*, 23, no. 6 (December 1983), 597–604.

[46] Arnold S. Brown, "Report on Navajo Elderly Abuse" (unpublished research report submitted to the Navajo Office on Aging, Window Rock, Arizona, Fall 1986), pp. 14–15, 18.

[47] Ruth Campbell and Elaine M. Brody, "Women's Changing Roles and Help to the Elderly: Attitudes of Women in the United States and Japan," *The Gerontologist*, 25, no. 6 (December 1985), 584–92.

[48] Elaine M. Brody and Claire B. Schoonover, "Patterns of Parent Care When Adult Daughters Work and When They Do Not," *The Gerontologist*, 26, no. 4 (August 1986), 372–81.

[49] Russell A. Ward, Susan R. Sherman, and Mark LaGory, "Informal Networks and Knowledge of Services for Older Persons," *Journal of Gerontology*, 39, no. 2 (March 1984), 216–23.

[50] Cantor, "Strain Among Caregivers," pp. 597–604.

[51] Beth J. Soldo and Jaana Myllyluoma, "Caregivers Who Live with Dependent Elderly," *The Gerontologist*, 23, no. 6 (December 1983), 605–11.

[52] Daisaku Maeda, "Family Care in Japan," *The Gerontologist,* 23, no. 6 (December 1983), 579–83.

[53] Rosalie A. Kane, "A Family Caregiving Policy: Should There Be One?" *Generations,* 10, no. 1 (Fall 1985), 33–36.

[54] Arnold S. Brown, "Increasing the Effectiveness of the Informal Support System in Rural Areas" (unpublished paper presented at the Western Gerontological Society, 31st Annual Meeting, Denver, Colorado, March 19, 1985).

[55] Howard P. Greenwald, "Cost Containment and Initiation of Care for Cancer in a Medicare-Eligible Population," *Public Administration Review,* 46 (November–December 1986), 651–56.

[56] David Teegarden, "Holistic Health and Medicine in the 1980s," in *The New Holistic Health Handbook: Living Well in a New Age,* eds. Shepherd Bliss et al., (Lexington, Mass.: Stephen Greene Press, 1985), pp. 14–19.

[57] Shepherd Bliss, "Enhancing and Prolonging Life," in *The New Holistic Health Handbook: Living Well in a New Age,* eds. Shepherd Bliss et al., (Lexington, Mass.: Stephen Greene Press, 1985), pp. 285–87.

[58] Ibid., p. 285.

[59] Hickey, *Health and Aging,* pp. 73–75.

14

Social-Service Provision in the Aging Network

INTRODUCTION

A major concern about elderly people in the United States in recent years has been the quality of their social lives. Regardless of their earlier social status, they tend to lose that status as they get older. Furthermore, concern about their social lives rests on the premise, quite prevalent today, that elderly people as a whole are socially, as well as physically and economically, dependent. Their very competence in relating to others is under question. It seems to many that, left to their own devices, the elderly typically become socially isolated and lose their social skills.

The prevailing assumption is that intervention is necessary. Consequently, we Americans have made it a policy to develop social-service programs for our aged, have made them available to those who fit that category, and have even encouraged them to participate. It is significant that the social relationships that are emphasized in these efforts are those within age-peer groups. Little is done to maintain or reestablish intergenerational relations.

In analyzing this aspect of the lives of the aged today, it is important to note that the prevailing view of the elderly as socially dependent represents a drastic change in perspective from that of the past. Clearly, there was a time in American history when older citizens were seen as more socially capable and respectable than any others in society. Far from being socially dependent, they were looked to as social leaders.

In light of the great change in society's view of elderly people, two basic questions become crucial to our understanding of their social standing today and in the future. First, what are the essential factors that have brought about such a switch in views about the social standing of the elderly? Second, what are the consequences to the elderly of the provision of social services?

PROCESSES IN DEFINING THE AGED AS SOCIALLY DEPENDENT

For over 100 years of American history, older people, as a whole, held especially privileged social status in the communities in which they lived. This can be best illustrated by the situation among the Puritans in Massachusetts Bay Colony. Drawing upon the Puritans' literary writings and historical records, Fischer reports that except for the poor, the ungodly, and widowed women, elderly people were not only highly respected and honored, but also treated with much veneration.[1] The environment in which they lived was relatively harsh, and very few lived to be old. Therefore, those who were able to live into old age were respected partly just for having survived. The longer they lived, the more they were respected.

More importantly, though, their respected and venerated positions in society were based on their Puritanical religious beliefs and orientation. Old age was an important sign to them that God had elected and blessed them to be among his chosen followers. From that religious perspective, then, elders also held special positions of power. The young readily rallied behind and obeyed the leadership of elderly "gray champions" in family matters, community affairs, and religious practices, and even into battles when necessary. The positions of power of the elderly patriarchs were also secured by the fact that they owned the land and controlled the economic processes.

There were problems and limitations to the social situations of elderly Puritans, however. For one, they, like everyone else, were very much subject to religious authority. Male heads of the households, no matter what their ages, were held strictly accountable to the church for how they ran their households and how their family members behaved. They lived in what has been called "closed communities and open families." Religious leaders in the strictly controlled communities had the right to enter the homes at any time to discipline family members, especially the heads of the households. Also, any family member had the right, and even the duty, to report any failures of the male heads to comply with the rules of the church.[2]

Another problem with the social status of elderly Puritans is that they tended to experience what Fischer described as "psychic infirmity."[3] While they tended to be respected, venerated, and obeyed, elders among the colonial Puritans were kept at an emotional distance from those under their control.

They were treated as strangers even among their closest relatives, and they enjoyed little or no social support for their authoritative actions. Younger people often resented their authority, and many elders were plagued with continual anxiety. Thus, there were strains in the system of social standing that elderly people in the colonial era enjoyed. Eventually, social change effectively challenged that system.

There have been different analyses of how age relations were challenged in the United States. Fischer contends that it has not been, as some have said, a modern phenomenon at all. Instead, he presents evidence that it began in revolutionary times with a radical redefinition of ideas. The concepts of both equality and liberty were defined as individual rights.[4] At least in principle, young adults no longer needed to feel compelled to follow the dictates of their elders.

These were not really new concepts that suddenly emerged in the United States in the mid-eighteenth century. European philosophers, particularly Immanuel Kant, were arguing that individuals were capable of controlling their own destinies through the use of reason.[5] Also, as Fischer acknowledges, these ideas were an inherent part of Protestant Christianity, which began in Europe and spread to the American colonies. Long before the days of the American Revolution, Roger Williams and others were expelled from Massachusetts Bay Colony for claiming the right of individual freedom. As early as 1636, Williams founded the colony of Rhode Island with a charter establishing individual freedoms.[6]

To a large degree, however, opportunities for the practical application of equality and liberty were rare in the colonial era. There were too many life-threatening dangers for white people in the New World for them to challenge the collective and hierarchical authority of the colonies. The revolutionary era was important because opportunities to expand beyond the colonies were becoming increasingly available, making it possible to challenge the colonial hierarchies. As Fischer analyzes the situation, "Once those great principles were set loose in the world, they developed an irresistible power."[7] The result of this emphasis on equality and individual liberty was a revolution in age relationships. According to Fischer's analysis, the years that followed saw the establishment not only of a cult of youth, but of a defiance of the authority of elders. Old age was increasingly viewed with disdain and disrespect. By the early part of the twentieth century, American literature portrayed the aged as pathetic, empty, and absurd.[8]

Achenbaum analyzes the loss of social status and respect among elderly people in the United States in terms of forces that have brought on "the obsolescence of old age." According to Achenbaum, these forces have been at work since the Civil War. They include (1) the theoretical and practical developments in medical science, (2) the increased social reliance on "experts" who base their expertise on the accumulation of knowledge rather than on experience, and (3) the increased reliance on what was believed to be the efficiency of youth compared with that of older people.[9] Debilitating diseases and the deteriorating results of physiological and mental aging challenged not only the physical capabilities of old people but the idea that they were in any way intellectually superior to younger people. Instead of being viewed as wise, they were increasingly seen as "old fogies" who were set in their ways and unable to learn new things and keep up with the growing body of knowledge. In that context, a lifetime of experience was seen as irrelevant compared to the knowledge that younger experts were able to gain through educational and training processes.

Cowgill has argued that the processes involved in the modernization of societies have brought about the loss of status among elderly people. As explained in Chapter 5, he cites four key variables to explain this phenomenon.[10] First, he points out that the development of health technology is an important component of modernization that has a detrimental effect on the social standing of older people. Health technology has made it possible for most people to live longer than they did in the past. Old age is therefore no longer rare and deserving of great respect by the young. Instead, it has become a symbol of dependency.

The second part of modernization that Cowgill says hurts old people's social standing is economic technology. With progressively newer productive technologies, work skills quickly become obsolete, leaving older workers at a continuous disadvantage. Retirement policies only accentuate the loss of status among elderly workers.

Urbanization is the third aspect of modernization that contributes to social losses among the aged, according to Cowgill. This, more than anything else, breaks up the extended-family system as a unit of intergenerational interdependency. While family relationships continue, independence of the generations is fostered, again leaving the aged at a social disadvantage.

The fourth process related to modernization from which Cowgill claims old persons experience loss of status is education. Each generation must learn more skills and accumulate more knowledge than the previous generation. As Achenbaum also pointed out, this renders the skills of each cohort of elderly people obsolete and even challenges the notion that wisdom rests with the life-long experiences of the aged. In general, as each of these factors illustrates, modernization is characterized by social change, and Cowgill explains that "rapid social change tends to undermine the authority and status of the elderly generation."[11]

The notion that the past was ideal for older people has been challenged in recent years. Analyses have shown that not all societies have honored their elders and that not all old people in any society at any one time have been respected.[12] There are elements of truth to that idea, but few would deny that, in general, the aged have experienced a loss of social status and that the emphasis on their social dependency has increased. The foregoing analyses provide at least part of the explanation for that phenomenon. It is clear from these analyses that the loss of status among old people is not merely an accident of recent history. Instead, it is the product of a long history of changing values and social relationships.

By the mid-1960s in the United States, the wisdom of the aged had effectively been challenged and their authority in society had been denied; moreover, they began to be seen as socially incompetent. Observations of the older population seemed to indicate that they were increasingly isolated, suffered from low self-esteem, and were often afraid and unable to interact meaningfully with others. They were looked upon as somewhat pathetic, as having lost their social skills, and as in need of professional help to have their social lives stabilized and reestablished.[13]

DEVELOPMENT OF SERVICE-PROVIDING NETWORKS

Concern for elderly Americans intensified throughout the 1950s. Their numbers were increasing dramatically and more and more of them were poor and in need of long-term health care. Furthermore, they generally appeared to be becoming progressively inactive and they seemed to be losing their sense of purpose in life. Old age quickly became an issue with which the federal government felt compelled to deal. A National Conference on Aging was held in 1950, an interdepartmental Committee on Aging and Geriatrics was soon formed, and the first official White House Conference was planned for 1961.[14] As explained in Chapter 9, the inactivity of the aged became a particular area about which it was assumed that some kind of intervention was needed. It seemed that the federal government ought to be able to somehow help to restore elderly people to social activity.

Consequently, in partial preparation for the 1961 White House Conference on Aging, the federal government funded a research demonstration project in Minnesota to organize and evaluate the effectiveness of senior citizens' activity centers. Under the leadership of Dr. Arnold Rose, sociologist at the University of Minnesota, centers were developed in five counties throughout the state. Elderly people were located and invited to participate, and the effects on their social lives were studied. It was found that while by no means all elderly people responded, center programs positively impacted the social lives of those who did.[15]

Their social lives were given new meaning in the context of peer-group relationships and activities. Rose saw this as a dynamic process from which a subculture of aging would eventually materialize.[16] This prediction has received little support among gerontologists, however. It rests on a view of the aged as possessing the kinds of interactional and social skills and initiatives that few people believe they have.

Restoring the social lives of the aged and keeping them active through programs of intervention was a major goal in the United States during the 1960s. Senior citizens' centers were developed in local communities across the country.

They served to draw elderly residents together in social activities and to deliver a variety of services that elderly people were assumed to need.

The Older Americans Act was passed in 1965 in response to the recommendations made by the delegates of the 1961 White House Conference on Aging. This piece of legislation committed the United States government, in cooperation with the states, to make it possible for older people "to secure equal opportunity to the full and free enjoyment" of income, health, housing, meaningful activities, social assistance, and a variety of community services.[17]

Title II of the Older Americans Act called for the creation of the Administration on Aging (AoA), a new federal agency responsible for programs on aging mandated by Congress. In provisions of the original and subsequent revisions of the Older Americans Act, many federal, state, regional, and local community agencies were tied together with the AoA into an interdependent working relationship. These agencies were expected to be run by trained planning personnel and were responsible to one another in a hierarchical order, from the top, down.[18]

The AoA was responsible to (1) develop program guidelines for each of the services outlined in the Older Americans Act and make them available to state agencies; (2) set funding allocations for the states based on old-age population figures and their written plans (annual, three-year, five-year, and so on); and (3) monitor state agencies' allocation expenditures and accomplishments. State agencies, in turn, were responsible to (1) develop written plans outlining what programs would be implemented, where they would be implemented, and what would be spent on each program; (2) set funding allocations for each Area Agency on Aging (AAA) within their states, based on written plans submitted by the AAAs; (3) monitor how AAAs spent their allocations and what was accomplished in their respective regions; and (4) submit regular reports of accomplishments to the AoA.

AAAs were, likewise, responsible to (1) develop written plans for their regions; (2) set funding allocations to local community agencies based on program proposals submitted by the local agencies; (3) monitor how local agencies spend their funds and meet their programs goals; and (4) submit regular reports of accomplishments.

Finally, local community agencies are responsible to (1) submit proposals requesting needed funds and outlining how services to the aged will be administered; (2) implement and administer services to the aged in their communities; and (3) submit regular reports of accomplishments to the AAAs.

The kinds of service programs typically provided for elderly people by local agencies with Older Americans Act support include activity centers, nutritional meals (congregate and meals-on-wheels), transportation, homemaker services, telephone reassurance, information and referral, legal services, and outreach. Probably the two most vital parts of this set of services are the centers and the meals programs.

Seniors' centers began as places to provide opportunities for elderly people to become and remain socially active. However, planners soon began to view them from a different perspective. They saw them as ideal places at which and from which many social services could be delivered. The focus was thus changed from what Taietz called the original "voluntary association model," with the major emphasis on social activities, to the "social agency model," with the major emphasis on outreach and provision of services to those with a variety of needs.[19] While participants, regardless of income levels, clearly preferred the voluntary association model, the social agency model has been mandated in Older Americans Act revisions and government policies. In the 1973 amendments to the act, centers began to be referred to as "multipurpose senior centers," and in 1976, Older Americans Act funds began to be made available for the construction of those kinds of centers.[20]

Among other things, seniors' centers have become nutrition sites where congregate meals are provided for senior citizens. Meals programs are the focus of a large percentage of Older Americans Act expenditure. They are seen as vital not only as a way to maintain the health of elderly people, but as a form of social intervention in their lives as well. It has been pointed out that meals have important cultural as well as nutritional significance. As Kart explains, "Food is important in the expression of group identity or solidarity."[21] For most people, therefore, meals are social events that take place either with families or with other culturally meaningful groups. However, many elderly people live alone and lack a social incentive to plan and prepare nutritious meals. Wentz and Gay made the point that "some older people feel so rejected and lonely that they lose the incentive to eat alone."[22] There are also practical reasons, such as lack of income and transportation, that many elderly people do not provide themselves with adequately nutritious meals. Therefore, congregate meals and meals-on-wheels programs for older people have become a vital part of the package of social services provided through the Older Americans Act. Meals are prepared according to strict nutritional guidelines, and transportation is provided to bring elderly people to the nutrition sites to participate in the congregate meals and to deliver the meals to the homebound.

INFLUENCES OF THE AGING NETWORK ON THE AGED

The services provided with Older Americans Act funds and the planning efforts of the aging network have indeed helped to meet some well-established needs of many older Americans. Many elderly people have come to rely on those services on a regular basis. For a good many of them, daily participation, especially in seniors' center activities and the meals programs, has become an enjoyable way of life upon which they depend. Lowy describes these centers as follows:

> The philosophy of the senior center is based on the premises that aging is a normal developmental process; that human beings need peers with whom they can interact and who are available as a source of encouragement and support; and that adults have the right to have a voice in determining matters in which they have a vital interest.[23]

However, important as they may seem to be and as institutionalized as they are today, by no means would all senior citizens agree with Lowy's optimistic assessment about the quality of services provided at seniors' centers. Evidence of that is the fact that a substantial percentage of older people in virtually every community in the United States choose not to participate in any of the programs offered at seniors' centers. Attention has been given to the problem of the underutilization of services by eligible elderly people. Holmes and his colleagues noted that this problem has been reported especially among minority elderly. They conducted a survey of community-based programs serving minorities to determine the extent to which they were participating. They discovered that utilization of services was somewhat greater in those programs in which outreach efforts were carried out. Most important, though, was the extent to which there were minority members on the program staffs.

The questions of whether or not potential elderly participants might define the services as necessary or appropriate and whether they were being delivered in acceptable ways were neither raised nor included as part of the survey. The primary conclusion of the project was that minority staff ought to be recruited.[24]

Underutilization of transportation services was also discovered in a special research-demonstration project in the early 1970s. The most troublesome factor was that those who obviously needed the services most—people isolated in their homes—were mostly the ones who failed to use the services. This was true even though part of the transportation system was specifically designed to target that group of elderly.[25]

It has been discovered that, while there are elderly people from all ethnic, racial, and social class groups who take advantage of senior citizens' center programs, few, if any, specific centers serve elderly people with different backgrounds. Fewer still serve the frail or confused elderly.[26]

It is noteworthy that two basic assumptions in the lack-of-utilization literature do not seem to even be questioned. First, it is assumed that social services will better meet the needs of the elderly recipients if they are planned and administered by professionals. Contrary to what Lowy reports about center programs allowing seniors a voice in matters that are vital to them, in reality, they generally neither control nor participate in the planning of the programs designed for them. Instead, program guidelines come from the government and are locally administered by professionals. It is true that some elderly people serve on advisory councils and in that role may exert a small amount of influence, but only within the limits set by professionally developed guidelines and agency policies.

The second basically unchallenged assumption that seems to be made in the lack-of-utilization literature is that failure to take advantage of services is somehow unreasonable and irrational. At best, the basis of noncompliance responses of the aged is assumed to be misunderstandings or unfounded fears about the real value of the programs.

The typical response of program planners and administrators is to improve their outreach efforts, add more services, or improve the service-delivery system. They attempt to make their programs even more professionally administered. In a study comparing seniors' centers in rural and urban areas, for example, Krout found that centers in rural areas offered fewer services because the sizes of their budgets and staffs were inadequate.[27] Taietz and Milton had found these kinds of rural–urban discrepancies and recommended that rural centers needed more staff, help from outside consultants, and seminars on grantsmanship.[28] In another study, Krout also discovered that even centers with large budgets were experiencing barriers to the goal of serving as a community "focal point" in behalf of the aged. Their efforts to develop linkages with other community agencies and to thereby serve more elderly people were also meeting with resistance. He concludes that ways must be found to overcome the problem of linkages in order to make it possible for centers to serve as community focal points.[29]

Schneider investigated what kept elderly people from participating in nutrition programs in Virginia, where an intensive outreach project had been carried out. He found that there was a combination of personal (attitudinal), environmental (racial differences), and programmatic barriers involved. His basic recommendation was that outreach workers needed to be better organized and informed about the community and the program.[30]

The Pennsylvania Office on Aging responded to the problem that they identified as a "fragmentation of services" with a state-wide organizational effort in the late 1970s. Their approach was focused on what they called "service management." Trained service managers were added to all of their AAA staffs throughout the state, professional consultants were made available, and all staff were trained in the service-management procedures. Each AAA could choose between two possible service-management models, depending on how they wanted to process their clients.[31] Gottesman and his fellow planners concluded that such a system is obviously "of real help" to clients since "it takes a professional with several years of experience to know when and how to access services."[32]

It is obvious from this analysis that the aging network operates almost exclusively from a professional orientation. Indeed, that is the orientation that was recommended by the 1971 White House Conference on Aging delegates. Even though they recommended "involvement of older people and independent agencies and organizations in the making of policies and in all aspects of planning," the more basic part of the recommendation was that "primary responsibility for planning and coordination of health, welfare, and other services for the older population should be placed in a public service agency with divisions at the federal, state, and local level with strong administrative authority and funding controls and the capability of functioning across departmental lines."[33]

To be sure, the professional approach to service delivery has accomplished much in identifying some types of needs and in efficiently providing vital services to the elderly. What is largely overlooked with this approach, though, is the effect of professionalism itself on the social and psychological lives of the elderly recipients. Specifically, attention needs to be paid to the ways in which it tends to create a sense of helplessness, powerlessness, and dependency. From that perspective, it ought to be obvious that decisions not to accept available services, by elderly people who are constantly sensitive to the risk of losing their independence, are entirely rational and deserve to be respected.

The professional approach to the planning and delivery of social services to the elderly is a dependency-creating process. That in itself raises serious questions about the validity of the ways in which professional service providers tend to define and attempt to meet the social needs of older people. It is commonly recognized that elderly people are overwhelmingly concerned about maintaining as much of their independence as possible. An increasingly prevalent way of trying to meet that need on the part of the aging network's professionally oriented personnel is to enable elderly people to remain in their own homes, a situation that has come to be labeled, and is presumed to epitomize, "independent living." This is made possible by professionally planned and delivered in-home services. Elderly individuals are thus enabled to remain at home by accepting given packages of services that are not at all unlike those they might receive in institutions (meals planned by someone else and delivered at specified times, housekeeping and friendly visitor services scheduled at the initiative and convenience of the service providers, and so on). While this approach may well be an acceptable and even necessary alternative to institutionalization, it is difficult to understand the logic of the claim that it represents independent living. It simply does not meet the need to remain independent. In fact, the more isolated these older people become in their homes, the more dependent they become on those who deliver services.

CROSS-CULTURAL COMPARISONS IN SERVICE PROVISION

A search of the cross-cultural literature on the provision of social services to the elderly reveals some patterns that are quite similar to those in the United States. This is especially true of the industrially developed nations of Europe and North America.

In the survey on aging in three industrial societies (Denmark, Great Britain, and the United States) carried out in the 1960s by an international team of investigators, it was discovered that social-service programs for older people had already been developed in all three countries. It is important to note that they were reported as welfare programs, included in the existing general welfare systems. Undoubtedly, that represents the prevailing view of elderly people in those countries.[34] The welfare perception of social services still prevails in European countries today.[35]

As reported in the 1960s international study, even though a majority of the social services were provided by the family members of the elderly, they were supplemented by community agencies. No matter who provided them, though, survey respondents reported a reluctance to accept assistance with personal affairs even when they needed the help. Many said that they would rather go without. The investigators interpreted that kind of response as an "obstinate" attempt to "preserve their independence."[36] While older people would perhaps prefer that such services come from family members rather than outsiders, they are apparently seen as a threat to independence regardless of the source.

In more recent years the provision of services has become increasingly professionalized in other modern Western societies besides the United States. In fact, Kane and Kane believe that we Americans could well learn from the professionally run system of care provided to elderly Canadians. They report that in three Canadian provinces (Ontario, Manitoba, and British Columbia), social workers and nurses, functioning as case managers, control social and other services to the aged.[37]

The services provided are free to the elderly participants. Because of this, some have worried that too great a demand will be made on them. It is reported, though, that this has not happened, because case managers basically control what services are used when.[38] Kane and Kane present this system of care as one that the United States might well adopt because it demonstrates that the kinds of services needed by elderly people can be provided when and where they are needed at affordable prices to the general society and certainly to the elderly people themselves. From the perspective of concern about accelerating costs and growing need for various levels of care on the part of the elderly, this is certainly a compelling argument. Case management is rapidly becoming seen as an efficient and effective welfare service-delivery system.

Nevertheless, it is a professionally controlled and administered system. As a system, it assumes that the elderly recipients, or "clients," are not capable of defining their own needs. Such a system fails to consider one of the most important social psychological needs of older people: the maintenance of their sense of independence. It is, instead, a dependency-creating system.

In a number of other cultures, there seems to be less emphasis on the provision of social services as such for older people, and less loss of social status and independence with age. Three aspects of older people's lives seem to directly contribute to those differences. One important factor is the intimate involvement of older people in the daily routines of their families, especially their children and grandchildren. This situation prevails in a number of countries where most older people live in three-generation households with their adult children. In that case, their social lives are basically oriented to their families, and their social needs are provided for by family members.

As we have already noted, a large majority of elderly Japanese live with their children, and their social status seems to be higher than it is for those in the industrialized nations of the West. The three-generation household is not only a tradition in Japan, but has become a part of government policy.[39] Maeda reports that the government has offered a number of incentives to families to encourage three-generation households: (1) tax deductions, and even exemptions, (2) loans for house remodeling, (3) provision of special equipment, (4) provision for short-term stays in nursing homes for emergencies, (5) daycare programs for the impaired elderly, (6) community home-help assistance, and (7) visiting nurses.[40]

Despite these efforts, the trend in Japan is, nevertheless, for fewer and fewer older people to live with their children. Between 1970 and 1980, the portion of the older population living with their children dropped from 76.9 percent to 68.7 percent, while those living with only their spouses rose from 12.1 percent to 18.9 percent, and those living alone increased from 5.5 percent to 8.2 percent. During that same decade, the number of beds for elderly in institutions more than doubled.[41] It is also true that, while respect for and authority of the elderly may still be an observed cultural tradition in Japan, the attitudes of many younger people seem to represent a challenge to that tradition. Campbell and Brody found, for example, that women—who are basically responsible for the care of elderly family members—tend to feel that old people are too powerful and do not gain in wisdom with age.[42] As the trends continue, it is reasonable to expect that Japanese elderly people will increasingly find themselves in dependency modes similar to those in modern Western nations.

The situation for the aged in Hong Kong is similar to that in Japan. Historically they have lived in the homes of their children, and this pattern was made government policy in 1965. There seemed to be no need for special social-service programs for the older population.[43] As their numbers grew and households were increasingly confined to nuclear units, however, government policies on aging changed. Many "care in the community" service programs have been developed for older residents, including community nursing home help, day care, laundry and canteen services, social and recreational activities at centers for the aged, and sheltered employment. Those over the age of 70 are now also eligible for a monthly income allowance.[44]

Clearly, the pattern of decreasing emphasis on families to provide for the social needs of the elderly and increasing reliance on publicly supported social-service programs also prevails in Hong Kong. The perception of the elderly as dependent will undoubtedly be a product of that trend. The growing perception of dependency does not merely stem from publicly supported services, however. The situations of older people in Japan and Hong Kong indicate, in fact, that it probably begins with the younger family members, who increasingly tend to view their older members as burdens, particularly in societies in which individual achievement is stressed. For that reason, it must be realized that intimate, daily involvement of older people with their families does not necessarily help to maintain their social status or keep them from becoming treated as dependent. It may, in fact, contribute to the perception that they are dependent.

Another aspect of elderly people's lives that tends to create a more positive perception of their social worth has to do with the systems of care under which they live. The American system of welfare has always placed, and continues to place, the emphasis on those with special needs. This sets welfare recipients apart from others and stigmatizes them as less competent and less worthy. In contrast, other nations have adopted welfare systems that are accepted as part of the everyday lives of all citizens. The philosophy behind this kind of system of care is that, like education, welfare serves basic, universal human needs. No one can do without it and no one independently has the resources that are necessary to meet those needs. In those countries that have developed systems of care based on this philosophy, the typical approach is to provide publicly supported, comprehensive, cradle-to-grave welfare programs at no charge or at minimal charge to recipients.

Many nations have established these kinds of healthcare systems, and virtually all socialist and communist countries provide all forms of social services on this basis. The advantage to elderly people of this kind of system of care is that it does not set them apart from the rest of the population as people with needs with which they are incapable of dealing. Being a recipient of welfare has no stigma attached to it. In fact, it has been pointed out that in the People's Republic of China, welfare to families and individuals of all ages is so much a part of their daily lives that elderly people are not only the recipients of it but also often dispense it to families in their neighborhoods.[45]

The third aspect of elderly people's lives that helps to maintain their social competency is the extent to which they are involved in interdependent and reciprocating relationships with others in their social settings. In the United States, elderly retired people offer their services in millions of hours of volunteer services. Yet the public perception of being old as a state of dependency and social incompetence continues partly because the elderly are seldom involved in direct reciprocal relationships. In contrast, the aged in a number of other societies do have those kinds of relationships in their daily lives, particularly with their families.

Kerns did an in-depth study of the Black Carib elderly in Belize, along the Caribbean coast of Central America.[46] She found an inconsistency between the attitudes of the people about old age and how they actually related to old people. On the one hand, they almost universally expressed negative attitudes about old age. On the other hand, most of them felt affection and a deep sense of obligation toward their elderly parents. As Kerns put it, "Filial responsibility to parents is a cultural ideal espoused by all."[47] The key to this sense of responsibility, though, is not so much that cultural tradition demands it. Instead, it is based on mutual helping relationships between parents, especially mothers, and their children that are developed over their years of living together. Widowed mothers, who typically have no source of economic security of their own, generously offer their helping services to their children as a base from which they can expect reciprocal help from their adult children when they need it. Thus, the elderly Black Carib are treated not as socially incompetent or dependent, but as interdependent partners.

Much is made of the idea that the ancient tradition of filial piety is still being practiced in China, and that older people are therefore respected and maintain high social status. This no doubt helps to explain the social respect they still enjoy. Perhaps more important, though, is the fact that they generally have all three of the previously mentioned living situations to enhance their social competence.

As we learned in Chapter 11, when elderly Chinese retire, they typically receive relatively high pensions. In addition, they continue to receive free medical and welfare services along with the rest of the population. They are thus no more economically dependent upon their children than their children are upon them. As we have also noted, almost all of them live in three-generation households with the family of one of their children. There they have roles that are vital to the welfare of the family. Besides child-care and housekeeping activities that they perform while their sons and daughters-in-law are at work, they also contribute on about an equal basis to family expenditures. Even though there are families in which there may be serious intergenerational problems on a personal level (such as between mothers-in-law and daughters-in-law), the relationships are characteristically interdependent and reciprocal.

This does not mean that life among Chinese elderly is ideal. Many of them live in poor financial and environmental conditions. However, they do not tend to be singled out and treated as though they were socially incompetent and dependent.

POTENTIAL FUTURE TRENDS IN SOCIAL-SERVICE PROVISION

What, then, is the future of the provision of social services for the aged? It cannot be denied that many of them do have special social needs, or that the programs of intervention that have been devised in recent years have helped to revitalize the social lives of many. This point can be illustrated by citing the example of a program in which this author was involved in the early 1970s in Butte, Montana.

Elderly participants could request a special bus, with stewards on board, to pick them up at their homes, deliver them to their destination, and return them home later. The purpose was to offer transportation to individuals who otherwise lacked it at a cost they could afford. In analyzing the utilization data from this project, it was learned that for many, the rides themselves became meaningful social events that they would not otherwise have had.[48] Almost certainly, the lives of most of those individuals once again became socially isolated when that part of the program was not re-funded and had to be discontinued.

Perhaps, then, elderly people in the United States who have social needs that they cannot satisfy on their own are simply doomed to live out their lives in an essentially dependent mode. Perhaps, as some trends already indicate, elderly people in other nations will be forced into that same dependency as their numbers grow and their social needs multiply. If that is indeed the inevitable future condition of older persons, then their lives will not only be affected negatively, but the burden of their care can do nothing but increase. The truth is that the more our service-providing systems promote dependency among the aged, the more dependent the aged become. This is true because we humans tend to lose our decision-making and planning skills when we cease to use them. Those kinds of skills keep life at any age vital and prevent us from becoming burdens to society. They make it possible for us to continue to make valuable social contributions.

A cross-cultural analysis reveals that older people in many societies continue to be intimately involved with and are respected by their families. This seems to keep them from becoming dependent upon societal benevolence for their social needs. Family involvement is still a prevalent tendency among some American ethnic groups. Johnson found this to be true, for example, in the immigrant environment of Italian Americans in Syracuse, New York.[49] Elderly Italian Americans are still respected and allowed to enjoy control over younger family members, even over those who have become educated, successful professional workers. This is accomplished by a strict family-oriented socialization that begins early in their lives, and by constant reminders by the family elders of younger members' family obligations.

This kind of family involvement on the part of elderly members has long been rejected by most elderly and younger family members alike in the United States, however. Decisions not to live with and not to interfere in the family affairs of their adult children constitute compliance with what has become a well-established social norm among elderly Americans. It is doubtful that traditionally oriented ethnic groups, such as Italian Americans, will be able to ignore that norm for very many generations. Furthermore, family involvement alone by no means assures elderly people that they will not be placed into situations of premature dependency. Indeed, the evidence seems to indicate that in most cases, family members are the first ones to express the idea that elderly people represent burdens of care rather than social assets to their families. This type of attitude seems to emerge in particular societies as the numbers of older people increase, even when it represents a serious break with centuries-old traditions, as is beginning to happen in Japan, for example. To be sure, families still offer elderly people a vital sense of security that is not available to them elsewhere. Families also often push older members into states of social dependency, however.

It has been proposed that chronological age should no longer be used as the criterion by which individuals become eligible to participate in publicly supported social-service programs. According to this argument, actual, documentable needs would be a better way of determining the populations to whom to target such programs.[50] The logic of this position is two-fold: (1) Making services available to all older people is too expensive; and (2) by doing so, we tend to reinforce the negative perceptions of old age. As Neugarten notes, that process may end up "stigmatizing rather than liberating older people from the negative effects of the label, 'old.' "[51]

Compelling as this argument may seem, there are good reasons that it is neither conceptually nor practically feasible. Conceptually, as the primary advocate for using need instead of age as the criterion, Neugarten fails to recognize how relative "needs" are to existing situations and our definitions of those situations.[52] She implies, but fails to adequately establish, that there are no needs that are unique enough to old people to warrant special attention in behalf of that population. Cook raises the issue of "specialness" in determining need among the aged with regard to victimization. She correctly reports that they are no more victimized than those of any age in terms of physical or financial losses, but that their level of fear about being victims of crime is indeed special for the aged.[53] Such experiences as retiring and becoming retired are unique enough to old age to be considered special, and both are associated with serious social adjustment problems. Practically, these are real situations that elderly people face today, and they represent some level of social need for many. The question is not whether elderly people do or do not have social needs (they do), but how those needs are treated.

Providing for the social needs of the elderly without also making them dependent may be close to impossible, given the present set of social and political circumstances. From a societal perspective, for example, there may be an important rationale for making elderly people dependent and treating them as dependent. From that perspective, formalized and professionalized provision of services for the aged becomes not so much a way of meeting their individual social needs as a form of social control. As Williams and his colleagues explain it, the public provision of services to elderly Americans has made it possible for them to remain somewhat independent of their adult children, but it did not make them less dependent. What has taken place is "an increase in dependence on and control by the state and its representatives in various government bureaucracies."[54] As the number of elderly retired people grows, they inevitably represent threats to many components of the existing societal power structures. Providing strictly controlled services to at least those who are the most apt to agitate for change makes them dependent on those providing the services. Creating that kind of dependency is an extremely effective way of exerting social control over a population. Dependent people seldom become change agents.

This is not to say that our systems of services were created as a conspiracy to control elderly trouble-makers. Neither do professionals perform their duties with that as their basic motivation. Nevertheless, the systems of care are indeed organized to operate that way. Service providers know that they must control the service-delivery processes for the sake of efficiency. If advisory boards are added to give elderly recipients a voice in how the programs will function, they become one more element of the process to manipulate and control. To be sure, our service-provision systems work efficiently and deliver important services to our elderly citizens. We need to understand, though, that they do not deal with one of the most basic social concerns of today's older population: the fear of becoming dependent.

The existing system of social-service provision is well institutionalized and thus could not easily be changed. A more important issue, however, is whether it is even possible to provide such services without making the elderly participants basically dependent. Providing services to individuals is a form of intervention into their lives, and the very notion that any form of intervention is necessary implies that, at least in that sense, they are dependent. The fact is, people of all ages are subject to some forms of intervention and dependency. It happens to all of us as a normal part of life. The issue with elderly people, then, is not whether they experience a certain amount of dependency or not. Rather, it is whether dependency permeates so much of their lives that they become labeled "dependent" and begin to see themselves as, and act as if they were, socially incompetent. Intervention, as such, does not bring this about, but some kinds and amounts can and do.

Clearly, if social services are to be offered to the elderly today in ways that enhance rather than diminish their social competency, then new approaches are necessary. At least two promising approaches are already available and deserve consideration.

One promising approach is what has been referred to as the self-help movement. Essentially, this means creating situations in which elderly people themselves are given the major responsibility for planning and even conducting the social services they need. One such approach, called a "network model," was put into operation in a residential area of San Francisco where over 20 percent of the residents were elderly.[55] Of central important to the success of the program called the Senior Block Information Service (SBIS), is a newsletter that provides a vital link to the social network for virtually all elderly people in the neighborhood. The newsletter provides information about available services and people in the network. Elderly volunteers are recruited from the neighborhood, and they provide much of the leadership in planning monthly meetings and special events. In reporting on this unique program, Ruffini and Todd conclude that "the network model, as represented by SBIS, works for a range of people. . . . Furthermore, it provides a latent structure that may be activated when necessary to mobilize large numbers in a crisis."[56]

Another promising approach for the enhancement of elderly people's social competency is to place special emphasis on intergenerational relationships that are reciprocal and interdependent. This is probably the most important lesson we can learn from the cross-cultural literature on the social standing of elderly people. In those societies in which the elderly are viewed as socially competent, they have family or community roles, or both, to fill in addition to their status as recipients of needed services. Reciprocal roles continue to tie together the older and younger generations in China, for example, in inter-dependent relationships and mutual respect. Johnson reports that interdependent relationships were also part of the basis for continued intergenerational respect among Italian Americans.[57] While most reciprocal relationships reported in the literature have taken place in the family setting, this approach could just as well be applied in the context of publicly supported social-service programs. This has already been suggested as a valuable additional emphasis in the programs for the aging in Hong Kong.[58]

CONCLUSION

In our critique of the work of the aging network in planning and providing services to the aged in the United States, we find reasons to be both optimistic and pessimistic about the condition of the aged in the future. The network has been criticized by some for inconsistency and inefficiency. Given the complexity of its structure, the enormity of its tasks, and the diversity of its clientele, its record on those counts is a relatively good one. Both the structure and the operational approaches of the network have become institutionally entrenched as part of the American service-provision system. Changes may be needed in social-service delivery methods, but they will not be made merely because new approaches may be more meritorious than existing ones.

Whether approaches such as those we have discussed here are considered for adoption will depend upon active advocacy on the part of those who are concerned about the social well-being of elderly people. It has been pointed out that older people have very little power or influence over policy issues related to them. Indeed, the dependency-creating forces that exist today may continue to effectively deny them the power needed to make the changes that they see as important. There are some indications, however, that they may now be beginning to take the necessary initiative to advocate effectively in their own behalf. If so, that in itself will help to demonstrate their social competency to the rest of society.

NOTES

[1] David H. Fischer, *Growing Old in America* (New York: Oxford University Press, 1978), pp. 30–40.

[2] Floyd M. Martinson, *Family in Society* (New York: Dodd, Mead, 1970), pp. 17–22.

[3] Fischer, *Growing Old in America*, pp. 72–73.

[4] Ibid., pp. 108–12.

[5] W. T. Jones, *A History of Western Philosophy* (New York: Harcourt, Brace, 1952), pp. 808–10.

[6] Kenneth S. Latourette, *A History of Christianity* (New York: Harper and Brothers, 1953), p. 953.

[7] Fischer, *Growing Old in America*, p. 110.

[8] Ibid., pp. 113–56.

[9] W. Andrew Achenbaum, "The Obsolescence of Old Age," in *Dimensions of Aging: Readings*, eds. Jon Hendricks and C. Davis Hendricks (Cambridge, Mass.: Winthrop, Inc., 1979), pp. 21–38.

[10] Donald O. Cowgill, "Aging and Modernization: A Revision of the Theory," in *Aging in America: Readings in Social Gerontology*, eds. Cary S. Kart and Barbara B. Manard (Sherman Oaks, Calif.: Alfred, 1981), pp. 111–32.

[11] Donald O. Cowgill, *Aging Around the World* (Belmont, Calif.: Wadsworth, 1986), p. 198.

[12] John B. Williamson, Linda Evans, and Lawrence A. Powell, *The Politics of Aging: Power and Policy* (Springfield, Ill.: Chas. C Thomas, 1982), pp. 51–71.

[13] Joseph A. Kuypers and Vern L. Bengtson, "Social Breakdown and Competence: A Model of Normal Aging," *Human Development*, 16 (1973), 181–201.

[14] Bennett M. Rich and Martha Baum, *The Aging: A Guide to Public Policy* (Pittsburgh: University of Pittsburgh Press, 1984), pp. 25–26.

[15] Bernard E. Nash and Gerald Bloedow, "The Five-County Demonstration Project," in *Aging in Minnesota*, ed. Arnold M. Rose (Minneapolis: University of Minnesota Press, 1963), pp. 21–33.

[16] Arnold M. Rose, "The Subculture of the Aging: A Framework for Research in Social Gerontology," in *Older People and Their Social World*, eds. Arnold M. Rose and Warren A. Peterson (Philadelphia: F. A. Davis, 1965), pp. 3–16.

[17] Donald E. Gelfand and Jody K. Olsen, *The Aging Network: Programs and Services* (New York: Springer, 1980), pp. 243–44.

[18] Marjorie Cantor and Virginia Little, "Aging and Social Care," in *Handbook on Aging and the Social Sciences*, eds. Robert H. Binstock and Ethel Shanas (New York: Van Nostrand Reinhold, 1985), p. 768.

[19] Philip Taietz, "Two Conceptual Models of the Senior Center," *Journal of Gerontology*, 31, no. 2 (March 1976), 219–22.

[20] Louis Lowy, *Social Policies and Programs on Aging* (Lexington, Mass.: Lexington Books, 1980), pp. 163–4.

[21] Cary S. Kart, *The Realities of Aging: An Introduction to Gerontology* (Boston: Allyn & Bacon, 1985), p. 222.

[22] Molly S. Wantz and John E. Gay, *The Aging Process: A Health Perspective* (Cambridge, Mass.: Winthrop, 1981), p. 287.

[23] Lowy, *Social Policies and Programs on Aging*, p. 164.

[24] Douglas Holmes et al., "The Use of Community-Based Services in Long-Term Care of Older Minority Persons," *The Gerontologist*, 19, no. 4 (August 1979), 389–97.

[25] Arnold S. Brown, "Final Report: The Problems of Mobilizing the Elderly with a Special Transportation Project" (unpublished report of demonstration-research grant #93-P-75063/8-02 to Title IV Research and Development Grants Program, Administration on Aging, Social and Rehabilitative Service, Department of Health, Education, and Welfare, Washington, D.C., 20201), October 1972.

[26] Dwight Frankfather, *The Aged in the Community* (New York: Praeger, 1977), pp. 36–39.

[27] John A. Krout, "Rural–Urban Differences in Senior Center Activities and Services," *The Gerontologist*, 27, no. 1 (February 1987), 92–97.

[28] Philip Taietz and Sande Milton, "Rural–Urban Differences in the Structure of Services for the Elderly in Upstate New York Counties," *Journal of Gerontology*, 3, no. 3 (May 1979), 429–37.

[29] John A. Krout, "Senior Center Linkages in the Community," *The Gerontologist*, 26, no. 5 (October 1986), 510–15.

[30] Robert L. Schneider, "Barriers to Effective Outreach in the Title VII Nutrition Programs, *The Gerontologist*, 19, no. 2 (April 1979), 163–68.

[31] Barbara Ishizaki, Leonard E. Gottesman, and Stacey M. MacBride, "Determinants of Model Choice for Service Management Systems," *The Gerontologist*, 19, no. 4 (August 1979), 385–88.

[32] Leonard E. Gottesman, Barbara Ishizaki, and Stacey M. MacBride, "Service Management: Plan and Concept in Pennsylvania, *The Gerontologist*, 19, no. 4 (August 1979), 379–85.

[33] "1971 White House Conference on Aging" (an unpublished report to the delegates from the Conference Sections and Special Concerns Sessions), p. 50.

[34] Ethel Shanas et al., *Old People in Three Industrial Societies,* (New York: Atherton Press, 1968), pp. 102–31.

[35] Cantor and Little, "Aging and Social Care," p. 769.

[36] Shanas et al., *Old People in Three Industrial Societies,* p. 115.

[37] Robert Kane and Rosalie Kane, *A Will and a Way* (New York: Columbia University Press, 1985), pp. 263–64.

[38] Ibid., p. 263.

[39] "The Japanese-Style Welfare System," *Japan Quarterly,* 30 (July–September 1983), 328–30.

[40] Daisaku Maeda, "Family Care in Japan," *The Gerontologist,* 23, no. 6 (December 1983), 579–83.

[41] Ibid., p. 580.

[42] Ruth Campbell and Elaine M. Brody, "Women's Changing Roles and Help to the Elderly: Attitudes of Women in the United States and Japan," *The Gerontologist,* 25, no. 6 (December 1985), 584–92.

[43] Nelson Wing-sun Chow, "The Chinese Family and Support of the Elderly in Hong Kong," *The Gerontologist,* 23, no. 6 (December 1983), 584–88.

[44] Ibid., p. 585.

[45] Bong-ho Mok, "In the Service of Socialism: Social Welfare in China," *Social Work,* 28, no. 4 (July–August 1983), 269–72.

[46] Virginia Kerns, "Aging and Mutual Support Relations Among the Black Carib," in *Aging in Culture and Society,* ed. Christine L. Fry (Brooklyn , N.Y.: J. F. Bergin, 1980), pp. 112–25.

[47] Ibid., p. 114.

[48] Brown, "Final Report."

[49] Colleen L. Johnson, "Interdependence and Aging in Italian Families," in *Growing Old in Different Societies: Cross-Cultural Perspectives,* ed. Jay Sokolovsky (Belmont, Calif.: Wadsworth, 1983), pp. 92–101.

[50] Bernice L. Neugarten, "Policy for the 1980s: Age or Need Entitlement?" in *Age or Need? Public Policies for Older People,* ed. Bernice L. Neugarten (Beverly Hills, Calif.: Sage, 1982), pp. 19–32.

[51] Ibid., p. 27.

[52] Alfred R. Lindesmith, Anselm L. Strauss, and Norman K. Denzin, *Social Psychology* (New York: Holt, Rinehart and Winston, 1977), pp. 255–58.

[53] Fay Lomax Cook, "Age as an Eligibility Criterion," in *Age or Need? Public Policies for Older People,* ed. Bernice L. Neugarten (Beverly Hills, Calif.: Sage, 1982), pp. 171–203.

[54] Williamson, Evans, and Powell, *The Politics of Aging,* p. 215.

[55] Julio L. Ruffini and Harry F. Todd, "A Network Model for Leadership Development Among the Elderly," *The Gerontologist,* 19, no. 2 (April 1979), 158–62.

[56] Ibid., p. 160.

[57] Johnson, "Interdependence and Aging in Italian Families," pp. 95–99.

[58] Nelson Wing-sun Chow, "The Chinese Family and Support of the Elderly in Hong Kong," p. 587.

15

Dying and Death as Experiences of the Aged

INTRODUCTION

As a child growing up on a farm in northern Montana, this author lived in the midst of death on an almost daily basis. Watching wild animals die was a common experience. Many pets died of accidents or problems of aging. Watching, and even participating in, the killing and butchering of domestic animals was also part of the rural life of those days.

Neither did human death escape my farm-boy experiences. A 26-year-old neighbor who lived only half a mile away suddenly caught bronchial pneumonia one cold winter day and died before his parents could get him to the hospital 40 miles away. Only a year later I was suddenly afflicted with the same disease and rode the 40 miles in an unheated automobile afraid that I would not make it in time either.

Death was no stranger in that neighborhood. It was something that happened to young and old alike. It took place where people lived, in their homes or places of work, more than anywhere else. Those who died were buried ceremoniously with the participation of the whole neighborhood, and survivors went on with their lives.

How different are the experiences of death and dying today? By and large, death now occurs among those who are old, and it is typically preceded by a somewhat extended period of dying. Furthermore, few people nowadays die either at home or where they work.

Death has thus become a subject in which gerontologists have become keenly interested. We want to explore how experiences with death have changed and how those changes have affected older people and their relationships.

DEATH AS A COMMON EXPERIENCE OF THE PAST

Many of today's students of death and dying point to the past as the time when death was not avoided but was dealt with realistically, meaningfully, and effectively. When the United States was basically an agrarian nation and technological development was limited, it was indeed difficult for most people to avoid direct experiences with death. The death of family members, close friends, and neighbors of all ages was also inescapable. Furthermore, people in the past typically died in their homes or work places, in the midst of family and friends who knew them intimately. Thus, survivors were often present as their loved ones died.

One distinct advantage that people in rural communities of the past had when someone close to them died was that they were almost always surrounded by the support of others. Families tended to be large, neighbors were often close friends, and communities were made up of people in daily contact with one another. Experience with death was rarely a lonely event. Even neighbors who were not close would pay their respects and express concern. Survivors were comforted, helped to make some common-sense meaning of death, and encouraged to move on with their lives.

Funerals tended to be highly meaningful events in the rural United States. They were events at which the total attention of communities was focused on the needs of survivors. They were also times when the lives of those who had died, even those not well liked, were ceremoniously honored and even celebrated. Their lives were put into the best possible perspective, providing assurances that they had not lived in vain but had made contributions to their families and communities.

To be sure, experiences with death in those kinds of settings in the past were real and vital. We must be careful, however, not to depict that as the ideal with regard to matters of death and dying. It was far from it.

The frequency of experiences with death in our past history by no means made them easy. The loss of close relatives and friends in death was traumatic and dreaded. Grief was shared, but it was nevertheless harsh and often viewed as unfair. The trauma of so much unpredicted death was neither easy nor understood, and was devastating to whole communities.[1] Baum and Baum suggest that, contrary to what is assumed in today's literature on death and dying, avoidance of the problems of death was probably more prevalent in the past than it is today. Elaborate funerals were perhaps more a way of avoiding death than actually coming to grips with it.[2] Moving through the rituals undoubtedly helped people to put the "why" questions aside unanswered and allowed them to get on with the problems of making a living and surviving.

People did not pursue the meaning of death or of the dying process. Dying as an elongated process was something few experienced. The few who did had little understanding of the agony involved and found little or no community support or empathy. People in the past faced death because they had very little choice, and dealt with it in practical ways that somewhat helped to alleviate the personal agony and the societal hardship. However, we would be mistaken if we supposed that they were any more emotionally or philosophically comfortable with death than we in modern societies are.

DYING AS AN OLD-AGE EXPERIENCE

A number of basic changes in our perception and experience of death have taken place in recent years. These changes, to a large extent, are directly related to the advancements that have been made in medical technology, particularly in the area of disease control. As a result of these advancements, the major causes of death have changed quite drastically.

In the not-too-distant past, the leading causes of death in the United States were acute, infectious diseases such as diphtheria, typhoid fever, and smallpox. Other acute problems, such as pneumonia and tuberculosis, also were common causes of death. Only a relatively few people survived all of the possible acute causes of death. As a result of the advances made in disease control technology and policies during this century (including immunization, vaccination, drugs, infection control, and so on), not only do few die from these diseases (see Table 15-1), but fewer and fewer are even afflicted with them. Few acute diseases take people's lives in modern societies.

TABLE 15–1   Three Leading Causes of Death and Percentage of Deaths by Each, 1900 and 1980

1900		1980	
Cause	Percent	Cause	Percent
Pneumonia, influenza, bronchitis	14.4	Heart disease	38.2
Tuberculosis	11.3	Cancer	20.9
Diarrhea and enteritis	8.1	Strokes	8.6

Source: E. M. Gee, "Living Longer, Dying Differently," *Generations,* 11, no. 3. (Spring 1987), 5. Reprinted with permission from *Generations,* 833 Market St., Suite 516, San Francisco, CA 94103. Copyright 1987 ASA.

Thus, while the death rate was once high among infants and spread across the age spectrum, death is now largely reserved for those who are old. Also, since there are fewer deaths at younger ages, more and more people live into old age and there are increasing numbers of deaths among the older population.[3]

Our experiences with death have changed not only in terms of who dies but also in terms of how they tend to die. The major causes of death have largely shifted from acute to chronic health problems. Gee refers to this shift as an "epidemiological transition" and explains that "when death rates are high and life expectancy low, the major takers-of-life are infectious diseases, which tend to select young victims. As death rates decline and life expectancy increases, the degenerative diseases of old age predominate."[4] That transition is shown in Table 15-1. Chronic problems are generally those that require long-term care and that elongate the dying process. Thus, the "dying trajectory" has become an important part of the death syndrome.[5] For many elderly people today, the suffering of dying is much worse than death itself.

One result of the growing recognition that death has become mostly a phenomenon of old age may be that it has also become more socially acceptable. Gadow describes three quite common ways of defining death among the aged: (1) as inevitable, (2) as natural, and (3) as peaceful. She suggests that it is, in fact, no more inevitable, natural, or peaceful in old age than at any age.[6] There is some evidence that would seem to support the notion that death tends to be more socially acceptable among the aged than it is among young people. Mumma and Benoliel, for example, compared the lifesaving efforts that were made in behalf of various types of dying patients. Among other findings, they noted that the older the patients were, the less the lifesaving efforts that were exerted in their behalf.[7]

We must be aware, though, that the so-called social acceptability of death is related to other factors as well as to age. Mumma and Benoliel found, for example, that the extent to which lifesaving treatments were provided was also related to how long the patients had been in the hospital and to the cause of dying. If they had had a relatively long stay in the hospital, and if they were afflicted with cancer, fewer efforts were made to save their lives.[8] It should not be too surprising that we are more willing today to accept the inevitability of death among those with chronic problems for which cures are relatively rare than among those with acute and correctable problems. Indeed, a movement for the right to reject many lifesaving practices and to die without having to endure the trauma of long dying trajectories is gaining widespread support today. Since death from chronic problems is more prevalent among the aged than others, it quite understandably becomes more acceptable among them than among others. That does not mean, of course, that any form of death among the elderly is acceptable, at least on the part of the aged themselves. That form of ageism undoubtedly exists to some degree in modern society, however.

PROFESSIONALIZING AND INSTITUTIONALIZING DEATH AND DYING

Death has increasingly become both professionalized and institutionalized. That is, how we die has largely come to be controlled by medical professionals, and death now takes place most often in medical institutions (mostly hospitals and nursing homes). The history of these trends is important.

These changes have taken place as a result of the development of modern medicine in the Western world. The emergence of the hospital as the place where modern medicine is administered and ailments are cured has been part of the change that has taken place. There was a time when people's homes were considered the best environment for recuperation. Centuries ago in Europe, hospitals began as lodging houses for travelers, and they were sponsored by religious organizations. They gradually turned into refuges for the poor and homeless, many of whom were physically ill, and health care began to be provided.[9] They also became opportune centers for medical research, and the poor and homeless became readily available experimental subjects. Thus, hospitals eventually became the primary locations of the latest medical technology and subsequently replaced people's own homes as the preferable places for rich as well as poor sick patients to receive the best medical care.

In the United States, the importance of hospitals in offering professional health care was greatly enhanced by the passage of the Hill-Burton Act in 1946. Under the provisions of this legislation, federal money was provided to build hospitals and to equip them with the best medical technology available. That legislation, and the Medicare and Medicaid laws, helped to make hospitals and nursing homes the acceptable places for elderly people with long-term chronic problems to turn for the care they needed.[10]

Medical institutions have not only become the places where health care is expected to be administered, but the provision of health care has also become more and more professionally oriented. Those in the practice of medicine became increasingly successful at curing illnesses and saving lives. Their expertise became unquestionably established. They, and they alone, diagnosed medical problems, operated the medical technology, and administered the appropriate treatments. Being cared for in the concerned and loving environment of their own homes became less and less important to those who were ill. Access to the latest medical technology and professional treatments was what was vital.

Despite their increasing success at curing the diseases and saving the lives of younger people, though, the lingering deaths of older people suffering from chronic diseases became a serious and troublesome dilemma for the practitioners of modern medicine. From their perspective, the inevitability of those kinds of deaths increasingly represented a failure of medical science, on which their expertise was based.

It has seemed logical that, because death tends to result from health problems, medical personnel would be the best qualified to deal with dying patients. It is true that their diagnostic expertise is vital in determining whether or not patients' conditions are terminal. Ironically, however, evidence indicates that they are no more qualified than many other types of people to provide appropriate care for the terminally ill. They are no better prepared than anyone else to deal with their own emotions concerning death. Indeed, the very goals of their professional work and the training they receive seem to make them even less qualified than other people to provide appropriate care for those who are dying.[11]

There are at least three types of evidence that tend to challenge the professionalization and institutionalization of death and dying: (1) the appropriateness of the institutional environments, (2) the attitudes of physicians and nurses about death, and (3) the kinds of relationships that physicians and nurses tend to have with dying patients.

For some time now, the idea of hospitals as appropriate environments for dying patients has been challenged. Part of the reason for this is that the overriding purpose of hospitals is to cure ailments as quickly and efficiently as possible, and they are almost exclusively organized toward fulfilling that purpose.[12] Mauksch has made the point that dying patients in that kind of setting tend to threaten the hospital and its personnel, and that the "routine orders, the predictable activities, when applied to the dying patient, cease to be meaningful, cease to be effective, and above all, cease to be satisfying either to the people doing them or to the patients who receive them."[13] Ironically, even though nursing homes are rapidly becoming the most typical place for dying people to spend their time before their deaths, they are essentially organized and operated from a hospital model.

There is evidence that the functional aspects of hospitals do, in fact, influence the attitudes of hospital workers about dying patients. Thompson studied nurses' attitudes about working with dying patients, for example. He found that whether their attitudes tended to be negative or positive depended more on which unit of the hospital in which they worked (palliative, surgical, or pediatric) than on the amount of experience they had had with dying people.[14] As might be expected, those assigned to the palliative unit, which provided hospice services, expressed the most positive attitudes. As Thompson explains, "Each unit approaches its work with the dying with its own philosophy or 'sentiment order,' where the emotional climate in a unit encourages a particular affective reaction to death."[15]

The attitudes of medical practitioners about death are partly personal as well as structural. The advisability of relying upon physicians and nurses as the primary caregivers for the elderly and for others who are dying has been challenged on the basis of the practitioners' own personal anxiety or fear of death. Studies have shown, in fact, that fear of death tends to be greater among physicians than among lay people and that many avoid thinking about or dealing with death in their own personal lives.[16]

The basic assumption is that, if medical practitioners have not come to grips with their own personal feelings and attitudes about death, then they will be inclined to avoid dealing with dying patients except as technicians. Glaser and Strauss observed that many physicians did, in fact, visit their dying patients only intermittently and briefly. They also reported that many nurses refused to talk to their patients about death because that meant to them that their patients had given up on life.[17]

It may be, however, that those kinds of avoidance behaviors have more to do with the particular circumstances concerning dying patients than with the fear of death physicians and nurses may feel. The avoidance behaviors reported by Glaser and Strauss, for example, were observed in the context of whether or not patients were aware of their terminal condition. Avoidance in these kinds of circumstances may have more to do with ambivalence about whether, when, and by whom patients ought to be told that they are dying than to physicians' and nurses' own fears of death.

Regarding that issue, physicians in general have tended to change their opinions since the 1950s. The majority in the 1950s would not tell their patients that they were dying, but by the mid-1960s, about half were disclosing terminal diagnoses to patients.[18] In a survey of family physicians and medical students, Eggerman and Dustin discovered that a large majority of both groups believed that dying patients ought to be told and that physicians were the ones who should inform patients. Nevertheless, both physicians and students were found to have substantial levels of death anxiety.[19]

Indeed, death anxiety and fear on the part of caregivers may not be a predictor of avoidance behavior at all. Thompson found, in fact, that nurses with the most experience with dying patients and the greatest willingness to work with them had the highest levels of death anxiety.[20] Momeyer contends that, contrary to the common notion that fear of death is abnormal, it is in fact a universal human experience. He also proposes that being anxious about one's own death can make a caregiver even more sensitive to dying patients' fears.[21]

From the viewpoint of philosophical theory, Momeyer's point makes good sense. Practically, though, it probably does not follow that the higher the level of fear and anxiety about death, the more understanding the practitioner will be of dying patients. Whether fear of death is normal or not, excessive amounts of it are functionally debilitating. It may be true, of course, that physicians and nurses are no more adversely affected by fear of death than other groups.

The issue about medical professionals is not so much whether their personal attitudes about death and dying are better or worse than anyone else's. The question is whether they are the best qualified to structure and control the situations in which elderly people will live through the dying trajectory. Given their goals as professionals and their lack of training in both gerontology and thanatology, it seems doubtful that they are. It was the judgment of one trained thanatologist that most of the physicians who treated his father during his dying experience "failed miserably." His father, he said, had come to see them as "simply uninterested in him as a dying, aged person."[22]

RELATIONSHIPS OF THE PUBLIC WITH DEATH AND DYING

How do most people in modern society relate to death and dying? What are their experiences with the processes of dying and with death itself? What are their attitudes and feelings about dying and death? These are questions to which a great deal of the thanatological literature is oriented.

Some authors have made the judgment that the United States is by and large a death-denying society.[23] Indications of this attitude include such tendencies as (1) speaking of the dead as "departed" or "deceased" rather than "dead," (2) letting people die in hospitals rather than at home with their families, (3) turning the management of dying and death over to professionals in preference to family involvement, and (4) having morticians use cosmetics to make corpses appear as life-like as possible. Furthermore, existentialists have argued that denial of death has become a necessity today because we, in our modern secularized society, have lost a meaningful interpretation of life and death.[24]

Others argue against the idea that the denial of death is a prevailing American characteristic. While acknowledging that our patterns of dealing with death may be problematic, Baum and Baum contend that they do not represent denial. Instead, they believe that because death happens primarily to old people and typically takes place in hospitals, most people rarely directly encounter it and are therefore "unprepared" for it.[25] Kübler-Ross similarly indicates that we are simply "unfamiliar" with death, because we seldom actually see it.[26] Backer, Hannon, and Russell conclude that "it is probably more accurate to say that instead of denial, we are ambivalent in our feeling toward death and dying."[27] Kalish submits that analysts have overemphasized the problem of denial because they have not carefully defined and distinguished between what they mean by such concepts as denial, fear, anxiety, and awareness of death.[28]

Even if the denial of death is not a problem, that does not mean that there is no anxiety or fear about dying and death. In order to avoid confusion about how these attitudes apply today, we must be clear about their meanings. In essence, anxieties and fears differ in that fears have quite specific objects while anxieties do not. We can identify what it is that we are afraid of, but we tend to be anxious about the unknown. In that sense, to the extent that we experience either, (and as already discussed, they are probably universal realities), fear tends to apply to dying and anxiety tends to apply to death.

There is probably no clear idea of the extent to which anxiety about death affects people today, but there can be little doubt that it bothers people of all ages to some degree, and more so today than ever before. Kastenbaum and Aisenberg contend that what bothers us most about death, for example, are thoughts of "annihilation, obliteration, and ceasing to be."[29] In a day when mass death is not uncommon and the danger of atomic destruction is very real, this kind of anxiety is particularly prevalent. Indeed, Bermann and Richardson found that between 1957 and 1976, there was a substantial growth in awareness of death, especially among young people.[30]

Fear of dying, however, is something else. That is something that is relatively easy for younger people to avoid since it is largely an experience of older people and typically takes place in isolation. It tends to become increasingly prevalent as people become older. Anxiety about death is apparently less troublesome to elderly people than the fear of dying. The processes of dying typically require having to face probable isolation from families and friends, possible pain, personal humiliation, and the loss of control over everyday life.[31]

Attitudes about the deaths of older people tend to be quite different from those about the deaths of younger people. Gadow argues that this is a form of discrimination. Although it is obviously inevitable for everyone, death is no more acceptable to older people than to younger people. Neither the time it happens nor how it takes place should ever be taken for granted.[32]

EXPERIENCES OF DYING AMONG THE AGED

As people grow older, they inevitably gain a growing awareness of their eventual impending death, and this awareness invariably has a major influence on their life experiences and their attitudes about death.

Kalish has identified at least five factors that tend to feed that awareness among elderly people. He says that as we age, we (1) have a shortened sense of the finiteness of life, (2) have a sense of being unworthy of further societal investments for our well-being, given the lack of a future, (3) experience a loss of roles, (4) have feelings of entitlement when we live beyond our life expectancy, and (5) feel lonely because of the loss of age peers. These feelings, he says, tend to create elements of fear and anxiety about death, especially on the part of elderly men and nonreligious people.[33]

Marshall accuses gerontologists of having basically ignored the importance of this awareness of death in older people, and of making assumptions about it that have not been tested for validity. It is totally ignored among activity theorists, for example, and treated by disengagement theorists as simply a natural part of aging.[34]

In a study of "awareness of finitude," he found, in fact, that it was related to age only indirectly. More important, subjects tended to calculate the times of their expected deaths on the basis of (1) the ages at which their parents had died, (2) the ages at which siblings might have already died, (3) ages at which friends of the same age had died, and (4) their perceived present health conditions.[35]

This kind of awareness is not so much the basis on which elderly people naturally and peacefully adjust to the inevitability of death, as disengagement theorists assume. More to the point, it represents the uneasy and often crisis-oriented anticipation of the dreaded dying process that may be ahead. This prospect would presumably be particularly poignant for those whose parents or siblings had died lingering deaths and for those who perceived their own health as poor.

Viney studied the relationships between illness and feelings of being threatened with "loss of life" and "loss of bodily integrity." Not surprisingly, she found that those of all ages who were ill were much more apt to feel both types of threats than those who were not ill. Somewhat surprisingly perhaps, she also found that these feelings of threat were stronger among those experiencing serious acute health problems, particularly if they were hospitalized or faced surgery, than among those with chronic problems. She found, further, that although both types of threats resulted in some expressions of anger and uncertainty, the threat to bodily integrity tended to be more personally devastating, typically leading to feelings of helplessness and hopelessness as well. It is of interest that those who felt the threat of loss of life tended to be more motivated toward socially active versus passive (dependent) social lives than those threatened with loss of bodily integrity.[36]

Apparently, death is not as threatening to people who are reminded of and forced to face their finitude as how dying may affect them in life. Apparently also, fear of the loss of bodily integrity is more apt than the prospect of the loss of life itself to make people have a sense of social incompetence. That awareness, in fact, seems to prompt people to pursue social interaction with those who matter to them even more actively than before.

Interaction with others may, in fact, help to alleviate some of the anxiety that often accompanies a growing awareness of death. In one study, for example, in which elderly nursing home residents were compared with those in public housing and in regular communities, it was discovered that anxiety about death was lowest among nursing home residents and highest among those living in the community. The researchers speculated that this was probably due in large part to the fact that those in nursing homes and public housing could alleviate their anxieties about death by talking about the meaning of death with their age peers. It is noteworthy, though, that those in nursing homes also expressed the least amount of "life satisfaction" of the three groups. While *death* was not a problem to them, *living* in that situation and in their conditions was.[37]

It is one thing for elderly people to become increasingly aware of death and dying and probably quite another to become a "dying person." In one sense, of course, everyone has a limited life span and can therefore be thought of as dying. That is not the way we normally view our lives, however. There is a special category of people who are defined in that way, and it is their lives that we want to examine here.

People become thought of, treated as, and live their lives as dying people when they are diagnosed as being terminally ill with only a limited time to live. Glaser and Strauss analyzed this "dying trajectory" as having two outstanding properties: "duration" and "shape." The duration, of course, depends upon type of illness and varies greatly from one dying person to another. Dying may take any of a number of different shapes. It may (1) move straight down quickly, (2) move slowly but steadily down, (3) vacillate slowly, or (4) move down, hit a plateau, and then suddenly plunge downward.[38] These analysts characterize the dying trajectory as a "status passage." It is not only a personal experience beset with extremely difficult emotional adjustments that individuals must make; it has also become part of the social structure and something of a unique way of life for those who experience it.[39] There are somewhat typical attitudes, behavioral patterns, and types of relationships that are expected of those who are dying.

An important issue related to the way of life of dying patients is whether or not they have a right, and ought, to be told about the terminal diagnosis. On the one hand, many physicians have been unwilling to tell them, or even to have someone else tell them, because of concern about how an awareness of their true condition might affect them physically as well as mentally. On the other hand, not telling them may well deprive them of the opportunity to put various aspects of their lives in order.[40] In the past, many people believed that those who were dying did not need to be told because they would quickly figure it out anyway. The problems with that assumption are that (1) it may simply not be true for many people, and (2) it does not facilitate open communication between the individuals who are dying and the significant other people in their lives.

Although, as previously discussed, there seems to be a growing sense among physicians and others that people have a right to be told, the issue has by no means been settled. A personal experience of this author seems appropriate to make the point that what is right in one case may not be in another.

A number of years ago, while on a business trip, I stopped off in Spokane, Washington, to visit some close friends and learned that the husband/father had terminal cancer and had only two months to live. No one had informed him of his terminal condition, but he obviously knew not only that he was dying but also that his time was very limited. He and I visited for more than two hours and talked openly about his religious convictions and how they helped him to face death. He also requested that I, as a trusted friend, help him to put some of his personal records in order so that his wife and family would be well cared for.

As a person who has always favored open communication in all situations between people who love each other, I was bothered that he and his family were denying each other the opportunity to share this important life-and-death matter. I asked myself, if he could talk to me about such matters, why not to his family? I considered getting them together and trying to facilitate open communication between them, but I didn't, hoping that they would eventually come to it themselves. I learned later that they never did, however, and for some time I regretted not having intervened.

In recent years, while studying more about the dynamics of the processes of dying and facing death, I have analyzed that situation again and again. Even though it is even now not completely settled in my mind, I now believe that it would not have been right to intervene. I drew this conclusion from my recollections of the kind of relationship that this man had had with his wife throughout their married life. He was a strong person who had always taken care of his wife, who to him was a loving but dependent person. The fact is that she proved to be a strong and decisive person through the process of his death, but he was better able to endure his time of dying by perpetuating the myth that he had to remain in charge. I believe that she intuitively understood that and was unwilling to destroy that myth in his mind. The kind of relationship that had made them a loving and satisfied couple throughout their married years was thus maintained until he died.

How individuals personally adjust to the fact that they are dying, once they become aware of it, is another issue related to death and dying. A combination of emotional and rational processes is involved. As a way of analyzing these processes in some kind of order and attributing to them some predictability, Kübler-Ross described individuals' responses to the reality that they are dying as moving through a number of developmental stages. A dying person's first response is characterized by denial and isolation, followed by anger, bargaining, depression, and finally acceptance.[41] In essence, this progression describes an active interplay between one's emotional reactions, a personal crisis, and one's attempts to rationalize and give meaning to that personal crisis. These reactions are not purely subjective. They inevitably have social dimensions as well. Denial and isolation, for example, might be as much a product of others' fear of death and dying as one's own.

Kübler-Ross's stage analysis of dying has been criticized because observations reveal that dying patients do not always experience all of the stages. Neither do they necessarily experience them in the order in which she presented them.[42] Most analysts are willing to concede that the clinical use of stage descriptions may be helpful to some patients, but even that overlooks a major conceptual falacy in this kind of typology. There is a very real danger, especially in clinical situations, that the stages will become reified as objective realities apart from the lives of the individuals involved. Individuals could be led to believe, on the one hand, that they are pathologically avoiding inevitable elements of normal adjustment if they have not experienced one of the stages in the right order. On the other hand, they may assume that all they have to do is passively wait out the stages and acceptance will finally come. What is actually required is active, not passive, involvement of one's rational capabilities, in the context of one's social environment.

Probably one of the most disturbing parts of living as a dying person is the social stigma that is often associated with it. According to Goffman, a stigmatized person is thought of as in some way "not quite human."[43] When people fail to interact with someone who is dying, their interaction is of course not to imply that the dying person is not quite human. Nevertheless, that is often the effect of such actions.

The observation has been made that, even though far more people die of heart disease than cancer, stigma is hardly ever attached to heart disease but is almost always attached to cancer. Some conjecture that it has to do with the difference in our perceptions of the two diseases. Cancer is seen as intractable and is therefore feared.[44] It is difficult to understand, though, how cancer is seen as any more intractable than heart disease. It would seem to be even more predictable than heart disease. Physicians seldom determine that heart patients will die within certain time frames but readily do so with cancer patients.

It is undoubtedly the diagnostic designation of the time of death that is the source of the stigma. That designation cogently labels individuals as dying, and that sets them apart from the rest of us. To be treated as different at a time when they are vulnerable and in need of social support can be devastating to those who are dying. The aged are often saddled with a double stigma—old age as well as dying.

HOSPICE MOVEMENTS AND THE RIGHT TO DIE

As we have seen, the dying trajectory has come to be an almost inevitable part of the death experience in recent years. At the same time, dying as a somewhat unique social process has come under critical scrutiny, and our awareness of the social psychological problems related to dying has grown.

Out of that awareness, two interrelated movements, have taken hold in the modern world. One has basically taken the form of a rather intensive philosophical discussion of the right of individuals to "die with dignity." The other has been an equally intensive promotion of the hospice program. While there are some differences between these two movements in terms of their philosophical and practical emphases, both represent powerful challenges to the institutionalized, cure-oriented medical model of dying that has become an entrenched part of modern culture.

The hospice movement began in London, England, with an organization called St. Christopher's Hospice. In this program, a caring environment was provided, totally unrelated to any hospital or traditional healthcare facility, in which the needs, desires, and values of dying patients and their families were respected and emphasized.

In 1972, a similar program was developed in New Haven, Connecticut, as the first hospice program in the United States. In the years that followed, programs were developed in many American communities, based on the same philosophy but with a variety of structural forms. An international task force, the International Work Group on Death and Dying (IWG), was eventually formed to study hospice and make policy recommendations. Their most important task was to recommend standards of care for dying people that would correct what they saw as inadequate, unrealistic, and humiliating traditional approaches. Their recommendations stress two major points: (1) that patients, family, and staff all have legitimate needs and interests; and (2) that the terminally ill person's own preferences and life-style must be taken into account in all decision-making.[45]

The National Hospice Organization, created in 1978, emphasized that hospice programs (1) should provide psychological, social, and spiritual, as well as physical, services to dying people and their families; (2) may provide these services in the homes of the dying clients as well as in institutions; (3) should offer bereavement services to families following the death of the dying persons; and (4) ought to use interdisciplinary teams to provide service.[46]

It should not be supposed that medical care is ignored by hospices. It is a vital part of the care that is provided. However, the purpose is not to attempt cures or postpone death, but to control pain and keep patients as functional as possible for as long as possible. Hospice teams are made up of both professionals and volunteers. They typically include physicians, nurses, social workers, clergy members, and community volunteers. Teams are expected to give the dying patients a sense of emotional and social security, to respect and honor their wishes as much as possible, and to provide opportunities for them to act as living, rather than dying, people.

The passage of the National Hospice Reimbursement Act, which became effective in 1983, is an indication of the amount of public support this movement has had in the United States. Under this act, the costs of professional services that elderly people receive in certified hospice programs may be covered by Medicare.

The federal government has also sponsored a comprehensive evaluation of hospice programs in the United States. The study, which was conducted by the Center for Health Care Research at Brown University, included 26 hospice programs across the country. A sizable majority (65 percent) of the recipients in the hospice programs studied were elderly. As many as 17.4 percent were over 75 years of age. Half of the elderly participants were women, and most were married.[47] These statistics reveal what might well be something of a serious failure of hospice to reach elderly people with the greatest need for social support: those who live alone in relative isolation. Labus and Dambrot conclude that this kind of discrimination is due to the admission requirements of most home-based hospice programs, which assume that the dying persons have family members in the home who will service as primary caregivers.[48]

The elderly participants in the Brown University study were found to be as mentally alert and received as much social support as those who were younger. However, their primary caregivers tended to be their daughters, spouses, or siblings, many of whom were elderly and physically at risk themselves. Investigators also found that elderly patients tended to get less intensive medical care than those who were younger. Mor concludes that, with this kind of statistic, "the possibility has been raised that the all-too-familiar pattern of age discrimination may have intruded itself into the terminal illness phase, even under hospice control."[49]

As a whole, though, hospice has been an enormous success. Even though, as Kastenbaum indicates, it is not the solution to every dying person's needs,[50] public support for the programs that thave been started is outstanding in terms of both finances and voluntary participation. Opposition to and even criticism of the program are minimal.

The movement for the right to die with dignity shares most of the philosophical assumptions on which hospice is based. Both stress the right of dying individuals to control their own destinies. Advocates of the right to die, however, tend to focus on somewhat different aspects of the claim of individual rights than those emphasized in hospice.

One goal of this movement is to influence state and national policy on how dying people are treated. It is important to clarify what is meant by the right to die with dignity. At issue here is whether dignity can be ensured by stipulating that certain actions are taken, such as refusing specific life-sustaining technology, or if it simply means adherence to the principle of self-determination. The President's Commission for the Study of Ethical Problems in Medicine and Biomedical and Behavioral Research considered this important issue. They reported that many advocates of the movement tend to have the vision that peaceful and aesthetically appealing death can be guaranteed simply by taking certain actions. Commission members cautioned that the major thrust of the movement must be to ensure "that the wishes of dying patients are solicited and respected."[51]

The point is made in the commissions's report that decisions about taking certain actions can never absolutely settle life-and-death considerations for anyone. Instead, they are made in the context of an inevitable tension between wanting to live as long as possible and fearing what the consequences of continued life might be. According to the authors of the commission's report, the crux of the matter is that individuals are "protected against decisions that make death too easy and quick as well as from those that make it too agonizing and prolonged."[52]

Two specific types of actions are stressed in this movement as options that dying people should have the right to exercise. One is the right to reject having their lives continued by the use of artificial life-sustaining equipment or treatments. The thrust of the argument in support of this claimed right is not that medical treatment as such is a bad thing. The point is, rather, that when the best medical knowledge available has already diagnosed someone's condition as terminal, then such treatment will not only be useless but will also rob that person of what meaningful life he or she may have left. To become temporarily dependent upon such technology may indeed be tolerable when there is the possibility of being cured and restored to normal life, but it has become defined as intolerable for increasing numbers of dying people for whom that possibility no longer exists. Medical treatments at that time make sense if they keep a person functional, but not if they hinder what functional capacities they may still have.

Some have argued that this is actually a passive form of euthanasia and is therefore morally unacceptable. That argument misses one important point, however. The reason for rejecting life-sustaining treatments is not to choose death, but to live life out to the fullest extent possible.

The other issue that the right-to-die movement has stressed is for individual dying persons to be allowed to die when and where they choose with the aid of members of their families. The argument is that when individuals can no longer function, when death is imminent, and/or when suffering can no longer be controlled or avoided, the continuation of life serves no good purpose. The advocacy of this type of euthanasia is quite controversial. It is vehemently opposed by most religious people and organizations, as well as by most of those in the medical community. The religious perspective is that we humans have no right to "play God" with matters of life and death. Fallible humans, even the most skilled physicians, can never stipulate that someone cannot be cured and has a specific time to live. The omniscient God is the only one who can determine when life no longer has purpose and it is time to die. While most religions teach that God relieves human suffering, they also teach that only he has the wisdom to determine when the mercy that death represents is appropriate. What is often overlooked by religious opponents, though, is that even they readily rely on many forms of human intervention to relieve suffering, some of which pose clear risks to people's lives (major surgery is an example).

Medical practitioners tend to oppose euthanasia from the ethical perspective of their professions. They practice medicine to save and preserve life, not to deliberately promote or contribute to death.

Even though euthanasia has been promoted by many and sometimes even practiced in one form or another in the United States, it has never been legalized in this country. One place in the world where it has been widely practiced by physicians is in Holland. Although it has not been legally sanctioned, it has been approved by the Royal Dutch Medical Association for those who are terminally ill and request it, provided they are mentally competent and a physician is willing to perform it.[53] The practice is permitted by the courts and is supported by more than two-thirds of the public, even among the Catholic laity.[54] Some in Holland, though, even among those who practice it, are fearful about where a euthanasia policy might lead. With a growing elderly population, the concern has been expressed that demented elderly patients might well be euthanized in the future for purely economic reasons.

BEREAVEMENT, MOURNING, AND GRIEF

Concerns about death and dying by no means end at the point of death. As important as what happens to people during the processes of dying is what happens to the survivors of those who have died. Interest in this aspect of death and dying has focused primarily on bereavement, mourning, and especially grief. These concepts are very much related but have different meanings. A review of the definitions of each of these concepts will help us to understand not only the personal experiences that survivors tend to have but something about their social significance as well.

To be *bereaved* means to experience some kind of loss. There are many kinds of losses that we humans normally experience that could be referred to as bereavement. The loss of someone through death is what is usually implied by the term, however.

Kastenbaum explains that this kind of bereavement is difficult for survivors not only because they personally miss the one who has died, but also because the survivor's social status has suddenly and drastically changed.[55] This is particularly true for those who experience the loss of their spouses through death. They are not only deprived of the intimacy they typically enjoyed with their spouses, but they are also suddenly thrust into the widowed status—a position in society for which most married people are not prepared.

This aspect of bereavement is largely ignored in the literature on death and dying. That is a regrettable omission because it could help to explain why some people continue to grieve the loss of spouse over a longer time than is normal—a phenomenon that psychological analysis alone has not been able to adequately explain. The point is that the loss of spouse, particularly among elderly people, is a major, socially disruptive event. It was discovered in one study that focused on elderly widowed people, for example, that becoming widowed caused the most abrupt and emotionally damaging disengagement patterns of any type of loss, largely because of the social disruption that it engendered.[56]

Mourning is another important part of the experience of those who have lost someone close to them. Kastenbaum defines mourning as "the culturally patterned expression of the bereaved person's thoughts and feelings."[57] We often feel sorry for those who mourn, and yet, to a large degree, mourning is a positive experience for most survivors. It involves them in rituals and ceremonies in which they tend to be surrounded by sympathetic supporters. This helps the survivors to celebrate the lives of those whom they have lost in death.

Funerals are a central component of the process of mourning. Contrary to the rather common notion that funerals are morbid experiences that people must endure in order to comply with social custom, evidence indicates that they are meaningful and helpful to most who are in grief. Kalish describes the funeral idealistically as "simultaneously a rite of passage for the dead person and a show of support for the survivors" and as having "a therapeutic value for survivors by permitting them to grieve openly and to advance their acceptance of the reality of death."[58] In one study on grief, newly widowed men and women reported having positive feelings about both planning and participating in the funerals of their spouses. They indicated that by planning and then moving through the ceremonies, they were able to publicly express their love, devotion, and attachment to their deceased spouses in meaningful ways. Most of them also said that funeral directors had been supportive to them, as were officiating clergy for those with religious orientations.[59]

The extent and severity of *grief* among people whose loved ones have died has been a subject of particular interest to students of death and dying. Studies have focused on such questions as why some people grieve more intensely than others, how excessive grief may affect people functionally and in terms of their health status, and why some people continue to grieve beyond what would be considered a normal period of time. Grief is defined as the typical personal response that people make to the losses they experience. We humans feel grief about many types of losses in our lives, but it is most often associated with losses due to death. Depending upon its severity, it not only affects individuals' mental state but also how they think, eat, and sleep. Severe grief clearly places people at physical risk.[60]

Studies indicate that the kinds of grief people suffer depend, at least in part, on three factors. First, it is related to whether or not the death of the person being grieved was expected or unexpected. As previously discussed, many people, especially among the aged, finally die after a period of dying. Those who grieve these people's deaths have usually been with them during the dying period and have learned to anticipate the death. Although their grief can still be difficult, it has been found to be less severe than that on the part of those for whom death was unexpected.[61] This assessment of the difference in severity between these types of bereaved persons is made after death has taken place, however. Grief related to expected deaths has been termed "anticipatory grief,"[62] implying that some grieving is experienced before as well as following death. The anticipatory grief of spouses who have served as primary caregivers is undoubtedly often just as severe as that experienced by those who grieve an unexpected death.

Another factor related to how survivors grieve is what has caused the death of those being grieved. One study, for example, compared the bereavement patterns of elderly survivors of spousal suicides with patterns of those who survive natural deaths. Findings showed that while they were no more depressed and suffered no greater mental or physical pathology, survivors of spousal suicide deaths had significantly higher levels of anxiety. The investigators speculated that the difference would probably have been even greater if the victims had been younger, and that over longer periods of bereavement, the grief of spousal suicide survivors might well be more severe than that of the other group, even among their elderly sample.[63] The primary differences in grief between those whose loved ones have died from different causes may be most dependent on the extent to which survivors can logically blame themselves and are therefore plagued with a sense of guilt. That is certainly true of many others besides survivors of those who have committed suicide.

The third and vital factor affecting the severity of grief is the level of social support that survivors enjoy. Wambuck makes the point that grief is not simply an individualized response to loss but is also, to a large extent, a "social construct" that "encompasses public expectations that can influence the grief experience of bereavement." That, she believes, helps to explain to individuals what they may not understand about their own grief.[64] Thus, be defining and explaining the process of grief, professional researchers and writers provide widows and others in grief with timetables and guides to follow. While these guides may turn out to be too rigid, they nevertheless provide a form of social support.

More important, though, are affective types of social support. This was illustrated in a study of the extent to which newly widowed elderly people in the Salt Lake City area were helped by supportive social networks during the first two years of widowhood. It was found that the qualitative, more than the structural, aspects of their social networks helped them to avoid depression, to cope, and to maintain satisfaction with life.[65]

Religious organizations are one source of social support for bereaved and grief-stricken people that might be expected to be readily available. Churches, probably more than any other societal institution, have historically been concerned about death and bereavement. However, a recent survey of Christian churches in northern California revealed that, although most pastors were supportive of survivors at the time of the funeral, very little was being done to provide sustained support over time. Typically, the ministers had not even received bereavement training in preparation for the ministry.[66]

The lack of sustained social support seems to typify our modern culture. It was found in the study of newly widowed people, referred to earlier, that those in the sample felt that they were left to reorganize their lives on their own without the help of those in their social networks. Indications from the study were that "community, colleagues, neighbors, and relatives are all inclined to turn back quickly to their ordinary concerns."[67]

In addition to the lack of sustained attention by the social network, newly widowed people report that those in their couple-oriented networks simply do not understand and are impatient with the problems involved in adjusting to life as widows.[68]

Part of the focus of the Salt Lake City study of elderly widows, just cited, was on those who had been widowed for more than two years. Part of that group were found to be "poor copers." They were still unable to accept the death of their spouses. They experienced intense emotions and tended to cry excessively. The investigators were unable to provide any better explanation for the behavior patterns of these people than that they were "not keeping busy."[69] It is very likely that the lack of understanding support groups was the major contributing factor.

Clearly, elderly widowed people are at special risk in coping with grief.[70] They not only face the grief related to the loss of a spouse, but they are typically also plagued with what Kastenbaum describes as "bereavement overload." As he so aptly points out, "Elderly men and women are more likely to develop a condition in which sorrow has been heaped upon sorrow, loss upon loss."[71]

CONCLUSION

The two themes that tend to dominate the study of death and dying today are: (1) the right of individuals to control their own destinies in death as well as in life, and (2) the importance of being relieved of the pain and suffering that so often accompanies the dying experience. Except for what can be found in the religious literature on the subject, discussions of the meaning of death seem to be largely missing from today's literature on death and dying. That may well represent an omission of the most vital aspect of this important subject.

Even with all of the rights we may have of self-determination and all the analgesic technology available today, death is still very much dreaded as a morbid event that raises the clear possibility in people's minds that life itself is futile. With some sense that death as well as life has meaning, however, even death with great pain and suffering seems to become not just tolerable but accepted, and sometimes even deliberately chosen. For example, Leviton reported that his father died an "appropriate death." By that he means that his father was allowed to die in a way that he himself deemed appropriate to his personal life. In contrast to many who claim the right of self-determination today, however, he deliberately chose not to take the pain-killing drugs that were readily available to him, and that his family urged him to take, during his final hours of life. Leviton reports that there were at least two possible reasons for his father to prefer to suffer the pain of death. He may have wanted either to symbolize his solidarity with his mother and sister, both of whom had suffered painful deaths, or similarly, to symbolize his identity with the suffering of Jews and other oppressed people everywhere.[72]

Perhaps, then, an appropriate conclusion to this chapter would be to review some of the most salient meanings of death we can find among individual and cultural interpretations. Probably the most obvious meanings assigned to death are those that are provided by religions that emphasize a belief in an after-life. Some religions believe in the immortality of the human soul and see death as the release of the soul from the body in which it is confined in this earthly life. Other religions, such as Christianity, see death as the ultimate punishment for human sin but also as a peaceful transition from this life to eternity for believers whom God has forgiven.

The Inuit Eskimo tribe in northern Canada has a religiously unique interpretation of the meaning of death. The elderly Inuits have been known for their fearless resignation to and acceptance of being abandoned by their families and left to die. The harshness of their cold environment has been given as the reason for this phenomenon. Guemple, an anthropologist, discovered, however, that instead it is because of their religious beliefs. They believe that the essence of life is not one's physical body but one's name, which gives one an immortal identity with all others who have had the same name. Death simply means returning to the eternal community of those who share a particular name.[73]

Religious beliefs such as these may seem primitive and naive to many people today, compared to the scientific body of knowledge about death and dying that we now have. After conducting a broad-based survey of the explanation of the origin of death in many primitive cultures, for instance, anthropologists Corcos and Krupka expressed dismay about how death was defined. They make the observation that primitive people observe people dying much more often than "civilized man" does, and yet "from the many observations primitive people could make, in general, they failed to deduce that all humans eventually die from natural, rather than supernatural, causes."[74]

One cannot help but wonder about the logic of such a conclusion. How can scientists draw a distinction between the natural and the supernatural without making nature something of an object of awe and devotion? They make the same logical error as do religious literalists who separate religion from nature. If death is a product of nature, which it is, there is nothing about that idea to contradict that it may also be the product of the supernatural. That is a matter of what we believe, not of scientific proof. Indeed, the point being made here is that religious belief is a very important definition of the meaning of death that provides people with assurances and the courage to face death.

Another prevalent theme about the meaning of death makes sense to both secularly oriented and religiously oriented people. It is the notion that death in some way or another makes, or ought to make, a contribution to the continuation of life. This general theme is found in a number of cultural settings. The traditional "good death" of the Irish is one example of this theme. They made a point of dying what Scheper-Hughes labeled "head-on"—fully awake and alert, slowly enduring whatever pain they had to, as a symbol of the way they had lived and the way they believe life ought to be lived. Following their death, wakes were held that were elaborate celebrations of their lives.[75]

Suicide has traditionally been a common pathway to death for elderly people as well as for others in Japan. It is important to understand, though, that this is done not out of personal despair, but from altruistic motives, as a sacrifice in behalf of the nation or of family well-being. Plath found that even today, a sizable percentage of Japanese elderly would be willing to sacrifice their own lives for the sake of the welfare of their families.[76]

Imara has probably best articulated the meaning of death as sacrifice for the sake of life in an analysis of "Dying as the Final Stage of Growth."[77] He points out that change is a necessary part of life, because living without change is not living at all. But changing entails abandoning old ways and breaking old patterns, and that, in essence, is a form of dying in order to grow and continue to live. Painful and agonizing as the physical dying process can be, he insists that it can nevertheless be packed with meaning if one conceives of it as the ultimate time of growth. To do that, he says, we must simply invest the remainder of our lives in creative and appreciative relationships with others, or in dying as a contribution to life.

Kastenbaum has recognized the importance of death having meaning for those who experience it. He suggests that how we die will never "really answer the existential 'why' of life," and that one important meaning that can be attached to death is that it happens in a way that preserves the values by which we have lived our lives.[78] Whatever the meaning that death has for any of us, it ought to be evident that the search for meaning is worth the effort if life and death are to have purpose.

NOTES

[1] Martha Baum and Rainer C. Baum, *Growing Old: A Societal Perspective* (Englewood Cliffs, N.J.: Prentice-Hall, 1980), p. 195.

[2] Ibid.

[3] Barbara A. Backer, Natalie Hannon, and Noreen A. Russell, *Death and Dying: Individuals and Institutions* (New York: John Wiley, 1982), p. 5.

[4] Ellen M. Gee, "Living Longer, Dying Differently," *Generations,* 11, no.3 (Spring 1987), 5–8.

[5] Barney G. Glaser and Anselm L. Strauss, *A Time for Dying* (Chicago: Aldine, 1968), pp. 5–6.

[6] Sally A. Gadow, "A Natural Connection?" *Generations,* 11, no. 3 (Spring 1987), 15–18.

[7] Christina M. Mumma and Jeanne Q. Benoliel, "Care, Cure, and Hospital Dying Trajectory," *Omega,* 15, no. 3 (1984–1985), 275–88.

[8] Ibid., pp. 282–84.

[9] Backer, Hannon, and Russell, *Death and Dying,* pp. 49–51.

[10] David L. Rabin and Patricia Stockton, *Long-Term Care for the Elderly: A Factbook* (New York: Oxford University Press, 1987), pp. 113–16.

[11] Backer, Hannon, and Russell, *Death and Dying,* pp. 81–110.

[12] Ibid., pp. 51–52.

[13] Hans O. Mauksch, "The Organizational Context of Dying," in *Death: The Final Stage of Growth,* ed. Elisabeth Kübler-Ross (Englewood Cliffs, N.J.: Prentice-Hall, 1975), pp. 9–10.

[14] Edward H. Thompson, "Palliative and Curative Care Nurses' Attitudes Toward Dying and Death in the Hospital Setting," *Omega,* 16, no. 3 (1985–1986), 233–42.

[15] Ibid., p. 234.

[16] Backer, Hannon, and Russell, *Death and Dying,* pp. 99–101.

[17] Barney G. Glaser and Anselm L. Strauss, *Awareness of Dying* (Chicago: Aldine, 1965), p. 45.

[18] Baum and Baum, *Growing Old,* p. 190.

[19] Sinda Eggerman and Dick Dustin, "Death Orientation and Communication with the Terminally Ill," *Omega,* 16, no. 3 (1985–1986), 255–65.

[20] Thompson, "Palliative and Curative Care Nurses' Attitudes," p. 236.

[21] Richard W. Momeyer, "Fearing Death and Caring for the Dying," *Omega,* 16, no. 1 (1985–1986), 1–9.

[22] Dan Leviton, "Thanatology Theory and My Dying Father," *Omega,* 17, no. 2 (1986–1987), 127–43.

[23] Ernest Becker, *The Denial of Death* (New York: Free Press, 1973).

[24] Baum and Baum, *Growing Old,* p. 185.

[25] Ibid., pp. 184, 192.

[26] Elisabeth Kübler-Ross, *Death: The Final Stage of Growth* (Englewood Cliffs, N.J.: Prentice-Hall, 1975), p. 5.

[27] Backer, Hannon, and Russell, *Death and Dying,* p. 1.

[28] Richard A. Kalish, "The Social Context of Death and Dying," in *Handbook of Aging and the Social Sciences,* eds. Robert H. Binstock and Ethel Shanas (New York: Van Nostrand Reinhold, 1985), pp. 149–70.

[29] Robert Kastenbaum and Ruth Aisenberg, *The Psychology of Death* (New York: Springer, 1972), p. 44.

[30] Sandra Bermann and Virginia Richardson, "Social Change in the Salience of Death Among Adults in America: A Projective Assessment," *Omega,* 17, no. 3 (1986–1987), 195–207.

[31] Backer, Hannon, and Russell, *Death and Dying,* pp. 33–35.

[32] Gadow, "A Neutural Connection?" pp. 15–18.

[33] Kalish, "The Social Context of Death and Dying," pp. 149–70.

[34] Victor W. Marshall, "Age and Awareness of Finitude in Developmental Gerontology," in

Understanding Death and Dying, eds. Sandra Galdier-Wilcox and Marilyn Sutton (Palo Alto, Calif.: Mayfield, 1984), pp. 150–51.

[35] Ibid., pp. 152–161.

[36] Linda L. Viney, "Loss of Life and Loss of Bodily Integrity: Two Different Sources of Threat for People Who Are Ill," *Omega,* 15, no. 3 (1984–1985), 207–22.

[37] Milton F. Nehrke, Georgette Bellucci, and Sally Jo Gabriel, "Death Anxiety, Locus of Control and Life Satisfaction in the Elderly: Toward a Definition of Ego-Integrity," *Omega,* 8, no. 4 (1977–1978), 359–68.

[38] Glaser and Strauss, *A Time for Dying,* pp. 5–6.

[39] Ibid., pp. 242–47.

[40] Glaser and Strauss, *Awareness of Dying,* pp. 5–11.

[41] Elisabeth Kübler-Ross, *On Death and Dying* (New York: Macmillan, 1969), pp. 34–121.

[42] Backer, Hannon, and Russell, *Death and Dying,* p. 23.

[43] Erving Goffman, *Stigma* (Englewood Cliffs, N.J.: Prentice-Hall, 1963), p. 5.

[44] Susan Sontag, *Illness as Metaphor* (New York: Random House, 1979), p. 5.

[45] Robert Kastenbaum, *Death, Society, and Human Experience* (Columbus, Ohio: Chas. E. Merrill, 1986), pp. 117–33.

[46] Ibid., p. 120.

[47] Vincent Mor, "Hospice," *Generations,* 11, no. 3 (Spring 1987), 19–21.

[48] Janet G. Labus and Faye H. Dambrot, "A Comparative Study of Terminally Ill Hospice and Hospital Patients," *Omega,* 16, no. 3 (1985–1986), 225–32.

[49] Mor, "Hospice," p. 21.

[50] Kastenbaum, *Death, Society, and Human Experience,* p. 130.

[51] Morris B. Abram, President's Commission for the Study of Ethical Problems in Medicine and Biomedical and Behavioral Research, *Deciding to Forego Life-Sustaining Treatment: A Report on the Ethical, Medical, and Legal Issues in Treatment Decisions* (Washington, D.C.: US Government Printing Office, March 1983), p. 24.

[52] Ibid., p. 23.

[53] "The Netherlands Debates the Legal Limits of Euthanasia," *The Los Angeles Times,* July 5, 1987, pt. 6, pp. 1, 8–9.

[54] Ibid., p. 1.

[55] Kastenbaum, *Death, Society, and Human Experience,* p. 135.

[56] Arnold S. Brown, "Socially Disruptive Events and Morale Among the Elderly" (unpublished paper presented at the Gerontological Society 27th Annual Meeting in Portland, Oregon, October 1974), Abstract printed in *The Gerontologist,* 14, no. 5, pt. 2 (October 1974), p. 72.

[57] Kastenbaum, *Death, Society, and Human Experience,* p. 138.

[58] Kalish, "The Social Context of Death and Dying," pp. 160–61.

[59] Kastenbaum, *Death, Society, and Human Experience,* pp. 142–43.

[60] Ibid., pp. 136–37.

[61] Howard T. Tokunaga, "Death Anxiety and Bereavement," *Omega,* 16, no. 3 (1985–1986), 267–80.

[62] Erick Lindemann, "The Symptomatology and Management of Acute Grief," *American Journal of Psychiatry,* 101, no. 2 (September 1944), 141–48.

[63] Norman L. Faberow et al., "An Examination of the Early Impact of Bereavement on Psychological Distress in Survivors of Suicide," *The Gerontologtist,* 27, no. 5 (October 1987), 592–98.

[64] Julie Ann Wambach, "The Grief Process as a Social Construct," *Omega,* 16, no. 3 (1985–1986), 201–11.

[65] Margaret Dimond, Dale A. Lund, and Michael S. Caserta, "The Role of Social Support in the First Two Years of Bereavement in an Elderly Sample," *The Gerontologist,* 27, no. 5 (October 1987), 599–604.

[66] Fred Sklar and Kathleen D. Huneke, "Bereavement, Ministerial Attitudes, and the Future of Church-Sponsored Bereavement Support Groups," *Omega,* 18, no. 2 (1987–1988), 89–102.

[67] Kastenbaum, *Death, Society, and Human Experience*, p. 143.

[68] Brown, "Socially Disruptive Events."

[69] Dale A. Lund, "Identifying Elderly With Coping Difficulties After Two Years of Bereavement," *Omega*, 16, no. 3 (1985–1986), 213–24.

[70] Richard A. Kalish, "Older People and Grief," *Generations*, 11, no. 3 (Spring 1987), 33–38.

[71] Kastenbaum, *Death, Society, and Human Experience*, p. 153.

[72] Leviton, "Thanatological Theory and My Dying Father," p. 140.

[73] Lee Guemple, "Growing Old in Inuit Society," in *Growing Old in Different Societies: Cross-Cultural Perspectives*, ed. Jay Sokolovsky (Belmont, Calif.: Wadsworth, 1983), pp. 24–28.

[74] Alain Corcos and Lawrence Krupka, "How Death Came to Mankind: Myths and Legends," *Omega*, 14, no. 2 (1983–1984), 187–98.

[75] Nancy Scheper-Hughes, "Deposed Kings: The Demise of the Rural Irish Gerontology," in *Growing Old in Different Societies: Cross-Cultural Perspectives*, ed. Jay Sokolovsky (Belmont, Calif.: Wadsworth, 1983), pp. 130–46.

[76] David Plath, " 'Ecstacy Years': Old Age in Japan," in *Growing Old in Different Societies: Cross-Cultural Perspectives*, ed. Jay Sokolovsky (Belmont, Calif.: Wadsworth, 1983), pp. 147–53.

[77] Mwalimu Imara, "Dying as the Last Stage of Growth," in *Death: The Final Stage of Growth*, ed. Elisabeth Kübler-Ross (Englewood Cliffs, N.J.: Prentice-Hall, 1975), pp. 147–63.

[78] Robert Kastenbaum, "The Search for Meaning," *Generations*, 11, no. 3 (Spring 1987), 9–13.

16

Future Trends in Aging

INTRODUCTION

By treating aging from the perspective of social processes, we become keenly aware that what it means to age and to become an old person has drastically changed throughout history. Patterns of changes have been identified by looking across the broad span of centuries as societies have progressed from nomadic groups on the edge of survival, to settled agrarian communities, to complex industrialized nations. Changes related to aging and old age have been particularly numerous and striking since the 1930s. Cross-cultural comparisons also show us that aging and old age differ in significant ways from one culture to another, but that changes have taken place within other cultures as well.

If the meanings connected to aging and old age have changed in the past, we can be sure that change will continue in the future. The problem is to predict what those changes will be. Exact predictions of the ways in which the social lives of elderly people will change are, of course, impossible. To try to offer such predictions would be an exercise in futility. However, we can gain some insights about possible future trends by summarizing some of the key social processes that we have examined here. By looking at past trends, present conditions, and cultural differences, potential future trends should become apparent.

One particular issue will orient this summary effort—whether and to what extent aging is viewed as merely a combination of losses or more as a transition to another potentially vital stage of life. This issue has been at the heart of the changes that have taken place in the past. It is also central to the meaning attached to old age at present, and will almost certainly continue to influence our assessment of aging in the future.

PAST TRENDS IN AGING AND OLD AGE

An analysis of aging from the broad perspective of history reveals a mixed emphasis on aging as loss versus development. It has recently been discovered that not all past societies honored, respected, or provided care for their older people, as has often been supposed. Instead, a curvilinear relationship characterizes the connection between the social status of the aged and types of societies over time, moving from low status for those in the most primitive and ancient societies, to relatively high status in more advanced and recent societies, and back again to low status for those in modern contemporary societies.

Indications are, for example, that many nomadic tribes of ancient times depended upon hunting and gathering activities in places where resources were scarce. Their lives were a never-ending struggle for survival. Having to support elderly members who could no longer do their share of the work was a threat to their abilities to survive. Thus, many such tribes abandoned their older members, leaving them behind to die. These were hard times, and relatively few people lived to be old. Abandonment and imminent death of those who did become old may seem cruel by present-day standards, but to them, young and old alike, it was a necessary part of their way of life. Abandonment of the elderly is still practiced among those who live in such harsh environments as the arctic regions of the far North.

With the development of agriculture, societies were able to settle into permanent communities. Division of labor became possible, and land ownership emerged. This was the kind of situation that favored the status and power of elderly people. They became the primary land owners and were thus able to control work and production processes as well as family life. These were times in history when old age was honorable and respected. The amount of control held by old people over economic and social institutions would be considered unnecessarily excessive to us today. There are also indications that their positions were associated with such high status that they were often denied the affectionate aspects of family life.

Two forces for change over the past 300 years have served to challenge the right of older people to control the economic and social lives of the rest of the population. The first was a movement for individual freedoms that began in the seventeenth century. It was a theme that was stressed in the philosophical and religious literature of that era, and it has been applied to the political and family structures in Europe and the United States ever since. Young adults could thus declare independence from their elders by marrying, raising families, and pursuing work careers.

Industrialization was the other major force that challenged the status and power held by the elderly. This movement revolutionized both economic and social institutions. Production moved from the family setting into factories, and families moved to the cities to find work. Ownership of businesses was transferred from patriarchial family heads to corporate structures. Workers were hired, not on the basis of their social standings, but because of their productive skills. In order for elderly people to become and remain employed at any level of production, they had to compete with all other available workers. As we have seen, asssumptions about old age incompetencies have placed older workers at a distinct competitive disadvantage. The establishment of the institution of retirement has served to remove them from the work place and to perpetuate assumptions that they are incompetent and, thus, dependent.

The notions that aging means loss and that old age is a time of dependency have also been nurtured by biological and neurological science in recent history. They have distinguished between diseases and physical and mental aging and have theorized that aging, apart from the effects of disease, is a gradual process that almost never results in death. Nevertheless, they have characterized it as a process of irreversible loss of the capacity to function mentally and physically. A further assumption is that the human organism becomes increasingly suscep- tible to ever more crippling chronic diseases of the body and the brain. The focus of scientific research and analysis to the present has been on the extent of loss, with little or no attempt to discover possible progressive development in the aging processes. Physically and mentally, then, as well as economically and socially, old age has come to be portrayed as a time of increasing loss and dependency. Ironically, the more that life expectancy has increased, the more old age has become characterized in that way.

These powerfully persuasive arguments have left us with the impression that elderly people have decreasing capacities to learn. They have also virtually destroyed the perception of earlier times that the aged possess special forms of knowledge or wisdom.

As a result of these kinds of analyses, a perception of old age as a time of dependency has grown in the recent past. That, in turn, has led to two deeply felt and paradoxical concerns that have permeated entire societies and have developed into political issues. On the one hand, concern for the physical, mental, social, and economic welfare of the elderly themselves has produced vast networks of services to take care of their monetary, social, and health needs. On the other hand, concern has also developed about the burden that their care places on society. It is as though our own perceptions of aging and old age have not only robbed older people of a basis of the meaning or purpose of life, but have also come to threaten the quality of life for the entire population.

PRESENT CONDITIONS OF AGING AND OLD AGE

An understanding of the present conditions in which today's elderly people find themselves gives us reason to be both pessimistic and optimistic about the future. We can best understand the possibilities for the future by analyzing present conditions from the perspective of a stuggle between those who view aging as loss and old age as dependency, and those who are beginning to define those entities much more positively. This very real struggle is complicated by both economics and politics. It is a struggle that is not well understood today, probably even by those who are involved. Yet the perceptions of old age and of the future position of the elderly in society are very much dependent upon its outcomes.

On one side of this struggle are well-established and enormously powerful institutions that design and control the services being provided to elderly people. Particularly prominent among these institutions are those that are represented in what has been labeled the medical industrial complex (discussed in Chapter 13). It also includes the aging network (discussed in Chapter 14).

It is not being suggested here that the motives of those involved are less than honorable. Neither is there any evidence of conspiracy on their part. There have, in fact, been major differences between some of the parties involved. Nevertheless, all of these institutions clearly have vested interests in continuing to define old age as a time of dependency. They were structured to serve a dependent population. Their continued existence and their profits depend upon the perpetuation of that definition. The relatively effective lobbying efforts of such groups as medical and hospital associations clearly demonstrate that, in addition to being motivated to serve, they are indeed deeply involved in a struggle for their own vested interests.

It is true, of course, that the elderly receive valuable services from these institutions. The social lives of many are restored and enhanced, and some are the recipients of the latest in lifesaving technology. The importance of these services is not the issue. At the heart of the present struggle are their costs to elderly recipients as well as to the society as a whole. Large economic entities exist for the sole purpose of making profits by providing medical services to elderly persons. Thus, the high costs of health care for the aged today are due in large part to profits realized by those private entities. Obviously, the more dependent older people become on those providers, the greater the potential profits to the providers. The major "cost" to the older recipients is the loss of independence they experience in order to receive the services.

There are forces on the other side of the struggle, however. A number of somewhat unrelated efforts are under way primarily on the part of the elderly themselves to maintain their independence and to restore the respect they feel they deserve. Some of these efforts are basically passive but quite effective means of resisting the dependency label. Others are active efforts to declare their independence from the dependency-building forces.

One viable and attractive option that older people today have is to passively choose a life-style that simply separates them from the institutions and people who may treat them as dependent. Low-income housing for the aged, retirement centers, retirement communities, and senior citizens' centers make it possible for both poor and wealthy elderly people to live retreatist life-styles. There they can confine their interactions to age peers, who share their concerns about remaining independent. In that kind of life-style, leisure provides enjoyable and meaningful activities. A retreatist subculture emerges, out of which they gain a renewed sense of belonging and self-worth. Consequently, they are able to escape the daily insistence, on the part of family members and service providers, that they are dependent. Passive retreat is the life-style for which many of the aged have opted today. It tends to be quite satisfying, at least for a time. It does not, however, diminish or even challenge the basic societal assumptions that the elderly are dependent. In times of economic or physical crisis, the elderly retreatists finally become dependent upon those who tend to define them that way.

Many today are also engaged in active challenges to the dependency-creating forces. One form of active involvement is the formation of and participation in self-advocacy groups on the part of elderly people. The combined efforts of these groups have the potential to greatly influence public perceptions of the elderly and also to have a strong and definitive voice about how they will be served. These advocates are found serving on advisory councils that help to set policy on aging at all levels of government. They are also at work at the grassroots level. Others are active lobbyists attempting to influence policies related to aging as legislation is being passed. Still others are actively challenging the images of old age that are being presented by the media and are attempting to educate the public about the actual capabilities of older people.

Another form of active resistance to the perception of old age as a time of dependency is practiced by groups that promote whole new definitions of aging, wellness, and dying. They see aging as characterized by potential growth and development, as well as loss. They emphasize the importance of research that focuses on the unique qualities, as well as the losses, of old age. They strongly advocate for the rights of elderly people, as well as others, to refuse services and treatments that they define as stripping them of their dignity. They are claiming the right to live as they choose until they die.

The combination of all of these emphases represents a potentially powerful force to change the perception of aging and old age as a set of losses. Each of these emphases is gaining popularity today. They do not as yet represent one identifiable overall organized effort however. As a result, their political clout thus far remains limited.

CROSS-CULTURAL INFLUENCES

When we look at aging cross-culturally, we find a mixture of beliefs about whether or not aging means loss and old age represents a time of dependency. As noted earlier, in many primitive societies aging is perceived as the loss of vital physical abilities, and older people are treated as dependents for whom the society cannot afford to provide care. At least it can be said that those societies do not attempt to keep their older members indefinitely alive and then decry the burden they represent. Instead, they tend to define death with some form of spiritual and sacrificial meaning to which those who are old can associate with dignity.

Throughout this analysis of aging, we have looked beyond primitive societies at a number of developing and developed countries that are vastly different from one another, both culturally and politically. It has been noted that most of them are at one or another stage of the modernization process, and some theorists have argued that this has negatively affected the status of older people, regardless of cultural background. Indeed, some of the available data indicate this to be true to some degree.

Neverthelesss, there are situations in some societies that still promote, rather than diminish, the social status of the aged. Oriental societies are particularly helpful to look at in this regard. Even in such an economically developed nation as Japan, for example, a large majority of the aged remain integrated into the extended family. They are still honored, respected, and cared for by family members, even though family members do experience a sense of burden as a result of the day-to-day responsibilities of providing the care.

From another perspective, it is noteworthy that, despite the very competitive, capitalistic atmosphere in which they live, quite a large percentage of Japanese elders seem ready and willing to sacrifice their own lives for the sake of their children and grandchildren. A sense of commitment to the family as a group is obviously still strong with elderly people as both participants and recipients. Consequently, their status remains pretty much intact.

The situation in the People's Republic of China provides us with further insights about the social status of older people in today's world. The Chinese elderly are also still very much a part of their extended families, but in a rather unique type of intergenerational interdependency. They share family roles and responsibilities with the adult children with whom they live, and they have an equal amount of authority. An approximately equal commitment of resources by both generations for the maintenance of their homes is also part of their interdependency. Within the family, then, elders are as vital to family life as any other family members.

The community roles that many elderly Chinese are called on to perform as volunteers constitute another source of social status. As they retire, at relatively young ages, they rarely if ever retreat to segregated life-styles. No opportunities exist for that possibility, nor are they motivated in that direction. Instead, they are actively recruited by the members of their local communities and by government entities to serve in community roles, many of which they are able to perform better than others could. A number of these roles are vital to the communities in which they live and represent positions of substantial authority. Furthermore, it is evident that more of the authoritative roles are filled by retired women than men. In a real sense, the elderly in the People's Republic of China are respected not so much because they are able to compete with younger adults for the same social positions, but because they are expected to hold positions that are unique to them. They are seen as having something to offer society precisely because they are older.

Health and health care constitutes still another important source of the positive emphasis on old age that prevails in the People's Republic of China today. Part of the agenda of communism in that country has been to promote good health for the total population. With limited healthcare resources available, a major emphasis was placed on prevention. The level of remedial health care that could be offered was made available to the total population as a right. Few, if any, sophisticated lifesaving technologies have even been available to the Chinese. Thus, long-term care as a social problem does not exist there. The relatively few with crippling, chronic problems are cared for at home until they die.

Consequently, while the life expectancy is lower in the People's Republic of China than in the United States, the elderly Chinese are generally healthy. Not as many live to ripe old ages, but those who do tend to be exceptionally healthy. That fact is quickly apparent to Westerners who visit the People's Republic of China today. Old people in the People's Republic of China give the clear impression of being physically vital.

IMPLICATIONS FOR THE FUTURE

Just as they have changed in the past, the processes of aging and old age will continue to change in the coming years. Some of those changes may well be relatively drastic. Progress in the scientific aspects of aging will surely continue to be made, but dramatic changes in that area do not seem to be on the horizon in the near future. The greatest changes, instead, are apt to be in our perceptions of aging and old age and, consequently, in the formation of public policy related to aging. In that regard, as previously noted, forces for change are already in place.

The direction and intensity of forthcoming changes are by no means certain, however. That depends mostly upon which sides of the political struggle prevail. On the one hand, those who have vested interests in continuing to define aging as a time of irreversible loss and old age as a time of dependency are extremely influential. They are highly respected professionally, and are politically well organized and powerful. On the other hand, those who advocate for more positive perceptions of aging and old age lack coordination. Their voices are intense and they are gaining popular support, but their influences on public policy are thus far quite limited.

Federal government officials, with their growing concerns about the costs of government, are likely to encourage a redefinition of old age as a time of necessary dependency. Many of them already claim that the majority of older people in the United States no longer live in poverty and have no greater needs than other age cohorts. With the pressure of rising federal budgets and competitive demands, the notion that old age is no longer necessarily a time of deprivation will likely become increasingly attractive to government officials involved in setting and implementing policy.

The kind of influence they are apt to have on the redefinitional process may well be more divisive than helpful, however. Their basic assumption seems to be that elderly people as a whole are in reality no different than others in terms of needs and capabilities and that they therefore have no more right to special entitlements than others. The consequence of this kind of position will almost certainly be to inflame the perception of unfairness among younger adults. It suggests that the old represent either an unfair burden or unfair competition. Furthermore, that characterization of old age does nothing to establish old age itself as a time of life with its own set of special qualities.

If more positive perceptions and policies on aging are to materialize, two fundamental changes will be necessary: (1) Better comprehensive and definitive information about the special qualities of the aged have to be provided; and (2) well-organized, coordinated advocacy efforts will have to be made by a coalition of those who are concerned, particularly elderly people themselves. In essence it will take the development of a social movement.

If there are, indeed, special qualities about aging, they will have to be supported by strong gerontological theories and research in order to challenge those that have in the past been oriented almost exclusively to the concept of loss. As we have seen, gerontologists have had a direct and substantial influence on policy through their theories and research. They have also helped to create the perception of aging as a time of loss and old age as a time of dependency. There is the same kind of potential for them to contribute to more positive perceptions of aging and old age. With an increasing volume of literature from such sources as other cultures, the holistic medicine movement, and the field of thanatology, there is ample information for gerontologists to use in developing new theories and in conducting research from a less negative approach.

The issue of retirement will no doubt be important in any reassessment of the meaning of aging that might be made in the future. Despite the many optimistic accounts about it from most of those who are retired today, it is a concept that has negative connotations for most other people. Thus it is at the heart of the perception that elderly people represent a burden to the younger population. The tendency in the future may well be to develop public policy that will discourage, if not do away with, retirement, with the idea that such policy will be in the best interests of older people. Once again, however, deemphasis on retirement will do nothing to demonstrate that old age has its own special qualities. It would only serve to thrust them into a competition for jobs, presumably as equals with younger workers.

Gerontologists will be called upon to treat retirement as the social institution that it has already in large part become. It is already seen as an institution that makes major contributions to society in the People's Republic of China. Much data exists to enable us to make the same point in the United States. Specific attention could be given to the economic contributions that retired people are making through their pension funds, and to the societally meaningful roles they are beginning to and potentially could play as volunteers. An important point to be made about volunteerism is that it provides opportunities for older people to perform roles for which they are uniquely capable. That is an emphasis that deserves to be made in the future as a way of testing the extent to which old age does indeed have unique qualities.

In order to be successful, the major impetus for coordination of efforts to advocate for more positive perceptions of aging will almost certainly have to come from the aged themselves. The recent history of advocacy by others in behalf of elderly people clearly indicates that it does not work. Not only do others often misunderstand and misrepresent the needs of the aged, but the process itself implies that older people are incapable of advocating for themselves.

A number of political scientists question how successful older people have been as their own advocates in the past and whether they can and will be successful in the future. The bases for this kind of pessimism are that older people are too diverse a group, that they do not tend to organize well enough for these kinds of efforts, and that, consequently, they lack the necessary political power. Only time will tell whether older people can and will provide the necessary leadership in advocating for more positive public perceptions of themselves. Some existing trends give us reason to be at least partially optimistic, however. Increasing numbers of them are already active advocates, as individuals and as groups. They are advocating at all levels—grassroots, city, county, state, and national. They have also usually been successful. This is important not just because of what they are able to accomplish with these efforts; even more important, their ability to be active and successful advocates serves as a clear demonstration of the positive potentials of old age.

A further reason to be optimistic about the future potential for older people to lead their own advocacy efforts has to do with their education. The educational level of the aged population is rising and will continue to rise dramatically in the years ahead. This is important for three reasons. First, the more education they have, the more apt they will be to have acquired the skills necessary to act as advocates. Second, education will tend to increase their knowledge about and sensitivity to the issues involved in aging. Third, education tends to create the desire to acquire more knowledge and learn new skills.

The potential for effective advocacy among the aged of the future is clearly in the works. Predictions of what will come of that potential are not easy to make with any promise of accuracy, however. Gerontology is a truly dynamic area of study. We can be assured that changes will occur, but we certainly cannot know the precise nature of these changes.

Index

Industrialized job-related poverty, 139
Industrialized societies, economic system prevalent in, 159–60
Industrial Revolution, 177
Industrial technology, 176–77
Inequity of services, 148–52
Infant or childhood mortality, 18
Infectious disease, 194, 238
Informal caregivers, 101, 209–10
Institution, retirement as social, 173–92
Institutionalization, 199, 203, 205
   of death and dying, 240–42
   dependence and, 68, 86
   loss of self-awareness and, 43
Insurance, health, 198
Interaction patterns of the aged, 51–52. See also Relationships; Role(s)
Interaction perspective of social psychology, 41
Interaction, symbolic, 41, 44, 50–51
Interdependency, 212, 232–33
   in family, 80–81, 228–29
   marital satisfaction and, 96
   peer-group, 82–85
International Work Group on Death and Dying (IWG), 248
Intimacy
   children as source of, 98–99
   at a distance, 80
   in marriage, 96
Inuit Eskimo tribe, 255
Ioway Indian tribe, 187
Isolation, 5
Italian Americans, elderly, 230, 233

Japan, aging in, 71, 265
   age identification, 47
   economics of, 167
   family and
      changes, 93, 129–30
      elderly parent-adult children relationships, 99–100
      extended-family households, 77–78, 226–27
      filial piety tradition, 93–94
      group membership and, 113–14
      health care institutions and, 130–31
      life expectancy, 130
      pension programs and, 179
      public provision of services and, 126–27, 132
      retirement and, 124–26, 128, 167
      suicide and, 256
      values and treatment of aged, 124–25
      welfare and, 124, 126
Jarrett, William, 101
Job characteristics as predictor of retirement, 180, 181
Job discrimination, age-related, 35
Johnson, Colleen L., 230

Kalish, Richard A., 68, 85, 244, 252
Kando, Thomas M., 177
Kane, Robert, 226
Kane, Rosalie, 226
Kant, Immanuel, 218
Kanter, Rosabeth M., 108
Karp, David A., 45
Kart, Cary S., 222
Kastenbaum, Robert, 243, 249, 252, 254, 256
Keith, Pat, 180–81
Keller, Helen, 42
Kerns, Virginia, 228
Kilty, Keith M., 181
Kitsuse, J.I., 148
Kleinman, Arthur, 206
Koh, James Y., 79
Kohn, Robert R., 28–29, 31, 32–33
Korean elderly in U.S., 79
Kornhaber, A., 102
Krout, John A., 112, 224
Krupka, Lawrence, 255–56
Kübler-Ross, Elisabeth, 243, 247
Kutner, Bernard, 43, 65, 68, 86
Kuypers, Joseph A., 36, 49, 66–67

Labeling, 43, 49, 66–68
Labor, division of, 175, 176
Labor, economics and, 158, 159
Labor unions, 177
Labus, Janet G., 249
Lai, Kwok Hung, 69, 146
Land ownership, 158
Language, 42
Lauffer, Armand, 138
Legal advocacy, 138
Legislation
   antimandatory retirement, 179
   health care, 201–3, 240
      Medicaid, 198, 199, 202, 203, 210, 240
      Medicare, 146, 198–99, 201–3, 209, 210, 240
      Social Security, 125–26, 139–40, 142, 143, 146, 161–63, 165, 169, 198, 199
Leisure
   activities, 62
   definition of, 185
   among retirees, 185–86
   roles, 186–89
Less-developed regions (LDRs)
   aged population in, 17–20
   old-age dependency ratio in, 19–20
   sex ratios in, 22
Levine, Solomon B., 167
Leviton, Dan, 255
Lewis, Myrna, 115, 207, 208
Lewkoff, Sue, 184
Life, stages of, 3, 32
Life cycle, marital satisfaction and family, 94–96
Life expectancy, 3, 12, 15, 18, 130–31, 140, 199, 208

Life satisfaction
   nursing home living and, 245
   personal-enhancement groups and, 112–14
   retirement and, 183, 184
Lifesaving and life-sustaining technology, 36, 200, 211, 250
Life spans, 36
Living situations, the aged in
   changing, 76–88
   dependent living, 85–86
   extended-family households, 77–79
   extended-family interdependency, 80–81
   independent living, 81–82
   peer-group interdependency, 82–85
Logue, Barbara, 18, 19, 23
Longevity, regions with claims to high, 18–19
Longino, Charles F., Jr., 84, 113
Long-term care, 6. See also Health and health care
Long-term memory, 30
Lopata, Helena Z., 62
Losses, age and, 36, 49, 57
Loss of major life roles theory, 61–64
Loss versus development, aging as, 261–62
Lowy, Louis, 222

McClelland, Kent A., 84, 113
Macht, Michael L., 34
Maddox, George L., 56, 60, 62
Maeda, Daisaku, 125, 167, 179, 209, 226
Mandatory retirement, 61–62, 127–28
Manton, Kenneth, 71
Mao Tse Tung, 123, 145, 175
Marital roles and relationships, 51, 91, 94–97
Marshall, Victor W., 244
Marx, Karl, 174, 175
Massachusetts Bay Colony, elderly of, 217–18
Mauksch, Hans O., 241
Meals programs, 222
Medicaid, 198, 199, 202, 203, 210, 240
Medical industrial complex, 197, 210–11, 263
Medical model, 30–31, 36, 197, 198, 200–201, 204, 211
Medical practitioners, attitudes about death, 241–42
Medicare, 146, 198–99, 201–3, 209, 210, 240
Medicine. See Health and health care
Memory, 30
Mental aging. See Psychology of aging
Mental dependency, 85
Mental illness, 29
Mentor role, 116

Mexican Americans, elderly
 parent-adult children
 relationships of, 99
Midlife crisis, 45
Migration among the aged, 20–21,
 23–24
Miller, Sheila J., 102
Miller, Stephen J., 176
Milton, Sande, 224
Minority elderly, 223. *See also* Native
 Americans
Modernization, effects of, 4–5, 79,
 219. *See also* Industrialization
Modernization theory, 70–72
Modified extended family, 97
Momeyer, Richard W., 242
Montgomery, James E., 96
Moon, Marilyn, 165
Mor, Vincent, 249
Morale, 183
More-developed regions (MDRs)
 aged population in, 17–20
 old-age dependency ratios in,
 19–20
 sex ratios in, 22
Morse, Nancy C., 174–75
Mother-daughter relationship, 99
Motivation to retire, 180–84
Motive talk, 44
Mourning, 252
Myllyluoma, Jaana, 209

National Association of Area
 Agencies, 143
National Association of Nutrition
 Directors, 143
National Association of State Units
 on Aging, 143
National Center for Black Aged, 143
National Conference on Aging
 (1950), 131, 142, 220
National Council of Senior Citizens
 (NCSC), 84, 142
National Council on Aging, 142
National Hospice Organization,
 248–49
National Hospice Reimbursement
 Act (1983), 249
National Indian Council on Aging,
 143
National Institute of Senior Centers,
 143
National Institutes of Health, 198
National Longitudinal Surveys in
 U.S., 183
National Pension Plan (Japan), 127
Native Americans, 64
 Inuit Eskimo tribe, 255
 Ioway Indian tribe, 187
 Navajo tribe, 52
 economic dependency among,
 168–69
 elder abuse, 169
 health care for, 204–6

political advocacy for, 140–41,
 150–51
 senior citizens' centers, 114
 Oto-Missouri tribe, 187
Navajo Council on Aging, 150–51
Navajo Tribal Council, 151
Need as criterion for service
 provision, 230–31
"Negotiated order," 49
Negotiation of roles, 99–100, 184–85
Neighborhoods, Chinese, 116
Neighbors, distinction between
 friends and, 109
Nestel, George, 34
Network model, 232
Networks
 development of service-providing,
 220–22
 peer-group, 49, 82–85
 social, 24, 109–14, 254
Neugarten, Bernice L., 58, 62, 102–3,
 231
New Deal, 161
Nomadic tribes of ancient times,
 elderly in, 261
Normative Aging Study, 181–82
Normative guidance, loss of, 49
Nuclear family, 91
Nursing homes, 86, 130, 198, 241,
 245
Nutrition programs, 208, 222, 224

O'Bryant, Shirley L., 109
Office of Aging Services, 151
Okrahu, Ishmael O., 80
Old age
 changing characteristics of, 3–5
 as social problem. *See* Social
 problem
 traditional conceptualizations of,
 3–4
Old Age Assistance (OAA), 162–63
Old-age dependency ratio, 19–20,
 22–24
Old Age Insurance (OAI) pension
 program, 162–63
Older American Resources Survey
 (OARS), 212
Older Americans Act (1965), 63, 131,
 138, 139, 143, 146–47, 149–50,
 208, 221–22
Old People's University (Shandung
 Province), 116–17, 188
Olson, Laura K., 164
One-child-per-couple policy in
 China, 12–13
Optimism, source of, 49
Orlander, E.B., 99
Oto-Missouri tribe, 187
Outreach projects, 223, 224. *See also*
 Social-service provision

Palmore, Erdman B., 7, 18–19, 47,
 71, 167, 180
Parker, Stanley, 178, 179

Participation, community. *See*
 Community
Paul, Carolyn E., 180
Peer group relationships, 48, 49, 52,
 68, 82–85, 113
Pendrell, Nan, 166–67
Penfield, Wilder, 30
Pennsylvania Office on Aging, 224
Pension plans, 23, 139, 161, 163–64,
 179
People's Republic of China, 141,
 265–66
 academic involvement of the aged
 in, 116–17
 age identification in, 47
 age stratification theory applied
 to, 69
 communism in, 78, 93, 113, 123
 community in, 113
 involvement of the aged in,
 115–16
 economic situation of the aged in,
 167–68
 elderly volunteers in, 186
 family in
 changing, 92–93, 129
 extended-family households,
 77–78
 grandparents, 103
 interdependency in, 229
 health and health care in, 36–37,
 130, 206–8, 266
 interaction patterns of aged in,
 51, 52
 life expectancy in, 130
 Marxian economic structure in, 175
 Old People's University in,
 116–17, 188
 one-child-per-couple policy in,
 12–13
 political advocacy in, 145–46,
 151–52
 public provision of services in,
 126, 132
 retirement in, 123, 128, 146, 152,
 168, 175, 182
 roles in old age in, 64, 100
 values and treatment of the aged
 in, 123–24
 welfare in, 123–24, 228
Pepper, Claude, 145, 179
Perceptions
 of aging and old age, 262, 263,
 266–68
 of dependency in old age, 123,
 227, 228, 262
 of self, changes with age in, 42–50
Perkins, Charles E., 82
Personal-enhancement groups and
 relationships, 109–14
Personal identity, quest for, 45. *See
 also* Self
Personality
 continuity theory and, 64
 self versus, 42

Rural areas, the aged in, 20, 21
Russell, Noreen A., 243

St. Christopher's Hospice, 248
Salt Lake City study of elderly
    widows, 254
Samoa, aging in, 71
Sandner, Donald F., 205
San Francisco, self-help movement
    in, 232
Satisfaction, role activity and, 62–63.
    See also Life satisfaction
Schaie, K. Warner, 31
Scheper-Hughes, Nancy, 256
Schneider, Robert L., 224
Schottland, Charles, 145
Schulz, James H., 161
Schwab, Karen, 183
Schweitzer, Marjorie M., 64, 186–87
Scientific investigation, 40
Scientific perspective on health,
    194–96. *See also* Medical model
Scientific technology, 177
Secondary aging, 29
Secondary relationships, 108
Self
    -awareness, loss of, 43
    basic concepts of, 42–43
    as cognitive process, 42
    I and me as active elements of, 44
    personality versus, 42
    real, 44–45
Self-advocacy groups, 264
Self-esteem, 48–50
Self-help movement, 232
Self-perception, 42–50
    age identification and, 45–48
    development of self and, 43–44
    evaluative aspect of self, 48–50
    subculture of aging and, 48
Self-worth, 48–50, 123
Senate Subcommittee on Aging, 142
Senescence, 32
Senility, 4
Senior Block Information Service
    (SBIS), 232
Senior citizens' centers, 111, 112,
    114, 221–22, 223
Senior companions, 186
Service Corps of Retired Executives
    (SCORE), 63, 143
Service management, 224
Services. *See* Social-service provision
Sex distributions of elderly
    populations, 21–22
Sexual equality/inequality of
    financial resources, 165, 166
Shanas, Ethel, 98, 100
Sharp, Henry S., 158
Sheehan, Nancy W., 110
Sheehan, Tom, 158
Sheehy, Gail, 45
Sheley, Joseph F., 183
Sheppard, Harold L., 170, 178
Short-term memory, 30
Sick role, 200–201

Siegel, Jacob S., 20, 22
Simic, Andrei, 60
Single-room occupancy hotels,
    84–85, 110
Skin, changes in, 35
Smith, Ken R., 165
Social adequacy, 162
Social advocacy, 138
Social agency model, 222
Social breakdown syndrome
    (labeling) model, 66, 67
Social dependency, 23–24, 35, 85,
    217–20
Social gerontology, development
    of, 57
Socialization in old age, 50, 60–61,
    62, 63, 184
Socially disruptive events
    loss of spouse as, 252
    theory, 65
Social networks, 109–14, 254
Social order, 41
Social policy
    advocacy as influencing, 141–46
    disengagement theory and, 59–60
    retirement policies and systems,
        emergence of, 177–79
    See also Government
Social problem
    defined, 120–21
    major elements of, 121
    old age as, 120–36
        aging network and, 131–32
        changing family roles and,
            128–30
        dominant social values and,
            122–25
        life expectancy and changing
            health problems, 130–31
        post-World War II retirement
            and, 127–28
        public provision of services and,
            125–27
Social-processes approach, 8–9
Social-psychological losses among
    elderly people, 5
Social psychological significance of
    work, 175
Social psychology, perspective of,
    40–41
Social psychology of aging, 40–55
    changing perceptions of self,
        42–50
    role transitions, 50–52
Social Security, 146, 165, 169, 199
Social Security Act (1935), 125–26,
    139, 142, 143, 161–63, 198
Social-service provision, 216–35
    advocacy to implement benefits
        equitably, 148–52
    cross-cultural comparisons in,
        225–29
    defining old age as social problem
        and, 125–27
    development of networks for,
        220–22

influences of aging network on the
    aged, 222–25
potential future trends in, 229–33
processes in defining the aged as
    socially dependent, 217–20
professional approach to, 224–25
utilization of services, 223–25
welfare perception of, 225
Social status. *See* Status
Social structures or systems
    approach, 8
Social theories of old age, 56–75
    activity theory, 58–59
    age stratification theory, 69–70
    continuity theory, 64
    disengagement theory, 59–61,
        62, 63
    emergence of, 56–58
    loss of major life roles theory,
        61–64
    modernization theory, 70–72
    reconstruction theory, 66–68
    socially disruptive events
        theory, 65
Social worth, perception of, 227–28
Socioeconomic status, retirement
    and, 180, 181
Sociological approaches, 8–9
Sokolovsky, Jay, 82
Soldo, Beth J., 209
Spector, M., 148
Spouses, relationships with, 51, 91,
    94–97. *See also* Family
Status
    achieved versus ascribed, 184
    changes, levels of modernization
        and, 70–72
    health and, 193
    loss of, 36
        forces creating, 4–5, 218–19
    past trends in aging and, 261–62
    roleless, 62
    survivor's social, 252
    in traditional societies, 158–59
    work ethic and, 122, 123
    See also Dependency
Stewart, David C., 201
Stigma of living as dying person,
    247–48
Stinnet, Nick, 96
Stratification, age, 69–70
Strauss, Anselm L., 242, 245
Stresses of aging, 65
Students, the aged as, 116–17,
    187–88
Subculture of aging, 36, 48, 68, 83,
    84, 193, 220
Suicide, 253, 256
Sullivan, Thomas J., 201
Sun-belt states, migration of the
    aged to, 21
Supplemental Security Income (SSI)
    program, 163, 169
Support
    informal caregivers, 101, 209–10
    from social networks, 24, 109, 110

Support (*cont.*)
   of survivors, severity of grief and,
      253–54
   See also Social-service provision
Survival curve, rectangular, 35
Survivors, bereavement, mourning
      and grief of, 251–54
Sussman, Marvin, 31, 34
Sweden, volunteers in, 187
Symbolic interaction, 41, 44, 50–51

Taietz, Philip, 222, 224
Tallman, Irving, 121
Tallmer, Margot, 65
Technology
   agricultural, 176
   changing concepts of work and,
      176–77
   economic, 219
   health and medical, 36, 70, 198,
      200, 211, 219, 238, 240, 250
   importance in industrialized
      society, 159–60
   industrial, 176–77
   scientific, 177
Teegarden, David, 211
Television commercials, portrayal of
      elderly in, 43
Terminal diagnosis, right to be told
      of, 246
Terminally ill, program for, 86
Texas, migration of aged to, 21
Theories. *See* Social theories of old
      age
Third-world countries, population
      control movement in, 15, 16
Thomas, Jeanne L., 102
Thompson, Edward H., 241, 242
Tian Jiyun, 124
Tobin, Sheldon S., 58, 62
Todd, Harry F., 232
Togonu-Bickersteth, Funmi, 47
Torack, Richard M., 29
Townsend, Francis, 125
Townsend movement, 83, 125,
      141–42, 180
Traditional societies, status of aged
      in, 158–59
Transportation services, 223, 229
Treas, Judith, 18, 19, 23, 167
Trends
   in aging, 260–68
      cross-cultural influences on,
         264–66
      implications for future, 266–68

past, 261–62
present conditions and, 263–64
demographic, 16–24
in social-service provision, 229–32
Troll, Lillian E., 29, 101, 102
Truman administration, 142
Trustee family, 90
Turner, Ralph H., 44–45, 50–51

Uehara, Edwina S., 166
Underutilization of services, 223–25
Unemployment
   effects of, 182
   in 1920s and 1930s, 160–61
   See also Economic dependency;
      Retirement
United States
   academic involvement of the aged
      in, 116, 187–88
   age identification in, 47
   as death-denying society, 243
   defining the aged as socially
      dependent in, 217–20
   financial support for the aged in,
      160–66
   healthcare system in, 196–99
   implementation of program
      benefits in, 148–51
   life expectancy in, 130
   political advocacy in, 141–45
   retirement in, 127–28, 175–76
   social theories of old age in, 56–75
   volunteer roles in, 186
Urbanization, the aged and, 20, 70,
      219

Values, the aged and changing, 79,
      122–25
Van Haitsma, Kim, 112
Varady, David P., 113
Vatuk, Sylvia, 61
Victimization, 231
Vilcabamba, Ecuador, 18
Viney, Linda L., 245
Voluntary association model, 222
Volunteer roles and programs, 23,
      111, 144, 186–87, 268
Volunteers in Service to America
      (VISTA), 151

Wang, Mr., 145
Wantz, Molly S., 222
Ward, Russell A., 47, 110–11
Warlick, Jennifer L., 165
War on Poverty era, 198

Weber, Max, 122, 174
Weinstein, Karol K., 102–3
Weiss, John P., 121
Weiss, Robert S., 174–75
Welfare perception of social services,
      225
Welfare systems, 228
   in China, 123–24
   in Japan, 124, 126
   in Western cultures, 122
   See also Social-service provision
Western cultures, values and
      treatment of the aged in,
      122–23. *See also* United States
Western Gerontological Society, 143
White House Conferences on Aging,
      131
   of 1961, 139, 142, 220, 221
   of 1971, 67, 139, 142, 147, 224
   of 1981, 145
Whittington, Frank, 71
Widowhood, 46, 98–99, 111, 165,
      166, 183, 252, 254
Williams, Roger, 218
Williamson, John B., 158, 231
Willis, Sherry L., 31
Wisdom of the aged, 3–4, 5, 33, 219,
      220
Wolfe, Paul R., 206–7
Women
   in China, community action of,
      115–16
   poverty among elderly, 165, 166
Wood, Vivian, 102
Work, changing concepts of, 174–77
Worker roles, loss of, 61–62. *See also*
      Retirement
Work ethic, 122, 123, 124, 159,
      174–75, 186
World War II, elderly workers
      during, 178
Wright, Burton, 121

Yi, Zeng, 78
Yin, Peter, 69, 146
Yin and yang, 206
Yoels, William C., 45
Yoruba culture in southwest Nigeria,
      aging in, 46–47
Youth bias, 139
Yugoslavia, social pattern among the
      aged in, 60, 61
Yu Guanghan, 207

Zick, Cathleen D., 165
Zusman, Zack, 66